W9-CLB-459

THE HISTORY OF
JIHAD

"Robert Spencer is one of my heroes. He has once again produced an invaluable and much-needed book. Want to read the truth about Islam? Read this book. It depicts the terrible fate of the hundreds of millions of men, women and children who, from the seventh century until today, were massacred or enslaved by Islam. It is a fate that awaits us all if we are not vigilant."

—Geert Wilders, member of Parliament in the Netherlands and leader of the Dutch Party for Freedom (PVV)

"From the first Arab-Islamic empire of the mid-seventh century to the fall of the Ottoman Empire, the story of Islam has been the story of the rise and fall of universal empires and, no less importantly, of never quiescent imperialist dreams. In this *tour de force*, Robert Spencer narrates the transformation of the concept of jihad, 'exertion in the path of Allah,' from a rallying cry for the prophet Muhammad's followers into a supreme religious duty and the primary vehicle for the expansion of Islam throughout the ages. A must-read for anyone seeking to understand the roots of the Manichean struggle between East and West and the nature of the threat confronted by the West today."

—Efraim Karsh, author of *Islamic Imperialism: A History*

2

"Spencer argues, in brief, 'There has always been, with virtually no interruption, jihad.' Painstakingly, he documents in this important study how aggressive war on behalf of Islam has, for fourteen centuries and still now, befouled Muslim life. He hopes his study will awaken potential victims of jihad, but will they—will we—listen to his warning? Much hangs in the balance."

—Daniel Pipes, president, Middle East forum and author of *Slave Soldiers and Islam: The Genesis of a Military System*

"Robert Spencer, one of our foremost analysts of Islamic jihad, has now written a historical survey of the doctrine and practice of Islamic sanctified violence. With crystal clarity and rigorous argument, he relentlessly marshals the facts that put the lie to the sophistries of apologists and the delusions of Western appeasers. To fight the enemy we must know the enemy, and Robert Spencer's page-turner is the place to start."

—Bruce Thornton, Research Fellow at Stanford's Hoover Institution and Professor of Classics and Humanities at the California State University

"The most important book you will read about the fifteen-hundred-year war that Islamic jihadists have waged on us. Spencer's brilliant book is also the only book you can read on this history, since appeasers of Islamic bigotry and bloodthirstiness have worked so diligently to suppress it."

—David Horowitz, founding president of the David Horowitz Freedom Center and author of *Radical Son: A Generational Odyssey*

"For those who still think—and, alas, there remain many—that Islamic Terrorism has emerged only in the last forty years or so, Robert Spencer's carefully researched work on jihad from the beginning of Muhammad's political and prophetical career to the acts of terrorism of September 11, 2001, will be a salutary shock. It will not be at all easy to refute Spencer's account since he, for the first three Islamic centuries, relies almost entirely on the Arabic sources, that is Muslim historians and scholars, such as Ibn Ishaq, Al-Tabari, Ibn Sa'd, Bukhari, Tirmidhi, and Muslim, who paint a grim picture of the early Islamic conquests. For the later Middle Ages, Spencer has also diligently consulted the primary sources where possible and has relied upon recognized modern scholars such as Ignaz Goldziher, Bernard Lewis, Bat Ye'or, and Steven Runciman, among others. Spanning centuries and continents, from the seventh to the twentieth century, from Spain to India, Spencer takes us on a tour of the global jihad that is Islamic history. Along the way, he shatters many myths, such as the myth of the Golden Age of Spain, a putative period of ecumenical harmony, a kind of perpetual medieval Woodstock Summer of Love. He also puts the Crusades into perspective and reminds us that the Crusades were a belated response to years and years of jihad, and persecution of Christians. Spencer brings the story up to modern times, not forgetting the Armenian genocides perpetuated by the Turks between 1915 and 1923.

"Robert Spencer's work is essential reading for all of us, for all those who want to defend our values from the relentless jihad that has not ceased for fourteen centuries. We must heed Spencer's final words if we are to succeed in saving Western Civilization:

> 'In the twenty-first century, the leaders of Europe, as well as many in North America, having brought almost certain doom on their countries no less unmistakable than that which befell Constantinople on May 29, 1453. Yet instead of taking responsibility for what they have done, they have stayed their course, and would have denounced the doomed Emperor Constantine XI, like his predecessor Manuel II, as "Islamophobic," and his exhortation to defend Constantinople to the death as "militaristic" and "xenophobic." In the twenty-first century, as the 1,400-year Islamic jihad against the free world continued to advance, the best allies the warriors of jihad had were the very people they had in their sights.'"

—**Ibn Warraq, author of** *The Origins of the Koran* **and** *The Quest for the Historical Muhammad*

"Jihad is not mere terrorism. Ironic as it may seem, that is Western wishful thinking. From its inception, as Robert Spencer incontestably illustrates, jihad has been the outward, aggressive expression of a conquest ideology. *The History of Jihad: From Muhammad to ISIS* is as relentless in relating unvarnished truth as is the phenomenon it tracks in seek ing domination—and never being satisfied with less, however long it takes. Those who care to preserve Western rationalism, civil liberties, and free societies must confront this history, and its implications, with eyes opened."

—Andrew C. McCarthy, bestselling author, former federal prosecutor, and *National Review* contributing editor

"In a time of cowardice and deliberate falsehood, the courageous and scholarly exposure of the greatest challenges and dangers of our time by Robert Spencer is priceless."

—Bat Ye'or, author of *The Dhimmi* and *The Decline of Eastern Christianity Under Islam*

THE HISTORY OF
JIHAD

FROM
MUHAMMAD
TO
ISIS

ROBERT SPENCER

A BOMBARDIER BOOKS BOOK
An Imprint of Post Hill Press
ISBN: 978-1-68261-659-8
ISBN (eBook): 978-1-68261-660-4

The History of Jihad:
From Muhammad to ISIS
© 2018 by Robert Spencer
All Rights Reserved

Cover Design by Cody Corcoran

Post Hill Press
New York • Nashville
posthillpress.com

Published in the United States of America

DEDICATION

*Dedicated to the untold millions of victims of jihad, from the
seventh century to today. May you somehow receive justice.*

CONTENTS

INTRODUCTION

This book attempts, for the first time in the English language, to provide a general overview of jihad activity from the time when the concept of jihad was invented (and arguably even before that) to the present day—from Arabia to North Africa and Persia, from Spain to India, from Tel Aviv to New York City.

In amassing this history of jihad from Muhammad to ISIS, I have endeavored wherever possible to quote the words of contemporary witnesses to the various events described, so that the reader may get some impression of how it was to experience the advance of jihad.

The accounts included in this book are as noteworthy for what they don't say as for what they do. The attentive reader will note that there is no period since the beginning of Islam that was characterized by large-scale peaceful coexistence between Muslims and non-Muslims. There was no time when mainstream and dominant Islamic authorities taught the equality of non-Muslims with Muslims, or the obsolescence of jihad warfare. There was no Era of Good Feeling, no Golden Age of Tolerance, no Paradise of Proto-Multiculturalism. There has always been, with virtually no interruption, jihad.

Nor is jihad in Islamic theology primarily, or even prominently, anything but warfare against unbelievers. The Qur'an contains numerous exhortations to fight against the infidels, as do all the *hadith* collections of Muhammad's words and deeds. It directs Muslims to "fight those who do not believe in Allah and the Last Day and do not forbid what Allah and his messenger have forbidden, nor practice the religion of truth, even if they are of the People of the Book, until they pay the jizya with willing submission and feel themselves subdued" (9:29). Nor does Muhammad mention any other pretext for an attack when he expands upon this passage with more detailed instructions on fighting against unbelievers:

> Fight in the name of Allah and in the way of Allah. Fight against those who disbelieve in Allah. Make a holy war; do not embezzle the spoils; do not break your pledge; and do not mutilate (the dead) bodies; do not kill the children. When you meet your enemies who are polytheists, invite them to three courses of action. If they respond to any one of these you also accept it and withhold yourself from doing them any harm. Invite them to (accept) Islam; if they respond to you, accept it from them and desist from fighting against them…. If they refuse to accept Islam, demand from them the jizya. If they agree to pay, accept it from them and hold off your hands. If they refuse to pay the tax, seek Allah's help and fight them.[1]

This triple imperative of conversion, subjugation, or death is reinforced in Islamic law. One manual of Islamic law that some of Sunni Islam's foremost authorities have certified as conforming to the "practice and faith of the orthodox Sunni community" states flatly that the "lesser jihad" means "war against non-Muslims."[2] The Muslim community is directed to make war "upon Jews, Christians, and Zoroastrians…until they become Muslim or pay the non-Muslim poll tax."[3]

Most Muslims are Sunnis. There are four schools of Sunni Muslim jurisprudence: the Shafi'i, Hanafi, Hanbali, and Maliki. These are not brick and mortar schools, but schools of thought, of interpretation of Islamic law. The legal manual quoted above originated with the Shafi'i school; a Hanafi authority, meanwhile, states that the infidels must first be called to embrace Islam, "because the Prophet so instructed his commanders, directing them to call the infidels to the faith." It adds that Muslims must not wage jihad in order to enrich themselves, but only for the cause of Islam. And when the infidels hear the call to Islam, they "will hence perceive that they are attacked for the sake of religion, and not for the sake of taking their property, or making slaves of their children, and on this consideration it is possible that they may be induced to agree to the call, in order to save themselves from the troubles of war."[4]

However, things will go badly for the non-Muslims who choose not to convert or pay the tax. Muslims must "make war upon them, because God is the assistant of those who serve Him, and the destroyer of His enemies, the infidels, and it is necessary to implore His aid upon every occasion; the Prophet, moreover, commands us so to do."[5]

Ibn Khaldun (1332-1406), a Maliki jurist as well as a pioneering historian and philosopher who authored one of the first works of historiography, likewise notes that "in the Muslim community, the holy war is a religious duty, because of the universalism of the Muslim mission and (the obligation to) convert everybody to Islam either by persuasion or by force." Islam is "under obligation to gain power over other nations."[6] And the Hanbali jurist Ibn Taymiyya (1263-1328) directed that "since lawful warfare is essentially jihad and since its aim is that the religion is God's entirely and God's word is uppermost, therefore according to all Muslims, those who stand in the way of this aim must be fought."[7]

These are old authorities, but none of these Sunni schools of jurisprudence have ever reformed or rejected these directives. The Shi'ite schools teach much the same things. Jihad as a spiritual struggle is a secondary concept at best for both, even though it bears the designation "greater jihad."

Only in our strange age has this quite obvious fact been controverted, with those who point it out being excoriated as bigots. Nonetheless, the historical record speaks for itself, even more loudly and clearly than it usually does. It is my hope that readers with an open mind and a willingness to consider unwelcome facts, as rare as those people may be nowadays, will see this record for what it is, and ponder carefully its implications for the future of free societies around the globe.

Robert Spencer
Sherman Oaks, California
January 2018

CHAPTER ONE

"I BRING YOU SLAUGHTER": THE BATTLES OF MUHAMMAD

Jihad, 622–632

VICTORIOUS WITH TERROR

"I have been made victorious with terror."[1]

Muhammad, the Prophet of Islam, died suddenly and unexpectedly, complaining that he felt the way he had several years earlier, when he was poisoned.[2] As death approached, the founder of Islam muttered those fateful words that could have been his epitaph: "I have been made victorious with terror."[3]

It was a fitting summation of his entire public career.

The beginnings of Islam are shrouded in mystery. There are thousands upon thousands of reports (*hadith*, plural *ahadith* or *hadiths*) of the words and deeds of Islam's Prophet Muhammad, but virtually all of them date from the eighth and ninth centuries, over a century and a half after Muhammad's death, which is traditionally set in 632. There is considerable reason to believe that the origins of Islam and the lives of its founding figures are quite different from how they're represented in Islamic sacred history.[4]

Yet for all that, those words and deeds of Muhammad as recorded in the *hadith* are indeed Islamic sacred history, and thus are believed and taken as fact by millions of Muslims, many of whom act upon those beliefs daily in various ways. Just as Jesus' words and deeds in the Gospels can be known and studied aside from the question of their historicity, so also can Muhammad's. The words and deeds of Islam's founder, and the various events that formed Islam as a religious and political force, form the foundation of Islamic faith to this day. As Islam is an ever-growing presence in the West, these elements of Islam should be known, regardless of their historical value or lack thereof.

Many of the key events of the life of Muhammad and the hundred years following his death as recorded by early Muslim historians most likely never happened, but as they are part of Islamic belief and the Islamic worldview to this day, it is important that those whose lives are increasingly affected by these teachings know and understand them.

NO REJECTION WITHOUT CONSEQUENCES

Islamic legend has it that Muhammad began as a preacher of religious ideas, expounding the simple and uncompromising message that there was only one true god and Muhammad was his prophet.

These were never claims one could reject without consequences.

First came warnings of hellfire. Then, when Muhammad's own people, the Quraysh tribe of Mecca, rejected his claim of being a prophet, his message began to take on a hard edge for the rejecters in this world. The jihad—Arabic for "struggle"—that Muhammad preached often began to refer specifically to warfare against those who denied his prophethood or the oneness of the deity.

One scorching day, Muhammad approached a group of Quraysh at the Ka'bah, the cube-shaped building in Mecca said to have been built by the patriarch Abraham and his son Ishmael. Muhammad kissed the black stone, the meteorite that the Arabs believed to have been thrown by Allah down to earth at that spot, and walked around the shrine three times. Then he fixed the Quraysh with a furious gaze and said: "Will you listen to me, O Quraysh? By him who holds my life in His hand, I bring you slaughter."[5]

And he did—not just to the Quraysh but to the entire world, as Muslims for fourteen hundred years heard his message of jihad warfare against the infidel and acted upon his words.

On another occasion, Muhammad sent men out to raid a Quraysh caravan, but they located it at Nakhla in Arabia only during a sacred month, when fighting was forbidden; nonetheless they decided to raid it anyway, whereupon Muhammad was furious and refused to accept his share of the booty.

But then a helpful revelation came from Allah, explaining that the Quraysh's opposition to Muhammad was worse than the Muslims' violation of the sacred month, and therefore the raid was justified:

> They ask you about the sacred month—about fighting therein. Say, "Fighting therein is great sin, but averting people from the way of Allah and disbelief in Him and al-Masjid al-Haram and the expulsion of its people therefrom are worse in the sight of Allah. And *fitnah* [disturbance, persecution] is greater than killing." (Qur'an 2:217)

Whatever sin the Nakhla raiders had committed in violating the sacred month was nothing compared to the Quraysh's *fitnah*. Muhammad's first biographer Ibn Ishaq explained: "They have kept you back from the way of God with their unbelief in Him, and from the sacred mosque, and have driven you from it when you were with its people. This is a more serious matter with God than the killing of those whom you have slain."[7]

Once he received this revelation, Muhammad took the booty and prisoners that Abdullah had brought him. This was a momentous incident, for it would set a precedent: if a group was guilty of *fitnah*, all bets were off, all moral principles could be set aside. Good became identified with anything that redounded to the benefit of Muslims and Islam, and evil with anything that harmed them.

INFLICT SLAUGHTER UPON THEM

The Muslims' raids on Quraysh caravans precipitated the first major battle the Muslims fought. Muhammad heard that a large Quraysh caravan, laden with money and goods, was coming from Syria. He again ordered his followers to raid it: "This is the caravan of the Quraysh possessing wealth. It is likely that Allah may give it to you as booty."[8]

Some of the Muslims were reluctant; Allah castigated them in a new revelation: "Those who believe say, 'Why has a *surah* [a chapter of the Qur'an] not been sent down?' But when a precise *surah* is revealed and fighting is mentioned therein, you see those in whose hearts is hypocrisy looking at you with a look of one overcome by death." (Qur'an 47:20)

Allah told the Muslims to fight fiercely: "So when you meet those who disbelieve, strike necks until, when you have inflicted slaughter upon them, then secure their bonds, and either favor afterwards or ransom until the war lays down its burdens." (Qur'an 47:4)

Muhammad set out toward Mecca to lead the raid. He knew that the Quraysh would be defending their caravan with an army this time, but he was confident: "Forward in good heart," he told his men, "for God has promised me one of the two parties"—that is, either the caravan or the army. "And by God, it is as though I now see the enemy lying prostrate."[9] When he saw the Quraysh marching toward the Muslims, he prayed: "O God, here come the Quraysh in their vanity and pride, contending with Thee and calling Thy apostle a liar. O God, grant the help which Thou didst promise me. Destroy them this morning!"[10] Abu Jahl (which means "Father of Ignorance," a name given him by Muslim chroniclers; his real name was Amr ibn Hisham), one of the Quraysh leaders, also felt a defining moment was at hand. Oiling a coat of chain mail before the battle, he declared: "No, by God, we will not turn back until God decides between us and Muhammad."[11]

BADR

The Quraysh came out to meet Muhammad's three hundred men at the village of Badr with a force of nearly a thousand.[12] Muhammad, panicking, warned Allah of the consequences of a Muslim defeat: "O God, if this band perish today Thou wilt be worshipped no more." But soon after that he expressed confidence in spiritual help that would guarantee the Muslims victory, telling his lieutenant Abu Bakr: "Be of good cheer, O Abu Bakr. God's help is come to you. Here is Gabriel holding the rein of a horse and leading it. The dust is upon his front teeth."[13]

Muhammad then gave his men a promise that would make them, and Muslim warriors after them throughout the ages, fight all the harder: "By God in whose hand is the soul of Muhammad, no man will be slain this day fighting against them with steadfast courage advancing not retreating but God will cause him to enter Paradise."[14]

His men believed him. One exclaimed: "Fine, Fine! Is there nothing between me and my entering Paradise save to be killed by these men?" He flung away some dates that he had been eating, rushed into the thick of the battle, and fought until he was killed. Another asked Muhammad: "O apostle of God, what makes the Lord laugh with joy at His servant?" Muhammad answered: "When he plunges into the midst of the enemy without mail." The man did so and fought until he was killed.[15]

Muhammad, far back in the ranks, picked up a few pebbles and threw them toward the Quraysh, saying, "Foul be those faces!" Then he ordered the Muslims to charge.[16] Despite their superior numbers, the Quraysh were routed. Some Muslim traditions say that Muhammad himself participated in the fighting; others, that it was more likely that he exhorted his followers from the sidelines. In any event, it was an occasion for him to avenge years of frustration, resentment, and hatred toward his people who had rejected him. One of his followers later recalled a curse Muhammad had pronounced on the leaders of the Quraysh: "The Prophet said, 'O Allah! Destroy the chiefs of Quraish, O Allah! Destroy Abu Jahl bin Hisham, Utba bin Rabi'a, Shaiba bin Rabi'a, Uqba bin Abi Mu'ait, Umaiya bin Khalaf [or Ubai bin Kalaf].'"[17]

KILLING MUHAMMAD'S ENEMIES

All the men Muhammad cursed were captured or killed during the Battle of Badr. One Quraysh leader named in this curse, Uqba, pleaded for his life: "But who will look after my children, O Muhammad?"

Muhammad at this point may have recalled that it had been Uqba who had thrown camel dung, blood, and intestines on him while he prostrated himself in prayer, as the Quraysh chiefs watched and laughed.[18] He had pronounced a curse on them at that time, and now it was being fulfilled. Who would care for Uqba's children? "Hell," Muhammad snarled, and ordered Uqba killed.[19]

Abu Jahl was beheaded. The Muslim who severed the head proudly carried his trophy to Muhammad: "I cut off his head and brought it to the apostle saying, 'This is the head of the enemy of God, Abu Jahl.'" Muhammad was delighted and thanked Allah for the murder of his enemy.[20]

According to another account, two young Muslims murdered Abu Jahl as he was "walking amongst the people." One of the murderers explained why: "I have been informed that he abuses Allah's Messenger. By Him in Whose Hands my soul is, if I should see him, then my body will not leave his body till either of us meet his fate." After they have done the deed, they went to see the Prophet of Islam, who asked, "Which of you has killed him?"

Both youths answered, "I have killed him."

Muhammad thought of a way to resolve the dispute, asking them: "Have you cleaned your swords?" They answered that they had not, so Muhammad inspected their weapons and announced: "No doubt, you both have killed him, and the spoils of the deceased will be given to Mu'adh bin Amr bin Al-Jamuh,'" who was one of the murderers.[21]

The bodies of all those named in the curse were thrown into a pit. As an eyewitness recalled: "Later on I saw all of them killed during the battle of Badr and their bodies were thrown into a well except the body of Umaiya or Ubai, because he was a fat man, and when he was pulled, the parts of his body got separated before he was thrown into the well."[22] Then Muhammad taunted them as "people of the pit" and posed a theological question: "Have you found what God promised you is true? I have found that what my Lord promised me is true." When asked why he was speaking to dead bodies, he replied: "You cannot hear what I say better than they, but they cannot answer me."[23]

ALLAH GRANTS VICTORY TO THE PIOUS

The victory at Badr was the turning point for the Muslims and became a cornerstone of the new religious community's foundational story. Many passages of the Qur'an draw lessons for all believers from this battle. Allah emphasized that it was piety, not military might, that brought victory at Badr: "Already there has been for you a sign in the two armies which met—one fighting in the cause of Allah and another of disbelievers. They saw with their eyes that they were twice their number. But Allah

10

supports with His victory whom He wills. Indeed in that is a lesson for those of vision." (Qur'an 3:13)

Another revelation had Allah announcing that armies of angels joined with the Muslims to smite the Quraysh, and that similar help would come in the future to Muslims who remained faithful to Allah: "And already had Allah given you victory at Badr while you were few in number. Then fear Allah; perhaps you will be grateful when you said to the believers, 'Is it not sufficient for you that your Lord should reinforce you with three thousand angels sent down?' Yes, if you remain patient and conscious of Allah and the enemy come upon you in rage, your Lord will reinforce you with five thousand angels having marks. And Allah made it not except as good tidings for you and to reassure your hearts thereby. And victory is not except from Allah, the Exalted in Might, the Wise." (Qur'an 3:123–126)

Allah told Muhammad the angels would always help the Muslims in battle and strike terror into the hearts of the enemies of the Muslims: "When you asked help of your Lord, and He answered you, 'Indeed, I will reinforce you with a thousand from the angels, following one another.'…When your Lord inspired the angels, 'I am with you, so strengthen those who have believed. I will cast terror into the hearts of those who disbelieved, so strike upon the necks and strike from them every fingertip.' That is because they opposed Allah and His Messenger. And whoever opposes Allah and His Messenger—indeed, Allah is severe in penalty." (Qur'an 8:9, 12–13)

Allah warned the Quraysh not to attempt another attack, telling them they would again be defeated no matter how much more numerous they were than the Muslims: "If you seek the victory, the defeat has come to you. And if you desist, it is best for you; but if you return, We will return, and you will never be aided by your company at all, even if it should increase, because Allah is with the believers." (Qur'an 8:19)

Allah revealed that the Muslims were not just aided; they were merely his passive instruments at Badr. Even the pebbles Muhammad threw toward the Quraysh were not thrown by him, but by Allah: "And you did not kill them, but it was Allah who killed them. And you did not throw, when you threw, but it was Allah who threw that He might test the believers with a good test. Indeed, Allah is Hearing and Knowing." (Qur'an 8:17)

Allah promised to grant such victories to pious Muslims even though they faced odds even more prohibitive than those they had overcome at Badr: "O Prophet, urge the believers to battle. If there are among you twenty steadfast, they will overcome two hundred. And if there are among you one hundred steadfast, they will overcome a thousand of those who have disbelieved, because they are a people who do not understand. Now, Allah has lightened the hardship for you, and He knows that among you is weakness. So if there are from you one hundred steadfast, they will overcome two hundred. And if there are among you a thousand, they will overcome two thousand by permission of Allah. And Allah is with the steadfast." (Qur'an 8:65–66)

Thus were first enunciated what would become recurring themes of jihad literature throughout the centuries to today: piety in Islam will bring military victory. Allah will send angels to fight with the believing Muslims, such that they will conquer even against overwhelming odds.

Flush with victory, Muhammad stepped up his raiding operations. During one of them, against the pagan Ghatafan tribe, he was surprised by an enemy warrior while resting. The warrior asked him: "Who will defend you from me today?"

Muhammad replied coolly, "Allah"—whereupon the warrior dropped his sword. Muhammad seized it quickly and asked, "Who will defend you from me?"

"None," said the warrior, and he recited the Shahada (the Muslim profession of faith) and became a Muslim.[24]

MUHAMMAD AGAINST THE JEWS

Now Muhammad turned his attention to the Jewish tribes of Medina, the Banu Qaynuqa, Banu Nadir, and Banu Qurayza, with whom he had made a covenant when he first arrived in the city.[25] He was beginning to chafe under that covenant, and Allah gave him a way out, in the form of a revelation allowing him to break treaties he had made with groups when he feared they would betray him, not just when any actual betrayal had taken place: "If you fear betrayal from a people, throw their treaty back to them on equal terms. Indeed, Allah does not like traitors." (Qur'an 8:58)

Muhammad announced, "I fear the Banu Qaynuqa," and resolved to strike them first.[26]

Striding into the Qaynuqa's marketplace, he issued a public warning: "O Jews, beware lest God bring upon you the vengeance that He brought upon Quraysh and become Muslims. You know that I am a prophet who has been sent—you will find that in your scriptures and God's covenant with you."

He added in a revelation from Allah, referring to the Battle of Badr: "Say to those who disbelieve, 'You will be overcome and gathered together to Hell, and wretched is the resting place.' Already there has been for you a sign in the two armies which met—one fighting in the cause of Allah and another of disbelievers. They saw with their eyes that they were twice their number. But Allah supports with His victory whom He wills. Indeed in that is a lesson for those of vision." (Qur'an 3:10)

The Qaynuqa Jews were not impressed, and replied: "O Muhammad, you seem to think that we are your people. Do not deceive yourself because you encountered a people with no knowledge of war and got the better of them; for by God if we fight you, you will find that we are real men!"[27]

Muhammad's forces laid siege to the Qaynuqa until they offered him unconditional surrender. But then a Muslim—classified as one of the Hypocrites, those who claimed to be Muslim but disobeyed Allah and opposed and even mocked Muhammad—pleaded that Muhammad be merciful with the Qaynuqa because he had business connections with many of them. Muhammad was angered, but he agreed to spare the Qaynuqa if they turned over their property as booty to the Muslims and left Medina.

However, Muhammad wanted to make sure this sort of thing did not happen again, and he received a revelation about the relationships that should prevail between Muslims and non-Muslims: "O you who have believed, do not take the Jews and the Christians as friends and allies. They are friends and allies of one another. And whoever is a friend and ally to them among you—then indeed, he is of them. Indeed, Allah guides not the wrongdoing people." (Qur'an 5:51)

Allah harshly scolded those who feared a loss of business prospects because of Muhammad's jihad, warning them not to hurry to the unbelievers' side: "So you see those in whose hearts is disease hastening to them, saying, 'We are afraid a misfortune may strike us.' But perhaps Allah will bring conquest or a decision from Him, and they will become, over what they have been concealing within themselves, regretful." (Qur'an 5:52).[28]

After the Battle of Badr and the action against the Qaynuqa Jews, Muhammad turned his wrath against a Jewish poet, Ka'b bin Al-Ashraf, who, according to Ibn Ishaq, "composed amatory verses of an insulting nature about the Muslim women."[29] Incensed, Muhammad asked his followers: "Who is willing to kill Ka'b bin Al-Ashraf who has hurt Allah and His Apostle?"[30]

A young Muslim named Muhammad bin Maslama volunteered; when the Prophet assented, Maslama made a request: "Then allow me to say a [false] thing [in effect, to deceive Ka'b]."

Muhammad granted his wish, and so Muhammad bin Maslama went to Ka'b and began to complain about the self-proclaimed prophet to whom he had dedicated his life: "That man [Muhammad] demands *sadaqa* [or *zakat*, alms] from us, and he has troubled us, and I have come to borrow something from you."[31] He worked hard to gain Ka'b's trust, and in order to get close enough to Ka'b to be able to kill him, professed to admire Ka'b's perfume: "I have never smelt a better scent than this.... Will you allow me to smell your head?" Ka'b agreed; Muhammad bin Maslama thereupon caught Ka'b in a strong grip and commanded his companions: "Get at him!" They killed Ka'b and then hurried to inform the Prophet, carrying Ka'b's head with them.[32] When Muhammad heard the news, he screamed, "*Allahu akbar!*" and praised Allah.[33]

After the murder of Ka'b, Muhammad issued a blanket command: "Kill any Jew that falls into your power."[34] This was not a military order: the first victim was a Jewish merchant, Ibn Sunayna, who had "social and business relations" with the Muslims. The murderer, Muhayissa, was rebuked for the deed by his brother Huwayissa, who was not yet a Muslim. Muhayissa was unrepentant. He told his brother: "Had the one who ordered me to kill him ordered me to kill you I would have cut your head off."

Huwayissa was impressed: "By God, a religion which can bring you to this is marvelous!" He became a Muslim.[35]

UHUD: ALLAH DOES NOT REWARD THE IMPIOUS

Muhammad would need his help. After their defeat at Badr, the Quraysh were itching for revenge. They assembled three thousand troops against one thousand Muslims at a mountain near Mecca named Uhud. Muhammad, brandishing a sword, led the Muslims into battle. This time, the Quraysh were far more determined, and the Muslims were routed. Muhammad's child bride, Aisha, later recounted that the Muslims were initially winning at Uhud, but then their lines collapsed in confusion due to a supernatural intervention: "Satan, Allah's Curse be upon him, cried loudly, 'O Allah's Worshippers, beware of what is behind!' On that, the front files of the [Muslim] forces turned their backs and started fighting with the back files."[36]

Muhammad himself had his face bloodied and a tooth knocked out; rumors even flew around the battlefield that he had been killed. When he was able to find water to wash the blood off his face, Muhammad vowed revenge: "The wrath of God is fierce against him who bloodied the face of His prophet."[37] When Abu Sufyan, the Quraysh commander, taunted the Muslims, Muhammad told his lieutenant Umar to respond: "God is most high and most glorious. We are not equal. Our dead are in paradise; your dead in hell."[38]

After Uhud came revelations to explain the setback. While Badr was Allah's victory, Uhud was not Allah's defeat but the result of the Muslims' failure of courage and lust for the things of this world, specifically in this case the spoils of war, the goods and women they hoped to win from the Quraysh: "And Allah had certainly fulfilled His promise to you when you were killing the enemy by His permission until when you lost courage and fell to disputing about the order and disobeyed after he had shown you that which you love. Among you are some who desire this world, and among you are some who desire the Hereafter. Then he turned you back from them that He might test you. And He has already forgiven you, and Allah is the possessor of bounty for the believers." (Qur'an 3:152)

Another revelation exhorted the Muslims to fight valiantly, assuring them that their lives were in no danger until the day Allah had decreed that they must die: "And it is not for one to die except by permission of Allah at a decree determined. And whoever desires the reward of this world, We will give him thereof; and whoever desires the reward of the Hereafter, We will give him thereof. And we will reward the grateful." (Qur'an 3:145)

Allah reminded them of his help given to the Muslims in the past, and reminded them that piety was the key to victory:

> And already had Allah given you victory at Badr while you were few in number. Then fear Allah; perhaps you will be grateful, when you said to the believers, "Is it not sufficient for you that your Lord should reinforce you with three thousand angels sent down?" Yes, if you remain patient and conscious of Allah and the enemy come upon you in rage, your Lord will reinforce you with five thousand angels having marks. And Allah made it not except as good tidings for you and to reassure your hearts thereby. And victory is not except from Allah, the Exalted in Might, the Wise, that He might cut down a section of the disbelievers or suppress them so that they turn back disappointed. (Qur'an 3:123–127)

The lesson was clear: the only path to success was Islam, and the cause of all failure was the abandonment of Islam. Allah promised that the Muslims would soon be victorious again, provided that they depended solely on him and rejected all accord with non-Muslims: "O you who have believed, if you obey those who disbelieve, they will turn you back on your heels, and you will become losers. But Allah is your protector, and He is the best of helpers. We will cast terror into the hearts of those who disbelieve for what they have associated with Allah of which He had not sent down authority. And their refuge will be the Fire, and wretched is the residence of the wrongdoers." (Qur'an 3:149–151)

DIVINE TERROR DEFEATS THE JEWS

Not long after the Battle of Uhud, some members of one of the Jewish tribes of Medina, the Banu Nadir, conspired to kill Muhammad by dropping a large stone on his head as he passed by one of their houses. However, some of the Muslims learned of the plot and notified Muhammad. Rather than appealing to the leaders of the Nadir to turn over the guilty men, Muhammad sent word to the Nadir: "Leave my country and do not live with me. You have intended treachery."[39]

Muhammad told the Muslims, "The Jews have declared war."[40] He ordered his men to march out against the tribe and lay siege to them.[41] Finally the Nadir agreed to exile themselves. Muhammad commanded them to turn over their weapons and allowed them to keep as much of the rest of their property as they could carry on their camels.[42] Some of the Nadir destroyed their houses, loading as much on the backs of their camels as they possibly could.[43] The rest of their belongings became Muhammad's personal property, which he distributed as booty among the *muhajiroun*, the Muslims who had emigrated with him from Mecca to Medina.[44]

In a revelation, Allah told Muhammad that it was divine terror that had defeated the Banu Nadir, and that they were all bound for hell:

> Whatever is in the heavens and whatever is on the earth exalts Allah, and He is the Exalted in Might, the Wise. It is He who expelled the ones who disbelieved among the People of the Book from their homes at the first gathering. You did not think they would leave, and they thought that their fortresses would protect them from Allah; but Allah came upon them from where they had not expected, and He cast terror into their hearts; they destroyed their houses by their hands and the hands of the believers. So take warning, O people of vision. And if not that Allah had decreed for them evacuation, He would have punished them in this world, and for them in the Hereafter is the punishment of the Fire. (Qur'an 59:2–3)

PROPHECY OF CONQUEST

After the expulsion of the Qaynuqa and Nadir Jews from Medina, some of those who remained approached the Quraysh, offering an alliance against Muhammad and the Muslims. The Quraysh readily accepted.[45] Muhammad, forewarned of this new alliance, had a trench dug around Medina. During the digging of the trench, Muhammad had visions of conquering the areas bordering Arabia. One of the earliest Muslims, Salman the Persian, the story goes, was working on the trench when he began having trouble with a particularly large rock. "The apostle," explained Salman, "who was near at hand, saw me hacking and saw how difficult the place was. He dropped down into the trench and took the pick from my hand and gave such a blow that lightning showed beneath the pick."[46] The flash of lightning "shot out, illuminating everything between the two tracts of black stones—that is, Medina's two tracts of black stones—like a lamp inside a dark room." Muhammad shouted the Islamic cry of victory, "*Allahu akbar*," and all the Muslims responded with the same shout.[47] This happened again and then a third time, in exactly the same way. Finally, Salman asked Muhammad: "O you, dearer than father or mother, what is the meaning of this light beneath your pick as you strike?"

The Prophet of Islam responded: "Did you really see that, Salman? The first means that God has opened up to me the Yaman; the second Syria and the west; and the third the east."[48] Or, according to another version of the same story: "I struck my first blow, and what you saw flashed out, so that the palaces of al-Hirah [in what is today southern Iraq] and al-Madai'in of Kisra [the winter capital of the Sassanian Empire] lit up for me as if they were dogs' teeth, and Gabriel informed me that my nation would be victorious over them." The second blow illuminated in the same way "the palaces of the pale men in the lands of the Byzantines," and the third, "the palaces of San'a"—that is, Yemen.[49] Gabriel promised Muhammad victory over each, repeating three times: "Rejoice; victory shall come to them!" To this Muhammad replied, "Praise be to God! The promise of One who is true and faithful! He has promised us victory after tribulation."

Decades later, when the countries named in this legend were indeed conquered by the warriors of jihad, an old Muslim used to say: "Conquer where you will, by God, you have not conquered and to the resurrection day you will not conquer a city whose keys God had not given beforehand to Muhammad."[50]

As the Quraysh, along with another tribe, the Ghatafan (known collectively in Islamic tradition as "the Confederates"), laid siege to Medina, the trench prevented their breaking through and entering the city, but the Muslims were unable to force them to end the siege. Meanwhile, the Banu Qurayza began collaborating with the Quraysh. As the siege dragged on (it lasted three weeks), the Muslims' situation grew more perilous. Conditions got so bad that one Muslim remarked bitterly about Muhammad's territorial ambitions and his designs on the two great powers that bordered Arabia, the Persian Empire of Chosroes and the Eastern Roman (Byzantine) Empire of Caesar: "Muhammad used to promise us that we should eat the treasures of Chosroes and Caesar and today not one of us can feel safe in going to the privy!"[51]

The Qurayzah agreed to attack the Muslims from one side while the Quraysh besieged them from the other. But then events took a turn for the Muslims. A strong wind blew up around this time, making it impossible for the Quraysh to keep their tents up or fires going. Abu Sufyan had had enough. He said to his men: "O Quraysh, we are not in a permanent camp; the horses and camels are dying; the [Banu] Qurayza have broken their word to us and we have heard disquieting reports of them. You can see the violence of the wind which leaves us neither cooking-pots, nor fire, nor tents to count on. Be off, for I am going!"[52] The Quraysh began to abandon their positions around Medina. Islam was saved.

MASSACRING THE JEWS

After the successful resolution of the Battle of the Trench, the angel Gabriel himself made sure that Muhammad settled accounts with the Qurayzah Jews. According to Aisha, "When Allah's Messenger returned on the day [of the battle] of Al-Khandaq [Trench], he put down his arms and took a bath. Then Jibril [Gabriel] whose head was covered with dust, came to him saying, 'You have put down your arms! By Allah, I have not put down my arms yet.' Allah's Messenger said, 'Where to go now]?' Jibril said, 'This way,' pointing towards the tribe of Bani Quraiza. So Allah's Messenger went out towards them."[53]

As his armies approached the fortifications of the Qurayzah, Muhammad addressed them in terms that have become familiar usage for Islamic jihadists when speaking of Jews today—language that, as we have seen, also made its way into the Qur'an: "You brothers of monkeys, has God disgraced you and brought His vengeance upon you?" The Qur'an in three places (2:62–65, 5:59–60, and 7:166) says that Allah transformed the Sabbath-breaking Jews into pigs and monkeys.

The Qurayzah Jews tried to soften Muhammad's wrath, saying: "O Abu'l-Qasim [Muhammad], you are not a barbarous person." But the Prophet of Islam was in no mood to be appeased. He told the Muslims who were with him that a warrior who passed by on a white mule was actually Gabriel, who had "been sent to Banu Qurayza to shake their castles and strike terror to their hearts." The Muslims laid siege to the Qurayzah strongholds for twenty-five days, until, according to Ibn Ishaq, "they were sore pressed" and, as Muhammad had warned, "God cast terror into their hearts."[54]

After the Qurayzah surrendered, Muhammad decided to put the fate of the tribe into the hands of the Muslim warrior Sa'd ibn Mu'adh. Sa'd pronounced: "I give the judgment that their warriors should be killed and their children and women should be taken as captives."

The Prophet of Islam was pleased. "O Sa'd! You have judged amongst them with [or, similar to] the judgment of the King [Allah]."[55] He confirmed Sa'd's judgment as that of Allah himself: "You have decided in confirmation to the judgment of Allah above the seven heavens."[56] Sa'd's sentence was duly carried out, with Muhammad himself actively participating. According to Ibn Ishaq, "The apostle went out to the market of Medina [which is still its market today] and dug trenches in it. Then he sent for [the men of the Qurayzah] and struck off their heads in those trenches as they were brought out to him in batches." One of the Prophet's fiercest enemies among the Qurayzah, Huyayy, proclaimed: "God's command is right. A book and a decree, and massacre have been written against the Sons of Israel." Then Muhammad struck off his head.

Sa'd's judgment had been to kill the men and enslave the women and children; one of the captives, Attiyah al-Qurazi, explained how the

Muslims determined who was a man and who wasn't: "I was among the captives of Banu Qurayzah. They [the companions] examined us, and those who had begun to grow hair [pubes] were killed, and those who had not were not killed. I was among those who had not grown hair."[57]

Ibn Ishaq puts the number of those massacred at "Six hundred or seven hundred in all, though some put the figure as high as eight hundred or nine hundred."[58] Another early biographer of Muhammad, Ibn Sa'd said, "They were between six hundred and seven hundred in number."[59] As the Qurayzah were being led to Muhammad in groups, someone asked Ka'b bin Asad what was happening. "Will you never understand?" replied the distraught leader of the Qurayzah. "Don't you see that the summoner never stops and those who are taken away do not return? By Allah it is death!"[60]

Allah also sent down a revelation referring obliquely to the massacre: "And He brought down those who supported them among the People of the Book from their fortresses and cast terror into their hearts. A party you killed, and you took captive a party." (Qur'an 33:26) Allah again claimed sole responsibility for the victory: "O you who have believed, remember the favor of Allah upon you when armies came to you and We sent upon them a wind and armies you did not see. And Allah ever sees what you do, when they came at you from above you and from below you, and when eyes shifted and hearts reached the throats and you assumed about Allah assumptions. There the believers were tested and shaken with a severe shaking." (Qur'an 33:9–11).

THE MUSLIMS TAKE SEX SLAVES

Meanwhile, Muhammad's cool head and trust in Allah when things looked bleakest for the Muslims stood him in good stead. Allah gave him a revelation, telling the Muslims to imitate him: "There has certainly been for you in the Messenger of Allah an excellent pattern for anyone whose hope is in Allah and the Last Day and remembers Allah often." (Qur'an 33:21)

Muhammad was now the undisputed master of Medina, and the Prophet of Islam enjoyed an immediate economic advantage. A *hadith* records that "people used to give some of their date-palms to the Prophet [as a gift], till he conquered Bani Quraiza and Bani An-Nadir, whereupon he started returning their favours."[61] But challengers to his consolidation of power over all Arabia remained. He received word that the Banu al-Mustaliq, an Arab tribe related to the Quraysh, were gathering against the Muslims, so he led the Muslims out to attack them. And Allah, according to Ibn Ishaq, "put the [Banu] al-Mustaliq to flight and killed some of them and gave the apostle their wives, children and property as booty."[62]

There were, according to Muslim warrior Abu Sa'id al-Khadri, "some excellent Arab women" among the captives of the Banu al-Mustaliq. "We desired them, for we were suffering from the absence of our wives, [but at the same time] we also desired ransom for them." The Qur'an permitted them to have sexual intercourse with slave girls captured in battle—"those captives whom your right hands possess" (4:24)—but if they intended to keep the women as slaves, they couldn't collect ransom money for them. "So," Abu Sa'id explained, "we decided to have sexual intercourse with them but by observing *azl*"—that is, *coitus interruptus*. Muhammad, however, told them this was not necessary: "It does not matter if you do not do it, for every soul that is to be born up to the Day of Resurrection will be born."[63] Conceptions and births were up to Allah alone. The enslavement and rape of the women were taken for granted.

THE TREATY OF HUDAYBIYYA

In 628, Muhammad and the Quraysh commenced a ten-year truce (*hudna*) with the treaty of Hudaybiyya. Muhammad wanted to make the pilgrimage to Mecca, and he was willing to make concessions to the Quraysh to be allowed to do so. When the time came for the agreement to be written, Muhammad called for one of his earliest and most fervent followers, Ali ibn Abi Talib, and told him to write, "In the name of Allah, the Compassionate, the Merciful." But the Quraysh negotiator, Suhayl bin Amr, stopped him: "I do not recognize this; but write 'In thy name, O Allah." Muhammad told Ali to write what Suhayl had directed.

When Muhammad directed Ali to continue by writing, "This is what Muhammad, the apostle of God, has agreed with Suhayl bin Amr," Suhayl protested again. "If I witnessed that you were God's apostle," Suhayl told Muhammad, "I would not have fought you. Write your own name and the name of your father." Again, Muhammad told Ali to write the document as Suhayl wished.

The treaty that was finally agreed to read this way:

> This is what Muhammad b. Abdullah has agreed with Su-
> hayl b. 'Amr: they have agreed to lay aside war for ten years
> during which men can be safe and refrain from hostilities
> on condition that if anyone comes to Muhammad without
> the permission of his guardian he will return him to them;
> and if anyone of those with Muhammad comes to Quraysh
> they will not return him to him. We will not show enmity
> one to another and there shall be no secret reservation or
> bad faith. He who wishes to enter into a bond and agree-
> ment with Muhammad may do so and he who wishes to
> enter into a bond and agreement with Quraysh may do so.

The Quraysh added: "You must retire from us this year and not enter Mecca against our will, and next year we will make way for you and you can enter it with your companions and stay there three nights. You may carry a rider's weapons, the swords in their sheaths. You can bring in nothing more."[64]

Muhammad shocked his men by agreeing that those fleeing the Quraysh and seeking refuge with the Muslims would be returned to the Quraysh, while those fleeing the Muslims and seeking refuge with the Quraysh would not be returned to the Muslims.

Muhammad insisted that the Muslims had been victorious despite all appearances to the contrary, and Allah confirmed this view in a new revelation: "Indeed, We have given you a clear conquest." (Qur'an 48:1) As if in compensation, Allah promised new spoils to the Muslims: "Cer-tainly was Allah pleased with the believers when they pledged allegiance to you under the tree, and He knew what was in their hearts, so He sent down tranquillity upon them and rewarded them with an imminent conquest and much war booty which they will take. And ever is Allah Exalted in Might and Wise. Allah has promised you much booty that you will take and has hastened this for you and withheld the hands of people from you—that it may be a sign for the believers and He may guide you to a straight path." (Qur'an 48:18–20)

Soon after this promise was made, a Quraysh woman, Umm Kulthum, joined the Muslims in Medina; her two brothers came to Muhammad, asking that she be returned "in accordance with the agreement between him and the Quraysh at Hudaybiya."[65] But Muhammad refused. He was following Allah's orders: "O you who have believed, when the believing women come to you as emigrants, examine them. Allah is most knowing as to their faith. And if you know them to be believers, then do not return them to the disbelievers; they are not lawful for them, nor are they lawful for them." This odd locution is generally understood as meaning that neither wives nor husbands are lawful for the disbelievers.

The passage continues: "But give the disbelievers what they have spent. And there is no blame upon you if you marry them when you have given them their due compensation. And hold not to marriage bonds with disbelieving women, but ask for what you have spent and let them ask for what they have spent. That is the judgment of Allah; He judges between you. And Allah is Knowing and Wise." (Qur'an 60:10)

In refusing to send Umm Kulthum back to the Quraysh, Muhammad broke the treaty, claiming that the treaty stipulated that the Muslims would return to the Quraysh any *man* who came to them, not any *woman*.[66] However, Muhammad soon began to accept men from the Quraysh as well, thus definitively breaking the treaty.[67] The breaking of the treaty in this way would reinforce the principle that nothing was good except what was advantageous to Islam, and nothing evil except what hindered Islam.

THE KHAYBAR RAID

Allah had promised the Muslims disgruntled by the Treaty of Hudaybiyya "much booty" (Qur'an 48:19). To fulfill this promise, Muhammad led them against the Khaybar oasis, which was inhabited by Jews—many of them exiles from Medina. One of the Muslims later remembered: "When the apostle raided a people he waited until the morning. If he heard a call to prayer he held back; if he did not hear it he attacked. We came to Khaybar by night, and the apostle passed the night there; and when morning came he did not hear the call to prayer, so he rode and we rode with him.... We met the workers of Khaybar coming out in the morning with their spades and baskets. When they saw the apostle and the army they cried, 'Muhammad with his force,' and turned tail and fled. The apostle said, 'Allah Akbar! Khaybar is destroyed. When we arrive in a people's square it is a bad morning for those who have been warned.'"[68]

The Muslim advance was inexorable. "The apostle," according to Ibn Ishaq, "seized the property piece by piece and conquered the forts one by one as he came to them."[69] Ibn Sa'd reports that the battle was fierce: the "polytheists...killed a large number of [Muhammad's] Companions and he also put to death a very large number of them.... He killed ninety-three men of the Jews."[70] Muhammad and his men offered the *fajr* prayer, the Islamic dawn prayer, before it was light, and then entered Khaybar itself. The Muslims immediately set out to locate the inhabitants' wealth. A Jewish leader of Khaybar, Kinana bin al-Rabi, was brought before Muhammad; Kinana was supposed to have been entrusted with the treasure of the Banu Nadir. Kinana denied knowing where this treasure was, but Muhammad pressed him: "Do you know that if we find you have it I shall kill you?" Kinana said yes, that he did know that.

Some of the treasure was found. To find the rest, Muhammad gave orders concerning Kinana: "Torture him until you extract what he has." One of the Muslims built a fire on Kinana's chest, but Kinana would not give up his secret. When he was at the point of death, Muhammad bin Maslama, killer of the poet Ka'b bin Al-Ashraf, beheaded him.[71]

Muhammad agreed to let the people of Khaybar go into exile, allowing them, as he had the Banu Nadir, to keep as much of their property as they could carry.[72] The Prophet of Islam, however, commanded them to leave behind all of their gold and silver.[73] He had intended to expel all of them, but some farmers begged him to let them stay if they gave him half their yield annually.[74] Muhammad agreed: "I will allow you to continue here, so long as we would desire."[75] He warned them: "If we wish to expel you we will expel you."[76] They no longer had any rights that did not depend upon the goodwill and sufferance of Muhammad and the Muslims. And indeed, when the Muslims discovered some treasure that some of the Khaybar Jews had hidden, he ordered the women of the tribe enslaved and seized the perpetrators' land.[77] A *hadith* notes that "the Prophet had their warriors killed, their offspring and woman taken as captives."[78]

During the caliphate of Umar (634–644), the Jews who remained at Khaybar were banished to Syria, and the rest of their land was seized.[79] To this day, Muslims warn Jews of impending massacres by chanting, "Khaybar, Khaybar. O Jews, the army of Muhammad will return."

MUHAMMAD'S SEX SLAVE

One of the Muslim warriors, Dihya ibn Khalifa, came to Muhammad and said: "O Allah's Prophet! Give me a slave girl from the captives." The Prophet of Islam was agreeable, telling Dihya: "Go and take any slave girl." Dihya chose a woman named Safiyya bint Huyayy.[80] Safiyya was the daughter of Huyayy bin Akhtab, who had induced the Banu Qurayzah Jews to repudiate their alliance with Muhammad. Muhammad had killed Huyayy along with the rest of the men of the Qurayzah. Safiyya's husband was Kinana ibn Rabi, who had just been tortured and killed by the warriors of jihad. Once captured herself, she had won the admiration of the warriors of Islam, who told their prophet: "We have not seen the like of her among the captives of war."[81] One man added: "O Allah's Messenger! You gave Safiyya bint Huyai to Dihya and she is the chief-mistress of [the ladies] of the tribes of Quraiza and An-Nadir, she befits none but you."[82]

Muhammad accordingly called for Dihya and Safiyya. When the Prophet of Islam saw Safiyya, he told Dihya: "Take any slave girl other than her from the captives." Muhammad then immediately freed her and married her himself—since she agreed to convert to Islam, she was able to be elevated beyond the position of a slave. That night Safiyya was dressed as a bride, and a wedding feast was hastily arranged. On the way out of Khaybar that night, Muhammad halted his caravan as soon as they were outside the oasis, pitched a tent, and consummated the marriage.[83] Safiyya went from being the wife of a Jewish chieftain to being the wife of the man who murdered her father and husband in a single day.

TAKING MECCA

Muhammad then marched on Mecca with an army of, according to some reports, ten thousand Muslims.[84] When the Meccans saw the size of their force, which Muhammad exaggerated by ordering his men to build many extra fires during the night as his men were assembled outside the city, they knew that all was lost. Many of the most notable Quraysh warriors now deserted and, converting to Islam, joined Muhammad's forces. As they advanced, they were met by Abu Sufyan himself, who had opposed Muhammad bitterly as a leader of the Quraysh; but now Abu Sufyan wanted to become a Muslim. Allowed into Muhammad's presence, Abu Sufyan recited a poem that included these lines:

> I was like one going astray in the darkness of the night,
> But now I am led on the right track.
> I could not guide myself, and he who with God overcame me
> Was he whom I had driven away with all my might.

According to Ibn Ishaq, when he got to the lines "he who with God overcame me / Was he whom I had driven away with all my might," Muhammad "punched him in the chest and said, 'You did indeed!' "[85] But when Muhammad said, "Woe to you, Abu Sufyan, isn't it time that you recognize that I am God's apostle?" Abu Sufyan replied, "As to that I still have some doubt."[86]

At that, one of Muhammad's lieutenants, Abbas, said to Abu Sufyan: "Submit and testify that there is no God but Allah and that Muhammad is the apostle of God before you lose your head." Abu Sufyan complied.[87]

When Muhammad "forced his entry" into Mecca, according to Ibn Sa'd, "the people embraced Islam willingly or unwillingly."[88] The Prophet of Islam ordered the Muslims to fight only those individuals or groups who resisted their advance into the city—except for a list of people who were to be killed, even if they had sought sanctuary in the Ka'bah itself.[89]

CONSOLIDATING POWER IN ARABIA

Muhammad was the master of Mecca, but there was one additional great obstacle between him and mastery of all Arabia. Malik ibn Awf, a member of the Thaqif tribe of the city of Ta'if, south of Mecca, began to assemble a force to fight the Muslims. The people of Ta'if had rejected Muhammad and treated him shabbily when he presented his prophetic claim to them ten years earlier. They had always been rivals of the Quraysh and viewed the conversion of the latter to Islam with disdain. Malik assembled a force and marched out to face the Muslims; Muhammad met him with an army twelve thousand strong, saying, "We shall not be worsted today for want of numbers."[90]

The two forces met at a *wadi*—a dry riverbed—called Hunayn, near Mecca. Malik and his men arrived first and took up positions that gave them an immense tactical advantage. The Muslims, despite their superior numbers, were routed. As they broke ranks and fled, Muhammad called out: "Where are you going, men? Come to me. I am God's apostle. I am Muhammad the son of Abdullah."[91] Some of the Muslims did take heart, and gradually the tide began to turn—although with tremendous loss of life on both sides.

The Muslims eventually prevailed, wiping out the last major force that stood between the Prophet of Islam and mastery of Arabia. After the battle, Muhammad received another revelation explaining that the Muslims had won because of supernatural help:

> Allah has already given you victory in many regions and on the day of Hunayn, when your great number pleased you, but it did not avail you at all, and the earth was confining for you with its vastness; then you turned back, fleeing. Then Allah sent down His tranquility upon His Messenger and upon the believers and sent down soldier angels whom you did not see and punished those who disbelieved. And that is the recompense of the disbelievers. Then Allah will accept repentance after that for whom He wills; and Allah is Forgiving and Merciful. (Qur'an 9:25–27)

With Malik defeated, the Muslims later conquered Ta'if with little re-sistance. On his way into the city, Muhammad stopped under a tree and, finding the area to his liking, sent word to the owner of the property: "Either come out or we will destroy your wall."[92] The owner refused to appear before Muhammad, so the Muslims indeed destroyed his proper-ty.[93] Endeavoring, however, to win the tribesmen of Ta'if to Islam, Mu-hammad was lenient toward them. In his distribution of the booty, he likewise favored some of the recent converts among the Quraysh, hop-ing to cement their allegiance to Islam. His favoritism, however, led to grumbling. One Muslim approached him boldly: "Muhammad, I've seen what you have done today…I don't think you have been just."

The Prophet of Islam replied incredulously: "If justice is not to be found with me then where will you find it?"[94]

CALLING THE WORLD TO ISLAM

Muhammad was determined to extend that justice to the world. Islamic tradition holds that he wrote to Heraclius, the Eastern Roman emperor in Constantinople:

> In the name of Allah, the most Gracious, the Most Mer-ciful. [This letter is] from Muhammad, the slave of Allah, and His Messenger, to Heraclius, the ruler of the Byzan-tines. Peace be upon him, who follows the [true] guidance. Now then, I invite you to Islam [that is, surrender to Al-lah], embrace Islam and you will be safe; embrace Islam and Allah will bestow on you a double reward. But if you reject this invitation of Islam, you shall be responsible for misguiding the peasants [that is, your nation].[95]

Then the letter quoted the Qur'an: "Say, 'O People of the Book, come to a common word between us and you—that we will not worship except Allah and not associate anything with Him and not take one another as lords instead of Allah.' But if they turn away, then say, 'Bear witness that we are Muslims.'" (3:64).

The letter contains a clear threat: "embrace Islam and you will be safe." Presumably, then, Heraclius and his people would not be safe if they did not embrace Islam. Heraclius, of course, did not accept Islam, and soon the Byzantines would know well that the warriors of jihad indeed granted no safety to those who made such a choice.

Muhammad sent a similar letter to Khosrau, the ruler of the Persians. After reading the letter of the Prophet of Islam, Khosrau contemptuously tore it to pieces. When news of this reached Muhammad, he called upon Allah to tear the Persian emperor and his followers to pieces.[96] He told his followers that they would enjoy the fruits of jihad victories over both Heraclius and Khosrau: "When Khosrau perishes, there will be no [more] Khosrau after him, and when Caesar perishes, there will be no more Caesar after him. By Him in Whose hands Muhammad's life is, you will spend the treasures of both of them in Allah's Cause."[97]

JIHAD AGAINST THE CHRISTIANS

Allah gave Muhammad a revelation commanding Muslims to fight even against Jews and Christians until they accepted Islamic hegemony, symbolized by payment of a poll tax (*jizya*) and discriminatory regulations that would ensure that they would be constantly reminded of their subordinate position: "Fight those who believe not in Allah nor the Last Day, nor hold that forbidden which has been forbidden by Allah and His Messenger, nor acknowledge the religion of truth, of the People of the Book, until they pay the jizya with willing submission, and feel themselves subdued." (Qur'an 9:29)

He told his followers to offer these unbelievers conversion to Islam, as he had offered to the rulers, and if they refused, to offer them the opportunity to pay tribute as vassals of the Islamic state, and if they refused that also, to go to war:

> Fight in the name of Allah and in the way of Allah. Fight against those who disbelieve in Allah. Make a holy war, do not embezzle the spoils; do not break your pledge; and do not mutilate [the dead] bodies; do not kill the children. When you meet your enemies who are polytheists, invite them to three courses of action. If they respond to any one of these, you also accept it and withhold yourself from do-

ing them any harm. Invite them to [accept] Islam; if they respond to you, accept it from them and desist from fighting against them.... If they refuse to accept Islam, demand from them the Jizya. If they agree to pay, accept it from them and hold off your hands. If they refuse to pay the tax, seek Allah's help and fight them.[98]

After commanding his followers to make war against Christians, Muhammad resolved to set an example for his followers by doing just that. In 631, he ordered the Muslims to begin preparations for a raid on the Byzantine Empire, at its northern Arabia garrison at Tabuk. The journey across the desert sands in the height of summer was arduous, and when Muhammad and his large Muslim force arrived at the Byzantine holdings in northwestern Arabia, they found that the Byzantine troops had withdrawn rather than trying to engage them.

On the way back, Allah gave Muhammad revelations scolding the Muslims who had declined to go along on the expedition. Allah reminded the Muslims that their first duty was to him and his prophet, and that those who refused to wage jihad would face terrible punishment:

> O you who have believed, what is with you that, when you are told to go forth in the cause of Allah, you adhere heavily to the earth? Are you satisfied with the life of this world rather than the Hereafter? But what is the enjoyment of worldly life compared to the Hereafter except a little. If you do not go forth, He will punish you with a painful punishment and will replace you with another people, and you will not harm Him at all. And Allah is over all things competent. (Qur'an 9:38–39)

Not that Muhammad needed their help, of course, because he had Allah on his side:

> If you do not aid the Prophet, Allah has already aided him when those who disbelieved had driven him out as one of two, when they were in the cave and he said to his companion, "Do not grieve; indeed Allah is with us." And Allah sent down his tranquility upon him and supported him

with angels you did not see and made the word of those who disbelieved the lowest, while the word of Allah, that is the highest. And Allah is Exalted in Might and Wise. (Qur'an 9:40)

THE PREEMINENCE OF JIHAD

Nonetheless, to go forth in jihad for the sake of Allah (*jihad fi sabil Allah*, which denotes in Islamic theology armed struggle to establish the hegemony of the Islamic social order) is the best deed a Muslim can perform:

Go forth, whether light or heavy, and strive with your wealth and your lives in the cause of Allah. That is better for you, if you only knew. (Qur'an 9:41)

The Prophet of Islam emphasized this on many occasions. Once a man asked him, "Guide me to such a deed as equals *Jihad* [in reward]."

Muhammad answered: "I do not find such a deed."[99]

Allah told Muhammad that the true Muslims did not hesitate to wage jihad, even to the point of risking their property and their very lives. The ones who refused to do this weren't even believers at all:

Those who believe in Allah and the Last Day would not ask permission of you to be excused from striving with their wealth and their lives. And Allah is Knowing of those who fear Him. Only those would ask permission of you who do not believe in Allah and the Last Day and whose hearts have doubted, and they, in their doubt, are hesitating. (Qur'an 9:44–45)

This "striving with their wealth and their lives" was, in the context of Muhammad's circumstances, unmistakably a military command—particularly in light of the fact that Allah was guaranteeing Paradise to those who would "fight in the way of Allah and shall slay and be slain" (Qur'an 9:111)—the Arabic word for "striving" being a form of the word "*jihad*." On another occasion he said: "I have been commanded to fight against people, till they testify to the fact that there is no god but Allah, and believe in me [that] I am the messenger [from the Lord] and in all that I have brought. And when they do it, their blood and riches are guaranteed protection on my behalf except where it is justified by law, and their affairs rest with Allah.[100] The obverse was also true: if they did not become Muslims, their blood and riches would not be guaranteed any protection from the Muslims.

"IF YOU ACCEPT ISLAM YOU WILL BE SAFE"

Muhammad was now the undisputed master of Arabia. The Arabian rulers and tribes that had not yet submitted to his authority now began to journey to Medina to accept his religion and pay him homage. To the lands of those who did not come, Muhammad sent jihad warriors. He sent the fearsome fighter Khalid bin al-Walid to the al-Harith tribe, instructing him to call them to accept Islam three days before he attacked them, and to call off the battle if they converted. Khalid duly told the tribe leaders: "If you accept Islam you will be safe"—whereupon the tribe converted. Khalid notified the Prophet of Islam and sent a deputation from the tribe to Medina to see Muhammad, who told them: "If Khalid had not written to me that you had accepted Islam and had not fought I would throw your heads beneath your feet."[101]

From Himyar in south Arabia came a letter informing Muhammad that the kings of the region had accepted Islam and waged war in Allah's name against the remaining pagans in the area. Muhammad was pleased, sending them a response informing them that "your messenger reached me on my return from the land of the Byzantines and he met us in Medina and conveyed your message and your news and informed us of your Islam and of your killing the polytheists. God has guided you with His guidance."

He detailed their obligations as Muslims and directed that Jews and Christians in their domains should be invited to convert to Islam, but if they refused, they were "not to be turned" from their religions.

Rather, the Jew or Christian in these newly Muslim lands "must pay the poll tax—for every adult, male or female, free or slave, one full dinar"—and he gave instructions for how that amount—"or its equivalent in clothes"—was to be calculated. He reminded the kings that the lives of the Jews and Christians depended on their payment of this tax: "He who pays that to God's apostle has the guarantee of God and His apostle, and he who withholds it is the enemy of God and His apostle."[102]

Ultimately the Prophet of Islam determined that Jews and Christians would no longer be allowed in Arabia at all. "I will expel the Jews and Christians from the Arabian Peninsula," he told his companions, "and will not leave any but Muslims."[103] He gave just such an order on his deathbed.

THE IMPORTANCE OF THE JIZYA

The jizya tax was so important because, besides raiding, which produced inconsistent results, it was the Muslims' chief source of income. This is clear in a letter Muhammad sent to a Jewish tribe, the Banu Janbah. He assured them that "under the guarantee of Allah and the guarantee of His Apostle there will be no cruelty or oppression on you. Verily, the Apostle of Allah will defend you." However: "Verily, for the Apostle of Allah will be the booty which you receive on making peace [with some party] and every slave you get, as well as animals and other objects, except that which the Apostle of Allah or his envoy remits. Verily, it is binding on you to pay one-fourth of the yield of your date-palms, and one-fourth of your game from the rivers, and one-fourth of what your women spin." But that was all: "besides that you will be exempt from *jizyah* and forced labour."[104] Likewise, to a Christian ruler Muhammad wrote:

> I will not fight against you unless I write to you in advance. So, join the fold of Islam or pay the *jizyah*. Obey Allah and His Apostle and the messengers of His Apostle, honour them and dress them in nice clothes.... Provide Zayd with good clothes. If my messengers will be pleased with you, I shall also be pleased with you.... Pay three *wasaq* of barley to Harmalah...[105]

The onerous tax burdens that Jews and Christians in Muslim domains bore simply for the privilege of being allowed to live in relative peace would become the key source of income for the great Islamic empires that carried Muhammad's jihad into Africa, Europe, and Asia. The *dhimmis* (or *zimmis*) were the "protected people" in the Islamic state, who paid the *jizya* and accepted discrimination and humiliation in exchange for permission to remain in their ancestral religions rather than convert to Islam.

MUHAMMAD'S BATTLES

Muhammad, according to Islamic tradition, died in 632. Ibn Ishaq reports that he had participated in twenty-seven battles. The parenthetical material below beginning with "T." refers to the version of the same material as recorded by another Muslim historian, Tabari.

The apostle took part personally in twenty-seven...raids:

Waddan which was the raid of al-Abwa'.
Buwat in the direction of Radwa. 'Ushayra in the valley of Yanbu'.
The first fight at Badr in pursuit of Kurz b. Jabir.
The great battle of Badr in which God slew the chiefs of Quraysh (T. and their nobles and captured many).
Banu Sulaym until he reached al-Kudr.
Al-Sawiq in pursuit of Abu. Sufyan b. Harb (T. until he reached Qarqara al-Kudr).
Ghatafan (T. towards Najd), which is the raid of Dhu Amarr.
Bahran, a mine in the Hijaz (T. above al-Furu').
Uhud.
Hamra'u'l-Asad.
Banu Nadir.
Dhatu'l-Riqa' of Nakhl.
The last battle of Badr.
Dumatu'l-Jandal.
Al-Khandaq.

Banul Qurayza.

Banu Lihyan of Hudhayl. Dhu Qarad. Banu'l-Mustaliq of Khuza'a.

Al-Hudaybiya not intending to fight where the polytheists opposed his passage.

Khaybar.

Then he went on the accomplished pilgrimage.

The occupation of Mecca.

Hunayn.

Al-Ta'if.

Tabuk.

In truth, he actually fought in nine engagements: Badr; Uhud; al-Khandaq; Qurayza; al-Mustaliq; Khaybar; the occupation [of Mecca]; Hunayn; and al-Ta'if.[106]

CHAPTER TWO

THE AGE OF THE GREAT CONQUESTS

Jihad in the Seventh Century

Shortly after the generally accepted date of Muhammad's death, 632, the Arab armies swept out of Arabia with immense force and embarked upon a series of conquests unparalleled in human history for their rapidity and scope. In detailing what happened, early historians contradict one another on numerous particulars, such that no reliable sequence of events can be definitively established, but there is no doubt that the two great world powers of the day, the Eastern Roman (Byzantine) Empire and the Persian Empire, suffered a series of staggering defeats, and by the end of the seventh century, the Arab invaders had amassed a huge empire of their own. Sassanid Persia was conquered altogether, and the Eastern Roman Empire was substantially reduced in size and placed in a state of ongoing siege, a state it would endure for the next seven hundred years.

These conquests began during what Muslim scholars generally regard as the first Islamic Golden Age, the period of the "Rightly-Guided Caliphs," Abu Bakr, Umar, Uthman, and Ali. Spanning 632 to 661, this period is held up to this day as the quintessential example of what an Islamic state is and ought to be.

It was anything but peaceful.

THE FIRST CALIPHATE CONTROVERSY

When Muhammad died, who should lead the nascent Muslim community was by no means clear. One party of the believers insisted that

Muhammad had chosen Ali ibn Abi Talib, his son-in-law (the husband of Muhammad's daughter Fatima) and one of his earliest followers, to succeed him. They presented as evidence a tradition in which Muhammad asked Ali, "Aren't you satisfied with being unto me what Aaron was unto Moses?"[1] The Qur'an depicts Moses saying to Aaron, "Take my place among my people" (7:142), so this meant, they argued, that Ali was to be Muhammad's successor (*khalifa*, or caliph).

Not everyone was convinced. Aisha, Muhammad's youngest and favorite wife, waved away Ali's claim to be Muhammad's successor by invoking her own closeness to the prophet in his dying moments. When, she asked, did Muhammad appoint Ali his successor? "Verily, when he died he was resting against my chest [or, in my lap] and he asked for a washbasin and then collapsed while in that state, and I could not even perceive that he had died, so when did he appoint him by will?"[2] She produced her own quotation from Muhammad regarding who should become the leader of the believers: "It is not befitting that a group, among whom is Abu Bakr, be led by other than him."[3] (This is, however, classified as a "weak" *hadith*, meaning that its authenticity is doubted.)

Meanwhile, the *ansar* (helpers), that is, those who became Muslim after Muhammad's *hijrah* to Medina, asserted that there should now be two rulers, one for them and one for the *muhajiroun* (emigrants), those from among the Quraysh tribe who had become Muslim in Mecca before the *hijrah*. The *ansar* chose one of their own, Sa'd ibn Ubadah, as their leader, but one of the *ansar* argued that there should be one ruler, and that ruler should be from among the *muhajiroun*: "In truth Muhammad was from Quraysh, and his people are more entitled...and more suitable."[4]

This was no staid gathering of courtly parliamentarians. The *ansar*, convinced that the *muhajiroun* should lead, rushed to swear their allegiance to Abu Bakr; in the excitement, Sa'd ibn Ubadah, who still refused allegiance, was pushed to the ground. Some of his followers exclaimed: "Be careful not to step on Sa'd!"[5]

At that, Umar, one of the *muhajiroun* and a fierce partisan of Abu Bakr, cried out, "Kill him! May God slay him!" He stepped on Sa'd's head and snarled: "I intend to tread upon you until your arm is dislocated." Sa'd, though caught on the ground, spat back: "By God, if you remove a single hair from it you'll return with no front teeth in your mouth." But then Abu Bakr urged Umar to show compassion—after all, Sa'd had a following that Abu Bakr wanted to bring into his fold—and a measure of calm was restored.[6]

Abu Bakr was one of Muhammad's closest and most fanatical followers. When a skeptic had doubted Muhammad's story about traveling to Jerusalem and then to Paradise on a winged white horse with a human head, Abu Bakr demonstrated the strength of his devotion: "If he says so then it is true. And what is so surprising in that? He tells me that communications from God from heaven to earth come to him in an hour of a day or night and I believe him, and that is more extraordinary than that at which you boggle!"[7]

But Abu Bakr's faith wasn't centered upon Muhammad. When the prophet of Islam died, Abu Bakr stood before the weeping Muslims and declared: "Whoever worshipped Muhammad, then Muhammad is dead, but whoever worshipped Allah, then Allah is alive and shall never die."[8]

Once he was definitively the caliph, Abu Bakr addressed the Muslims, making sure they knew that he was not claiming to have inherited Muhammad's prophetic powers: "Oh people, I am just like you…God chose Muhammad above the worlds and protected him from evils, but I am only a follower, not an innovator. If I am upright, then follow me, but if I deviate, straighten me out…. I have a Satan who takes possession of me; so when he comes to me, avoid me so I may have no effect on your hair and your skins"—that is, not harm them.[9]

Abu Bakr exhorted the Muslims: "Abandon not jihad, when the people hold back from jihad, they are put to disgrace."[10]

THE APOSTASY WARS

Not all the Muslims were impressed. Self-proclaimed prophets, disdaining to be ruled by a mere successor of a prophet, had already arisen all over Arabia during the time of Muhammad's final illness. After Abu Bakr became caliph, they rejected not only his authority but Islam itself. Maslama bin Habib (derisively dubbed "Musaylima" or "little Maslama" in Muslim accounts) and his wife Sajah bint al-Harith declared themselves to be new prophets in the eastern Arabian oasis of Yamamah. Aswad al-Ansi in Yemen and Tulayhah ibn Khuwaylid of the Asad tribe in north central Arabia announced that they were new prophets as well. They began demanding the allegiance of those who had been Muslim.[11]

Many of the tribes of Arabia that Muhammad had recently subdued saw in his death their chance to reassert their autonomy. Numerous, and sometimes all, members of every Arab tribe except two—the Quraysh and the Thaqif—left Islam at this point.[12] They declared that their pledge of allegiance to Muhammad had ended with his death, and that neither Abu Bakr nor anyone else had any right to claim it. Some declared that they would maintain Islamic prayers but withhold *sadaqah*, the supposedly voluntary alms-giving that was in effect a payment of tribute to the leaders of the Muslims.

Abu Bakr rejected this proposal. He and his followers countered that these Arabs had not pledged allegiance to Muhammad as a person but as a prophet, and that the religion they had embraced still existed. What's more, Muhammad himself had mandated that anyone who left that religion should be put to death: "Whoever changed his Islamic religion, then kill him."[13]

Abu Bakr sent his most skillful warrior, Khalid ibn al-Walid, to subdue the apostates and bring them back into the fold of Islam. Abu Bakr gave these instructions to the Muslim armies: "When you come upon one of the people's abodes, and then hear the call to prayer in it, desist from its people until you have asked them for what reason they were hostile. But if you do not hear the call to prayer, then launch a raid such that you kill and burn."[14] He added that if Muslims did not hear a people make the call to prayer, they had no choice but to "raid them" and "kill them by every means, by fire or whatever else." And if they refused to pay the alms tax, there would be no choice but to "raid them without any word" of warning.[15]

Khalid carried out his assignment with dispatch, aided by some skillful diplomacy that turned some of the rebels back to Islam and considerably swelled his ranks. He marched across Arabia subduing the rebellious tribes with relative ease, calling people to Islam and killing those who resisted.[16]

The Muslims captured one of the chieftains of the rebels, Malik ibn Nuwayrah; Malik made the Islamic profession of faith, but Khalid had him beheaded anyway and took his wife, Umm Tamim bint al-Minhal, for himself. Back in Medina, the headquarters of Muslims, Abu Bakr's lieutenant and eventual successor Umar was incensed. He hurried to Abu Bakr and raged against Khalid: "The enemy of God transgressed against a Muslim man, killing him and then leaping upon his wife."[17] Abu Bakr kept his counsel.

Khalid returned to Medina as a conquering hero, wearing as a trophy his turban festooned with the apostate arrows that had been shot at him. But instead of marveling at his valor, Umar in fury pulled the arrows from his turban and broke them, and raged at Khalid: "What hypocrisy, to kill a Muslim man and then leap upon his wife! By God, I would pelt you with stones."[18]

The Qur'an (which, according even to Muslim accounts, had not been collected by this time) forbids a Muslim to kill a fellow Muslim (4:92). In the face of Umar's anger, Khalid said nothing, but he worried that Abu Bakr would agree with Umar; however, when granted an audience with the caliph, Khalid found himself pardoned. Abu Bakr explained to his lieutenant: "Oh Umar, I will not sheathe a sword that God has drawn against the unbelievers."[19]

That sword was still needed. The Muslims met the forces of the rival "prophet" Musaylima at Yamamah. Amid the battle melee, one of the Muslim commanders made it very clear what the fight was about: "Oh company of the Muslims, you are the party of God, and they are the parties of Satan."[20] The apostates were defeated, and the rebellion collapsed. It was all over by March 18, 633, just a year after the death of Muhammad. Abu Bakr ordered Khalid to have all the adult men of the Banu Hanifah, a powerful tribe that had supported Musaylima, put to death.

Khalid, however, concluded a treaty with them instead, and pressed one of the Banu Hanifah chieftains, Mujja'ah: "Give me your daughter in marriage." Mujja'ah warned Khalid that he was destroying his reputation in the eyes of Abu Bakr. Khalid had no patience for this, shouting, "Marry her to me, man!"[21] But Mujja'ah was right: soon a letter arrived from Abu Bakr, reminding him of the Muslims' losses in the apostasy wars: "Upon my life, oh son of Khalid's mother, are you so free as to marry women, while in the court of your house is the blood of 1,200 men of the Muslims that has not yet dried?"[22]

Khalid thought he detected the influence of his rival, muttering, "This is the work of the little left-handed man"—that is, Umar.[23] Abu Bakr's most notable achievement may have been maintaining an uneasy peace between the little left-handed man and the great general, as both played a large role in what was to come next. Umar declared that Abu Bakr (not Khalid) had "successfully waged the apostasy wars, and thanks to him, Islam is now supreme in Arabia."[24] But the apostasy wars were simply a process of recapturing what had already been won for Islam, and then lost again; now the Muslims' gaze turned outward. There were many, many more unbelievers outside Arabia than there had ever been within it, and Khalid would soon unsheathe the sword of Allah against them.

THE CONQUEST OF IRAQ

Abu Bakr needed Khalid too much to stay angry with him over his amatory adventures. While his general was still at Yamamah, the caliph sent him new orders: "Go on toward Iraq until you enter it. Begin with the gateway to India, which is al-Ubdullah.[25] Render the people of Persia [Fars] and those nations under their rule peaceable."[26]

Iraq was within the domains of Sassanid Persia; it would become the first land outside of Arabia to experience jihad. Khalid stormed through the land, defeating the Persians in four initial battles. In May 633, he reached the city of al-Hirah, the capital of the northern Euphrates region; its Sassanian governor, Qabisah ibn Iyas, and the noblemen of the city came to welcome him. Khalid wasted no time explaining why he and his men were there: "I call you to God and to Islam. If you respond to the call, then you are Muslims: You obtain the benefits they enjoy and take up the responsibilities they bear. If you refuse, then [you must pay] the *jizyah*. If you refuse the *jizyah*, I will bring against you tribes of people who are more eager for death than you are for life. We will then fight you until God decides between us and you."[27] Another account has Khalid saying, "If you refuse the jizyah, then we will bring against you a people who love death more than you love drinking wine."[28]

Qabisah was unprepared for war. "We have no need to fight you," he told Khalid. "Rather, we will keep to our religion and pay you the *jizyah.*"[29] The people of al-Hirah, a Christian stronghold within a Zoroastrian empire, agreed to pay the Muslims ninety thousand dirhams.

In presenting Qabisah with this triple choice, Khalid was obeying the commands of the Qur'an and Muhammad: offer the People of the Book (Jews, Christians, and Zoroastrians) conversion to Islam; subjugation under the rule of the Muslims, signified by the payment of the tax, the *jizyah*, from which the Muslims were exempt; or war. Given the paucity of contemporary evidence of Muhammad's life, or of the existence of the Qur'an before the early eighth century, it is quite possible that Khalid was the originator of this triple choice, rather than a believer obediently following the dictates of his prophet; in any case, this choice became codified in the Qur'an and Islamic law, and remains the primary stance of Islam toward the People of the Book to this day.

Khalid wrote more harshly to the Sassanian rulers: "From Khalid b. al-Walid to the rulers of the Persians: Peace be upon whosoever follows right guidance."[30] This was to become the mandated greeting for Muslims toward non-Muslims; when greeting a fellow Muslim, Muslims were to say, "Peace be upon you." But to a non-Muslim, a Muslim was to wish peace only upon "whoever follows right guidance," that is, the Muslims. Khalid continued:

> Praise be to God, Who has scattered your servants, wrested your sovereignty away, and rendered your plotting weak. Whoever worships the way we worship, faces the direction we face in prayer, and eats meat slaughtered in our fashion, that person is a Muslim and obtains the benefits we enjoy and takes up the responsibilities we bear. Now then, when you receive this letter, send me hostages and place yourself under my protection. Otherwise, by Him other than Whom there is no god, I will most certainly send against you a people who love death just as you love life.[31]

The Sassanian rulers soon realized these were not empty words. Khalid stormed through Persia, offering the Persians the same ultimatum: convert to Islam, pay the *jizya*, or face war. He defeated the Persians in numerous battles. At the fortress of Dumah, a force of Christian Arabs joined the locals in defense against the Muslims; Khalid defeated them as easily as he had everyone else, beheaded their commander, and bought his daughter, who was renowned for her beauty, as a sex slave.[32]

In December 633, Khalid arrived at al-Firad, a Persian fortress on the Sassanians' border with the other great power of the day, the Byzantine Empire. The Byzantines, seeing the Muslim advances all over Iraq, decided to aid the Persians against Khalid, even though they had just fought a series of exhausting wars against each other. The ninth-century Muslim historian Tabari has the Persians and Byzantines exchanging intelligence about Khalid: "This is a man who is fighting on the basis of religion. He has intelligence and knowledge. By God, he will most definitely be victorious, whereas we will most certainly fail."[33]

It is doubtful that seventh-century Roman and Persian commanders were actually that defeatist, but they were certainly correct that Khalid was "fighting on the basis of religion." Everywhere he had gone in Persia, he had called the people to accept Islam or pay the *jizya*; for Khalid, the invasion of Persia was an expedition to bring Islam to the Sassanid Empire, or to subjugate the Zoroastrians and Christians in Persia under the rule of the Muslims.

The Persians and Byzantines had every reason to be concerned. Khalid told his men: "Press your pursuit of them. Do not grant them any respite."[34] The Muslims won a decisive victory; Tabari notes that "the cavalry commander would corner a group of them with the spears of his men; having collected them, they would kill them. On the day of al-Firad, one hundred thousand men were slain in the battle and the pursuit."[35]

After this, Khalid returned to Arabia and made the pilgrimage to Mecca, giving thanks to Allah for granting him so many great victories for Islam. He planned then to return to Persia and complete its conquest, first by attacking Qadissiyah, a Persian fort that lay between him and the imperial capital of Ctesiphon. As it turned out, however, he was needed elsewhere. The Muslim armies had entered Syria, a Byzantine province, but they were not facing as easy a time of it as Khalid had encountered in Persia. The Byzantine emperor Heraclius was assembling a massive force to meet them, and Abu Bakr wasn't confident that any of the generals he had in Syria were up to the challenge. But he knew a man who was: "By Allah," he exclaimed, "I shall destroy the Romans and the friends of

Satan with Khalid Ibn Al Walid."[36] He ordered Khalid to put his plans for Persia on hold for the time being and go to Syria.

Khalid did so and his men won battle after battle, reaching Damascus in August 634 and laying siege to it. But then his most important supporter, the caliph Abu Bakr, fell mortally ill. Tabari says it was the handiwork of those whom the Qur'an designates (at 5:82) to be the worst enemies of the Muslims: "The cause of his death was that the Jews fed him poison in a grain of rice; it is also said in porridge."[37]

"THE LITTLE LEFT-HANDED MAN" TAKES OVER

On his deathbed, Abu Bakr appointed his most trusted lieutenant, Umar ibn al-Khattab, to succeed him as caliph. As far as Umar was concerned, his first job upon becoming caliph was to put his enemy in his place. Umar's hatred for Khalid ibn al-Walid had not dimmed; even as Khalid was defeating Byzantine armies that were larger and better equipped in Syria, "the little left-handed man" finally had his chance: Umar sent word that he was relieving Khalid of command.[38]

Khalid complied humbly, staying with the Muslim armies as a lesser commander; however, the great general had the last laugh later, when Abu Ubaydah, whom Umar had appointed commander of the Muslim armies, heeded Khalid's advice regarding the placement of the Muslim armies against the Byzantines in the decisive battle of Yarmouk, and ultimately placed him in command of the Muslim forces at Yarmouk. Khalid, always behaving deferentially toward Abu Ubaydah, continued to win victory after victory over the infidels; he became a hero among the Muslims and was hailed as "the sword of Allah." There was one person, however, whom he never entirely won over: Umar, now the caliph of the Muslims.

TAKING SYRIA

The Byzantines amassed a massive force to meet the Muslims at Yarmouk in Syria, once again far outnumbering the Muslim armies.[39] Before the battle, one of the Muslims, Miqdad, stood before the Muslims and recited the eighth chapter of the Qur'an, "The Spoils of War," also known as "The Chapter of Jihad," in order to instill in them the fighting spirit.[40] It was said that Muhammad had begun after the Battle of Badr to recite this chapter before battles, and as he remained the "excellent example" (33:21) for the Muslims, the practice continued.

In this chapter, Allah reminds the Muslims to remember, "When your Lord inspired to the angels, 'I am with you, so strengthen those who have believed. I will cast terror into the hearts of those who disbelieved, so strike upon the necks and strike from them every fingertip.'" (8:12) It exhorts the Muslims to "fight them until there is no fitnah [disturbance, rebellion] and the religion, all of it, is for Allah." (8:39) And it reminds them that Muhammad is to receive a fifth of the goods and women they capture from the enemy: "And know that anything you obtain of war booty—then indeed, for Allah is one fifth of it and for the Messenger and for near relatives and the orphans, the needy, and the traveler." (8:41)

Another Muslim commander, Abu Sufyan, went among the troops exclaiming: "God, God! You are the defenders of the Arabs and the supporters of Islam. They are the defenders of the Romans and the supporters of polytheism. O God, this is a day from among your days. O God, send down your help to your worshipers."[41]

Thus inspired, the Muslims rushed to engage the Byzantines in battle. In the latter camp, morale was not so high. The Byzantine emperor Heraclius, meanwhile, was worried. He told his lieutenants: "Did I not tell you, 'Do not fight them'? You have no staying power with these people. Their religion is a new religion that renews their persistence, so that no one will stand up to them but he will be tested."[42]

Indeed. Khalid and his men won a decisive victory at Yarmouk, drastically weakening the Christian empire and paving the way for more Arab conquests.[43] The Muslims then struck a further blow to the Christians by expelling the Christian community at Najran in Yemen from the Arabian Peninsula, in accord with what were recorded as Muhammad's deathbed words: "If I live—if Allah wills—I will expel the Jews and the Christians from the Arabian Peninsula."[44]

The Muslims moved on to a swift conquest of Damascus; the native Christian population was forced to pay the *jizya* (tax), and Khalid assured them that they would be safe as long as the money kept flowing:

"The Muslims and their Caliph will practice nothing but good to the people of Damascus while they keep paying the *jizyah*."[45]

Umar likewise emphasized that the Muslims must be sure to collect the *jizya* from the subjugated peoples, as it was nothing less than the Muslims' source of livelihood: "I advise you to fulfill Allah's *dhimma* [financial obligation made with the *dhimmi*] as it is the *dhimma* of your Prophet and the source of the livelihood of your dependents [that is, the taxes from the *dhimmi*.]"[46]

TAKING PERSIA

With Syria now almost entirely under the control of the invaders, the Muslims could turn their attention back to Persia. But many were reluctant, according to Tabari: "The Persian front was among the most disliked and difficult of the warfronts for them, because of the strength of the Persians' sovereignty, their military force, their might, and their subjection of the nations."[47] Finally Umar himself made an appeal, basing it firmly upon Islam:

> The Hijaz is not a home for you except for foraging, its inhabitants do not survive in it except by that. Where are the impulsive migrants for the sake of God's promise? Travel in the land that God has promised you in the Book to make you heirs to, for He has said, "That he may make it [Islam] triumph over all religion" [cf. Qur'an 9:33, 48:28, 61:9]. God is the one who grants victory to His religion, strengthens His helper, and commits to His people of the inheritances of the nations. Where are the righteous worshippers of God?[48]

Many Muslims heeded the call, and as far as they could tell, Umar's words proved true. The Muslims met a vastly superior Persian force at Buwaib on the Euphrates; Muslim sources recorded that the Persian army was devastated, losing one hundred thousand men to the Muslims' one hundred.[49] Soon after that, the armies approached each other again at another town on the Euphrates, Qadisiyya. Despite their earlier losses, the Persians still vastly outnumbered the Muslims and were vastly better equipped.

As seven thousand Muslims encamped to face a Persian force of thirty thousand, the Persians were derisive. Seeing the thinness of the Arabs' arrows, the Persians laughed, saying the invaders had come armed with spindles. Some of the Persians called out to the invading warriors: "You have no might or power or weapons. What has brought you here? Turn back!"[50] The Arabs responded: "We shall not turn back. We are not the kind of people who turn back."[51]

The Persians invited the Muslims to send an emissary to explain why they had come. The Muslims sent a warrior named Al-Mughirah, who explained to Rustam, the Persian commander, and his men about Islam and added: "If you kill us, we shall enter Paradise; if we kill you, you shall enter the Fire, or hand over the poll tax."[52] The Persians snorted derisively and retreated to the battle lines.

But the Persian emperor, Yazdegerd III, was intrigued. He summoned the Muslim envoys to his court and asked them what they wanted. When the rough jihadis entered, clad in rustic cloaks and sandals and carrying whips, the perfumed, splendidly clad Persian courtiers were as amazed as they were contemptuous.[53]

Yazdegerd, however, was in no mood for mockery. He asked the Muslims point-blank: "Why did you come here? What induced you to attack us and covet our country?"

A member of the Muslim delegation, Al-Nu'man ibn Muqarrin, answered by telling him about the prophet, whom he did not name, who "promised us the goodness of this world and of the next," and who brought all the tribes of Arabia under his sway, "willingly or unwillingly." The prophet, said Al-Nu'man, "ordered us to start with the nations adjacent to us and invite them to justice." He added:

> We are therefore inviting you to embrace our religion. This is a religion which approves of all that is good and rejects all that is evil. If you refuse our invitation, you must pay the poll tax. This is a bad thing, but not as bad as the alternative; if you refuse, it will be war.[54]

Yazdegerd was incensed. He responded: "But for the custom not to kill envoys, I would have killed you. I have nothing for you."[55] He told them that the Persians would "punish you severely as an example for others."[56]

But it was not to be. At Qadisiyya, the Persians were again decisively defeated. The Muslims' control over Iraq was now virtually total, and the warriors of jihad continued moving against what remained of the Sassanid Empire, pursuing the shattered remnants of the Persian army into Persia itself.

When the Muslims took the Persian imperial capital of Ctesiphon in 636, they entered the emperor's White Palace, had the throne replaced with a pulpit, proclaimed that there was no god but Allah and Muhammad was his prophet, and said Friday prayers there. One of them quoted (or, given the lack of contemporary historical evidence of the existence by this time of the Muslim holy book, perhaps composed) verses of the Qur'an about the opulence they had conquered: "How much they left behind of gardens and springs and crops and noble sites, and comfort wherein they were amused. Thus. And We caused another people to inherit it. And the heaven and earth did not weep for them; nor were they reprieved." (44:25–29).

When the Arabs took Basra in Iraq, Umar instructed his lieutenant Utbah bin Ghazwan to offer the people choices essentially identical to those Khalid had previously offered the Persians: "Summon the people to God; those who respond to your call, accept it from them, but those who refuse must pay the poll tax out of humiliation and lowliness. If they refuse this, it is the sword without leniency. Fear God with regard to what you have been entrusted."[57]

With Persia largely subdued, Umar declared proudly: "The Empire of the Magians has become extinct this day and from now on they will not possess a span of land to injure the Muslims in any way."[58] However, he warned the Muslims that their ability to hold the land, and to conquer more, depended entirely upon their adherence to the will of Allah and to the religion that the deity had declared "perfected" (Qur'an 5:3): "Muslims do keep in mind not to admit any change in your way of life; otherwise, Allah the Almighty will take the sovereign power from you and give it to others."[59] The ability to gain and retain political power was directly tied to one's obedience to Allah and Islam.

TAKING JERUSALEM

The modern-day Muslim historian Akbar Shah Najeebabadi portrays the Muslim conquerors of the seventh century as magnanimous, beneficent, and tolerant:

> Whenever the Muslim army halted for a few days, the populace of that territory rose to welcome the Muslims as providers of peace and prosperity. When the defeated nations watched with their naked eyes, the blessings of peace, morality, divine affection, justice, mercy, courage and the ambition of their victories, they put themselves in their service. It is an undeniable fact of history that humanity saved itself only through the marching steps of the Arab forces.[60]

The inhabitants of Jerusalem in the year 636 would undoubtedly have had a different view.

At that point, it looked as if Allah was pleased with the Muslims' level of devotion and ready to grant them more victories; it was now the turn of Jerusalem. According to Tabari, Umar wrote its inhabitants a conciliatory letter:

> In the name of God, the Merciful, the Compassionate. This is the assurance of safety [aman] which the servant of God, Umar, the Commander of the Faithful, has granted to the people of Jerusalem. He has given them an assurance of safety for themselves, for their property, their churches, their crosses, the sick and the healthy of the city, and for all the rituals that belong to their religion. Their churches will not be inhabited [by Muslims] and will not be destroyed. Neither they, nor the land on which they stand, nor their cross, nor their property will be damaged. They will not be forcibly converted. No Jew will live with them in Jerusalem. The people of Jerusalem must pay the poll tax [jizya] like the people of the [other] cities, and they must expel the Byzantines and the robbers.[61]

That's Tabari's version, but sources dating from the actual time of the conquest do not depict the conquerors as being quite so magnanimous. Sophronius, the patriarch of Jerusalem who, according to legend, turned the city over to a magnanimous and tolerant Umar after the Arab conquest in 637, lamented the advent of "the Saracens who, on account of our sins, have now risen up against us unexpectedly and ravage all with cruel and feral design, with impious and godless audacity."[62]

In a sermon in December 636 or 637, Sophronius deplored "so much destruction and plunder" and the "incessant outpourings of human blood." He said that churches had been "pulled down" and "the cross mocked," and that the "vengeful and God-hating Saracens…plunder cities, devastate fields, burn down villages, set on fire the holy churches, overturn the sacred monasteries, oppose the Byzantine armies arrayed against them, and in fighting raise up the trophies [of war] and add victory to victory."[63] Strikingly, he made no mention of the conquerors' coming with a new prophet, religion, or holy book.

Islamic legend, widely taken as fact, has it that Sophronius escorted Umar around Jerusalem. When they reached the Church of the Holy Sepulchre, which Christians said housed Christ's tomb and was the site of his resurrection from the dead, Sophronius invited Umar to pray inside the great church. Umar magnanimously turned him down, explaining that his followers would use his prayer as a pretext to turn the church into a mosque, and that he wanted to leave it for the Christians instead.[64] In his actual writings, Sophronius never mentioned this incident; nor did he even mention Umar at all.

According to Islamic tradition, however, Umar and Sophronius concluded a pact in which the Christians were not allowed to build new churches, carry arms, or ride on horses, and must pay the *jizya*, but were generally allowed to practice their religion and live in relative peace.[65] Although this "Pact of Umar" is not likely to be authentic, it reflected the core tenets of the Islamic legal system of the *dhimma*, or contract of protection, which to this day remains part of Islamic law. "Protection" was meant in the sense more of Mafiosi than of benefactors, since the *dhimmi*'s life would be spared only if he converted to Islam or paid the *jizya*.

"The little left-handed man" was not so magnanimous when it came to Khalid ibn al-Walid. He accused him of wrongfully appropriating funds that belonged to Muslims, and Umar summoned him to Medina. Khalid, maintaining his innocence, was incensed, and confronted the caliph: "I have complained about you to the Muslims. So help me God, Umar, you have treated me like dirt!"[66]

Umar was in no mood to argue with Khalid over his treatment and stuck to the matter at hand, asking the great general, "Where did you get the money?"[67] Khalid insisted that it had come from the spoils of war, lawfully distributed, and that Umar's share was ready for him to take it. Umar assessed Khalid's possessions and found this to be true. He declared that Khalid was an honorable man but relieved him permanently from his command anyway, explaining his reasoning (because of Khalid's great fame among the Muslims):

> I have not relieved Khalid from his post because he has
> caused me displeasure or because of deceit on his part. But
> the people were captivated by illusions on account of him,
> so I was afraid that they would confer too much trust upon
> him and would consequently be tested. I wanted them to
> realize that it is God who is the creator of all things and I
> did not want them to be subject to an illusion.[68]

Khalid ibn al-Walid retired to Emesa in Syria. Despite Umar's cosmetic explanation, it was clear to everyone that he had been dismissed in disgrace. His contempt for Umar burned brighter than ever; he told his wife: "Umar appointed me over Syria until it turned to wheat and honey; then he dismissed me!"[69] He wondered why Allah had not allowed him the glory of a death on the battlefield as a martyr. Khalid, one of the most successful generals in history, died in his bed a few years later, an embittered and broken man.

TAKING EGYPT

The jihad continued. When the Muslim armies entered Egypt in 639, they behaved much the same way as they had elsewhere. The leader of the invasion, Amr ibn al-As, was extremely brutal. John of Nikiou, a seventh-century Coptic Christian bishop, recounted in the 690s about what happened when Umar's army arrived in Egypt some fifty years before:

Amr oppressed Egypt. He sent its inhabitants to fight the inhabitants of the Pentapolis [Tripolitania] and, after gaining a victory, he did not allow them to stay there. He took considerable booty from this country and a large number of prisoners.... The Muslims returned to their country with booty and captives. The patriarch Cyrus felt deep grief at the calamities in Egypt, because Amr, who was of barbarian origin, showed no mercy in his treatment of the Egyptians and did not fulfill the covenants which had been agreed with him.[70]

When they arrived in John's native town of Nikiou, they were no more merciful:

Then the Muslims arrived in Nikiou. There was not one single soldier to resist them. They seized the town and slaughtered everyone they met in the street and in the churches—men, women and children, sparing nobody. Then they went to other places, pillaged and killed all the inhabitants they found.... But let us now say no more, for it is impossible to describe the horrors the Muslims committed when they occupied the island of Nikiou...[71]

Amr's men began to demand payment of the *jizya*:

Amr's position became stronger from day to day. He levied the tax that had been stipulated.... But it is impossible to describe the lamentable position of the inhabitants of this town, who came to the point of offering their children in exchange for the enormous sums that they had to pay each month, finding no one to help them because God had abandoned them and had delivered the Christians into the hands of their enemies.[72]

Similarly, an eyewitness to the conquest of a village near Alexandria recounted:

> We assembled all those captives who were still in our care, and the Christians among them were grouped together. Then we began to bring forward every single man from among them and we gave him the choice between Islam and Christianity. When he chose Islam, we all shouted, "God is great," even louder than we had done when that village was conquered, and we gathered him within our ranks. When he opted for Christianity, the Christians would snort and pull him back into their midst, while we imposed the jizyah on him.[73]

In light of all this, it is understandable that some of the captive people did not see the conquerors as pious, but as hypocritical. The Panegyric of the Three Holy Children of Babylon, a Christian homily dating from soon after the Arab conquest of Egypt, said that the Arab conquerors "give themselves up to prostitution, massacre and lead into captivity the sons of men, saying: 'We both fast and pray.' "[74]

Accordingly, the conquered people did not welcome their new overlords. Umar asked a Muslim who complained about the expenditures they were making to conquer these vast new territories: "Do you think that these vast countries, Syria, Mesopotamia, Kufa, Basra, Misr [Egypt] do not have to be covered with troops who must be well paid?"[75] Apparently the troops were needed in order to keep the captive populations in line.

Persia and Egypt were not by any means the only theater of jihad at this point; the Muslims were proceeding northward as well. When the Arabs conquered Armenia in 642, they behaved no less brutally than they had elsewhere, killing untold numbers of people and taking captive many more: "The enemy's army rushed in and butchered the inhabitants of the town by the sword.... After a few days' rest, the Ismaelites [Arabs] went back whence they had come, dragging after them a host of captives, numbering thirty-five thousand."[76]

The Arabs were now a global force, controlling much of Syria and the Levant, as well as most of Persia and Egypt. In the process of amassing this vast empire, they had smashed one great power, the Sassanian Empire, and greatly weakened the other, the Byzantine Empire. And much, much more victory in jihad was to come.

Yet Umar did not have long to savor his victories: his harsh treatment of the peoples he had conquered ended up killing him. In 644, Fayruz al-Nihawandi (aka Abu Luluah), a Christian slave who had been captured by the Muslims during the conquest of Persia, stabbed Umar many times while he was leading prayers in the mosque in Medina. He died three days later.[77]

UTHMAN: THE THIRD "RIGHTLY-GUIDED CALIPH"

Another early follower of Muhammad, Uthman ibn Affan, was chosen as the next caliph. Ali was once again passed over, as he had been when Abu Bakr was chosen. They did not formally leave the fold of Uthman's followers, but Ali's partisans, the party of Ali (*shiat Ali*, whence the word "Shia"), never accepted Uthman as the legitimate caliph.

Ali's supporters mocked Uthman for cowardice, saying that he had run away during some of the early battles of the Muslims, "like a donkey runs from the lion."[78] Uthman didn't deny this; he just said he had permission: a *hadith* depicts a Muslim asking the caliph Umar's son Abdullah, who was an old man by this time, if he was aware that Uthman fled from the Battle of Uhud, was absent also from the Battle of Badr, and didn't even attend when Muhammad's closest companions pledged their fealty to him. Abdullah explains that Allah had "excused" Uthman from Uhud, that Uthman's wife was ailing and Muhammad asked him to stay behind from Badr to care for her, as she was also Muhammad's daughter, and that Uthman had also been on assignment from Muhammad when his companions gathered to pledge their loyalty.[79]

However implausible these explanations may have sounded to many of the early Muslims, Uthman had no trouble marshaling forces to continue the jihad. The Muslims completed the conquest of Egypt and kept moving in North Africa, taking the former Roman territories of North Africa and imposing the payment of the *jizya* upon those who refused to convert to Islam. The jihadis also completed the conquest of Armenia.

Uthman's caliphate saw the beginning of jihad on the high seas, as well as the jihadis' first incursion into Europe, albeit its outlying islands.

An enterprising young commander named Muawiya prevailed upon Uthman in 649 to allow a jihadi naval expedition to Cyprus. The Muslims defeated the Byzantines on the island easily, imposed the *jizya*, and carried off much booty; then they proceeded to Rhodes, the site of one of the ancient wonders of the world, the 108-foot-tall Colossus of Rhodes, a statue of the sun god Helios that had been constructed in 280 BC to stand bestride the harbor entrance, so that ships entering the harbor would pass between its enormous legs. This magnificent effect lasted only 54 years, however, as the Colossus toppled over in an earthquake in 226 BC.

Even though toppled, the statue was still valued by the inhabitants of Rhodes, even after they converted to Christianity, and because of its immense size, it became a tourist attraction. But the Muslims had no patience for such trifles: as far as Islam is concerned, all the artifacts of pre-Islamic civilization are the products of *jahiliyya*, the society of unbelievers, retaining no value whatsoever. The Qur'an even sees the ruins of pre-Islamic civilizations as a sign of the judgment of Allah upon the unbelievers: "Many were the ways of life that have passed away before you: travel through the earth, and see what was the end of those who rejected truth" (3:137). Muawiya unsentimentally had the pieces of the Colossus carted off the island and sold as scrap metal to a Jewish merchant, who loaded the metal onto nine hundred camels and took it to Emesa.[80]

Appointed governor of Syria by Uthman, Muawiya wrote to the Byzantine emperor Constantine "the Bearded" in 651, calling on him to renounce Christianity and take up Abrahamic monotheism, or else:

> If you wish to live in peace…renounce your vain religion, in which you have been brought up since infancy. Renounce this Jesus and convert to the great God whom I serve, the God of our father Abraham.… If not, how will this Jesus whom you call Christ, who was not even able to save himself from the Jews, be able to save you from my hands?[81]

Meanwhile, the Egyptian city of Alexandria, having earlier agreed to submit to Muslim rule and pay the *jizya*, revolted and had to be subdued with extreme violence. Other revolts broke out as well, in the newly subdued African province and in Persia. Nonetheless, the Arab empire was growing with astonishing rapidity; according to Islamic tradition, Uthman moved to ensure that Islam would grow with it by compiling the Qur'an as it stands today. It is said that he began this initiative in the early 650s after a Muslim named Hudhaifa bin al-Yaman warned Uthman that the Muslims were in danger of becoming like the Jews and Christians: "O chief of the Believers! Save this nation before they differ about the Book [Qur'an] as Jews and the Christians did before."[82]

Uthman appointed a commission to standardize and codify the Qur'anic text, and once this work was done in 653, Uthman is supposed to have distributed the final version to all the Islamic provinces and burned all the variants.[83] Yet contrary to this account, which most historians to this day take for granted as true, the Qur'an isn't mentioned anywhere for several more decades. If it was indeed standardized, copied, and distributed in the year 653, it is extremely strange that no one seems to have taken notice of the fact, and that neither the Arabs nor the people they conquered mentioned that the conquerors came with a new religion, prophet, and holy book.

Uthman was assassinated in 656 by some Muslims who had rebelled against his rule. His detractors accused him of the sin of *bid'a* (innovation) for changing some of the practices to which the Muslims had become accustomed. This was a serious offense for those who believed in a religion that proclaimed its own perfection ("This day I have perfected your religion for you," Allah says in the Qur'an, 5:3.) When he saw the forces arrayed against him, Uthman wrote in desperation to Muawiya, one of his top generals, equating obedience to himself with adherence to Islam: "The Medinese have become unbelievers; they have abandoned obedience and renounced their oath of allegiance. Therefore send to me the Syrian soldiers who are at your disposal, on every camel you have, whether docile or stubborn."[84]

Muawiya, however, knowing that some of the Companions of Muhammad (that is, Muhammad's earliest and closest disciples) did not support Uthman, delayed action on the caliph's order. Muawiya had his eye on the prize himself, but it would be a few years before he attained it. In the meantime, after Uthman's death, Ali ibn Abi Talib, the fourth and last of the "Rightly-Guided Caliphs," finally got his chance.

ALI'S TROUBLED CALIPHATE

After so many spectacular conquests, now the jihad turned inward, as the Muslims became more preoccupied with fighting among themselves than with fighting infidels. Ali immediately faced challenges to his rule so severe that his caliphate came to be known as the period of the First Fitna (disturbance)—a time of chaos and civil war. Muhammad's youngest and favorite wife, Aisha, hated Ali with burning intensity because of an incident late in Muhammad's life, when Aisha was accused of adultery, and instead of defending her, Ali advised Muhammad to forget about her and let her be stoned to death. After all, the prophet of Islam could always get other women.

Over two decades later, Aisha was not happy to hear that Ali was now caliph. She had started out from her home in Mecca to make the journey to Medina, but when she heard the news, she returned to Mecca; when its governor, Abdallah ibn Amir al-Hadrami, asked her why she had returned, she answered: "The fact that Uthman has been killed unjustly and that as long as the mob rules, order will not be established." She cried out to Abdallah: "Seek revenge for the blood of Uthman, and you will strengthen Islam!"[85]

Aisha now embarked upon a jihad of her own, organizing an armed revolt against Ali. She had no difficulty finding people who were willing to join her, enraged at the murder of Uthman and unwilling to accept Ali as caliph; despite Muawiya's inaction when Uthman asked him for help, they supported him for caliph instead of Ali. Those who thought Uthman had been rightly killed as an innovator in Islamic practice supported Ali.

At the Battle of the Camel in Basra on November 7, 656, Aisha directed her forces from the back of a camel, on which she was sitting fully veiled and concealed inside a howdah. Ali, victorious perhaps because he could move and see much more easily than she could, spared her life.

This magnanimous act, however, won him no supporters among his enemies.[86] Aisha's defeat did not unite the Muslims under Ali's leadership. Muawiya continued to press his claim to the caliphate; he and Ali battled in 657 in Siffin, a village on the banks of the Euphrates River in Syria.

Tabari, writing two centuries after the events he was recounting supposedly occurred, recounted that when addressing Muawiya's forces, Ali framed the entire controversy as one of obedience or disobedience to Islam: "I have given you time so that you might revert to the truth and turn to it in repentance. I have argued against you with the Book of God and have called you to it, but you have not turned away from oppression or responded to truth."[87] Speaking to his own men on the eve of battle, he framed the conflict as an act of religious devotion: "Tomorrow you will meet the enemy, so lengthen the night standing in prayer, make abundant recitation of the Qur'an, and ask God for help and steadfastness."[88]

The battle was hotly contested and protracted; finally, when it looked as if victory was in sight for Ali, one of Muawiya's commanders, the conqueror of Egypt, Amr ibn al-As, offered his chief a plan: in battle his forces would raise aloft their copies of the Qur'an and proclaim, "Their contents are to be authoritative in our dispute." When Muawiya's men did this, Ali claimed that Muawiya was ignorant of the true religion, calling his enemies "men without religion and without *qur'an*."[89] He charged that the raising up of copies of the Qur'an was a ruse: "They do not exalt them and do not know what it is that they contain. They have raised them up to you only to deceive you, to outwit you, and to trick you." He insisted: "The only reason I have fought against them was so that they should adhere to the authority of this Book, for they have disobeyed God in what He has commanded and forgotten His covenant and rejected His Book."[90]

Both sides finally agreed to arbitration based on the Qur'an. However, a third party in this dispute registered disapproval of the entire process. The Khawarij, or Kharijites, were an especially fervent and violent party of Muslims who had initially supported Ali but ultimately broke with him. At this point, they complained to Ali that Muawiya and his supporters had "always rejected our appeals when we summoned them to the Book of God."[91] Thus they considered Muawiya and his followers heretics who "should be killed or repent," pressing Ali on what they considered to be a violation of the Qur'an's command, a contradiction of his promises to abide by the word of Allah's Book.[92] The Kharijites were saying that Muawiya should not be negotiated with but simply fought—as the Qur'an commanded. They were angry with Ali for submitting to arbitration instead.

The arbitration was inconclusive anyway. Muawiya returned to Syria and maintained an uneasy peace with Ali. But the Kharijites, enraged at what they considered to be the deviation of both parties from obedience to the Qur'an, murdered Ali in 661 (they tried to kill Muawiya and Amr as well but failed). At that point, Muawiya became caliph.

The story is full of legendary elements. This battle and the subsequent arbitration are supposed to have taken place only eight years after Uthman codified the contents of the Qur'an and distributed the standardized copy to the provinces. It is extremely unlikely that Muawiya's men would have had so many copies of the Qur'an, in an age when every book had to copied out by hand, that they could raise them on their lances, and unlikely that they would have risked damage to the books by doing so. However, Tabari's account shows that by the ninth century, when the historian was writing his account, Islamic warfare was considered wholly in terms of obedience and disobedience to Islam.

MUAWIYA AND THE UMAYYAD CALIPHATE

With the death of Ali ended the period of the "Rightly-Guided Caliphate." After Ali was killed, the people of Iraq hailed his son Hasan ibn Ali as caliph; Muawiya made Hasan a gift of five million dirhams, and his rival renounced his claim.[93] Muawiya was not magnanimous in victory; he told his lieutenant al-Mughira: "Do not tire of abusing and insulting Ali and calling for God's mercifulness for Uthman, defaming the companions of Ali, removing them and omitting to listen to them; praising, in contrast, the clan of Uthman, drawing them near to you and listening to them."[94]

Someone in Muawiya's camp composed a *hadith* in which no less an authority than Muhammad himself declared that Ali's father and Muhammad's guardian, Abu Talib, was burning in hell: "Perhaps my intercession will be of use to him at the day of resurrection, so that he may be transferred into a pool of fire which reaches only up to the ankles but which is still hot enough to burn his brain."[95] Muawiya's opponents, not to be outdone, invented their own *hadith* in which Muhammad refers to Hasan and his younger brother Husayn as his own children and says that they were "Imams whether they stand up or sit down"—that is, whether they actually ruled over the Muslims or not.[96]

Muawiya was the first caliph who was not a Companion of Muhammad; he had been but a youth when the Prophet of Islam was alive, and once almost became the recipient of Allah's curse. Muawiya's father, Abu Sufyan, was commander of the Quraysh during some of their wars with Muhammad and the Muslims. Once, when a captive Muslim, Khubayb ibn Adi, was being tortured, he cried out: "Allah, count them well. Kill them all, one by one, and let not one escape!" Abu Sufyan and young Muawiya were standing nearby; Abu Sufyan immediately threw Muawiya to the ground and held him there facedown, so that when Allah passed by to curse all the enemies of the Muslims, he would not be able to tell who the boy was and would, therefore, not know whom to curse.[97]

Muawiya thus survived long enough to become caliph. Befitting the man who first took jihad to the seas, he ordered the construction of ships and mounted the Muslims' first siege of Constantinople around 670. Having taken down the Persian Empire, the Muslims were determined to destroy the Byzantine Empire as well. A *hadith* depicts Muhammad promising "the first army amongst my followers who will invade Caesar's city [Constantinople] will be forgiven their sins."[98] This statement was almost certainly put into Muhammad's mouth long after the first Muslim siege of Constantinople, but there is no doubt that it reflected an aspiration that those early jihadis shared, for to destroy Constantinople in 670 would have meant that the Arabs had defeated both of the world's great powers within the span of three decades.

The invaders had not, however, reckoned with the mysterious weapon known as Greek Fire, which the Byzantines wielded against any Arab ship that got too close to the great city. The Muslims tried sporadically to breach the city's defenses, but they proved too formidable; ultimately the jihadis had to admit that they were defeated, an unusual occurrence in the seventh century, and they retreated.

KARBALA AND THE SUNNI/SHI'ITE SCHISM

Muawiya found more success in dealing with internal enemies and uniting most of the Muslims under his authority. He conducted campaigns against the Kharijites and prevailed upon Hasan ibn Ali's wife, Jada bint al-Ashat, to kill her husband by poisoning in 670, establishing a precedent that would be repeated many times in the coming years with rulers of the *shiat Ali*.[99]

The jihad also continued elsewhere. The Muslims took Crete, advanced in North Africa, and won great victories in central Asia, pressing beyond Persia into Afghanistan. One of Muawiya's most notable achievements, meanwhile, was that he made the caliphate into a family dynasty, which became known as the Umayyad Caliphate (after Umayya ibn Abd Shams, patriarch of the Umayyad clan of Mecca). The immediate reaction to this development was not uniformly positive; it touched off another period of civil war, the Second Fitna, as some of the Muslims refused to accept the hereditary accession to the caliphate.[100]

Ultimately, the dispute came down to two hereditary successors: in 680, when Muawiya's son, Yazid I, succeeded him, the second son of Ali, Husayn, was not willing to accept Yazid's authority. He gathered supporters and stood at Karbala in Iraq against Yazid's forces, which vastly outnumbered the *shiat Ali*.

One of Muawiya's men at Karbala, Abdullah ibn Umayr, expressed impatience with all of this infighting. When he saw troops being assembled and was told that they were going to fight Husayn, Abdullah exclaimed: "By God! I was anxious to make holy war [jihad] against the polytheists. I hope that making holy war against these people, who are attacking the son of the daughter of the Prophet, will be no less rewarded with God than His reward would be to me for making holy war against the polytheists."[101] He fought for Husayn at Karbala.

Both sides at Karbala justified their fighting against other Muslims by declaring them not Muslims at all. As the battle raged, several of Muawiya's warriors got close enough to Husayn to ask him if he expected to burn in hell when he died.[102] One of the followers of Husayn fought while repeating: "I believe in the religion of Ali."[103] A follower of Muawiya attacked him, crying: "I follow the religion of Uthman."[104] The response: "Rather you follow the religion of Satan." The follower of Husayn then killed Muawiya's man.[105]

At Karbala, Husayn and his two sons, one who was just six months old, were killed—but Husayn's followers refused to accept Yazid's authority, and the split in the Muslim community became permanent: the *shiat Ali,* that is, the Shia, and the majority Sunnis went their separate ways, with both sides condemning and cursing the other as heretical, and sporadically waging jihad against each other. The Shi'ites followed not caliphs but Imams, all descended from Ali and believed to be imbued with prophetic infallibility and a portion of Muhammad's prophetic spirit. The history of the Imamate, as might be expected, is one long story of Sunni persecution.

CONQUERING NORTH AFRICA

While much of Yazid's attention was taken up with subduing Husayn and his followers, he did not neglect the larger jihad against infidels. In 682, he sent the general Uqba ibn Nafi with ten thousand jihadis from Damascus into North Africa. Like his uncle Amr ibn al-As, Uqba marched forward fearlessly, winning victory after victory. Entering the former Roman province of Mauritania Tingitana, Uqba found its native inhabitants to be desperately poor—too poor to provide much in the way of spoils of war besides their girls, who were renowned for their beauty and who ultimately fetched a thousand gold pieces each in the caliphate's sex-slave markets.[106]

Pressing on as far as he could possibly go, Uqba ultimately reached land's end. Flush with victory, he rode his horse out onto the beach and into the waves, where he stopped to exclaim that he wanted more: "Great God! If my course were not stopped by this sea, I would still go on, to the unknown kingdoms of the West, preaching the unity of thy holy name, and putting to the sword the rebellious nations who worship any other Gods than thee."[107]

But his course was stopped not just by the sea. The native North African Berbers were unwilling to accept subjugation and Islamization and rose up against the invaders. The Byzantines allied with the Christian Ber-

ber king Kusaila in hope of preventing a Muslim conquest of the great
ancient city of Carthage. Uqba, heading westward, was ambushed in 682
at the town of Vescera (Biskra in modern-day Algeria). The Muslims were
defeated, Uqba was killed, and the Muslims were driven out of the Berber lands of modern-day Tunisia. The warriors of jihad suffered losses so
extensive that they were forced to withdraw also from Crete and Rhodes.

But the losses proved to be temporary. In 698, the Muslim general
Hasan ibn al-Nu'man defeated the Byzantines at Carthage and took the
city for Islam. Hasan could not, however, complete the Muslim conquest
of North Africa; he was defeated at Meskiana in Algeria by the Berber
queen Dahya, to whom the Muslims referred with a mixture of contempt
and fear as al-Kahina, the soothsayer. It was only by her black arts, they
said, that she was able to defeat the Muslims. Some said that she was
Jewish, a claim that many a jihadi would make about his foes throughout
the history of Islam.[108] Since the Qur'an declared that the Jews would be
the worst enemies of the Muslims (5:82) and depicted them as scheming
indefatigably against Allah and his messenger, all their most determined
and resourceful foes *had* to be Jewish.

Hasan was determined as well. In 700, he returned to North Africa,
defeated Dahya and her forces, and put an end to her independent Berber kingdom. The stage was set for the Muslims to spread Islam beyond
North Africa, as Uqba had exclaimed was his hope to do as his horse
tramped amidst the waves.

As all of this was going on, the infighting among the Muslims continued as well. After Yazid's death in 683, rival claimants to the caliphate waged jihad against one another. The Khawarij remained a nagging
problem. There were ongoing troubles from the Shi'ites as well.

SUBJUGATING THE CHRISTIANS

But amid it all, the jihad advanced, and the jihadis were determined to
keep what they seized; they worked assiduously to Islamize the lands
they now ruled. In the late 680s, the Muslim rulers of Egypt issued a
series of orders for the Christians in their domains: churches could no
longer bear crosses, and all crosses that could be publicly seen must be
destroyed. All churches had to post signs on their doors reading: "Mu-

hammad is the great apostle of God, and Jesus also is the apostle of God. But truly God is not begotten and does not beget"—that is, Jesus was not the only begotten Son of God. The Muslims were forcing the Christians to deny the faith on the very doors of their houses of worship.[109] The caliph Muawiya II (683–684) began a persecution of Christians in Iraq and destroyed many churches after the Catholicos of the Assyrian Church refused his demand for gold. The persecution continued under his successor, Abd al-Malik (685–705).

This persecution was transforming the conquered lands by making conversion to Islam an easy option for relief from discrimination, harassment, and constant threat. By the end of the seventh century, the Muslims controlled and were rapidly Islamizing an immense area stretching from North Africa to Central Asia, all of which they had won in a period of six decades. It was an extraordinary achievement, and much more jihad was to come.

CHAPTER THREE

THE JIHAD COMES TO SPAIN AND INDIA

Jihad in the Eighth and Ninth Centuries

I. THE JIHAD IN SPAIN BEGINS

Count Julian's rage

Once North Africa was secured for Islam, the ancient Roman province of Spain, now under Visigoth rule, was within reach. Here again, the available accounts contradict one another and are overlaid with legend, but a general outline of events can be known, and even some of the legends are illustrative of both the mindset of the day and some lingering tendencies.

The jihad in Europe, still raging today, began in 711, when Musa al-Nusayr, the governor of the Muslim provinces of North Africa under the caliph Walid, sent Muslim forces under the command of a freed Berber slave named Tariq ibn Ziyad to cross the narrow strait that separated Africa from Europe and take the land for Allah.

According to one Muslim chronicler, the Muslims came to Spain at the invitation of an enraged Christian who was hungry for revenge. Ibn Abd al-Hakam, writing in the ninth century, said that Tariq "with his female slave of the name Umm Hakim" arrived in Tangiers some time before Walid sent him to Spain, and "remained some time in this district, waging a holy war."[1] He eventually made the acquaintance of a Christian, "Ilyan, Lord of Septa," Count Julian of Ceuta, who had a proposition for him.

Count Julian was a ruler of some of the remaining Christian domains in North Africa, subject to Roderic, the reigning (and last) Visigothic king of Spain. According to Ibn Abd Al-Hakam, Julian was "the governor of the straits between this district and Andalus" and "also the governor of a town called Alchadra, situated on the same side of the straits of Andalus as Tangiers."[2]

Tariq established contact with Count Julian. According to Ibn Abd al-Hakam, Tariq "treated him kindly, until they made peace with each other." Eventually Tariq won Julian's confidence to the extent that the count told him of his personal sorrow. Julian, per Ibn Abd al-Hakam, "had sent one of his daughters to Roderic, the Lord of Andalus, for her improvement and education." Like many a powerful man presented with a comely intern, however, Roderic had taken advantage of the girl, and "she became pregnant by him." When he learned of the violation of his beloved daughter, who became a vivid and controversial figure in Spanish legend under the name Florinda La Cava, presented variously as victim, seductress, and even prostitute, Julian was enraged. He was determined to take revenge upon Roderic. It didn't take him long to come up with a plan: Roderic had destroyed his daughter, so he would destroy Roderic's kingdom. "I see for him no other punishment or recompense, than that I should bring the Arabs against him."[3]

Julian contacted his friend Tariq ibn Zayed and offered his help for a jihadi invasion of Spain. Tariq was skeptical, telling Julian: "I cannot trust you until you send me a hostage."[4] Julian had no problem with that, and sent Tariq his two daughters; apparently, the prospect of their becoming the sex slaves of a Muslim ruler didn't trouble him as much as Roderic's behavior. In any case, the reception of the girls convinced Tariq of Julian's sincerity, and the plan went forward.

Julian also met with Musa ibn Nusayr and got his approval. Then the traitor provided the Muslims with ships to carry the warriors of jihad across the strait that would not arouse the notice of any Spanish sentries. These were preferable to the Muslims' own ships for being familiar to the Spanish people. Ibn Abd al-Hakam explained: "the people of Andalus did not observe them, thinking that the vessels crossing and recrossing were similar to the trading vessels which for their benefit plied backwards and forwards."[5]

As he crossed the strait himself, Tariq spotted an island and left his female slave, Umm Hakim, there with a division of troops. These troops immediately sent a message to the people of that island, and to all of Spain, that the invaders would not hesitate at any brutality. Finding no one on the island except a group of vinedressers, they took them all prisoner; then they chose one of them at random, whom they killed and dismembered. Then they boiled the pieces of his body, while meat was boiling in other cauldrons. Out of the sight of their prisoners, they threw out the boiled pieces of their victim's body, and then, as their prisoners watched, began eating the meat they had been boiling. The vinedressers were convinced that the Muslims were eating the flesh of the man they had killed, and the Muslims freed them to spread this tale far and wide, so as to "strike terror in the enemies of Allah." (Qur'an 8:60)[6]

Tariq's boats

Tariq and his men landed at the Mons Calpe, a rock formation at the southern tip of the Iberian Peninsula; ultimately, the conquering Muslims would rename it Jabal Tariq in his honor—the mountain of Tariq, from which is derived the word "Gibraltar." It has become part of Tariq's legend as an indomitable warrior that he ordered the Muslims to burn the boats that Count Julian had supplied, that had just carried them to Europe. The Muslims were going to take Spain from Islam or die there, but there was no going back. Tariq posed this choice to his troops:

> Oh my warriors, whither would you flee? Behind you is the
> sea, before you, the enemy. You have left now only the hope
> of your courage and your constancy. Remember that in this
> country you are more unfortunate than the orphan seated at
> the table of the avaricious master. Your enemy is before you,
> protected by an innumerable army; he has men in abun-
> dance, but you, as your only aid, have your own swords, and,
> as your only chance for life, such chance as you can snatch
> from the hands of your enemy.[7]

He reminded them of the rewards that awaited them if they won. The Qur'an allowed a Muslim to have sexual intercourse not only with his wives but with the "captives of the right hand" (4:3, 4:24, 23:1–6) that were the spoils of war (33:50), and there were plenty of young women in Spain who could be used in this way:

> You have heard that in this country there are a large number of ravishingly beautiful Greek maidens, their graceful forms are draped in sumptuous gowns on which gleam pearls, coral, and purest gold, and they live in the palaces of royal kings.[8]

The caliph, meanwhile, was forsaking his rightful share of the booty; the only thing he wanted was for Islam to be established in Spain:

> The Commander of True Believers, Alwalid, son of Abdalmelik, has chosen you for this attack from among all his Arab warriors; and he promises that you shall become his comrades and shall hold the rank of kings in this country. Such is his confidence in your intrepidity. The one fruit which he desires to obtain from your bravery is that the word of God shall be exalted in this country, and that the true religion shall be established here. The spoils will belong to yourselves.[9]

Tariq ended his address by calling upon his men to kill Roderic. There were others on the Christian side besides Count Julian who wanted him dead as well. Roderic was a usurper, and some of the chronicles of the Muslim invasion of Spain have the sons of a previous Visigothic king, Witiza, aiding the Muslim armies against Roderic. Also helping the Muslims was Witiza's brother Oppas, the archbishop of Toledo and Seville. Whatever the historical value of these accounts, there has never been a shortage of non-Muslims willing to aid the jihad for their own purposes.

The two armies met near the Guadalete River in the lower Guadalquivir valley. As seemed always the case in the days of the early jihad conquests, the Muslims were vastly outnumbered. Roderic appeared on the field of battle dressed as if he were certain of victory: he was arrayed in a gorgeous gold robe, with a crown of pearls on his head, and was carried on a litter of ivory. But the battle did not go well for the defenders. According to Ibn Abd al-Hakam: "And there was never in the West a more bloody battle than this. The Moslems did not withdraw their swords from Roderic and his companions for three days."[10]

As the Visigoths' losses mounted, Roderic fled the field of battle; his magnificent crown and robe were found on the riverbank, but there was no trace of the king. The Muslims concluded that Roderic had drowned in the river; they beheaded someone else, sending the head back as Roderic's to the caliph Walid, who was headquartered in Damascus, as a symbol of his triumph.[11]

Conquering Spain

Count Julian's thirst for revenge was not slaked by Roderic's death. He went to Tariq and urged him to press on and conquer all of Spain: "The king of the Goths is slain; their princes are fled before you, the army is routed, the nation is astonished. Secure with sufficient detachments the cities of Boetica; but in person and without delay, march to the royal city of Toledo, and allow not the distracted Christians either time or tranquillity for the election of a new monarch."[12] Toledo was at that time the capital of Spain. Tariq heeded his advice and marched north, meeting very little resistance and capturing Toledo with relative ease. Among the spoils he seized was a table of emeralds that was said to have belonged to King Solomon, taken from the Temple in Jerusalem by the Romans as they were destroying it in AD 70.

Back across the strait, Musa heard of Tariq's astonishing victories and grew envious. Not to be upstaged, he landed in Spain with an army of eighteen thousand Muslims and began seizing towns and cities that Tariq had bypassed, most notably Seville. Some Christian turncoats who had entered Seville posing as refugees opened the gates of the city for Musa and his men, and the plunder began.[13] Leaderless, dispirited, riven with short-sighted factionalism and beset with widespread treason, Visigothic Spain collapsed with amazing speed before the invading Muslims. By 718, just seven years after Tariq and his men burned their boats and determined to take the land for Islam or die, they had done so: Spain was almost entirely subdued.

The Holdout

Almost entirely. In Asturias in northwestern Spain, those among the Visigoths who were not utterly defeated or traitorous in 718 chose as their leader a man named Pelayo, who immediately told the local Muslim overlords that he would not pay the *jizya*. He established what he called the Kingdom of Asturias and began to attack the Muslim bases in the area. The warriors of jihad made only perfunctory attempts to find and kill Pelayo and destroy his little kingdom, for they didn't regard it as significant enough: they were pressing on into France, and a few Christian fanatics in a remote, mountainous region of Spain didn't worry them.

However, after the harassment from Pelayo's men caused a Muslim governor, Munuza, to flee the area, the Muslims had had enough. Munuza returned with a Muslim commander, al-Qama, and an army, to put an end to Pelayo's Kingdom of Asturias once and for all. Al-Qama and Musa brought with them the renegade bishop Oppas. According to an early tenth-century account, Oppas sought out Pelayo in his mountain hideaway and told him resistance was futile: "I believe that you understand how the entire army of the Goths cannot resist the force of the Muslims; how then can you resist on this mountain? Listen to my advice: abandon your efforts and you will enjoy many benefits alongside the Moors."[14]

Pelayo was unmoved by this appeal to defeatism. He made a counter-appeal to Oppas' putative religion: "Have you not read in Sacred Scripture that the Church of the Lord is like the mustard seed, which, small as it is, grows more than any other through the mercy of God? Our hope is in Christ; this little mountain will be the salvation of Spain and of the people of the Goths; the mercy of Christ will free us from that multitude."[15]

At first it appeared as if the Muslims would have no trouble overcoming this little rebellion, as they regained control of much of the area with little or no resistance. But Pelayo and his force of only three hundred men were hiding deep in the mountains; they swept into the valley at the village of Covadonga and surprised the Muslim forces, which vastly outnumbered them. In a turnabout of the usual scenario in early jihad attacks, the Christians were both outnumbered and victorious. After another defeat at his hands, the Muslims decided to leave Pelayo and his tiny kingdom alone.

Pelayo's words to Oppas proved prophetic. That Kingdom of Asturias and Battle of Covadonga were the beginning of the seven-hundred-year effort by the Christians of Spain to drive the Muslims out: the Reconquista.

Treatment of the Conquered People

As the conquest of Spain was being completed, the Umayyad caliph Umar ibn Abd al-Aziz sent out a message to the governors of the various Islamic provinces, denouncing non-Muslims:

> O ye who believe! The non-Moslems are nothing but dirt. Allah has created them to be partisans of Satan; most treacherous in regard to all they do; whose whole endeavor in this nether life is useless, though they themselves imagine that they are doing fine work. Upon them rests the curse of Allah, of the Angels and of man collectively.[16]

According to the thirteenth-century Muslim jurist Ghazi ibn al-Wasiti, Umar also "commanded that both Jews and Christians should be forbidden to ride upon saddles; that no one belonging to the 'Protected People' should be allowed to enter a public bath on Friday, except after Prayer-time. He ordered, further, that a guard should be set to watch both Jews and Christians whenever they slaughtered an animal, so that the guard should mention the name of Allah and of his Prophet [at such a slaughter]."[17]

The Umayyad caliphate began large-scale dealing in slaves, requiring not only physical laborers but sex slaves for the harems of the caliphs and other high officials, as well as eunuchs who could be trusted to guard these harems. The warriors of Islam drew these slaves beginning in the eighth century from regular raids in three principal areas: Central Asia, the northern fringes of Sub-Saharan Africa, and Central and southeastern Europe, which they called Bilad as-Saqaliba, slave country. The ethnic designation "Slav" is derived from the Arabic "*saqlab*," or slave.[18]

II. THE JIHAD IN INDIA BEGINS

Conquering Sindh

In 711, the same year that Tariq ibn Ziyad and his men crossed the Strait of Gibraltar in Count Julian's boats and began the jihad against Spain, the Umayyad Empire was expanding eastward as well. Hajjaj ibn Yusuf, the governor of Iraq, sent the general Muhammad ibn Qasim into Sindh, modern-day western Pakistan. It was the beginning of the jihad conquest of India.

Hajjaj gave his commander ruthlessly precise instructions:

> My ruling is given: Kill anyone belonging to the combatants [*ahl-i harb*]; arrest their sons and daughters for hostages and imprison them. Whoever submits…grant them *aman* [protection] and settle their tribute [*amwal*] as *dhimmah*.[19]

This policy severely discouraged resistance. The Muslim invaders of India treated the native population with extraordinary harshness. In jihad campaigns in Europe, as well as in the Middle East and Persia, the warriors of jihad had subjugated the local populations and collected the *jizya* from them—the Qur'an-mandated (9:29) poll tax to be paid by the People of the Book, that is, the monotheistic Jews, Christians, and Zoroastrians. But the Hindus, Jains, and Buddhists whom Muhammad ibn Qasim and his jihadis encountered in Hindustan were not People of the Book, and hence no *jizya* could be demanded from them. Their only choices were to convert to Islam or face the sword of Islam.

The Indians quickly realized just how ruthless their foe really was. As the Muslims besieged the city of Brahmanabad, its inhabitants saw the writing on the wall:

> If we unite and go forth to fight, we will be killed: for even if peace is [subsequently] made, those who are combatants [ahl-i silat] will all be put to death. As for the rest of the people; aman is given to the merchants, artisans, and agriculturalists. It is better that we be trusted. Therefore, we

should surrender the fort to him on the basis of a secure covenant [ahd-i wathiq].[20]

However, not all of the Sindhis were that willing to give up without a struggle, even at Brahmanabad. The Muslim response was just as fierce; Muslims massacred between six thousand and twenty-six thousand Sindhis at Brahmanabad, six thousand more at Rawar, four thousand at Iskalandah, and six thousand at Multan.

As Muhammad ibn Qasim's jihad in India continued, however, it proved to be impractical to offer all the people in India the choice of conversion to Islam or death: there were simply too many people in India for them all to be converted to Islam or killed. Consequently, an adjustment had to be made, and Muhammad ibn Qasim ultimately granted the Hindus the status of the People of the Book, accepting their submission and payment of the *jizya*, with the ultimate objective remaining to bring all of these people into the fold of Islam.[21]

The jihadis, however, were unremittingly ruthless toward Hindu temples. The Qur'an says: "And were it not that Allah checks the people, some by means of others, there would have been demolished monasteries, churches, synagogues, and mosques in which the name of Allah is much mentioned." (22:40) The Qur'an regards Jesus and the prophets of Hebrew Scriptures as prophets and the Torah and Gospel as legitimate revelations, although it contends that the Jews and Christians twisted their prophets' words and altered the scriptures they received. Consequently, while many churches and synagogues were seized throughout the history of jihad and turned into mosques, this was never a thoroughgoing or universal policy. Hindu temples, by contrast, were always considered to be centers of idolatry, in which the "name of Allah" was not "much mentioned," and consequently they were to be destroyed whenever possible.

At Daybul, the Muslims faced a force of four thousand Rajputs (Indian warriors) and two to three thousand Brahmins (Hindu priests) defending a Hindu temple. Once victorious, Muhammad ibn Qasim had the temple destroyed and the Brahmins circumcised so as to convert them to Islam. However, seeing that his new converts were resisting, rather than embracing, their new religion, he ordered all of them over the age of seventeen to be executed.[22] The victorious jihadis began a massacre so intensive that it lasted three days.[23] Young women and children were enslaved, but in a rare act of mercy, older women were freed outright.[24]

Seeing the immensity of the task before him, Muhammad ibn Qasim began encouraging the locals to surrender rather than fight; but this aroused the ire of his boss. Hajjaj wrote to Muhammad urging him to be more discriminating between those who had surrendered sincerely and those who had not, and charged that his practice of granting protection was un-Islamic:

> I am appalled by your bad judgment and astounded by your policies. Why are you so intent on giving *aman*, even to an enemy whom you have tested and found hostile and intransigent? It is not necessary to give *aman* to everyone without discrimination.... In any case, if [the Sindis] sincerely request *aman* and desist from treachery, they will surely stop fighting. Then income will meet expenditures and this long situation will be concluded.... It is acknowledged that all your procedures have been in accordance with religious law [*bar jadah-yi shar*] except for the one practice of giving *aman*. For you are giving *aman* to everyone without distinguishing between friend and foe.[25]

His instructions to Muhammad ibn Qasim were ruthlessly precise:

> God says, "Give no quarter to infidels but cut their throats." Then you shall know that this is the command of the great God. You shall not be too ready to grant protection, because it will prolong your work. After this give no quarter to any enemy except those of rank.[26]

Muhammad ibn Qasim may have been too lenient for Hajjaj's taste, but as he subdued Sindh he was ruthless against manifestations of non-Muslim religion. At Nirun, he had a mosque built on the site of a Buddhist temple, and appointed an imam to instruct converts in the new, dominant religion. After a series of victories over Dahir, king of Sindh, Muhammad wrote triumphantly to Hajjaj:

The forts of Siwistan and Sisam have been already taken. The nephew of Dahir, his warriors, and principal officers have been dispatched, and infidels converted to Islam or destroyed. Instead of idol temples, mosques and other places of worship have been built, pulpits have been erected, the Khutba [Islamic Friday sermon] is read, the call to prayers is raised so that devotions are performed at the stated hours. The takbir ["*Allahu akbar*"] and praise to the Almighty God are offered every morning and evening.[27]

At Multan, Muhammad ibn Qasim ordered the destruction of an immense idol made of gold, with eyes of rubies. According to the *Chach Nama*, a twelfth-century Persian history of the conquest of Sindh that may have been based on an earlier Arabic original, "Two hundred and thirty *mans* of gold were obtained, and forty jars filled with gold dust. This gold and the image were brought to the treasury together with the gems and pearls and treasures which were obtained from the plunder of Multan."[28]

Muhammad ibn Qasim left another idol in place at Multan because of its popularity, intending to profit from the many offerings left there; however, to show his horror at Hindu superstition, and seeing that the cow was sacred to Hindus, he ordered that the idol's necklace be removed and replaced with a piece of cow's flesh.[29] The idol did not protest. The great general and his followers told the Hindus that was a sign that their idols were false and the harsh god of the invaders was the only true god.

The conquering jihad commander sent some of his massive haul back to the caliph Walid, along with two choice sex slaves, the daughters of the Sindhi king Dahir himself. One of them, named Janaki, particularly caught the caliph's eye, but when he took her to bed, the panicked girl told him that she had already been raped by Muhammad ibn Qasim.

Walid was enraged. Muhammad ibn Qasim had dared to send him damaged goods. Immediately he ordered that the victorious general, victories or no, be sewn up into a rawhide sack and shipped to his court. By the time the sack containing Muhammad ibn Qasim arrived, he was already dead.

The cause of Walid's monumental fit of temper, Janaki, was appalled. "The king has committed a very grievous mistake," she exclaimed, "for he ought not, on account of two slave girls, to have destroyed a person who had taken captive a hundred thousand modest women like us and who instead of temples had erected mosques, pulpits and minarets."[30]

In any case, the killing of Muhammad ibn Qasim stalled the jihad in India. But the subcontinent was never forgotten. A century or so after Muhammad ibn Qasim's jihad in Sindh, words were put into the mouth of Muhammad, the Prophet of Islam, emphasizing the importance of jihad in India. Abu Huraira, one of Muhammad's companions, is depicted in a *hadith* as saying: "The Messenger of Allah promised that we would invade India."[31] In another *hadith*, Muhammad himself says: "There are two groups of my Ummah whom Allah will free from the Fire: The group that invades India, and the group that will be with Isa bin Maryam [Jesus Christ], peace be upon him."[32]

III. THE JIHAD IN CONSTANTINOPLE BEGINS

The Second Siege of Constantinople

With Islam on the march in the East, as the warriors of jihad conquered Sindh, and in the West, with the Islamic conquest of Spain nearly completed and the jihadis pressing on into France, the Muslims were at a pinnacle of confidence: it looked as if Allah had indeed granted them hegemony over the entire world; all they had to do was seize it. And so, in 717, they made their second attempt to capture the jewel of Christendom and the capital of the great empire that still stood as the foremost obstacle to their plans: Constantinople.

The caliph Suleyman appointed his brother, Maslama, as commander of the Muslim forces for the siege. Maslama set out for Constantinople with a force of over one hundred thousand men and a huge fleet. As the siege began, the Byzantine general Leo the Isaurian, soon to be Emperor Leo III, asked for negotiations; Maslama sent a Muslim commander named Ibn Hubayrah.

The negotiations proceeded as a game of verbal chess. Ibn Hubayrah tried to maneuver Leo into admitting that resistance to the Muslim armies was foolish, asking him: "What do you consider to be the height of stupidity?"[33]

Instead of admitting that the Byzantines' situation was hopeless, however, Leo responded: "The man who fills his stomach with everything that he finds"—a slap at the Muslims' apparently insatiable desire for conquest.[34]

Ibn Hubayrah replied that he was only following orders: "We are men of religion, and our religion calls for obedience to our leaders."[35]

Leo then offered to pay the Muslims to leave: one dinar for the head of everyone in the great city. Maslama, however, rejected this offer, whereupon Leo came back to him with a new one. He told Maslama: "The people [of Constantinople] know that you will not advance against them in a bold attack and that you intend to prolong the siege as long as you have food. But if you were to burn the food, they would submit," as they would be afraid that the Muslims were burning their food because they were not planning to stay long but were preparing an imminent attack.[36]

Maslama believed him and burned the Muslims' food supplies. But the Byzantines did not surrender. According to the historian Tabari, during the difficult winter of 718, the jihadis camped around Constantinople "ate animals, skins, tree roots, leaves—indeed, everything except dirt."[37] The winter was so severe that Suleyman could not send the Muslims supplies or reinforcements.

The caliph Suleyman died with the Muslims still besieging Constantinople; his successor, Umar ibn Abd al-Aziz, recognized that the Muslim armies were ill-supplied and ill-equipped to deal with the Greek Fire that the Byzantines were using to destroy much of the Muslim fleet. On August 15, 718, the Muslims ended the siege, which the grateful citizens of Constantinople attributed to the aid of the Virgin Mary, whose falling asleep and departure from this world, or Dormition, was celebrated on that day.

IV. DEFEATS AND INTERAL STRIFE

The jihadis' failure at Constantinople was costly. The Muslims limped back to Umayyad domains with their fleet mostly destroyed. The Byzantines took immediate advantage of this, driving the Muslims out of Sicily and conducting raids in Syria and Egypt.

Meanwhile, the warriors of jihad were losing elsewhere as well: in 720, the Turkic Turgesh warrior Kursul defeated them in battle near Samarkand. Four years later, the jihadis, harassed by a superior Turkic force, beat a hasty retreat to the river Jaxartes in Transoxiana (modern Tajikistan), only to find their path back to Umayyad domains blocked by hostile forces. Knowing this would be a fight to the death, the Muslims burned their supplies, valued at one million dirhams, and fought successfully to break through despite increasing hunger and thirst in what would come to be known as the Day of Thirst—a humiliation that would burn in the memories of many Muslims until long after the Muslim losses were regained and their prestige restored.

The Muslim presence in Central Asia was now substantially diminished, albeit only temporarily.[38] The Umayyads continued to send forces into Khurasan and Transoxiana (modern-day northeast Iran, Uzbekistan, Tajikistan, and the surrounding areas), but they were hampered in their ability to secure the region by some of their own policies.

The Umayyads have gone down in Islamic history as notably irreligious, a curious charge for a dynasty that was established within thirty years of the generally accepted date of Muhammad's death, raising the inevitable questions of why the fervor for Islam was lost so quickly after its founding, and how the Umayyads retained power over the Muslims for nearly a century while continually flouting or ignoring core precepts of the religion. The most plausible explanation for this is that the Umayyads were not actually irreligious, but that Islam itself was at the time of their reign in an inchoate state, with even the Qur'an and the elements of the life of Muhammad that would become the sources and foundation of Islamic doctrine not set in their final form until the Umayyads had ruled for four or five decades. Later, however, when it became accepted even among non-Muslim historians that Uthman had codified and distributed the Qur'an in 653, and statements attributed to Muhammad that appear only in the eighth or ninth centuries were taken for granted as having actually been spoken by him in the seventh, the only explanation for the Umayyads' apparent indifference to all of this material was that they were impious and sinful.

One example of this Umayyad impiety was that they imposed the *jizya* and the *kharaj*, a land tax, upon non-Arab converts to Islam in

Central Asia. Muslim rulers who tried to reverse this policy faced complaints from Arab settlers in Khurasan, as well as an inevitable decline in tax revenues that threatened to make their position fiscally untenable. In the late 720s, the Umayyad governor of Khurasan, Ashras ibn Abdallah al-Sulami, promised the Soghdians, a Central Asian people among whom were Zoroastrians, Buddhists, and Nestorian Christians, equal tax rates with the Arabs if they converted to Islam. The mosques were flooded with converts, but local non-Arab rulers began to complain to Ashras that they could not meet their own tax quotas, since so many of their people were "becoming Arabs."[39]

Unnerved, Ashras began placing more stringent requirements upon converts, most notably that they provide proof of circumcision. Just ten years before, the caliph Umar ibn Abd al-Aziz had forbidden this, saying, "God sent Muhammad to call men to Islam, not as a circumciser," and commanding that non-Arab converts to Islam be placed on an equal footing with the Arabs, but pressures from the Arabs themselves, and the need to keep tax revenues up, often led to these commands' being ignored.[40]

However, Ashras' reneging on his initial offer led to an uprising of the non-Arab Muslims, aided by sympathetic Arabs, including a warrior named al-Harith ibn Surayj, who in 734 led a large-scale revolt against Umayyad rule in Khurasan and Transoxiana, promising equality of non-Arab Muslims with Arabs, and other reforms.

The Arab response was swift and brutal. Arriving at Balkh, the ancient Bactria in what is now northern Afghanistan, the Muslim commander Juday al-Kirmani likened the people of the city to "the adulterous woman who gives access to her leg to whomever comes to her" for allying with al-Harith.[41] He vowed that if he discovered anyone who was sending messages to al-Harith, "I will cut off his hand and foot and crucify him"—the punishment that the Qur'an (5:33) prescribes for those who "wage war against Allah and his messenger.[42] The governor of Khurasan, Asad ibn Abdallah al-Qasri, ordered al-Kirmani to send him fifty of the leaders of Balkh, whom he immediately killed. Asad directed al-Kirmani to divide the rest of the men of the city into three groups, and to crucify one group, cut off the hands and feet of the second, and cut off the hands only of the third. Al-Kirmani complied, killing and crucifying four hundred men and auctioning off their property.[43]

Despite the brutality of the Umayyads, the revolt continued. In 736, a Muslim named Ammar ibn Yazid, who called himself Khidash, arrived in Marw in Khurasan and began calling believers to allegiance not to the Umayyad caliph Hisham ibn Abdel Malik but to the Shi'ite leader, the fifth Imam, Muhammad ibn Ali. Khidash, however, was quickly captured and brought to Asad, who ordered him blinded and his tongue cut out. Asad told the rebel commander: "Praise be to God who has taken revenge on you for Abu Bakr and Umar."[44] Asad then ordered Khidash killed and the body crucified, and for good measure, had Muhammad ibn Ali, who was living quietly in Medina, murdered by poisoning.[45]

Asad died in 738, and his successor, Nasr ibn Sayyar, stymied the rebellion by defeating and killing both Kursul and al-Harith. He also moved to take the wind out of the rebels' sails by promising to end the collection of the *jizya* from non-Arab Muslims, and the widespread exemption of non-Muslims from paying the *jizya*. At Marw, Nasr declared:

> Verily, Bahramsis was the protector of the Magians [*majus*]; he favored them, protected them and put their burdens on the Muslims. Verily, Ashbdad son of Gregory was the protector of the Christians, just as Aqiva the Jew protected the Jews. But I am protector of the Muslims. I will defend them and shield them and make the polytheists carry their burdens. Nothing less than the full amount of the *kharaj* as written and recorded will be accepted by me. I have placed Mansur b. Umar b. Abi al-Kharqa as my agent [*amil*] over you and I have ordered him to act justly toward you. If there is a man amongst you who is a Muslim and from whom *jizyah* has been levied, or who has been charged an excessive amount of *kharaj*, thus lightening the burden for the polytheists, then let him raise that with Mansur b. Umar so that he may take the burden away from the Muslim and place it upon the polytheist.[46]

Mansur acted quickly. "By the following Friday," per Tabari, "Mansur had dealt with thirty thousand Muslims who had been paying the *ji-*

zyah and eighty thousand polytheists who had been exempted from the *jizyah*. He imposed the *jizyah* on the polytheists and removed it from the Muslims."[47] The impetus of the revolt had been removed and a key element of Islamic law codified, placing the burden for filling the Islamic treasury squarely upon non-Muslims, and the rebellion was crushed.

The Loss of France

Nonetheless, Umayyad hegemony was weakening across the board. In the West, the Muslims faced more and even greater difficulties. After their defeat at Covadonga, the Muslims decided no longer to bother with Pelayo's tiny band of holdouts in the mountains; a Muslim chronicler said derisively, "What are thirty barbarians perched on a rock? They must inevitably die."[48] The warriors of jihad had already entered France, where they conquered the ancient Roman province of Septimania in southwestern France without much difficulty, moved into Aquitaine, and pressed on. The people of southern France were poor and could offer little in the way of booty to the invaders, so the Muslims began despoiling churches and monasteries, as well as the popular shrine of St. Hillary of Poitiers, taking what they believed to be their due from the treasure of the infidels.

There was another shrine that was a favored site of pilgrims and contained a good deal of silver and gold: that of St. Martin of Tours, in north-central France. In 732, the Muslims under the command of Abdul Rahman al-Ghafiqi, governor of al-Andalus, proceeded to march there.

Frankish authorities, seeing their advance, were not sure if the jihadis constituted simply a raiding party determined to carry away the loot at St. Martin's shrine or an actual invading force. Ultimately, however, there was little difference. Inspired by the exhortations of the Qur'an and Muhammad, the warriors of Islam ultimately intended to seize and hold every bit of land on earth and were determined to continue their jihad wherever and whenever possible. Whether they intended to hold Tours in 732 or not, they intended to do so eventually, and advance farther, as far as the land and sea would take them.

In any case, it was the Muslims who made a far greater miscalculation, drastically underestimating the strength of the forces that gathered between Tours and Poitiers to stop them. The commander of those forces was a Frankish duke named Charles, who gained the name Martel, "The Hammer," for his decisive victory there. October 25, 732 was a bitterly cold day, and the Franks routed the jihadis, who had come dressed for a Spanish summer. Al-Ghafiqi and the remnants of his army beat a scorched-earth retreat back to al-Andalus, burning and looting everything in sight.

But the Franks would rebuild. The Muslims' defeat was near total, and would be total before long. In 734, they lost Avignon in southern France, and not long thereafter were driven out of France altogether, even as they were strengthening and consolidating their hold on Spain.

The Battle of Tours in 732 may have stopped the complete conquest and Islamization of Europe. The warriors of jihad would appear again in France, but they would not come close again to gaining control of the whole country until many centuries later, by vastly different means, when there was no longer a Charles Martel to stop them. The Muslim warriors had traversed immense distances and, in all of Europe, there were, in the early seventh century, no significant forces that could have stopped them were it not for the Battle of Tours. Eighteenth-century English historian Edward Gibbon envisioned the continent's complete Islamization had the Franks lost at Tours thus:

> A victorious line of march had been prolonged above a thousand miles from the rock of Gibraltar to the banks of the Loire; the repetition of an equal space would have carried the Saracens to the confines of Poland and the Highlands of Scotland; the Rhine is not more impassable than the Nile or Euphrates, and the Arabian fleet might have sailed without a naval combat into the mouth of the Thames. Perhaps the interpretation of the Koran would now be taught in the schools of Oxford, and her pulpits might demonstrate to a circumcised people the sanctity and truth of the revelation of Mahomet.[49]

One twentieth-century European, however, was disappointed that Charles Martel had defeated the warriors of Islam, for the same reason that Gibbon was relieved. He exclaimed:

> Had Charles Martel not been victorious at Poitiers—already, you see, the world had fallen into the hands of the Jews, so gutless a thing was Christianity!—then we should in all probability have been converted to Mohammedanism, that cult which glorifies heroism and which opens the seventh heaven to the bold warrior alone. Then the Germanic races would have conquered the world. Christianity alone prevented them from doing so.[50]

The man expressing that regret was Adolf Hitler.

The Fall of the Umayyads

The setbacks of the Muslims in Central Asia and Western Europe led to increasing dissatisfaction with the Umayyads, who were finally overthrown by a rival clan and an Islamic revivalist movement, the Abbasids, in 750. The Abbasids gained supporters by arguing that they had a superior claim to the caliphate than the Umayyads did, as they were members of Muhammad's household, descendants of his uncle, Abbas ibn Abd al-Muttalib, while the Umayyads were descendants of Abu Sufyan, the Quraysh chieftain who had fought Muhammad at the Battle of Uhud and the Battle of the Trench.

This line of reasoning, had the Abbasids followed it to its logical conclusion, would have led them to acknowledge that the Shi'ites had the best claim of all to the caliphate, as their Imams were descended from Ali ibn Abi Talib, Muhammad's son-in-law. Of course, they did not go that far.

The Abbasids also accused the Umayyads of impiety and promised to rule strictly in accord with the Qur'an and the teachings of Muhammad; and so, it was that they defeated the Umayyads in several battles and finally captured and killed the Umayyad caliph Marwan ibn Muhammad on August 6, 750. Abbasid warriors cut off the impious Marwan's head and sent it as a trophy to the Abbasid caliph, the pious Abu al-Abbas.[51]

Almost immediately, it looked as if Allah was favoring the Abbasids and blessing their seizure of the caliphate. In July 751, at the Talas River on the border of present-day Kazakhstan and Kyrgyzstan, the forces of the new caliphate met those of the Chinese Tang dynasty, in what was to be the decisive battle for hegemony over Central Asia. China's Westward expansion was stopped, and the region was definitively secured for Islam. The Buddhist and Christian presence in Central Asia went into rapid decline. The area would be Islamic ever after.

V. UMAYYAD SPAIN

Meanwhile, the Umayyads, vanquished as they were, were not prepared to vanish from history. Abd al-Rahman, an Umayyad prince and the grandson of the caliph Hisham ibn Abdel Malik, escaped Abbasid assassination squads and fled to al-Andalus, where he succeeded in gathering a force of Muslims who did not want to give their allegiance to the Abbasids; ultimately, he established himself as emir of Córdoba and continued to pursue jihad warfare against the Christian domains in Spain.

The Abbasid caliph Mansur was not willing to take the loss of Spain lightly, and directed the commander Ala'a ibn Mughith, who was stationed in North Africa, to invade Spain and destroy the Umayyad upstart. Abd al-Rahman, however, captured Ala'a ibn Mughith and other Abbasid commanders. He had each beheaded, and then had their heads placed in finely decorated boxes that were sent to Mansur. In the box containing Ala'a ibn Mughith's head, Abd al-Rahman placed Mansur's letter ordering his North African commander to go to Spain and fight Abd al-Rahman, along with a fragment of the black flag of jihad that Mansur sent Ala'a ibn Mughith to be his standard. Mansur, receiving this macabre package, murmured, "Thank Allah there lies a sea between Abdur Rahman and me," and made no more attempts to secure Spain for the Abbasids.[52]

Charlemagne at Saragossa

The ongoing war between the Christians and Muslims in Spain became part of Western Europe's foundational legend and myth. In 778, the grandson of Charles Martel, Charles, the King of the Franks, who became known to history as Charles the Great or Charlemagne, led an expedition into Spain at the invitation of a group of Muslim rulers who would not accept the authority of Abd al-Rahman: Husayn, the governor of Saragossa; Suleyman al-Arabi, governor of Barcelona and Girona; and Abu Taur, governor of Huesca. They promised fealty to Charlemagne if he would aid them against Abd al-Rahman; Charlemagne, like so many Christian leaders much later lulled into complacency by their Muslim partners in "interfaith dialogue," trusted them and went on the march.

When Charlemagne arrived at Saragossa, however, al-Arabi offered him his fealty as promised, but Husayn did not, claiming that he had never agreed to do so, and the gates of the city were not opened to him as promised. Charlemagne's forces laid siege to Saragossa, but when the Frankish king learned that the Saxons were revolting against his rule in northern France, he opted to abandon the siege and retreat across the Pyrenees.

On his way out of Spain, however, Charlemagne's men destroyed the walls of Pamplona, the city of the Basques, out of fear that forces opposed to the king were coalescing there. In revenge, the Basques, probably allied with some Muslim forces, ambushed the Franks at Roncevaux Pass, inflicting more severe losses on Charlemagne than he suffered at any other time in his career.

Over time, as century after century passed filled with aggression from the warriors of jihad, the Battle of Roncevaux Pass became in legend a Muslim ambush on Charlemagne's retreating army. In the eleventh century, three hundred years after the battle, the French epic poem known as *The Song of Roland* appeared, describing the heroism of Charlemagne's nephew Roland, who is leading the rear guard of Charlemagne's forces and is caught up in the Muslim ambush. Roland has an *oliphant*, a horn made of an elephant's tusk, which he can use to call for help, but he initially declines to do so, thinking it would be cowardly. Finally, Roland does blow his horn. Charlemagne, way ahead of the rear guard, nonetheless hears Roland's horn and hurries back, but it is too late: Roland and his men are dead, and the Muslims victorious. Charlemagne, however, pursues and vanquishes the Muslims, and captures Saragossa.

Thus, the legend. *The Song of Roland* was enormously popular and inculcated in the Christians who sang and celebrated it in what came to be known (in the European Middle Ages) as knightly virtues: loyalty, courage, and perseverance, even in the face of overwhelming odds. These were virtues that would be needed if Europe was to hold out against the ever-advancing jihad.

VI. RAIDING BYZANTIUM

Harun al-Rashid at Chalcedon

Some Christians were ready to display those virtues. In the late 770s, the Abbasid caliph al-Mahdi traveled to Aleppo, where twelve thousand Christians greeted him with great honor. Al-Mahdi, however, was not disposed to respond in kind, and told them: "You have two options. Either die or convert to our religion."[53] Most of the Christians chose to die rather than embrace Islam. In and around Baghdad, he noticed that the Assyrian Christians had built new churches since the Muslim conquest, in violation of *dhimmi* laws; he ordered them destroyed; five thousand Christians in Syria were given the choice of conversion to Islam or death. Many stayed true to their ancestral faith and chose death.

However, loyalty, courage, and perseverance were not always in evidence. In 782, al-Mahdi sent his son, Harun al-Rashid, into Byzantine territory. Harun advanced swiftly, taking seven thousand Christian slaves and getting all the way to Chalcedon, right across the Bosporus from Constantinople.[54] He seemed on the verge of achieving what the warriors of jihad had tried and failed to do twice before: conquer the imperial city and destroy the Eastern Roman Empire. However, the Byzantine logothete Staurakios was able to move Byzantine troops to a position east of Harun's forces and surround the Muslims, cutting off their path to return to the caliphate.

Harun's position seemed desperate, but then he received help from an unexpected quarter: another in a long and continuing line of short-sighted and opportunistic non-Muslims who saw the jihad as their chance to line their pockets or improve their standing. The Byzantine Empire at this point was riven by the iconoclast controversy: a fierce dispute over whether it was permissible or proper to create and venerate images of Christ, the Virgin Mary, and the saints. The Byzantine general Tatzates, an iconoclast, feared that the iconodule empress regent Irene was going to dismiss him; she was indeed removing iconoclasts from positions of influence. In the jihadis' advance he saw an opportunity: with Harun's army encircled, Tatzates deserted and joined the Muslims, taking much of his army with him.

This momentous desertion was kept secret, so that Harun could use Tatzates to lure Staurakios and other Byzantine officials to the negotiating table. When the Byzantines arrived for the negotiations, Harun took them hostage and used them as bargaining chips to extract favorable terms from Irene.[55] Harun was ultimately able to proceed unmolested back to Abbasid domains, taking with him a substantial sum of Byzantine gold and Irene's promise to pay the Muslims seventy thousand dinars in *jizya* each year for the next three years.[56] Harun rewarded Tatzates by appointing him governor of Armenia.

During his twenty-three-year reign as Abbasid caliph (786–809), Harun al-Rashid invaded the Byzantine Empire eight times. Each time, he demanded the submission of the territories his armies entered and the payment of the *jizya*. If the Christians refused, his forces would plunder the area thoroughly, making sure to take more than they would have collected in tribute.[57] Meanwhile, the *jizya* still came annually from the imperial court in Constantinople. In 802, however, the empress Irene was deposed and exiled, and her successor, Nicephorus, sent envoys to Harun in Baghdad with a defiant message. It said that Irene "considered you as a rook, and herself as a pawn. That pusillanimous female submitted to pay a tribute, the double of which she ought to have exacted from the Barbarians. Restore therefore the fruits of your injustice or abide the determination of the sword."[58]

After they delivered this message to Harun in his legendarily sumptuous court in Baghdad, Nicephorus' messengers threw a bundle of swords at the caliph's feet. Harun reacted coolly. He smiled, unsheathed his scimitar, and declared: "In the name of the most merciful God, Harun al Rashid, commander of the faithful, to Nicephorus, the Roman dog. I have read thy letter, O thou son of an unbelieving mother. Thou shalt not hear, thou shalt behold, my reply."[59]

In 806, Harun made good on his threat, leading a massive Muslim force into the Byzantine Empire. At Cilicia in southern Asia Minor, he ordered sixteen churches demolished and used their stones to shore up the fortifications along the border between the caliphate and the Christian empire.[60] Near Samosata in southeast Anatolia, he ordered all the churches in the area to be destroyed; at Keysun, the Muslims destroyed a magnificent church with fifteen altars that was said to have been constructed by the apostles of Christ themselves. They used the stones to build a fortress at the town of Hadath.[61] At Tyana in Cappadocia, Harun had a mosque built, a declaration of his intentions to hold and Islamize the land.[62] And he kept going, destroying not just the Christians' churches, but also Byzantine fortresses, wherever he could.

Harun advanced with alarming speed across Asia Minor, getting as far as Heraclea Pontica, just 175 miles from Constantinople. Nicephorus, thoroughly alarmed, saw that he was going to have to eat his words: it was he, not Harun, who was going to have to abide by the determination of the sword. He sued for peace and agreed to resume paying the *jizya*; Harun, according to the ninth-century Byzantine chronicler Theophanes the Confessor, was immensely pleased, as the money was a "token that he had subjected the Roman Empire."[63] Nicephorus also agreed not to rebuild the fortresses that the jihadis had destroyed, but once Harun withdrew, he rebuilt them anyway. Harun, hearing of Nicephorus' perfidy, seized the city of Thebasa in Lycoania and the island of Cyprus, where he destroyed all the churches and forcibly resettled the Cypriots elsewhere.[64]

As Harun carried out his jihad campaigns, he heeded the advice of a Muslim jurist, Abu Yusuf, who advised him:

> Whenever the Muslims besiege an enemy stronghold, establish a treaty with the besieged who agree to surrender on certain conditions that will be decided by a delegate, and this man decides that their soldiers are to be executed and

their women and children taken prisoner, this decision is lawful. This was the decision of Sa'ad b. Mu'adh in connection with the Banu Qurayza. The decision made by the chosen arbitrator, if it does not specify the killing of the enemy fighters and the enslavement of their women and children, but establishes a poll tax, would also be lawful; if it stipulated that the vanquished were to be invited to accept Islam, it would also be valid, and they would therefore become Muslims and freemen. It is up to the imam to decide what treatment is to be meted out to them and he will choose that which is preferable for the religion and for Islam. If he esteems that the execution of the fighting men and the enslavement of their women and children is better for Islam and its followers, then he will act thus, emulating the example of Sa'ad b. Mu'adh.[65]

Sa'd ibn Mu'adh was the Companion of Muhammad who pronounced the judgment that the men of the Qurayzah Jewish tribe be executed, and the women and children enslaved, after which Muhammad beheaded between six hundred and nine hundred men.

None of this has become part of the legend of Harun al-Rashid. According to the historian Karen Armstrong, "Harun al-Rashid was a patron of the arts and scholarship and inspired a great cultural renaissance. Literary criticism, philosophy, poetry, medicine, mathematics and astronomy flourished not only in Baghdad [where the Abbasids had placed their capital] but in Kufah, Basrah, Jundayvebar and Harran."[66] In the West, Harun al-Rashid may be the best known of all the caliphs, and his name is generally associated with cultural advancement, scholarship, and poetry. After *The Arabian Nights* brought his name and legend to the West, he became a mythical philosopher-king on the order of King Arthur. Alfred Lord Tennyson and William Butler Yeats celebrated him in verse. Even the novelist Salman Rushdie, in hiding after the Islamic Republic of Iran offered a reward for his murder for his "blasphemous" 1988 novel *The Satanic Verses*, followed up in 1990 with *Haroun and the Sea of Stories*, in which the two main characters are called Haroun and Rashid in a tribute to Harun al-Rashid and an Islamic culture that Rushdie considered more enlightened than that of Ayatollah Khomeini.

Yet Harun al-Rashid had another side. History does not record how many Christians and other non-Muslims this most enlightened of caliphs subjected to lives of slavery and degradation, or to immediate death after a defeat in battle. No one at his opulent court looked askance at this: the subjugation of the conquered peoples was taken for granted. It was the will of Allah.

VII. MORE JIHAD FORAYS INTO EUROPE

Hisham at Narbonne

The warriors of jihad had not given up on France. In 791, the Umayyad emir of Córdoba, Hisham al-Reda, the son of Abd al-Rahman, declared jihad against the Franks, and determined for good measure to strike a hard blow against the nagging problem of the Christian Kingdom of Asturias. He led forty thousand jihadis across the Pyrenees and advanced as far as Narbonne and Carcassone in southern France, but was unable to go farther or hold the territory. He did, however, carry back an immense haul of plunder: forty-five thousand gold coins and many enslaved Christians. When his men sacked Oviedo, the new capital of the Kingdom of Asturias, they added even more to the booty. To show his gratitude to Allah for this bounty, Hisham gave a large part of the gold to finance the construction of the Great Mosque of Córdoba.[67]

The Jihad in Crete and Sicily

By this time, however, the jihad in France was largely over, at least until the twenty-first century. Elsewhere, however, it was just beginning. In 825, ten thousand Muslims from al-Andalus took to the sea and began to engage in the jihad of piracy, raiding infidel ships in search of booty and setting the pattern for jihad pirates down through the ages, including the Barbary pirates, who waged war against the newly independent United States, and the Somali pirates, who terrorized the waters around east Africa in the twenty-first century. Eventually they landed in Alexandria, where they plundered churches and Abbasid mosques, both considered to be the domains of infidels at war with the rightful Islamic authority, the Umayyads of Córdoba, and seized and sold six thousand Christians as slaves.[68]

Driven out of Alexandria in 827 by the Abbasid caliph al-Ma'mun, the pirates set their sights on Crete, an outpost of the Byzantine Empire. The Muslims thought they were merely plundering the island until their chief, Abu Hafs, took a page from Tariq ibn Ziyad's book and set fire to their ships.

The jihadi sailors were enraged. Abu Hafs, however, quickly mollified them, saying: "Of what do you complain? I have brought you to a land flowing with milk and honey. Here is your true country; repose from your toils, and forget the barren place of your nativity."

The jihadis countered: "And our wives and children?"

Abu Hafs had a ready answer: "Your beauteous captives will supply the place of your wives, and in their embraces you will soon become the fathers of a new progeny."[69] The idea that the Muslims might lose doesn't seem to have entered anyone's mind.

Apparently convinced by Abu Hafs' promise of "beauteous" spoils of war, the jihadis began to fight for control of the island. A former monk who had converted from Christianity to Islam led them to Chandax, an area of the island that was suitable for the construction of a fortress. The Byzantines were quickly defeated; the Emperor Michael II the Stammerer, alarmed at the loss of a land so strategically placed in the Mediterranean, sent several expeditions to recapture Crete, but none were successful. Abu Hafs established the Emirate of Crete, giving nominal obeisance to the Abbasid caliph while essentially ruling on his own. The Emirate of Crete would be a thorn in the side of the Byzantines for the next century and a half, harassing Byzantine shipping in the eastern Mediterranean and serving as a base for jihad raids elsewhere, until it was finally recaptured in a Byzantine offensive in 961.

The Muslim conquest of Sicily began the same year as the conquest of Crete, 827. As with the jihad into Spain, a renegade Christian was its impetus. According to legend, a young man named Euphemius had become entranced with a young cloistered nun; unable to control himself, he kidnapped her from her cloister and married her, all against her will. News of this outrage reached the ears of the emperor Michael himself, who stammered out that the lust-drunk libertine Euphemius must be punished by having his tongue cut out.[70]

Euphemius was not resolved to suffer such a punishment in silence. He fled Sicily, but knew that wherever he went in Byzantine domains, he was likely to be caught and punished even more severely than Michael had ordered. He went instead to North Africa, where he appealed for help from the Muslims, who were happy to oblige. Euphemius returned to Sicily in style with ten thousand new friends and one hundred ships. While initially successful, Euphemius and the Muslims soon encountered fierce resistance, and the traitor Euphemius was killed.

By 829, the jihadi invaders had been almost completely driven off the island when they received unexpected help: an invading Muslim army from al-Andalus, led by Asbagh ibn Wakil. Although they ultimately took Palermo, the Muslims were not able to secure the eastern part of Sicily, stymied both by the ferocity of the native population and their own inability to unite their various factions. The fighting went on for decades.

In 878, the Muslims finally took Syracuse, and the booty was immense. According to Gibbon, "the plate of the cathedral weighed five thousand pounds of silver; the entire spoil was computed at one million of pieces of gold [about four hundred thousand pounds sterling]." Along with the treasure, the Muslims enslaved over seventeen thousand Christians. The exact number is not known, but according to Gibbon, it exceeded the number of the seventeen thousand Christians who were captured and sent to Africa to lead lives of slavery when the Muslims took Taormina.[71]

The warriors of jihad were finally able to secure complete control of Sicily in 902. The conquerors treated their new domains with extreme severity, brutally suppressing the Greek language and forcibly converting thousands of young boys to Islam.

Jihad in Asia Minor

The successors of Harun al-Rashid continued the jihad against the Byzantine Empire, but for a considerable period this took the form of raids into Byzantine territory in Asia Minor, in which the Muslims would capture treasure and slaves and then return to the caliphate. In the 830s, the Byzantine emperor Theophilus asked the Abbasid caliph al-Ma'mun for a peace accord, but al-Ma'mun's response hewed to the Islamic tripartite choice for the People of the Book, and made it clear yet again that the Muslims were not fighting the Byzantines simply out of a desire for conquest:

> I should make the answer to your letter [the dispatch of] cavalry horses bearing steadfast, courageous and keen-sighted riders, who would contend with you over your destruction [*thuklikum*], to seek God's favor by spilling your blood.... They have the promise of one of the two best things: a speedy victory or a glorious return [to God as martyrs in battle]. But I consider that I should proffer you a warning, with which God establishes clearly for you the decisive proof [of Islam], involving the summoning of you and your supporters to knowledge of the divine unity and the divine law of the religion of the *hanifs* [pre-Islamic monotheists]. If you refuse [to accept this offer], then you can hand over tribute [literally: a ransom] which will entail the obligation of protection [*dhimmah*] and make incumbent a respite [from further warfare]. But if you choose not to make that [payment or ransom], then you will clearly experience face-to-face our [martial] qualities to an extent which will make any effort [on my part] of eloquent speaking and an exhaustive attempt at description superfluous. Peace be upon him who follows the divine guidance![72]

To al-Ma'mun's bellicose message, Theophilus prudently did not reply. Then, perhaps recalling (or coining) Muhammad's dictum "War is deceit," al-Ma'mun set out to harass Theophilus in a different way. In Cilicia in southern Asia Minor, a Christian approached the caliph and convinced him that he was Theophilus' son and would be his vassal. Al-Ma'mun gave him a costly bejeweled crown and ordered Job, the Patriarch of Antioch, to consecrate the imposter emperor of the Romans. Job, knowing that his choice was to go along with the charade or be killed, complied, consecrating the new "emperor" with full pomp; when the Patriarch of Constantinople heard about what had happened, he excommunicated Job. Al-Ma'mun and his sham Byzantine emperor kept up the pretense for two years, but when they saw that none of the Byzantines were falling for the imposture and rising against Theophilus, they gave it up, and the false emperor converted to Islam.[73]

In 833, al-Ma'mun ventured into Byzantine territory and made significant gains. He retook the city of Tyana for the Muslims, where Harun al-Rashid had built a mosque, but which the Muslims had evacuated when Nicephorus sued for peace. When he had originally conquered it in 831, al-Ma'mun had ordered the city destroyed, after which the Muslims again withdrew from the area. When he took it yet again in 833, however, al-Ma'mun realized its value as a fortress and base for further operations against the Byzantines and ordered it rebuilt yet again. According to the twelfth-century chronicler Michael the Syrian, "He started to rebuild it through taxes demanded from the country so harshly that every tongue cursed him."[74]

Al-Ma'mun, if he heard these imprecations, was undoubtedly unmoved; it was the will of Allah that the *dhimmi* People of the Book pay for the upkeep and works of the Muslims. But shortly thereafter, the caliph died suddenly and unexpectedly at the age of forty-seven, after eating green dates while relaxing on a riverbank.[75]

Not long thereafter, two Muslim commanders, Nasr and Babak, converted to Christianity with a portion of their troops and offered themselves to Theophilus' service. Theophilus, delighted and emboldened, conducted several raids into caliphate territory.

Al-Ma'mun's successor as caliph, al-Mu'tasim, was enraged. He led a huge army into Asia Minor, conquered Ancyra (modern Ankara), and proceeded on to Amorium, a major city at that time, which he put under siege. After twelve days, a Christian prince named George betrayed the city, allowing it to fall into al-Mu'tasim's hands. The caliph gave full vent to his rage upon the city's inhabitants. The Muslims raided the monasteries and took thousands of nuns as sex slaves, killed eighteen thousand people, and destroyed the city's churches. Then al-Mu'tasim's son Daoud, a devout young man, prevailed upon his father to restrict the lives of the captive Christians even more than they had been already, forbidding funeral processions, church bells, the open display of the cross on church buildings, the public celebration of the Divine Liturgy, and the consumption of pork.[76] With the exception of the last, these became part of Islamic law for the treatment of Christians in Islamic lands.

Yet even after this, Theophilus again tried to make peace. He sent the caliph gifts and asked that he exchange Byzantine prisoners for Muslim ones. Al-Mu'tasim sent the emperor gifts in return but rejected a one-for-one prisoner exchange: "It is not the Arab custom to exchange [one] Arab for a Byzantine since the Arabs have greater value. But if you give up our [people] then I will return many of your people."[77]

It remains part of Islamic law to this day that the life of a Muslim is worth more than that of a non-Muslim. A manual of Islamic law certified as reliable by al-Azhar, the foremost authority in Sunni Islam today, specifies that "the indemnity paid for a Jew or Christian is one-third the indemnity paid for a Muslim. The indemnity paid for a Zoroastrian is one-fifteenth that of a Muslim."[78]

Theophilus agreed to an unequal prisoner exchange, and for a brief period there was peace in Asia Minor.

The Jihad in Rome

As the jihad against Sicily continued, Muslims also began jihad raids on the Italian mainland. In 846, they attacked Rome, the grandest city in Christendom aside from Constantinople, but were unable to get through its walls. The basilicas of St. Peter and St. Paul Outside the Walls, however, as the latter's name indicated, were outside the city's defenses. The jihadis plundered both, taking as much silver and gold as they could, including a sumptuous silver altar from St. Peter's. But finding Rome's walls too strong to breach, they continued down the Appian Way to nearby Fondi, which they plundered, and Gaeta, which they besieged.

Although the jihadis had left the immediate vicinity of Rome, the people in the great city were thoroughly alarmed. Despite the Muslims' inability to break through into the heart of the city, the Romans criticized Pope Sergius for not doing enough to keep the city safe. When he died in 847, his successor, Pope Leo IV, swiftly began shoring up Rome's defenses, building new walls and repairing the existing ones, as well as repairing the damage the Muslims had done to St. Peter's and St. Paul's.

That all this was necessary was taken for granted by everyone. The jihad forces were still in Italy, and the threat was urgent; it had not yet become customary for the Roman Pontiff to proclaim the peacefulness of Islam and benign character of the Qur'an, and to decry the building of walls. If anyone had been skeptical about the need for Pope Leo's new walls, they were no longer so in 849, when Muhammad Abu'l Abbas, the emir of the Aghlabid dynasty that ruled in North Africa, ostensibly under the authority of the Abbasid caliph, sent a fleet to the mouth of the Tiber River, just sixteen miles from Rome. Leo, however, had formed an alliance with several Italian princes, as well as with the Byzantines, and a significant Christian force was there to meet the forces that the Christians called the Saracens. In battle at Ostia, a district of Rome, and aided by a storm that destroyed much of the Muslim fleet, the Christians were victorious, and the conquest and Islamization of Rome was prevented, at least for the foreseeable future.

Elsewhere, the Christians were not so fortunate. Gibbon recounted the habitual savagery of the conquerors:

> It was the amusement of the Saracens to profane, as well as to pillage, the monasteries and churches. At the siege of Salerno, a Mussulman chief spread his couch on the communion-table, and on that altar sacrificed each night the virginity of a Christian nun. As he wrestled with a reluctant maid, a beam in the roof was accidentally or dexterously thrown down on his head; and the death of the lustful emir was imputed to the wrath of Christ, which was at length awakened to the defence of his faithful spouse.[79]

Enforced subjugation

Meanwhile, the Christians who were living in the domains of the caliphate demonstrated why it was so important for the Christians elsewhere to resist the jihadi onslaught. The eleventh-century Muslim historian al-Maliki noted that in the ninth century, a *qadi* (Sharia court judge) "compelled the *dhimmis* to wear upon their shoulder a patch of white cloth [*riqa'*] that bore the image of an ape [for the Jews] and a pig [for the Christians], and to nail onto their doors a board bearing the sign of a monkey."[80]

These were not singular instructions issued at only one time and in one location. In 850, the caliph al-Mutawakkil issued a decree designed to make sure that the *dhimmis* knew their place, and that the Muslims knew how to keep them in their place:

> It has become known to the Commander of the Faithful that men without judgment or discernment are seeking the help of *dhimmis* in their work, adopting them as confidants in preference to Muslims, and giving them authority over the subjects. And they oppress them and stretch out their hands against them in tyranny, deceit, and enmity. The Commander of the Faithful, attaching great importance to this, has condemned it and disavowed it. Wishing to find favor with God by preventing and forbidding this, he decided to write to his officers in the provinces and the cities and to the governors of the frontier towns and districts that they should cease to employ dhimmis in any of their work and affairs or to adopt them as associates in the trust and authority conferred on them by the Commander of the Faithful and committed to their charge…
>
> Do not therefore seek help from any of the polytheists and reduce the people of the protected religions to the station which God has assigned to them. Cause the letter of the Commander of the Faithful to be read aloud to the inhabitants of your district and proclaim it among them, and let it not become known to the Commander of the Faithful that you or any of our officials or helpers are employing anybody of the protected religions in the business of Islam.[81]

Al-Mutawakkil was not innovating. He was extrapolating all of this from the directions of the Qur'an itself: "Let not believers take disbelievers as friends and protectors rather than believers. And whoever does that has nothing to do with Allah, except when taking precaution against them in prudence." (3:28)

The caliph was determined to ensure that the *dhimmis* lived in a constant state of humiliation, as befitting those who had rejected the truth of Allah and his prophet, and to be readily recognizable for what they were, so that they would not be mistakenly accorded respect by an unwitting Muslim. While he issued the decree above, according to Tabari, the caliph also:

> ...gave order that the Christians and the *dhimmis* in general be required to wear honey-colored hoods and girdles; to ride on saddles with wooden stirrups and two balls attached to the rear; to attach two buttons to the caps of those who wear them and to wear caps of a different color from those worn by the Muslims; to attach two patches to their slaves' clothing, of a different color from that of the garment to which they are attached, one in front on the chest, the other at the back, each patch four fingers in length, and both of them honey-colored. Those of them who wore turbans were to wear honey-colored turbans. If their women went out and appeared in public, they were only to appear with honey-colored head scarfs. He gave orders that their slaves were to wear girdles and he forbade them to wear belts. He gave orders to destroy any churches which were newly built, and to take the tenth part of their houses. If the place was large enough it was to be made into a mosque; if it was not suitable for a mosque it was to be made into an open space. He ordered that wooden images of devils should be nailed to the doors of their houses to distinguish them from the houses of the Muslims. He forbade their employment in government offices and on official business where they would have authority over the Muslims. He forbade their children to attend Muslim schools or that any Muslim should teach them. He forbade the display of crosses on their Palm Sundays and Jewish rites in the streets. He ordered that their graves be made level with the ground so that they should not resemble the graves of the Muslims.[82]

VIII. SEIZING THE STONE

The Qarmatians at Mecca

In the second half of the ninth century, the jihad against infidels largely gave way to a jihad against Muslim rivals. The Abbasid caliphate was beset with internal strife, with four caliphs ruling between 861 and 870, as rival factions vied for power. In the mid ninth century, the Abbasids were so weakened by their internal divisions that the Byzantines were able to go on the offensive and recapture the provinces of Illyricum, Greece, Bulgaria, Northern Syria, Cilicia, and Armenia, which they had previously lost to the jihad.[83]

Despite all their dissension and disunity, however, the Abbasids still had the time and energy to continue to persecute the Shi'ite minority. The caliph al-Mutawakkil forced the tenth Shi'ite Imam, Ali ibn Muhammad al-Naqi, to move from his home in Medina to Samarra, which the Abbasids had made their capital in 836. Once he had him close by, Al-Mutawakkil had al-Naqi mistreated, ridiculed, and tortured. Al-Mutawakkil died in 861, but the persecution continued until the caliph al-Mu'tazz bi-'llah had al-Naqi poisoned to death in 868.[84] His successor as Imam of the Shi'a, Hasan ibn Ali al-Askari, lived under house arrest in Samarra until his death, also by Sunni poisoning, in 874.

Shi'ite tradition holds that the prophecy that the twelfth Imam would be the Mahdi, the savior figure of Islam awaited by both Sunnis and Shi'ites, was widely known—so al-Askari was kept under wraps lest he father a son who could claim that title.[85] Shi'ites believe, however, that he managed to have a son anyway, although there are differing traditions about who his wife was and where she was from, and no one is sure how she got to the Imam under the watchful eyes of the Sunnis.

However it happened, the twelfth Imam, Muhammad ibn Hasan al-Mahdi, was born, and great things were expected of him. However, his father was killed when he was just four years old and, soon afterward, the long-awaited boy himself disappeared—probably also murdered by Sunnis, like most of the Imams before him. In the Shi'ite view, however, he went into "occultation," unable to be seen by ordinary human eyes but still very much alive. Four men known as his special deputies claimed to be in contact with him, and they led the Shi'ite community for the next seventy years, always in an atmosphere of persecution from the Sunnis. The return of the twelfth Imam, and the triumph of the Shi'a over the Sunnis and all infidels, became a staple of Shi'ite apocalyptic literature.

Meanwhile, a schism among the Shi'ites caused more trouble for the Abbasids. The sixth Imam, Jafar al-Sadiq, who reigned from 733 to 765, designated his son Ismail ibn Jafar as his successor. Ismail, however, died before Jafar did, and so Jafar was succeeded by his brother, Musa ibn Jafar al-Kazim. However, a party of the Shi'ites believed that since their Imams were infallible, Ismail was the rightful successor of Jafar, as Jafar would not have designated him otherwise, and that the Imamate belonged not to Musa, but to Ismail's son Muhammad ibn Ismail.

This Shi'ite group came to be known as the Ismailis, and they were beset by internal divisions as well. In the late ninth century, one group of Ismailis—known as Qarmatians, after their founder Hamdan Qarmat— preached an apocalyptic vision centered upon the imminent return of Muhammad ibn Ismail as the Mahdi, the savior figure of Islamic apocalyptic literature. The Qarmatians were fierce and fanatical, seeing even the pilgrimage to Mecca as idolatrous, because while there the pilgrims venerated the Black Stone of the Ka'aba, the sacred meteorite that Allah, it was said, had thrown down to that spot from Paradise.[86]

In 899, the Qarmatians captured Hajr, the capital of Bahrain, and established Bahrain as their stronghold, setting up a utopian society with no Friday services and, indeed, no mosques at all; apparently, they jettisoned Islamic practices in anticipation of the Mahdi's arrival and the consummation of all things.[87] Thirty thousand black slaves did the work, and another twenty thousand served as the army. No taxes were levied, as the community relied on plunder for its sustenance. The Qarmatians were energetic in pursuing that plunder: the Qarmatians began raiding the caravans of pilgrims to Mecca. In 906, they killed twenty thousand pilgrims who were returning from Mecca, and in 924 massacred another pilgrim caravan. They also began seizing Abbasid strongholds, sacking Kufa in 925 and coming close to taking Baghdad in 927.[88]

In 928, the Qarmatians struck their mightiest blow yet against Abbasid power: they stormed Mecca and stole the Black Stone from the Ka'aba, carrying what they considered a focus of idolatry back to Bahrain. The theft of the Black Stone signified, the Qarmatians said, the end of Islam and the commencement of the age of the Mahdi. They were, however, willing to return it for a ransom back to Mecca, but the Abbasids never made any effort to pay up.

Finally, in 950, on the orders of the Fatimid Shi'ite caliph who had established himself in Cairo and whose authority they had accepted, the Qarmatians threw the Black Stone into the Great Mosque of Kufa in central Iraq, along with a note saying, "By command we took it, and by command we have brought it back."[89] It had been in three pieces when it was taken; perhaps from the impact of being thrown into the mosque, it had now broken into seven, but fragmentary or no, it was still the Black Stone, or the closest thing to the Black Stone that anyone actually possessed.

The Abbasids, no doubt breathing a sigh of relief that it had finally been returned to Kufa, restored it to its place for veneration at the Ka'aba in Mecca. And that was that. Abbasid power was severely shaken, but the jihad imperative remained and would eventually be taken up again.

CHAPTER FOUR

CONSOLIDATION AND OPPRESSION

Jihad in the Tenth and Eleventh Centuries

I. THE JIHAD IN SPAIN

Islam in Power in Spain

The jihad in Spain slowed down considerably in the late ninth and early tenth centuries. In fact, the Christian domains in Spain were growing, but very slowly and amid many setbacks. As in all wars, long and short, matters became complicated; on occasion, Christians and Muslims forged alliances for short-term goals. Whatever the utility of these coalitions of convenience, and however successful they were, the jihad imperative remained a constant, and there was never any shortage of Muslims in al-Andalus who were ready to pursue it.

In 920, the forces of the Emirate of Córdoba routed the Christians of the Kingdom of León, the successor to Pelayo's Kingdom of Asturias, at Valdejunquera. But those who were determined to resist the jihad were by no means wiped out, and they fought on.

From 929 on, the Umayyad rulers of Spain styled themselves as caliphs of Córdoba. That caliphate, and Islamic al-Andalus in general, has become a potent myth in the twenty-first century. Historians have painted it as a paradise of protomulticulturalism: Karen Armstrong, author of *Islam: A Short History*, claims that "until 1492, Jews and Christians lived peaceably and productively together in Muslim Spain—a coexistence that was impossible elsewhere in Europe."[1] Historian María Rosa Menocal asserts that the Muslim rulers of Spain "not only allowed Jews and Christians to survive but, following Quranic mandate, by and large protected them."[2]

This myth has come to be taken for granted in the West. In his June 4, 2009, outreach speech to the Muslim world from Cairo, U.S. president Barack Obama said: "Islam has a proud tradition of tolerance. We see it in the history of Andalusia."[3]

Yet Umayyad Spain was hardly a comfortable place for the Christians and Jews who were subjugated there under the rule of Islam. Several decades after the Umayyads proclaimed their caliphate in Córdoba, the Holy Roman emperor Otto I sent an emissary, John of Gorze, to Muslim Spain. John of Gorze noted that the Christians of al-Andalus were living in fear and suffering under the burden of systematic discrimination.[4] But when he proposed informing Otto I about the plight of the Christians in al-Andalus, a Spanish bishop told him that to do so would only make matters worse. "Consider," he told John, "under what conditions we live. We have been driven to this by our sins, to be subjected to the rule of the pagans. We are forbidden by the Apostle's words to resist the civil power. Only one cause of solace is left to us, that in the depths of such a great calamity they do not forbid us to practise our own faith.... For the time being, then, we keep the following counsel: that provided no harm is done to our religion, we obey them in all else, and do their commands in all that does not affect our faith."[5]

Dhimmis throughout the ages have enunciated a similar philosophy: just stay quiet, or matters will get even worse. Islamic law forbade the *dhimmis* to complain about their state, on pain of forfeiting their contract of "protection"; *dhimmi* communities, therefore, learned to put up with the most humiliating degradation in silence, for fear that if they said anything about their condition to anyone, it would only become even more precarious and dangerous.

Even Menocal grants that the lives of the *dhimmis* in al-Andalus were severely restricted:

> The *dhimmi*, as these covenanted peoples were called, were granted religious freedom, not forced to convert to Islam. They could continue to be Jews and Christians, and, as it

turned out, they could share in much of Muslim social and economic life. In return for this freedom of religious conscience the Peoples of the Book (pagans had no such privilege) were required to pay a special tax—no Muslims paid taxes—and to observe a number of restrictive regulations: Christians and Jews were prohibited from attempting to proselytize Muslims, from building new places of worship, from displaying crosses or ringing bells. In sum, they were forbidden most public displays of their religious rituals.[6]

The Umayyad laws were designed to emphasize that Muslims had the dominant position in society, and that the Christians of Spain were decidedly inferior.[7] It was made unpleasant, expensive, and dangerous to live daily life as a Christian, so that the victory and supremacy of Islam was readily observable and regularly reinforced. *Dhimmi* Christians also knew that all they had to do to end this daily discrimination and sporadic harassment and persecution was convert to Islam.

Many did convert, because it was miserable to live as a Christian in al-Andalus. Christians could never be sure that they would not be harassed. One contemporary account tells of priests being "pelted with rocks and dung" by Muslims while on the way to a cemetery.[8] The *dhimmis* also suffered severe economic hardship. Paul Alvarus, a ninth-century Christian in Córdoba, complained about the "unbearable tax" that Muslims levied on Christians.[9]

Nor could Christians say anything about their lot, because it was proscribed by Islamic law, and criticizing Islam, Muhammad, or the Qur'an in any manner was a death-penalty offense.[10] In 850, Perfectus, a Christian priest, engaged a group of Muslims in conversation about Islam; his opinion of the conquerors' religion was not positive. For this, Perfectus was arrested and put to death. Not long thereafter, Joannes, a Christian merchant, was said to have invoked Muhammad's name in his sales pitch. He was lashed and given a lengthy prison sentence.[11] Christian and Muslim sources contain numerous records of similar incidents in the early part of the tenth century. Around 910, in one of many such episodes, a woman was executed for proclaiming that "Jesus was God and that Muhammad had lied to his followers."[12]

The Christians outside of the caliphate did not forget their oppressed brethren, and there were periodic confrontations, large and small, between those who wanted to restore Christian Spain and the warriors of jihad who continued to strike out at the resistance they were facing in conquering the northern portion of the Iberian Peninsula for Allah. In 939, the Christians under the leadership of King Ramiro II of León met the forces of jihad under the command of Abd al-Rahman III, the caliph of Córdoba, at Simancas (also known as Alhandega) in northwestern Spain.

Abd al-Rahman was a scrupulous, doctrinaire Muslim ruler. The eleventh-century Muslim historian Ibn Hayyan of Córdoba recounted:

> God protected the people of al-Andalus, preserving their religion from calamities thanks to…the Prince of the Believers [Abd al-Rahman III]…whom [God] wanted as a Caliph…who followed in the steps of his ancestors, adhering closely to Scripture and proclaiming the Sunnah…so that no devilish heresy would arise that he would not destroy, no flag of perdition was raised that he did not humble, so that with him God kept the community of Islam together, obedient, peaceful…. He expelled innovation and gathered in his capital [Córdoba] the most perfect culture of the times, as never before existed, and he attended to matters of religion, investigating the behavior of the Muslims…and their gatherings in the mosques by means of spies whom he ordered to penetrate the most intimate secrets of the people, so that he could know every action, every thought of good and bad people, and…the explicit and hidden views of the different groups of the population…. God showered gifts upon him…because of his keeping of the law and his subjugating of men, so they sang his praise and his defense of the people's hearts against heresy…following the true and witnessed traditions [ahadith] attributed to greatest of all Imams, Malik ibn Anas, Imam of the people of Medina…. [These traditions] are the ones that have benefited this country, and purified the people from those tendencies which [Abd al-Rahman III] punished in those who

held them, and he ordered his zalmedina [Muslim judge in charge of patrolling the public spaces to enforce Sharia] Abdallah b. Badr, his mawla, to interrogate the accused and carry out an Inquisition against them…terrifying them and punishing them severely.[13]

It is not surprising, considering his careful adherence to Islamic law, that Abd al-Rahman III was harsh with his Christian prisoners. Ibn Hayyan detailed a typical incident:

Muhammad [one of the officers of Abd al-Rahman III] chose the 100 most important barbarians [that is, Christians] and sent them to the alcazar of Córdoba, where they arrived Friday, 7 of the *yumada* I [March 2, 939], but since an-Nasir [Abd al-Rahman III] was vacationing in the orchard of an-Naura [La Noria], they were taken there, their marching coinciding with the people's exiting from the aljama mosque of Córdoba, upon the conclusion of the Friday prayer, so that many gathered and followed to see what end the prisoners would have, and it turned out that an-Nasir was installed on the upper balcony over the orchard facing the river…to watch the execution. All the prisoners, one by one, were decapitated in his presence and under his eyes, in plain sight of the people, whose feelings against the infidels Allah alleviated, and they showered their blessings on the Caliph. The death of these barbarians was celebrated in a poem by Ubaydallah b. Yahya b. Idris [one of the many sycophantic intellectuals in the pay of the Umayyads who relentlessly praised their greatness], saying:

Defeated the prisoners arrived,
Carried and shackled by *Allah*,
Like an angry lion you looked at them,
Surrounded by wild lions and dragons,
And in plain sight of everyone your sword annihilated them,
Among blessings and praises to *Allah*.[14]

Abd al-Rahman III was also notorious for his cruelty toward the *dhimmis*. Ibn Hayyan related one sadly representative incident:

> I must say that I have heard from ulama, generationally
> close to that dynasty [the Umayyads], about the brutal-
> ity of an-Nasir li-din [that is, "the defender of the faith
> of Allah," Abd al-Rahman III] towards the women that
> were under his protection and discretion, similar to what
> he showed in public toward men, according to the word of
> the principal ones among his most intimate servants—eu-
> nuchs who lived in his house and witnessed his personal
> life: a female slave who was one of his most highly regard-
> ed favorites, but whose haughty personality did not bend
> easily to his vanity, having remained with him alone in one
> of his leisure days to drink in the garden of az-Zahra [a
> palace that Abd al-Rahman III had built for his favorite
> sexual slave that contained three hundred baths, four hun-
> dred horses, fifteen thousand eunuchs and servants, and a
> harem of 6,300 women], sitting by his side until drinking
> had an effect on him, and he threw himself upon her face
> to kiss and bite her, and she got disgusted by this and
> turned her face away, raining on his parade; this so pro-
> voked his anger that he ordered the eunuchs to seize her
> and put a candle to her face, burning and destroying her
> beauty...until they destroyed her face, burning her badly
> and finishing with her—one of his worst actions.[15]

The tenth-century Catholic nun Hrotsvitha von Gandersheim recorded that Abd al-Rahman also happened upon a thirteen-year-old Christian boy who had been taken hostage. Entranced by the boy's beauty, the caliph made amorous advances upon him, only to be rejected; enraged, he had the boy tortured and then beheaded.[16]

On another occasion, another one of Abd al-Rahman's sex slaves found herself bearing the brunt of the caliph's anger. Ibn Hayyim recounted:

> His executioner, Abu Imran [Yahya], whom he always had
> at the ready with his "instruments," said that one night he

called him to his room in the palace of an-Naura, where Yahya had slept with his sword and leather floor mat. [Yahya] then entered the room where [Abd al-Rahman III] was drinking and found him squatting, like a lion sitting on his paws, in the company of a girl, beautiful like an onyx, who was being held by his eunuchs in a corner of the room, who was asking for mercy, while he answered her in the grossest manner. He then told [Yahya] "Take that whore, Abu Imran, and cut her neck." [Yahya] said, "I procrastinated, asking him again, as was my custom, but he told me, "Cut it, so may *Allah* cut your hand, or if not, put down your own [neck]." And a servant brought her close to me, gathering up her braids, so that with one blow I made her head fly; but the strike of the blade made an abnormal noise, although I had not seen it hit anything else [but the neck]. Afterwards they took away the body of the girl, I cleaned my sword on my leather mat, I rolled up the mat, and I left; but when I entered my own room and I unfolded the mat, there appeared in it pearls big and shiny, mixed with jacinths and topazes that shone like red-hot coals, all of which I gathered in my hands and I hurried to take it to an-Nasir; he rejected it immediately and told me, "We knew they were there, but we wanted to give them to you as a gift; take it and may Allah bless it to you." And with it I bought this house.[17]

Abd al-Rahman III was no more merciful toward his own people. According to Ibn Hayyan, "I must also mention a horror with which an-Nasir terrorized people, which was by means of lions to make their punishment even more terrible, an action more proper of the tyrannical kings of the Orient, in which he imitated them, having the lions brought to him by the little kings on the North African coast, since they are not animals proper to al-Andalus."[18]

The eleventh-century Muslim cleric Ibn Hazm of Córdoba added that Abd al-Rahman's cruelty sometimes had a racial element:

Abd al-Rahman an-Nasir was not far from his great grand-
father al-Hakam b. Hisam in the way he threw himself
into sin and committed doubtful acts, abusing his subjects,
giving himself cynically to pleasure, punishing with cruelty
and caring little for the effusion of blood. He was the one
who hanged the sons of the blacks from the well of his palace as a sort of counterweight to draw water, making them
die; and he had his impudent buffoon Rasis in a cortege,
with sword and helmet, when in fact she was a shameless
old woman, not to mention other hideous things, that *Allah*
knows better.[19]

In a small bit of retribution for all this savagery, Abd al-Rahman III and
the Muslims were badly beaten at Simancas, and the jihadi army utterly
wiped out. Abd al-Rahman III managed to escape with his life, but although he remained caliph of Córdoba until his death in 961, he never
again led the warriors of jihad onto the field of battle against the infidels.

This was no indication, however, that he blamed himself for the
disaster at Simancas. Upon his return to Córdoba after the defeat, the
caliph ordered the crucifixion of three hundred of his top officers.[20] Ibn
Hayyan recounted that he ordered an attic built above the highest floor
of one wing of his palace, specifically for this purpose:

He put almenas [turrets] and ten door-like openings in
it.... Having prepared ten high crosses, each one placed in
front of each door of the attic, an arrangement that awed
the people, who did not know his purpose, and therefore
more people came to watch than ever before. When the
army arrived, he ordered the zalmedina to arrest 10 of the
principal officers of the army, the first ones to break ranks
on the day of Alhandega, who were there in the ranks,
whom he named and ordered to be placed on the crosses, which was done by the executioners right away, leaving
them crucified, among their supplications for mercy and
pardon, which only increased his anger and insults, while
letting him know they had let him down.[21]

Crucifixion was the punishment the Qur'an prescribed (5:33) for those who "make war upon Allah and his messenger"; apparently Abd al-Rahman considered that they had done that by their incompetent management of the battle against the Christians at Simancas. An onlooker later recalled: "I was caught in the midst of the crowd...I turned away my eyes, almost fainting with horror at the sight...and such was my state, that a thief stole my pack [without my noticing it].... It was a terrible day that scared people for a long time afterwards."[22]

However, even with the decimation of the caliphate's army, the Christians were too riven by infighting to take full advantage of the situation. The caliphate of Córdoba continued to exist, and to "strike terror in the enemies of Allah," as the Qur'an ordered (8:60). In 981, the de facto Córdoban ruler Almanzor, who had usurped the caliph's powers, sacked Zamora and killed four thousand Christians, leveling a thousand Christian villages and destroying their churches and monasteries.[23]

This roused the twenty-year-old King Ramiro III of León, who had become king at age five upon the death of his father, Sancho the Fat, to action. But Almanzor was far more experienced, knowledgeable, and ruthless than Ramiro, who showed how outmatched he was as Almanzor defeated him three times in quick succession.[24] Emboldened by victory, Almanzor began conducting regular jihad raids into Christian lands. In 985, he sacked Barcelona; the following year, he destroyed León, burning monasteries as he went.[25]

As he pursued the jihad against the Christian domains of northern Spain, Almanzor also determined to enhance the glory of his capital. He set a squadron of Christian slaves, their legs in irons, to the task of expanding and beautifying the Great Mosque of Córdoba.[26] In 997, he destroyed Santiago de Compostela, the city that housed the famous shrine of St. James, known as Santiago Matamoros, or St. James the Moor-Slayer. As the warriors destroyed the shrine, they saved the gates and bells for the mosque at Córdoba; Islam forbade bells, but they could be melted down and put to other uses. Newly enslaved Christians, captured at Santiago de Compostela, carried these precious spoils back to Córdoba on their shoulders.[27]

Almanzor continued to pursue the jihad against the Christians of Spain with consistent success, becoming notorious among the Christians of Spain as he did so; when he died, a Christian monk, bitter over the devastation he had wrought upon the native population of Spain, wrote him a succinct epitaph: "Almanzor died in 1002; he was buried in hell."[28]

After the death of Almanzor, there was no leader of comparable strength ready to take his place. The Muslims in Spain were beset with infighting. Berbers from North Africa entered Spain and challenged Umayyad authority; taking Córdoba in 1013, they began massacring Jews, and initiated a wholesale slaughter of Jews in Granada.[29]

The caliphate of Córdoba came to an end in 1031, as the last Umayyad caliph, Hisham III, was imprisoned and exiled, and the Muslim chieftains who ruled the various regions of Muslim Spain could not agree on a successor. Al-Andalus henceforth became a collection of small Muslim emirates and fiefdoms. In the early 1060s, King Fernando I of León won a series of victories over the four most important of these small Muslim states (*taifas*): Zaragoza, Toledo, Badajoz, and Valencia. In a turnabout of the *jizya*, he forced them to pay tribute. In 1064, he successfully laid siege to the fortress city of Coimbra and freed most of Portugal from Islamic rule.[30] After he died, those who were grateful for his stand against the jihad began to refer to him as Ferdinand the Great.

Pogrom in Granada

Meanwhile, the disarray, lack of central authority, and overall weakness of Muslim Spain in the middle of the eleventh century led to no lessening of the plight of religious minorities, since that plight was mandated in the core texts of Islam.

Jews in al-Andalus sometimes had it even worse than Christians did. In the middle of the eleventh century, a Jew named Samuel ibn Naghrila gained the trust of the Muslim rulers and was granted political power in Granada. Later, Samuel's son Joseph also held positions of great honor and responsibility. Islamic law mandated that a non-Muslim could not hold authority over a Muslim, but as with all legal systems, there are some people who flout the rules and periods of relaxation in which the rules are simply ignored.

However, the Muslims in Granada knew Islamic law and were considerably resentful of the power of Samuel, and later of Joseph.[31] The Muslim jurist Abu Ishaq composed verses addressed to the Berber king Badis that vividly demonstrate the Muslim conviction that Muslims must enjoy a place superior to that of the *dhimmis*, who must endure a state of humiliation. Of Granada's Muslim ruler, Abu Ishaq wrote:

> He has chosen an infidel as his secretary / when he could, had he wished, have chosen a Believer. / Through him, the Jews have become great and proud / and arrogant— they, who were among the most abject. / And have gained their desires and attained the utmost / and this happened suddenly, before they even realized it. / And how many a worthy Muslim humbly obeys / the vilest ape among these miscreants. / And this did not happen through their own efforts / but through one of our own people who rose as their accomplice. / Oh why did he not deal with them, following the example set by worthy and pious leaders? / Put them back where they belong / and reduce them to the lowest of the low, / Roaming among us, with their little bags, / with contempt, degradation and scorn as their lot, / Scrabbling in the dunghills for colored rags / to shroud their dead for burial… / These low-born people would not be seated in society / or paraded along with the intimates of the ruler.…/ God has vouchsafed in His revelations / a warning against the society of the wicked. / Do not choose a servant from among them / but leave them to the curse of the accurst! / For the earth cries out against their wickedness / and is about to heave and swallow all. / Turn your eyes to other countries / and you will find the Jews are outcast dogs. / Why should you alone be different and bring them near / when in all the land they are kept afar?… / I came to live in Granada / and I saw them frolicking there. / They divided up the city and the provinces / with one of their accursed men everywhere. / They collect all the revenues, / they munch and they crunch. / They dress in the finest clothes / while you wear the meanest. / They are the

trustees of your secrets, / yet how can traitors be trusted? / Others eat a dirham's worth, afar, / while they are near and dine well..../ Their chief ape has marbled his house / and led the finest spring water to it. / Our affairs are now in his hands / and we stand at his door. / He laughs at God and our religion..../ Hasten to slaughter him as an offering, / sacrifice him, for he is a precious thing..../ Do not consider it a breach of faith to kill them, / the breach of faith would be to let them carry on. / They have violated our covenant with them..../ God watches His own people / and the people of God will prevail.[32]

Abu Ishaq referred to the Jews as "apes" because the Qur'an depicts Allah transforming Sabbath-breaking Jews into apes and pigs (2:63–65; 5:59–60; 7:166).

The Muslims of Granada heeded Abu Ishaq's call. On December 30, 1066, rioting Muslims, enraged by the humiliation of a Jew ruling over Muslims, murdered four thousand Jews in Granada. The maddened Muslim mob crucified Joseph ibn Naghrila and plundered the homes of the Jews.[33]

The Almoravids and El Cid

The Christians continued to advance in Spain. In a major defeat for Islamic al-Andalus, the forces of King Alfonso VI of Castile and León captured Toledo, the old capital of Visigothic Spain, in 1085. The leaders of the various *taifas*, alarmed, in 1086 called for help from the Almoravids, a Berber Muslim dynasty that had taken control of Morocco and its environs in the middle of the eleventh century.

The Almoravids, fearsome in appearance for their practice of wearing veils over the lower half of their faces, which they did to protect themselves from the twin threats of desert sands and evil spirits, entered Spain swiftly. Their king, Yusuf ibn Tashfin, sent a messenger to Alfonso VI, offering him the standard Islamic choices for the People of the Book: conversion to Islam, submission to the hegemony of the Muslims, or war.[34] Alfonso wrote back a contemptuous refusal; when Yusuf received the paper containing this message, he turned it over and wrote on the back, "What will happen, you shall see."[35]

What Alfonso saw was nothing that he wanted to see. The battle, at the village of Sagrajas north of Badajoz, was an unmitigated disaster for the Christians. Alfonso lost over half of his army. When it was over, the Muslims beheaded the Christian corpses and arranged their heads into piles; the muezzins then climbed atop the piles of heads to call the Muslims to prayer, displaying once again in the blood and gore of the Christians' heads the victory and superiority of Islam.[36]

Yusuf and the Almoravids had stopped the momentum of the Christians in Spain and ensured that Islamic al-Andalus would endure. But the whole situation was nonetheless unprecedented. The forces of jihad had never had this much trouble holding a territory they had conquered for Islam, and seldom, if ever, would again. Even as the Almoravids united the *taifas* under their rule and continued to wage jihad against the Christians, the Muslims were still quite often on the defensive. The Christians were determined not to let Spain be Islamized, and they kept pushing against the Muslim domains.

Alfonso VI was thus determined even in defeat. In the wake of the disaster, he sent out appeals for help to Christian leaders all over Spain and France, warning them that the Almoravid advance deeply endangered Christianity in Spain, and asking them to come join him in the defense of Christendom. Alfonso sent one of these appeals to Rodrigo Díaz de Vivar, a Castilian warrior with whom Alfonso had a long history.

Rodrigo had been a Castilian commander under King Sancho II of Castile, the son of Fernando I, Ferdinand the Great. Fernando had been king of Castile and León; when he died, Sancho became king of Castile, and his brother Alfonso became king of León. (A third brother, Garcia, became king of Galicia.) Sancho, suspecting that Alfonso intended to make war upon his two brothers and unite their kingdoms under his rule, struck preemptively: his commander Rodrigo defeated Alfonso in battle, and Sancho became king of León as well as Castile.

Soon afterward, however, Sancho was murdered. Since he had no children, his kingdoms passed into the possession of his eldest brother, who was none other than the one he had just warred against and deposed, Alfonso. Rodrigo and a group of other Castilian noblemen then forced Alfonso to swear, solemnly and repeatedly, that he had not been involved in Sancho's murder. Alfonso had no choice but to comply, but his heart began to burn in bitter resentment toward those who had humiliated him—principally Rodrigo, whom he eventually exiled.

Rodrigo was a Christian. He knew well what the warriors of jihad had in store for the Christians of Spain. But the Christian king whom he had served had exiled him. Whether out of necessity or a desire for revenge, or both, Rodrigo offered his services to Yusuf al-Mu'taman ibn Hud, the king of the Muslim *taifa* of Zaragoza. He fought so valiantly in the service of the Muslims that they began to call him El Sayyid (The Master), which in Spanish folklore became El Cid.

By that name, El Cid, Rodrigo Díaz de Vivar has become one of the great heroes of Spanish history, and the central figure of the *Cantar de Mio Cid*, the renowned Spanish epic poem. For when he received Alfonso's appeal, he returned and again took up the struggle against the Almoravids. He took the city of Valencia from the Muslims, and in 1097 defeated the jihadis decisively at Bairén, near Gandia in southeast Spain.

When El Cid died in 1099, the Christians of Spain controlled two-thirds of the Iberian Peninsula. The momentum of the jihad had been decisively broken. And the impetus for more initiatives against the Muslims came continuously from the systematic mistreatment of the Christians who still lived in the Islamic domains. Even when they were not facing active persecution, if Christians and Jews didn't abide by the restrictions placed upon them as *dhimmis*, they could in accordance with the Sharia be lawfully killed or sold into slavery.[37]

Around 1100, the Muslim governing official and poet Ibn Abdun detailed the rules for *dhimmis* in Seville:

> A Muslim must not act as a masseur to a Jew or Christian; he must not clear their rubbish nor clean their latrines. In fact, the Jew and the Christian are more suited for such work, which are degrading tasks. A Muslim must not act as a guide or stableman for an animal owned by a Jew or Christian; he must not act as their donkey-driver or hold the stirrups for them. If it be noticed that a Muslim contravenes these prohibitions, he shall be rebuked....

It is forbidden to sell a coat that once belonged to a leper, to a Jew or Christian, unless the buyer is informed of its origin; likewise, if this garment once belonged to a debauched person.

No tax-officer or policeman, Jew or Christian may be allowed to wear the dress of an aristocrat, nor of a jurist, nor of a wealthy individual; on the contrary they must be detested and avoided. It is forbidden to accost them with the greeting "Peace be upon you [as-salam alayka]!" In effect, "Satan has gained the mastery over them, and caused them to forget God's Remembrance. Those are Satan's party; why, Satan's party, surely they are the losers!" (Koran 58:20) A distinctive sign must be imposed upon them in order that they may be recognized and this will be for them a form of disgrace.

The sound of bells must be prohibited in Muslim territories and reserved only for the lands of the infidels....

It would be preferable not to let Jewish or Christian physicians be able to heal Muslims.[38]

If the *dhimmis* violated any of these provisions or any of the others that enforced and reminded them daily of their subjugation, they could be sold into slavery. In 1126, several thousand Christians were sent to Morocco to serve as slaves. Once again, the Muslim leadership was acting within the bounds of its right to kill or enslave *dhimmis* who violated the terms of their protection agreement.[39]

Indeed, Umayyad Spain became a center of the Islamic slave trade. Muslim buyers could purchase sex-slave girls as young as eleven years old, as well as slave boys for sex as well, or slave boys raised to become slave soldiers. Also for sale were eunuchs, useful for guarding harems.[40] Blonde slaves seized in jihad raids on Christian nations north of al-Andalus were especially prized, and fetched high prices. Slave traders would use makeup to whiten the faces and dye to lighten the hair of darker slaves, so that they could get more money for them.[41]

A twelfth-century witness of the sale of sex slaves described the market:

The merchant tells the slave girls to act in a coquettish manner with the old men and with the timid men among the potential buyers to make them crazy with desire. The

> merchant paints red the tips of the fingers of a white slave;
> he paints in gold those of a black slave; and he dresses them
> all in transparent clothes, the white female slaves in pink
> and the black ones in yellow and red.[42]

If the girls did not cooperate, of course, they would be beaten or killed.

The Andalusian slave market became particularly important in the eleventh century, when two of the other principal markets from which the Muslims drew slaves, Central Asia and southeastern Europe, dried up. The Slavs by this time had converted to Christianity and were no longer interested in selling their people as slaves to Islamic traders. In Central Asia, meanwhile, the Turks had converted to Islam. The primary market for slaves among Muslims was for non-Muslims, as enslaving fellow Muslims was considered a violation of the Qur'an's requirement to be "merciful to one another" (48:29); hence Muslim slave traders had to look elsewhere for merchandise.[43]

II. THE JIHAD IN INDIA

Quiescence, Not Reform

Outside of Spain, the jihad, at least against infidels, was relatively quiet during the tenth century, as the Abbasids struggled to hold on to their domains, battling not only the Qarmatians but the Shi'ite Fatimid caliphate that had been established in 909 and ultimately wrested much of North Africa and the Middle East from Abbasid control.

That the jihad against unbelievers went through a period of relative quiet was not due to any reform in Islam, or to reconsideration or rejection of the exhortations in the Qur'an and the teachings of Muhammad to wage war against and subjugate unbelievers. It wasn't pursued as relentlessly as it had been in the seventh and eighth centuries solely because the various Muslim factions were preoccupied with infighting, such that they did not have the resources to carry the battle to the infidels the way they once had done. But the jihad would be taken up again as soon as any significant number of Muslims had the will, the unity, and sufficient resources to do so.

The Jihad Against India

At the beginning of the eleventh century, there arose a Muslim commander who was like Tariq ibn Ziyad in two important ways: he was full of zeal for Islam, and had the valor and ruthlessness to bring that zeal to jihad warfare. His name was Mahmud of Ghazni (971-1030), a native of Khurasan who revived the long-dormant jihad against India and greatly extended Islam's presence on the subcontinent. For thirty years, Mahmud terrorized non-Muslims in what is today northeast Afghanistan, Pakistan, and northwest India.[44]

In 994, Mahmud became governor of Khurasan. Bestowing upon himself the title of sultan (governmental power), Mahmud swiftly began to expand his domains—all in the name of Islam.[45] Mahmud's domains were nominally under the suzerainty of the Abbasid caliph; when Mahmud secured the caliph al-Qadir bi-'llah's recognition in 999, he pledged annual jihad raids against India.[46] He didn't manage to invade that frequently, but he did lead seventeen large-scale jihad incursions into the subcontinent.[47]

The thirteenth-century Muslim historian Minhaj al-Siraj Juzjani, author of the *Tabaqat-i Nasiri*, a history of Islam's rise, noted that as Mahmud waged jihad in India, "he converted so many thousands of idol temples into masjids [mosques]."[48] Mahmud broke the idols whenever he could, so as to demonstrate the power of Islam and the superiority of Allah to the gods of the people of India. When he defeated the Hindu ruler Raja Jaipal in 1001, he had Jaipal "paraded about in the streets so that his sons and chieftains might see him in that condition of shame, bonds and disgrace; and that the fear of Islam might fly abroad through the country of the infidels."[49]

Mahmud of Ghazni made an immense effort to conquer Gujarat, according to Zakariya ibn Muhammad, another thirteenth-century Muslim historian, because he hoped that if he was able to destroy Gujarat utterly, its inhabitants would be shocked and demoralized into submission, and would convert to Islam en masse.[50] The people of Gujarat, however, did not submit but resisted, and fifty thousand were killed.[51] Entering one Hindu temple in Gujarat, Mahmud was overcome with anger at seeing the idols; raising his battle-axe, he hit one with full force, breaking it into pieces. The pieces were carried to Ghazni and placed at the threshold of the mosque as a sign of the victory of Islam over the idols and the superiority of Allah to them.[52]

Mahmud proceeded with a massive army of jihadis to Thanessar in Hindustan, where he had heard that there was a magnificent temple in which was placed an idol, Jagarsom, that people from all over the region venerated. Anandapala, the Hindu ruler of the Shahi dynasty in modern-day eastern Afghanistan and northern Pakistan, heard of Mahmud's advance and sought to make peace, sending an envoy to Mahmud offering the Sultan fifty elephants if he would abandon the jihad against Jagarsom. Mahmud ignored the offer, but when he and his men arrived in Thanessar, they found the city entirely empty of people.

Nonetheless, there was plenty to plunder. The Muslims roamed the empty streets, seizing and destroying all the idols from the temples. They transported Jagarsom to Ghazni, where Mahmud ordered that the now broken idol be set in front of the mosque, so that the Muslims would trample upon its pieces on their way in and out for prayer.[53]

The *Kitab i Yamini*, an eleventh-century account of Mahmud of Ghazni's reign up to 1020 by the Muslim historian Abu Nasr Muhammad al-Utbi, contains another account of Mahmud's attacking Thanessar, apparently during one of his other invasions of India. Al-Utbi recorded that the leader of Thanessar "was obstinate in his infidelity and denial of God. So the Sultan marched against him with his valiant warriors, for the purpose of planting the standards of Islam and extirpating idolatry."[54]

Mahmud and his jihadis showed no mercy: "The blood of the infidels flowed so copiously that the stream was discoloured, notwithstanding its purity, and people were unable to drink it."[55] Al-Utbi was sure this was a sign of the divine favor upon the Muslims: "The victory was gained by God's grace, who has established Islam forever as the best of religions, notwithstanding that idolaters revolt against it."[56]

The same historian boasted that Mahmud "purified Hind from idolatry, and raised mosques therein," but the Sultan wasn't finished. In

1013, he marched with a large jihadi army toward Lahore, the capital of Hindustan, where he found a Buddhist temple. Inside the temple was a stone bearing an inscription saying, according to al-Utbi, "that the temple had been founded fifty thousand years ago." Mahmud of Ghazni "was surprised at the ignorance of these people, because those who believe in the true faith represent that only seven thousand years have elapsed since the creation of the world."[57]

Mahmud and his men went on to Nandana, the capital of the Kabul Shahi kingdom under King Anandapal. Here again, the jihadis slaughtered the population indiscriminately and destroyed the temples. Al-Utbi recounted: "The Sultan returned in the rear of immense booty, and slaves were so plentiful that they became very cheap and men of respectability in their native land were degraded by becoming slaves of common shopkeepers. But such is the goodness of Allah, who bestows honour on his own religion and degrades infidelity."[58]

Five years later, Mahmud entered Hindustan again and marched toward the fortress of Mahaban. Al-Utbi said that "the infidels...deserted the fort and tried to cross the foaming river...but many of them were slain, taken or drowned.... Nearly fifty thousand men were killed."[59]

Then at Mathura, al-Utbi added, "the Sultan gave orders that all the temples should be burnt with naptha and fire, and levelled with the ground."[60] At Kanauj, the Muslim historian continued, "there were nearly ten thousand temples.... Many of the inhabitants of the place fled in consequence of witnessing the fate of their deaf and dumb idols. Those who did not fly were put to death. The Sultan gave his soldiers leave to plunder and take prisoners."[61] Then, at Shrawa, "the Muslims paid no regard to the booty till they had satiated themselves with the slaughter of the infidels and worshippers of sun and fire. The friends of Allah searched the bodies of the slain for three days in order to obtain booty.... The booty amounted in gold and silver, rubies and pearls nearly to three thousand *dirhams*, and the number of prisoners may be conceived from the fact that each was sold for two to ten *dirhams*. They were afterwards taken to Ghazni and merchants came from distant cities to purchase them, so that the countries of Mawaraun-Nahr, Iraq and Khurasan were filled with them, and the fair and the dark, the rich and the poor, were commingled in one common slavery."[62]

Al-Utbi concluded with satisfaction that Mahmud of Ghazni "demolished idol temples and established Islam. He captured...cities, killed the polluted wretches, destroying the idolaters, and gratifying Muslims. He then returned home and promulgated accounts of the victories he obtained for Islam." Mahmud repeated the vow he had made to the Abbasid caliph that "every year he would undertake a holy war against Hind."[63]

In 1023, Mahmud prayed to Allah for assistance and invaded India again, this time with a force of thirty thousand jihad warriors on horseback.[64] After crossing a desert, the Muslims came upon a fort, inside of which were wells and abundant water. The people inside the fort came out and tried to appease Mahmud's wrath, but the sultan was having none of it: he killed all the inhabitants and broke their idols into pieces.[65]

According to Minhaj al-Siraj Juzjani, "He led an army to Nahrwalah of Gujarat, and brought away Manat, the idol, from Somnath, and had it broken into four parts, one of which was cast before the entrance of the great Masjid at Ghaznin, the second before the gateway of the Sultan's palace, and the third and fourth were sent to Makkah and Madinah respectively."[66]

In Somnath there was a magnificent temple of Shiva; Manat was the name of one of the pre-Islamic goddesses of Mecca. It was rumored among the Muslims that when Muhammad cleansed the Ka'aba of its pre-Islamic idols and transformed it into a Muslim shrine, and idol worship was extinguished in Arabia, an idol of Manat was transported to India and set up in the temple in Somnath. Thus Mahmud, in destroying this temple, was doing something particularly great in Muslim eyes, as he was extinguishing the last remnant of Arabian idol worship and completing a job begun by none other than Muhammad himself.[67]

In any case, the spoils, in both treasure and human beings, were once again immense: Ghazni was filled with stolen Indian goods that the jihadis had appropriated, and even though the Muslims killed fifty thousand people at Somnath, Hindu slaves were again so plentiful that they sold for as little as two or three dirhams.[68]

The Muslim advance was relentless. Conquering a fortress of Bhim, a Gujarati king, Mahmud and the Muslims plundered it thoroughly, carrying away one hundred gold and silver idols. Mahmud had one of the more impressive and splendid golden images melted down to make grand new gold doors for the mosque of Ghazni, replacing the old iron ones.[69] At Mathura in Uttar Pradesh, Mahmud stripped the Hindu temples of all their gold and silver and then had all the temples set ablaze.[70]

Triumphant, Mahmud had coins minted that proclaimed: "The right hand of the empire, Mahmud Sultan, son of Nasir-ud-Din Subuk-Tigin, Breaker of Idols."[71] Like that of Harun al-Rashid, Mahmud's court became a center of culture and learning, with the sultan patronizing scientists and poets, including the renowned Ferdowsi.[72] This element of Mahmud's legacy tends to be remembered in the contemporary West more than his bloody ventures into India.

Mahmud of Ghazni died in 1030, having made immense gains for Islam in the Punjab and Sindh, and establishing a foothold also in Kashmir and Gujarat. His son Masud followed in his footsteps. In 1037, Masud led a jihad force into Hindustan and sacked the Hindu fort of Hansi. According to the eleventh-century *Tarikh-us-Subuktigin*, "The Brahmins and other high-ranking men were slain, and their women and children were carried away captive, and all the treasure which was found was distributed among the army."[73]

During all of his jihad ventures into India, however, Mahmud had neglected to protect his home base, and by the time Masud ventured into India in 1037, Ghazni itself was vulnerable. While Masud and his men were enjoying this great jihad victory, the Seljuk Turks, who had converted to Islam in the late tenth century, sacked Ghazni and overran most of Masud's Western domains. The jihad against India would come to a halt, albeit, as always, only temporarily.

III. THE SHI'ITE FATIMID CALIPHATE

In the early tenth century, Ismaili Shi'a claiming descent from Fatima, Muhammad's daughter, secured control of large expanses of North Africa, and later over Egypt and the Levant. The Fatimid caliphate existed in an almost perpetual state of jihad against its Sunni neighbors, but it imposed the strictures of dhimmitude upon its non-Muslim subjects no less rigorously than they did. In the early twelfth century, the Fatimid caliph Al-Amir bi-Ahkamillah issued this edict:

Now, the prior degradation of the infidels in this world before the life to come—where it is their lot—is considered an act of piety; and the imposition of their poll tax [*jizya*], "until they pay the tribute out of hand and have been humbled" (Koran 9:29) is a divinely ordained obligation. As for the religious law, it enjoins the inclusion of all the infidels in the payment of the *jizya*, with the exception, however, of those upon whom it cannot be imposed; and it is obligatory to follow in this respect the line laid down by Islamic tradition.

In accordance with the above, the governors of the provinces in their administration must not exempt from the *jizya* a single *dhimmi*, even if he be a distinguished member of his community; they must not, moreover, allow any of them to send the amount by a third party, even if the former is one of the personalities or leaders of their community. The *dhimmi*'s payment of his dues by a bill drawn on a Muslim, or by delegating a real believer to pay it in his name will not be tolerated. It must be exacted from him directly in order to vilify and humiliate him, so that Islam and its people may be exalted and the race of infidels brought low. The *jizya* is to be imposed on all of them in full, without exception.[74]

IV. THE JIHAD IN ASIA MINOR

In the early tenth century, the patriarch of Constantinople Nicholas I Mystikos made an early attempt at interfaith outreach, writing to the Abbasid caliph Muqtadir in cordial terms: "The two powers of the whole universe, the power of the Saracens and that of the Romans, stand out and radiate as the two great luminaries in the firmament; for this reason alone we must live in common as brothers although we differ in customs, manners and religion."[75]

Like later attempts at interfaith outreach, this one was for naught. The jihad continued.

The End of Christian Rule in Asia Minor: Armenia

The Seljuks took Baghdad in 1055. The Abbasids, essentially power-less in the face of growing Seljuk power, granted the Seljuk leaders the title of sultan; the Seljuk sultans paid nominal fealty to the Abbasid caliphs and set out to amass a considerable empire, taking up the jihad against infidels.

The Christians made this easier for them than it might have been by fighting among themselves. In the middle of the eleventh century, the Byzantines seized a substantial portion of Armenia, primarily because they believed that this mountainous region of northeastern Asia Minor would serve as an effective barrier against the warriors of jihad.

The Armenian historian Aristakes Lastivertsi (1002–1080) recalled with anguish the harshness of the invaders:

> In these days Byzantine armies entered the land of Armenia four times in succession until they had rendered the whole country uninhabited through sword, fire, and captive-tak-ing. When I think about these calamities my senses take leave of me, my brain becomes befuddled, and terror makes my hands tremble so that I cannot continue my composi-tion. For it is a bitter narration, worthy of copious tears.[76]

Even worse, the Byzantine emperor Constantine IX, frustrated with the continued resistance of the Armenians, secretly contacted the Seljuk sultan Tugrul Beg in 1044 and urged him to attack the Armenian capi-tal, Ani.[77] Meanwhile, the Byzantines began a systematic persecution of the Armenians. This was because the Armenians held to Monophysite Christianity, which had been declared a heresy by the Council of Chal-cedon in 451, to which the Byzantines adhered. The Byzantine perse-cution of the Armenians became so severe that many Armenian troops upon which the Byzantines were relying to man the border defenses deserted their posts, leading Lastivertsi to lament: "The cavalry wanders about lordlessly, some in Persia, some in Greece, some in Georgia."[78] Some Armenians even joined the Seljuks in their jihad raids into Byz-antine territory.[79]

While all of this was going on, a portion of the Byzantine army re-belled against the emperor Michael VI. The warriors of jihad were only too happy to exploit all of this internal dissension among the Christians. Noted Lastivertsi: "As soon as the Persians realized that [the Byzantine nobles] were fighting and opposing one another, they boldly arose and came against us, ceaselessly raiding, destructively ravaging."[80]

By "Persians," he was referring to the Seljuk Turks. In 1048, they seized the Armenian city of Ardzen. According to Matthew of Edes-sa, a twelfth-century Armenian chronicler, the rampaging jihadis killed 150,000 people, and Matthew lamented "the sons taken into slavery, the infants smashed without mercy against the rocks, the venerable old men abased in public squares, the gentle-born virgins dishonoured and car-ried off."[81] This was the kind of treatment Constantine IX was inviting when he had urged Tugrul Beg to attack Ani.

Constantine IX died in 1055, so he did not live to see his wish ful-filled, but it was fulfilled indeed, and in a manner that visited yet more horror upon the Armenians: in 1064, Tugrul Beg's successor as sultan of the Seljuks, Muhammad bin Dawud Chaghri, who for his exploits in jihad earned the honorific Alp Arslan, or Heroic Lion, besieged Ani.

The Armenians, whatever their distaste for the Byzantines may have been, knew that their treatment at the hands of the Muslims would be worse, and initially resisted with everything they had. But the siege last-ed for twenty-five days, and the people of Ani grew progressively more desperate. At one point they sent their comeliest young men and women out to Alp Arslan, hoping to appease him with this sumptuous offering of sex slaves; the jihad commander, however, would not turn aside from his goal. Once the Muslims broke through the city's defenses, they were merciless. The thirteenth-century Muslim historian Sibt ibn al-Jawzi re-counted the testimony of an eyewitness:

> The army entered the city, massacred its inhabitants, pil-laged and burned it, leaving it in ruins and taking prison-er all those who remained alive.... The dead bodies were so many that they blocked the streets; one could not go anywhere without stepping over them. And the number of prisoners was not less than 50,000 souls. I was determined

to enter the city and see the destruction with my own eyes. I tried to find a street in which I would not have to walk over the corpses; but that was impossible.[82]

The Debacle at Manzikert

Something even worse was coming. In 1071, Alp Arslan besieged the Byzantine fortress of Manzikert, in eastern Asia Minor, but was not trying to provoke a large-scale war with the Byzantines, whose history, going back to Julius Caesar and before that, was legendary, and whose immense might was respected. The Eastern Roman Empire of the late eleventh century was just a shadow of that former glorious entity, but the extent of its weakness was not yet fully known. In any case, instead of engaging with the Byzantines and risking a disaster, Alp Arslan turned south, determined to confront and destroy the Ismaili Shi'ite Fatimid caliphate.

Alp Arslan was besieging Aleppo when the news came that the Byzantine emperor Romanos IV Diogenes was heading east from Constantinople with a massive force. The sultan hurriedly broke off his siege and headed north, losing a good bit of his army along the way: the jihadis who had been looking forward to the spoils that would come from the plunder of Aleppo knew that the haul would be substantially smaller for defeating a Byzantine army in a dusty outpost of Asia Minor, away from any major city, advancing without their treasure and without their women. A substantial number of the Seljuk forces peeled off.[83]

But Romanos' army, which was made up of a large number of foreign mercenaries, was growing smaller as well. The eleventh-century Byzantine historian Michael Attaleiates recounted that as the imperial army traveled eastward, Romanos began to alienate his own men: "He became a stranger to his own army, setting up his own separate camp and arranging for more ostentatious accommodation."[84]

Discontent was growing in the Byzantine ranks, and it was compounded by confusion: Alp Arslan had extraordinarily good intelligence on the ground in Asia Minor, and knew exactly where Romanos and his forces were and where they were heading at any given time; by contrast, the Byzantines did not have the vaguest idea of where the jihadis were, or of how many of them there were, until it was far too late.[85]

The Byzantine forces were routed. Romanos himself was captured. Brought before Alp Arslan, Romanos was exhausted from the battle, his once fine clothes tattered and covered with dust. Alp Arslan couldn't believe that this bedraggled prisoner was the Byzantine emperor; once he was convinced, however, he ordered Romanos to kiss the ground before him, and then put his foot on the defeated sovereign's neck.[86]

The humiliation of the emperor, however, was little more than a ritual formality, a public demonstration of the victory and supremacy of Islam. Once it was completed, Alp Arslan ordered that Romanos be treated with the respect due his station. He was, after all, still the emperor of the Romans, even if captured.

However, worse was in store for Romanos. Alp Arslan asked him what he would do if the tables were turned: "What would you do if I was brought before you as a prisoner?"

The emperor responded frankly: "Perhaps I'd kill you, or exhibit you in the streets of Constantinople."

To that, Alp Arslan said: "My punishment is far heavier. I forgive you, and set you free."[87]

Alp Arslan was not being ironic. He was completely serious: it would have been a far lighter punishment for Romanos to have been killed at Manzikert than to have returned to his imperial capital. This became immediately clear when Romanos did return to Constantinople. The Byzantine army was devastated and Asia Minor essentially defenseless before the Seljuk advance, all because of Romanos' decision to confront the Seljuks at Manzikert.

His rivals in Constantinople immediately took advantage of his weakness; Romanos was deposed and blinded, and he died of his wounds soon thereafter. His legacy was nothing like anything he would have been able to endure imagining: his failure at Manzikert enabled Asia Minor, which had been populated by the Greeks since time immemorial, ultimately to become Turkey, and before that the seat of the last great Islamic caliphate, in which the native Greeks and Armenians were *dhimmis*, living precariously under the overlordship of Islam.

The Aftermath of Manzikert

Alp Arslan did not take immediate advantage of his victory, but it was only a matter of time. The Byzantine presence in Asia Minor was history, and for them, the situation was going to get worse still. In 1076, the Turks conquered Syria; in 1077, Jerusalem. Victorious, the Seljuk emir Atsiz bin Uwaq promised not to harm the inhabitants of Jerusalem, but once the jihadis had entered the city, they murdered three thousand people.[88] Meanwhile, in 1075, Seljuk sultan Suleymanshah established the sultanate of Rum (Rome, referring to the New Rome, Constantinople) with its capital in Nicaea, the once great Christian city that had been the site of two ecumenical councils of the Church and was perilously close to Constantinople itself.[89] From here they continued to threaten the Byzantines and harass the Christians all over their new domains.

The situation was desperate, and desperate times called for desperate measures. Back in 1054, the Church of Rome and the Church of Constantinople, after having had a rocky relationship with each other for centuries, issued mutual excommunications, and what came to be known as the Great Schism between the Eastern and Western Churches began. Necessity, however, tended to make the differences between the two seem less important than the more pressing matter of simple survival, at least for the Byzantines.

The emperor Alexius I Comnenus, who reigned from 1081 to 1118, fought back against the Seljuk advance and met with some success, but he didn't have the resources to follow through to victory, and the Turkish presence in Asia Minor was like a knife at the empire's throat. Accordingly, in 1095, Alexius sent envoys to Piacenza in northern Italy, where the Church of Rome was holding a synod. Addressing the assembled bishops and eminent laymen, the Byzantine ambassadors explained the situation and the need, and asked for help, stressing that to come to the aid of the venerable Christian empire would be a great service to God and the Church.

Pope Urban II and his entourage listened intently and were intrigued. The envoys had come at a time when the leaders of Western Europe were quite concerned with what was happening in the East. Besides helping the Byzantines, the Westerners were interested in liberating Jerusalem, where Christians had suffered for centuries. A few examples: in the early eighth century, sixty Christian pilgrims from Amorium were crucified; around the same time, the Muslim governor of Caesaria seized a group of pilgrims from Iconium and had them all executed as spies—except for a small number who converted to Islam; and Muslims demanded money from pilgrims, threatening to ransack the Church of the Resurrection if they didn't pay. Later in the eighth century, a Muslim ruler banned displays of the cross in Jerusalem. He also increased the *jizya* that Christians had to pay and forbade them to engage in religious instruction of their own children and fellow believers.[90]

In 772, the caliph al-Mansur ordered Christians and Jews in Jerusalem to be stamped on their hands with a distinctive symbol. In 789, Muslims beheaded a monk who had converted from Islam and plundered the Bethlehem monastery of St. Theodosius, killing many more monks. In the early ninth century, the persecutions grew so severe that large numbers of Christians fled to Constantinople and other Christian cities. Fresh persecutions in 923 saw more churches destroyed, and in 937, Muslims went on a rampage in Jerusalem on Palm Sunday, plundering and destroying the Church of Calvary and the Church of the Resurrection.[91]

In the 960s, the Byzantine general Nicephoras Phocas (a future emperor) carried out a series of successful campaigns against the Muslims, recapturing Crete, Cilicia, Cyprus, and even parts of Syria. In 969, he recaptured the ancient Christian city of Antioch. The Byzantines extended this campaign into Syria in the 970s.[92]

Saif al-Dawla, ruler of the Shi'ite Hamdanid dynasty in Aleppo from 944 to 967, launched annual jihad campaigns against the Byzantines. He appealed to Muslims to fight the Byzantines on the pretext that the Byzantines were taking lands that belonged to the House of Islam. This appeal was so successful that jihadis from as far off as Central Asia joined the jihads.[93]

In 1004, the sixth Fatimid caliph, Abu Ali al-Mansur al-Hakim (985–1021) turned violently against the faith of his Christian mother and uncles (two of whom were patriarchs) and ordered the destruction of churches, the burning of crosses, and the seizure of church property. He moved against the Jews with similar ferocity. Over the next ten years, thirty thousand churches were destroyed, and untold numbers of Christians converted to Islam simply to save their lives. In 1009, al-Hakim gave his most spectacular anti-Christian order: he commanded that the Church of the Holy Sepulcher in Jerusalem be destroyed, along with several other churches (including the Church of the Resurrection). The Church of the Holy Sepulcher, rebuilt by the Byzantines in the seventh century after the Persians had burned an earlier version, marks the traditional site of Christ's burial. Al-Hakim commanded that the tomb inside be cut down to the bedrock. He ordered Christians to wear heavy crosses around their necks (and Jews heavy blocks of wood in the shape of a calf). He piled on other humiliating decrees, culminating in the order that Christians accept Islam or leave his dominions.[94]

The erratic caliph ultimately relaxed his persecution and even returned much of the property he had seized from the Church.[95] Nevertheless, Christians were in a precarious position, and pilgrims remained under threat. In 1056, the Muslims expelled three hundred Christians from Jerusalem and forbade European Christians from entering the Church of the Holy Sepulcher.[96] The disaster at Manzikert followed a decade and a half after that. The Byzantine Empire's subsequent loss of Asia Minor made it all the more urgent, as far as Pope Urban II was concerned, for the Christians of the West to act to defend their brethren in the East. It was a necessity born of charity.

Outside of the Reconquista in Spain, which would not fully realize its goal for three hundred more years, the Crusades were the first significant attempt to reverse the gains of the jihad.

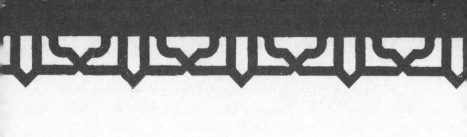

CHAPTER FIVE

THE VICTIMS OF JIHAD STRIKE BACK

Jihad in the Twelfth and Thirteenth Centuries

I. THE CRUSADES

Calling the First Crusade

Pope Urban II called the First Crusade at the Council of Clermont in 1095, saying that without military action, "the faithful of God will be much more widely attacked" by Muslim forces:

> For your brethren who live in the east are in urgent need of your help, and you must hasten to give them the aid which has often been promised them. For, as most of you have heard, the Turks and Arabs have attacked them and have conquered the territory of Romania [the Greek empire] as far west as the shore of the Mediterranean and the Hellespont, which is called the Arm of St. George. They have occupied more and more of the lands of those Christians and have overcome them in seven battles. They have killed and captured many and have destroyed the churches and devastated the empire. If you permit them to continue thus for awhile with impunity, the faithful of God will be much more widely attacked by them. On this account I, or rather the Lord, beseech you as Christ's heralds to pub-

lish this everywhere and to persuade all people of whatever rank, foot-soldiers and knights, poor and rich, to carry aid promptly to those Christians and to destroy that vile race from the lands of our friends.... Moreover, Christ commands it.[1]

The Pope spoke of an "imminent peril threatening you and all the faithful which has brought us hither":

From the confines of Jerusalem and from the city of Constantinople a grievous report has gone forth and has repeatedly been brought to our ears; namely, that a race from the kingdom of the Persians, an accursed race, a race wholly alienated from God, 'a generation that set not their heart aright and whose spirit was not steadfast with God,' violently invaded the lands of those Christians and has depopulated them by pillage and fire. They have led away a part of the captives into their own country, and a part...they have killed by cruel tortures. They have either destroyed the churches of God or appropriated them for the rites of their own religion. They destroy the altars, after having defiled them with their uncleanness.... The kingdom of the Greeks is now dismembered by them and has been deprived of territory so vast in extent that it could be traversed in two months' time.... This royal city, however, situated at the center of the earth, is now held captive by the enemies of Christ and is subjected, by those who do not know God, to the worship [of] the heathen. She seeks, therefore, and desires to be liberated and ceases not to implore you to come to her aid. From you especially she asks succor, because as we have already said, God has conferred upon you above all other nations great glory in arms.[2]

He invoked the Muslim destruction of the Church of the Holy Sepulcher: "Let the holy sepulcher of our Lord and Saviour, which is possessed by unclean nations, especially arouse you, and the holy places which are now treated with ignominy and irreverently polluted with the filth of the unclean."[3]

The People's Crusade

The Crusades initially came together as pilgrimages: Crusaders embarked on a pilgrimage to the Holy Land, intending to defend themselves if attacked. Many took religious vows. Indeed, the first Crusader foray into Muslim lands, the so-called People's Crusade, was more religious revival meeting than military force. It began with preaching, as a charismatic preacher known as Peter the Hermit traversed France and Germany with a scorching message of hellfire and redemption and the necessity of the Crusade.

As Peter preached, he began to attract followers—women and children as well as soldiers. The "People's Crusaders" crossed Europe and arrived in Constantinople in August 1096, by then thirty thousand strong. Entering the domains of the Turks, they were quickly massacred near Nicaea, while Peter the Hermit was still in Constantinople discussing strategy with Alexius Comnenus. The principal Crusader force of actual military men had not yet even arrived in the region.[4]

As the People's Crusaders crossed Europe, Peter the Hermit became famous and attracted imitators. Many of these new Crusade leaders, however, were not interested primarily in defending the Christians in the Middle East, but in lining their own pockets at the expense of the Jews of Germany. In Mainz, forces under the command of Count Emicho of Leiningen found the Jews under the protection of the local bishop, who had heard that they were coming and brought the Jews in the area into his palace. Undeterred, these "Crusaders" stormed the bishop's palace and massacred the Jews inside it.

An eleventh-century historian of the First Crusade, Albert of Aix, recounted that they "killed the women, also, and with their swords pierced tender children of whatever age and sex."[5] A Crusader explained his thinking to a rabbi: "You are the children of those who killed the object of our veneration, hanging him on a tree; and he himself had said: 'There will yet come a day when my children will come and avenge my blood.'"[6]

There is no record of Jesus Christ ever saying such a thing. The Crusader massacres of Jews in Europe were not only an outrageous crime but a disastrous miscalculation. Had the warriors of jihad succeeded in Europe, they would have subjugated the Christians and the

Jews in the same way. Had the Crusaders traversed Europe inviting help from the Jews rather than killing them, the Crusaders might have arrived in the Middle East far stronger, and the history of the world would have been different in incalculable ways. But this was not by any means the only time in the history of jihad warfare that the Muslims benefited from disunity and infighting among those who stood between them and their goal.

The Muslims were disunited as well. The thirteenth-century Muslim historian Ibn al-Athir even recorded speculation that the Crusaders had come only at the bidding of the Fatimid Shi'ites, in order to disrupt the growth of the Sunni Seljuk Turkish domains: "Some say that when the masters of Egypt saw the expansion of the Seljuk empire, they took fright and asked the Franj [Franks, or Crusaders] to march on Syria and to establish a buffer between them and the Muslims. God alone knows the truth."[7]

Crusader Barbarism

According to Ibn al-Athir, as the Crusaders approached Antioch, the Muslim ruler of Antioch, Yaghi-Siyan, demonstrated for future historians that he knew exactly what the conflict was about, and it wasn't about land or treasure: he "feared possible sedition on the part of the Christians of the city. He therefore decided to expel them."[8]

It was to no avail. Antioch fell to the Crusaders, who, lacking adequate food supplies, proceeded to nearby Ma'arra to secure them. Ibn al-Athir said that "for three days they put people to the sword, killing more than a hundred thousand people and taking many prisoners."[9] This is impossible, as Ma'arra likely was home to no more than ten thousand people, but jihad preachers were already finding the exaggeration of atrocity stories and casualty figures to be a useful tool in recruitment efforts.

The Crusaders, meanwhile, were not finished in Ma'arra. Not finding the stores of food they had hoped to find, and increasingly desperate, they fell to cannibalism. The twelfth-century Frankish chronicler Radulph of Caen recounted: "In Ma'arra our troops boiled pagan adults in cooking-pots; they impaled children on spits and devoured them grilled."[10] A coterie of leading Crusaders reported less graphically to

Pope Urban II: "A terrible famine racked the army in Ma'arra, and placed it in the cruel necessity of feeding itself upon the bodies of the Saracens."[11] Exclaimed Albert of Aix: "Not only did our troops not shrink from eating dead Turks and Saracens; they also ate dogs!"[12]

This ghastly event spread far and wide in Muslim lands, contributing to the popular image of the Crusaders among Muslims that was enunciated by the twelfth-century chronicler Usamah ibn Munqidh: "All those who were well-informed about the Franj saw them as beasts superior in courage and fighting ardour but in nothing else, just as animals are superior in strength and aggression."[13]

Even had the horrific events in Ma'arra never taken place, however, it would have been difficult for the Crusaders to make a better impression: the characterization of non-Muslims as akin to animals was not original to Usamah ibn Munqidh, but could be found in the Qur'an itself: "For the worst of beasts in the sight of Allah are those who reject him; they will not believe." (8:55)

The Crusaders in Jerusalem

In any case, the Crusaders scarcely behaved better as they continued their conquests. After a five-week siege, the Crusaders entered Jerusalem on July 15, 1099. An anonymous contemporary account by a Christian recounted what happened next:

> One of our knights, Letholdus by name, climbed on to the wall of the city. When he reached the top, all the defenders of the city quickly fled along the walls and through the city. Our men followed and pursued them, killing and hacking, as far as the temple of Solomon, and there was such a slaughter that our men were up to their ankles in the enemy's blood....
>
> The emir who commanded the tower of David surrendered to the Count [of St. Gilles] and opened the gate where pilgrims used to pay tribute. Entering the city, our pilgrims pursued and killed the Saracens up to the temple of Solomon. There the Saracens assembled and resisted fiercely all day, so that the whole temple flowed with their blood. At last the pagans were overcome and our men seized many men

and women in the temple, killing them or keeping them alive as they saw fit. On the roof of the temple there was a great crowd of pagans of both sexes, to whom Tancred and Gaston de Beert gave their banners [to provide them with protection]. Then the crusaders scattered throughout the city, seizing gold and silver, horses and mules, and houses full of all sorts of goods. Afterwards our men went rejoicing and weeping for joy to adore the sepulchre of our Saviour Jesus and there discharged their debt to Him...[14]

Three principal Crusade leaders—Archbishop Daimbert; Godfrey, Duke of Bouillon; and Raymond, Count of Toulouse—boasted to Pope Paschal II in September 1099 about the Crusaders' Jerusalem exploits: "And if you desire to know what was done with the enemy who were found there, know that in Solomon's Porch and in his temple our men rode in the blood of the Saracens up to the knees of their horses."[15] Balderic, a bishop and the author of an early-twelfth-century history of Jerusalem, reported that the Crusaders killed between twenty thousand and thirty thousand people in the city.[16]

The story of this massacre has grown over the centuries. Around 1160, two Syrian chroniclers, al-Azimi and Ibn al-Qalanisi, wrote separately of the sack. Al-Azimi said only that the Crusaders "turned to Jerusalem and conquered it from the hands of the Egyptians. Godfrey took it. They burned the Church of the Jews." Ibn al-Qalanisi added a bit more detail: "The Franks stormed the town and gained possession of it. A number of the townsfolk fled to the sanctuary and a great host were killed. The Jews assembled in the synagogue, and the Franks burned it over their heads. The sanctuary was surrendered to them on guarantee of safety on 22 Sha'ban [14 July] of this year, and they destroyed the shrines and the tomb of Abraham."[17]

Ibn al-Jawzi, writing about a hundred years after the event, said that the Crusaders "killed more than 70,000 Muslims" in Jerusalem. Ibn al-Athir recounted: "The population of the holy city was put to the sword, and the Franj spent a week massacring Muslims. They killed more than seventy thousand people in al-Aqsa mosque."[18] The fifteenth-century historian Ibn Taghribirdi recorded one hundred thousand. Former U.S. President Bill Clinton claimed in November 2001 that the Crusaders murdered not just every Muslim warrior or even every Muslim male, but "every woman and child who was Muslim on the Temple mound" until the blood was running "up to their knees."[19]

The Crusaders' cruelty was not unique for the savage warfare of the period, but that does not excuse it. The cannibalism at Ma'arra has largely been forgotten in the West, but the sack of Jerusalem and the burning of the Jews inside their synagogue has not. The Crusaders' savagery in Jerusalem in 1099 was, according to journalist Amin Maalouf in *The Crusades Through Arab Eyes*, the "starting point of a millennial hostility between Islam and the West."[20] Islamic scholar John Esposito declares: "Five centuries of peaceful coexistence elapsed before political events and an imperial-papal power play led to centuries-long series of so-called holy wars that pitted Christendom against Islam and left an enduring legacy of misunderstanding and distrust."[21]

We have already seen how false these statements are. Islam, as the jihads in Spain, France, Italy, and Asia Minor show, was hostile to the West from its inception. There was no peaceful coexistence; there were only brief periods in between jihad invasions. Christian overtures to establish a lasting peace accord were invariably answered by a repetition of the triple choice: conversion, submission, or war. To ascribe a thousand years of hostility between Islam and the West to the Crusaders is to fall prey to the peculiar modern Western malady of civilizational self-loathing and blaming the West for all the ills in the world.

Yet the Crusaders' record is by no means spotless. No one's is. Wars never allow one side to claim all of the moral high ground. The sins of the Crusaders, however, are taken today to be so very great, and the Crusaders' very mission so imperialistic, colonialist, and wrongheaded, that those who view the period of the Crusades with unalloyed pride are hard to find. This shame, however, is itself a relatively new development; as recently as the middle of the twentieth century, schools all over the U.S. called their sports teams Crusaders, and students were aware that defense against the jihad was noble and worthwhile, even if all those who participated in it weren't. But that was when the West was made of sterner stuff.

Crusader states

After the conquests of Antioch and Jerusalem, the poet Ibn al-Khayyat lamented the devastation the Crusaders had wrought and exhorted Muslims to respond:

> The polytheists have swelled in a torrent of terrifying extent.
> How long will this continue?
> Armies like mountains, coming again and again, have ranged
> forth from the lands of the Franks....
> Do you not owe an obligation to God and Islam, defending
> thereby young men and old?
> Respond to God! Woe to you! Respond![22]

Initially, the response was not overwhelming. The Crusaders met with a good deal of success at first and established four states of their own in quick succession: the County of Edessa and the Principality of Antioch in 1098, the Kingdom of Jerusalem in 1099, and the County of Tripoli in 1104. Collectively they were known in Europe as Outremer, the lands beyond the sea.

The Crusaders' original intention was not to establish states. Pope Urban II decreed that lands recovered from the Muslims would belong to Alexius Comnenus and the Byzantine Empire, not to the Western Europeans who conquered them. He envisioned the First Crusade as an act of Christian charity and sacrifice; hence the common parlance that a warrior joining the Crusade was "taking up the cross."[23]

Some of the Crusaders saw their struggle in the same way. Godfrey of Bouillon, the duke of Lower Lorraine, one of the more prominent European lords who took up the cross, sold off many properties in order to finance his trip, but he clearly planned to come home rather than settle in the Holy Land, as he did not give up his title or all of his holdings.[24]

When the Crusade leaders met with Alexius Comnenus, he prevailed upon them to agree individually, in accord with Urban's wishes, that any lands they conquered would revert to the Byzantine Empire. But as the Crusaders' siege of Antioch dragged on through the winter and Muslim armies advanced north from Jerusalem, the Crusaders waited for the promised Byzantine troops to arrive. The emperor, however, received a report that the Crusaders' situation in Antioch was hopeless and turned back his forces. The Crusaders felt betrayed and reneged on their earlier agreement to return the lands they won to Byzantine rule.

Although they existed in a state of more or less constant war, the Crusader states managed to allow many of their citizens to go about living normal lives. In the 1180s, a Muslim from al-Andalus, Ibn Jubayr, visited the Crusader domains on his way to Mecca. To his dismay, he found that Muslims were living better in the Crusader lands than they were in the neighboring Islamic areas:

> Upon leaving Tibnin [near Tyre], we passed through an unbroken skein of farms and villages whose lands were efficiently cultivated. The inhabitants were all Muslims, but they live in comfort with the Franj—may God preserve them from temptation! Their dwellings belong to them and all their property is unmolested. All the regions controlled by the Franj in Syria are subject to this same system: the landed domains, villages, and farms have remained in the hands of the Muslims. Now, doubt invests the heart of a great number of these men when they compare their lot to that of their brothers living in Muslim territory. Indeed, the latter suffer from the injustice of their coreligionists, whereas the Franj act with equity.[25]

To preserve Muslims from this temptation, the jihad to destroy these entities began immediately after they were established. The Principality of Antioch fell to the warriors of jihad in 1268; the County of Tripoli, in 1289; and the Kingdom of Jerusalem, in 1291.

Zengi, Nur ed-Din, and the Second Crusade

The first Crusader state that was established, the County of Edessa, was the first to go. The Turkish jihad leader Imad ad-Din Zengi, *atabeg* (governor) of Mosul, laid siege to Edessa in 1144, and conquered it after a four-month siege. The Syrian bishop Basil was present as the victors plundered the Crusaders' churches:

Everything was taken from the Franj…gold, silver, holy vases, chalices, patens, ornamented crucifixes, and great quantities of jewels. The priests, nobles, and notables were taken aside, stripped of their robes, and led away in chains to Aleppo. Of the rest, the artisans were identified, and Zangi kept them as prisoners, setting each to work at his craft. All the other Franj, about a hundred men, were executed.[26]

The Crusader advance had been definitively halted, making Zengi a hero of Islam. A contemporary inscription at Aleppo hailed him as the "tamer of the infidels and the polytheists, leader of those who fight the Holy War, helper of the armies, protector of the territory of the Muslims."[27] Ibn al-Athir hailed Zengi in extravagant terms, attributing it all to the intervention of Allah, as the Qur'an does regarding the Battle of Badr:

> When Almighty God saw the princes of the Islamic lands and the commanders of the Hanafite [monotheistic] creed and how unable they were to support the one [true] religion and their inability to defend those who believe in the One God and He saw their subjugation by their enemy and the severity of their despotism…He then wished to set over the Franks someone who could requite the evil of their deeds and to send to the devils of the crosses stones from Him to destroy and annihilate them [the crosses]. He looked at the roster of valiants among His helpers and of those possessed of judgement, support and sagacity amongst His friends and He did not see in it [the roster] anyone more capable of that command, more solid as regards inclination, stronger of purpose and more penetrating than the lord, the martyr [*al-shahid*] Imad al-Din.[28]

Allah may have used Zengi for his own purposes, yet the *atabeg* was not always a model of piety. One night not long after he conquered Edessa, he drank a large quantity of wine and fell asleep, only to be awakened to the sight of one of his Frankish slaves, Yarankash, sneaking some wine from Zengi's own goblet. Enraged, Zengi vowed to punish the slave in the morning, and fell asleep again—whereupon Yarankash, thoroughly frightened at the prospect of his master's wrath, stabbed him multiple times and fled.[29]

. The death of Zengi did not blunt the renewed momentum of the jihad. Pope Eugene III in December 1145 called for a second Crusade, and an army was amassed, but it was soundly defeated by the Turks in Asia Minor and never even got close to achieving its objective of recapturing Edessa. Zengi's son Nur ed-Din worked hard to revive the spirit of jihad among the Muslims, using a combination of threats and enticements. One emir who received his call to aid him in jihad against the Franks complained:

> If I do not rush to Nur al-Din's aid, he will strip me of my domain, for he has already written to the devotees and ascetics to request the aid of their prayers and to encourage them to incite the Muslims to *jihad*. At this very moment, each of these men sits with his disciples and companions reading Nur al-Din's letters, weeping and cursing me. If I am to avoid anathema, I must accede to his request.[30]

Unlike his father, Nur ed-Din was strict in his observance of Islam. Not only did he not partake of alcohol, he forbade it to his troops as well, along with, in the words of the chronicler Kamal al-Din, "the tambourine, the flute, and other objects displeasing to God." (In accord with statements attributed to Muhammad, Islam forbids musical instruments as well as alcohol.) The *atabeg* also "abandoned luxurious garments and instead covered himself with rough cloth."[31] Before battles, he would pray, "O God, grant victory to Islam and not to Mahmud [his given name; Nur ed-Din is a title meaning Light of the Religion]. Who is this dog Mahmud to merit victory?"[32]

Appealing to a rival Turkish commander amid ongoing disputes between rival Muslim factions, Nur ed-Din again demonstrated his piety: "I desire no more than the well-being of the Muslims, jihad against the infidels, and the release of the prisoners they are holding. If you come over to my side with the army of Damascus, if we help each other to wage the jihad, my wish will be fulfilled."[33] It was. His forces captured Damascus from Muslim rivals in 1154.

Jockeying for Egypt

The Crusaders, however, were by no means a spent force. At least not yet. Realizing the feebleness of the Shi'ite Fatimid caliphate in Cairo, King Amalric of the Kingdom of Jerusalem led troops into Egypt in 1164, where he faced the forces of Shirkuh, the general whom Nur ed-Din had sent to seize the Fatimid domains for himself. Hoping to relieve the pressure on Shirkuh, Nur ed-Din moved quickly toward Antioch and defeated a large Crusader army in the outskirts of the great city.

It was a standoff. Amalric agreed to withdraw from Egypt if Shirkuh would as well, and so it was done. But the great game was not over. In 1167, Nur ed-Din sent Shirkuh into Egypt again. By this time, the Fatimid caliph was just a figurehead, like his Sunni Abbasid counterpart; the real ruler of Egypt was Shawar, whom Nur ed-Din had sent into Egypt only to see him turn against his patron. Shawar appealed to Amalric for help; the Crusaders again entered Egypt, and Shawar agreed to pay an annual tribute to the Christians for protection against Nur ed-Din. However, this arrangement was not to last either. When Shirkuh died in 1169, his nephew assumed his authority, and defeated a combined force of Crusaders and Byzantines at Damietta in Egypt. The Crusaders were driven from Egypt, and Shirkuh's nephew was only beginning to take the jihad to them and to roll back what they had gained.

The Assassins

The Crusaders faced other foes as well. In 1175, the king of Germany and Holy Roman emperor Frederick Barbarossa sent an envoy to Egypt and Syria, who reported back to him about a strange and dangerous Shi'ite Muslim sect, the Nizari Ismailis, commonly known as the Assassins. With their planned murders of many of their individual opponents, the Assassins gave the English language its word for one who commits planned, premeditated murder, and foreshadowed the individual jihad terror attacks of the twenty-first century. Barbarossa's envoy wrote:

Note that on the confines of Damascus, Antioch and Aleppo there is a certain race of Saracens in the mountains, who in their own vernacular are called *Heyssessini*, and in Roman *segnors de montana* [elders of the mountains]. This breed of men live without law; they eat swine's flesh against the law of the Saracens, and make use of all women without distinction, including their mothers and sisters. They live in the mountains and are well-nigh impregnable, for they withdraw into well-fortified castles. Their country is not very fertile, so that they live on their cattle. They have among them a Master, who strikes the greatest fear into all the Saracen princes both far and near, as well as the neighboring Christian lords. For he has the habit of killing them in an astonishing way. The method by which this is done is as follows: this prince possesses in the mountains numerous and most beautiful palaces, surrounded by very high walls, so that none can enter except by a small and very well-guarded door. In these palaces he has many of the sons of his peasants brought up from early childhood. He has them taught various languages, as Latin, Greek, Roman, Saracen as well as many others. These young men are taught by their teachers from their earliest youth to their full manhood, that they must obey the lord of their land in all his words and commands; and that if they do so, he, who has power over all living gods, will give them the joys of paradise. They are also taught that they cannot be saved if they resist his will in anything. Note that, from the time when they are taken in as children, they see no one but their teachers and masters and receive no other instruction until they are summoned to the presence of the Prince to kill someone. When they are in the presence of the Prince, he asks them if they are willing to obey his commands, so that he may bestow paradise upon them. Whereupon, as they have been instructed, and without any objection or doubt, they throw themselves at his feet and reply with fervor, that they will obey him in all things that he may command. Thereupon the Prince gives each one of them a golden dagger and sends them out to kill whichever prince he has marked down.[34]

Several years later, Archbishop William of Tyre wrote a history of the Crusader states in which he included this:

There is in the province of Tyre, otherwise called Phoenicia, and in the diocese of Tortosa, a people who possess ten strong castles, with their dependent villages; their number, according to what we have often heard, is about 60,000 or more. It is their custom to install their master and choose their chief, not by hereditary right, but solely by virtue of merit. Disdaining any other title of dignity, they called him the Elder. The bond of submission and obedience that binds this people to their Chief is so strong, that there is no task so arduous, difficult or dangerous that any one of them would not undertake to perform it with the greatest zeal, as soon as the Chief who has commanded it. If for example there be a prince who is hated or mistrusted by this people, the Chief gives a dagger to one or more of his followers. At once whoever receives the command sets out on his mission, without considering the consequences of the deed nor the possibility of escape. Zealous to complete the task, he toils and labours as long as may be needful, until chance gives him the opportunity to carry out his chief's orders. Both our people and the Saracens call them Assissini; we do not know the origin of this name.[35]

We do. The word "assassin" is derived from "*hashashin*," or hashish smokers, a name given to the group by its foes and based on stories about their novel method of recruiting new members. In the early thirteenth century, the German chronicler Arnold of Lübeck revealed more about the group's mysterious leader:

I shall now relate things about this elder which appear ridiculous, but which are attested to me by the evidence of reliable witnesses. This Old Man has by his witchcraft so bemused the men of his country, that they neither worship nor believe in any God but himself. Likewise he entices them in a strange manner with such hopes and with promises of such pleasures with eternal enjoyment, that they prefer rather to die than to live. Many of them even, when standing on a high wall, will jump off at his nod or command, and, shattering their skulls, die a miserable death. The most blessed, so he affirms, are those who shed the blood of men and in revenge for such deeds themselves suffer death. When therefore any of them have chosen to die in this way, murdering someone by craft and then themselves dying so blessedly in revenge for him, he himself hands them knives which are, so to speak, consecrated by this affair, and then intoxicates them with such a potion that they are plunged into ecstasy and oblivion, displays to them by his magic certain fantastic dreams, full of pleasure and delights, or rather of trumpery, and promises them eternal possession of these things in reward for such deeds.[36]

The fullest account of how the Assassins recruited their fanatical killers comes from Marco Polo's late-thirteenth-century *Travels*:

Mulehet is a country in which the Old Man of the Mountain dwelt in former days; and the name means "*Place of the Aram*." I will tell you his whole history as related by Messer Marco Polo, who heard it from several natives of that region.

The Old Man was called in their language *Aloadin*. He had caused a certain valley between two mountains to be enclosed, and had turned it into a garden, the largest and most beautiful that ever was seen, filled with every variety of fruit. In it were erected pavilions and palaces the most elegant that can be imagined, all covered with gilding and exquisite painting. And there were runnels too, flowing freely with wine and milk and honey and water; and numbers of ladies and of the most beautiful damsels in the world, who could play on all manner of instruments, and sung most sweetly, and danced in a manner that it was charming to behold. For the Old Man desired to make his people believe that this was actually Paradise. So he had fashioned it after the description that Mahommet gave of his Paradise, to wit, that it should be a beautiful garden running with conduits of wine and milk and honey and water, and full of lovely women for the delectation of all its inmates. And sure enough the Saracens of those parts believed that it *was* Paradise!

Now no man was allowed to enter the Garden save those whom he intended to be his *Ashishin*. There was a Fortress at the entrance to the Garden, strong enough to resist all the world, and there was no other way to get in. He kept at his Court a number of the youths of the country, from 12 to 20 years of age, such as had a taste for soldiering, and to these he used to tell tales about Paradise, just as Mahommet had been wont to do, and they believed in him just as the Saracens believe in Mahommet. Then he would introduce them into his garden, some four, or six, or ten at a time, having first made them drink a certain potion which cast them into a deep sleep, and then causing them to be lifted and carried in. So when they awoke, they found themselves in the Garden.[37]

According to the legend that surrounded the Assassins, the "potion" that made these young men susceptible to the suggestion that they had visited Paradise was hashish.[38] The Old Man would get his potential recruits high on hashish—an experience they didn't understand and for which they had no cultural referent—and then introduce them to his gardens, which, as Marco Polo related, had been scrupulously designed to correspond to the Qur'an's descriptions of Paradise: fruits, women, and all:

> Indeed, you [disbelievers] will be tasters of the painful punishment,
>
> And you will not be recompensed except for what you used to do—
> But not the chosen servants of Allah.
> Those will have a provision determined—

Fruits; and they will be honored
In gardens of pleasure
On thrones facing one another.
There will be circulated among them a cup from a flowing
spring,
White and delicious to the drinkers;
No bad effect is there in it, nor from it will they be intox-
icated.
And with them will be women limiting their glances, with
large eyes,
As if they were eggs, well-protected. (37:38–49)

The Old Man of the Mountain, according to Marco Polo's account, used his young recruits' experience of Paradise to manipulate them into doing his murderous bidding:

> When therefore they awoke, and found themselves in a place so charming, they deemed that it was Paradise in very truth. And the ladies and damsels dallied with them to their hearts' content, so that they had what young men would have; and with their own good will they never would have quitted the place.

But eventually the hashish wore off, and the girls were gone, and the Old Man of the Mountain would then explain to the bewildered and disappointed young men who had been so enjoying Paradise what had just happened:

> Now this Prince whom we call the Old One kept his Court in grand and noble style, and made those simple hill-folks about him believe firmly that he was a great Prophet. And when he wanted one of his Ashishin to send on any mission, he would cause that potion whereof I spoke to be given to one of the youths in the garden, and then had him carried into his Palace. So when the young man awoke, he found himself in the Castle, and no longer in that Paradise; whereat he was not over well pleased. He was then conducted to the

Old Man's presence, and bowed before him with great veneration as believing himself to be in the presence of a true Prophet. The Prince would then ask whence he came, and he would reply that he came from Paradise! and that it was exactly such as Mahommet had described it in the Law. This of course gave the others who stood by, and who had not been admitted, the greatest desire to enter therein.[39]

This was all to induce the young men to commit murder:

So when the Old Man would have any Prince slain, he would say to such a youth: "Go thou and slay So and So; and when thou returnest my Angels shall bear thee into Paradise. And shouldst thou die, natheless even so will I send my Angels to carry thee back into Paradise." So he caused them to believe; and thus there was no order of his that they would not affront any peril to execute, for the great desire they had to get back into that Paradise of his. And in this manner the Old One got his people to murder any one whom he desired to get rid of. Thus, too, the great dread that he inspired all Princes withal, made them become his tributaries in order that he might abide at peace and amity with them.[40]

The Old Man could plausibly promise these young men that if they killed at his bidding and were killed in the process, they would enter Paradise, because that same promise is in the Qur'an: "Indeed, Allah has purchased from the believers their lives and their properties; for that they will have Paradise. They fight in the cause of Allah, so they kill and are killed." (9:111)

Although they mainly killed rival Muslim leaders, Assassins murdered the Latin king of Jerusalem, Conrad of Montferrat, in 1192. They became in the consciousness of the Crusaders the epitome of the ruthless and terrible fanatics against whom they were fighting. Twenty-first-century individual jihadis have frequently boasted, "We love death more than you love life." The Assassins would have agreed.

Saladin

Meanwhile, a jihad commander was on the scene who would turn the tide in the Holy Land decisively against the Crusaders. Shirkuh's ambitious young nephew was named Saladin. Once in control in Egypt, he began enforcing the laws subjugating Christians as *dhimmis*: Michael the Syrian recounted that Saladin "issued an order in Egypt that Christians must always appear in public wearing a [distinguishing] belt as a sign of servitude, and that they could not mount a horse or mule."[41]

Saladin was to become one of the most celebrated and renowned Muslim warriors in the entire history of jihad, and one of the few whose name is known in the West.

In modern-day mythmaking, Saladin is to individual Muslims what al-Andalus is to Muslim polities. He has become the prototype of the tolerant, magnanimous Muslim warrior, historical proof of the nobility of Islam. In *The Crusades Through Arab Eyes*, Amin Maalouf describes Saladin as "always affable with visitors, insisting that they stay to eat, treating them with full honours, even if they were infidels, and satisfying all their requests. He could not bear to let someone who had come to him depart disappointed, and there were those who did not hesitate to take advantage of this quality. One day, during a truce with the Franj, the 'Brins,' lord of Antioch, arrived unexpectedly at Saladin's tent and asked him to return a district that the sultan had taken four years earlier. And he agreed!"[42]

But he was not always so magnanimous. Saladin set out to conquer Jerusalem in 1187 in response to Crusaders under the command of Reynald of Chatillon's taking a page from the Islamic prophet Muhammad's book and raiding caravans—in this case, Muslim caravans. The rulers of the Kingdom of Jerusalem ordered Reynald to stop, because they knew that his actions endangered the very survival of their kingdom. Yet he persisted, and finally Saladin had had enough.[43]

He struck hard. When Saladin's forces defeated the Crusaders at Hattin on July 4, 1187, he ordered the mass execution of his Christian opponents. According to his secretary, Imad ed-Din, Saladin "ordered that they should be beheaded, choosing to have them dead rather than in prison. With him was a whole band of scholars and Sufis and a certain number of devout men and ascetics; each begged to be allowed to kill one of them, and drew his sword and rolled back his sleeve." The great jihad warrior took particular satisfaction in the scene: "Saladin, his face joyful, was sitting on his dais; the unbelievers showed black despair."[44] The warriors of jihad captured the True Cross and displayed it in Damascus, upside down.[45]

However, when Saladin recaptured Jerusalem for the Muslims in October 1187, he treated the Christians with magnanimity—in sharp contrast to the behavior of the Crusaders in 1099. Yet magnanimity was not his initial plan; he had originally intended to put to death all the Christians in the city. However, the Christian commander inside Jerusalem, Balian of Ibelin, threatened in turn to destroy the city and kill all the Muslims there before Saladin could get inside, so Saladin relented—but once inside the city, he did enslave many of the Christians who could not afford to buy their way out.[46] Each Christian had to raise a ransom payment in order to leave the city; those who remained who were not enslaved had to pay the *jizya*.[47]

Saladin also took Acre and Jaffa, greatly reducing the Crusaders' territory. The tide had turned definitively against the Crusaders, and the end of their presence in the Middle East was only a matter of time. Alarmed by Saladin's victories, Pope Gregory VIII called the Third Crusade, and won the active participation of King Henry II of England and Philip II of France, who had previously been warring against each other.

But what began in a demonstration of Christian unity was doomed by Christian disunity: also participating was Frederick Barbarossa, by now seventy years old. His title of Holy Roman emperor, which all the successors of Charlemagne in Germany had taken, may have played well at home, but in the East it was a different story: the Byzantine emperors still considered themselves to be the sole rightful emperors of the Romans. The Roman emperor Isaac II thus viewed the Roman emperor Frederick Barbarossa as an upstart and a pretender. Isaac granted Frederick permission to pass with his Crusader forces through Byzantine domains, but once Frederick was there, Isaac did all he could to make his passage difficult. So offended was Isaac, emperor of the Romans, by the appropriation of his title that he contacted Saladin himself and concluded a secret treaty with the Muslim commander; Isaac agreed to do everything he could to hinder Frederick's advance.[48]

As promised, provisions failed to appear, and Byzantine troops actively interfered with the Crusaders' advance. Frederick became infuriated and warned Isaac that if the harassment didn't stop, the Crusaders would attack Byzantine territory. Isaac asked for negotiations, but these became mired in arguments over who exactly was the Roman emperor, and so Frederick ultimately made good on his threat and captured Adrianople. Isaac then agreed that if the Crusaders withdrew from his city, he would provide them provisions and other aid against the Muslims.[49]

Frederick was then able to advance across Asia Minor, defeating the Turks in one battle before it all came to naught when the elderly Holy Roman emperor drowned while crossing a river in Armenia. His Crusade came to nothing. The other forces of the Third Crusade managed to recapture Acre and Jaffa, but they failed to retake Jerusalem.

Saladin, meanwhile, had visions of extending his jihad far beyond the Holy Land. He understood his fight against the Crusaders as part of the larger jihad that was indeed global, and he wanted to pursue that as well. His friend Baha ed-Din recalled that once, standing on the shores of the Mediterranean with Saladin, the great commander had said to him: "I think that when God grants me victory over the rest of Palestine I shall divide my territories, make a will stating my wishes, then set sail on this sea for their far-off lands and pursue the Franks there, so as to free the earth of anyone who does not believe in God, or die in the attempt."[50]

The Fifth Crusade

Saladin did not live to realize his aspiration to take the jihad to the lands of the Franks; he died in Damascus in 1193. Other Muslims, however, had the same goal and would pursue it indefatigably. In April 1213, nine years after the Fourth Crusade went disastrously awry, with the Crusaders getting involved in a Byzantine dynastic dispute and ending up sacking Constantinople, Pope Innocent III called a Fifth Crusade. In his bull *Quia Maior*, he articulated the reasons for the conflict as he saw them, in the virtual obverse of Saladin's aspirations for global jihad. Innocent noted that "the Christian peoples, in fact, held almost all the Saracen provinces up to the time of Blessed Gregory"—that is, Pope Gregory the Great, who reigned from 590 to 604.[51] "But since then," Innocent continued, "a son of perdition has arisen, the false prophet Muhammad, who has seduced many men from the truth by worldly enticements and the pleasures of the flesh."[52]

He thought that the end of Islam was approaching: "Although [Muhammad's] treachery has prevailed up to the present day, we nevertheless put our trust in the Lord who has already given us a sign that good is to come, that the end of this beast is approaching, whose 'number', according to the Revelation of St. John, will end in 666 years, of which already nearly 600 have passed." Nonetheless, it was imperative to resist the Saracens: "And in addition to the former great and grave injuries which the treacherous Saracens have inflicted on our Redeemer, on account of our offences, the same perfidious Saracens have recently built a fortified stronghold to confound the Christian name on Mount Thabor, where Christ revealed to his disciples a vision of his future glory; by means of this fortress they think they will easily occupy the city of Acre, which is very near them, and then invade the rest of that land without any obstructive resistance, since it is almost entirely devoid of forces or supplies."[53]

This Crusade, too, was ultimately unsuccessful, as were subsequent forays. The warriors of jihad from the Mamluk sultanate took Jerusalem in 1244. The remaining Crusader kingdoms were in serious peril, and there was no help in sight. The jihadis pursued their quarry ruthlessly: in 1268, when the jihad forces of the Mamluk sultan Baybars took Antioch from the Crusaders, Baybars was annoyed to find that the Crusader ruler, Count Bohemond VI, had already left the city. So he wrote to Bohemond to make sure he knew what his men had done in Antioch:

> You would have seen your knights prostrate beneath the horses' hooves, your houses stormed by pillagers and ransacked by looters, your wealth weighed by the quintal, your women sold four at a time and bought for a dinar of your own money! You would have seen the crosses in your churches smashed, the pages of the false Testaments scattered, the Patriarchs' tombs overturned. You would have seen your Muslim enemy trampling on the place where you celebrate the Mass, cutting the throats of monks, priests

and deacons upon the altars, bringing sudden death to the Patriarchs and slavery to the royal princes. You would have seen fire running through your palaces, your dead burned in this world before going down to the fires of the next, your palace lying unrecognizable, the Church of St. Paul and that of the Cathedral of St. Peter pulled down and destroyed; then you would have said, "Would that I were dust, and that no letter had ever brought me such tidings!"[54]

As the last cities of Outremer were facing conquest and Islamization in 1290, an offer of help came from Arghun, the Mongol ruler of Persia and client of the great Mongol emperor Kublai Khan.

In 1258, Hulagu Khan, the brother of Kublai Khan and grandson of Genghis Khan, sacked Baghdad and toppled the Abbasid caliphate. (The Mamluks restored the Abbasids in Cairo in 1261, but the Abbasid caliphate in Egypt was never much more than a figurehead and a pawn of vying Islamic factions.[55]) Hulagu's mother was a Nestorian Christian, and Hulagu himself maintained a positive stance toward Christianity. Two years later, a Christian Mongol leader named Kitbuka seized Damascus and Aleppo for the Mongols. Arghun, a Buddhist, wanted to try to raise interest among the Christian kings of Europe in making common cause to wrest the Holy Land from the Muslims once and for all. Arghun's closest friend was the Catholicos, the chief prelate of the Nestorian Church. His vizier was a Jew. Arghun had come to power in Persia by toppling the Muslim ruler Ahmed (a convert from Nestorian Christianity) after Ahmed made attempts to join forces with the Mamluks in Cairo.[56]

Arghun had written to Pope Honorius IV in 1285 to suggest an alliance between the Mongols and the Christians of Europe against the Seljuk Turks and the Mamluks of Egypt, but the pope did not answer.[57] The Mongol ruler then sent an emissary, Rabban Sauma, a Nestorian Christian from Central Asia, to Europe to discuss the matter personally with the pope and the Christian kings.

Sauma's journey was one of the most remarkable in the ancient world: he started out from Trebizond and traveled all the way to Bordeaux to meet with King Edward I of England. Along the way, he met the Byzantine emperor Andronicus in Constantinople (whom he referred to as King Basileus, or King King, demonstrating that thirteenth-century translators weren't infallible); traveled to Naples, Rome (where Honorius IV had just died and a new pope had not yet been chosen), and Genoa; went on to Paris, where he dined with King Philip IV of France; met with Edward I in Bordeaux; and returned to Rome for a triumphant meeting with the new pope, Nicholas IV.[58]

All the European leaders liked Rabban Sauma's proposal of a Mongol–Christian alliance to free the Holy Land. Philip IV offered to march to Jerusalem himself at the head of a Crusader army. Edward I was likewise enthusiastic: Sauma was proposing an alliance that the king himself had called for in the past. Pope Nicholas showered Sauma and Arghun with gifts. But what none of these men, or anyone else in Europe, could decide was a date for this grand new Crusade. Their enthusiasm remained vague; their promises, nonspecific.[59]

The crowned heads of Europe were too disunited and distracted with challenges at home to take up the Mongols' offer; perhaps they were also suspicious of a non-Christian king who wanted to wage war to liberate the Christian Holy Land. They may have feared that once they helped the wolf devour the Muslims, the wolf would turn on them in turn. But in any case, it was an opportunity missed. Dissatisfied with the results of Rabban Sauma's journey, Arghun sent another emissary, Buscarel of Gisolf, to Europe in 1289.[60]

He asked Philip IV and Edward I for help, offering to take Jerusalem jointly with soldiers sent by the Christian kings; he would then hand the city over to the Crusaders. Edward's answer, which is the only one that survives, was polite but noncommittal. Dismayed, Arghun tried yet again in 1291, but it was too late: in that year, Outremer fell. By the time the emissaries returned, Arghun himself was dead.[61]

An alliance with the Mongols was a lost opportunity for the Christian Europeans. In the early fourteenth century, the renowned Islamic jurist Ibn Taymiyya composed a fatwa, that is, a religious ruling on a disputed issue, against the Muslims of Mardin, who had been conquered by the Mongols in 1260, for not waging jihad against their new overlords. Ibn Taymiyya fulminated against the people of Mardin, saying that "in spite of their pretension to be Muslims—[they] not only glorify Chinghis-Khan but they also fight the Muslims. The worst of these infidels even give him their total and complete obedience; they bring him their properties and give their decisions in his name.... Above all this they fight the Muslims and treat them with the greatest enmity. They ask the Muslims to obey them, to give them their properties, and to enter [into the obedience of the rules] which were imposed on them by this infidel polytheistic King..."[62]

But by that time, there was no Christian presence anywhere in the area that could conceivably have allied with the Mongols to fight against the warriors of jihad. The fourteenth-century Muslim historian Abu'l Fida rejoiced over the end of the Crusader presence in the Holy Land: "With these conquests the whole of Palestine was now in Muslim hands, a result that no one would have dared to hope for or desire. Thus the whole of Syria and the coastal zones were purified of the Franks, who had once been on the point of conquering Egypt and subduing Damascus and other cities. Praise be to God!"[63]

Indeed, there were many times when the Crusaders seemed on the verge of an immense victory, only to have it snatched from them. Nevertheless, neither Abu'l Fida nor anyone else at the time seemed to have noticed the greatest achievement of the Crusades: from the time Pope Urban II called the First Crusade in 1095 to the fall of the last of Outremer in 1291, there were no jihad forays into Europe. The Reconquista in Spain continued to reduce the size of Islamic al-Andalus, and so in sharp contrast to the jihad forays into Europe and against the Byzantine Empire that had been a regular feature in the centuries before the Crusades, the two centuries of the principal Crusader period saw the forces of jihad both in Spain and in the Holy Land in an unfamiliar posture: on the defensive.

This did not, of course, make any difference to the Christians and Jews who had the misfortune of living within Islamic domains. The influential Islamic jurist Ibn Qayyim al-Jawziyya, who died in 1350, reiterated the restrictions on the *dhimmis* from the Abbasid capital of Damascus:

> Those who are of the opinion that to pray in a church or synagogue is loathsome also say that they are places of great infidelity and polytheism. Indeed, their loathsomeness is greater than that of bathhouses, cemeteries or dunghills since they are places of Divine Wrath.... Moreover,

are they not the houses of the enemies of Allah, and Allah is not to be adored in the houses of his enemies...?

They [the Christians] are prohibited to sound bells except noiselessly in the depths of their churches...for the sound of bells is the banner of infidelity, as well as its outward sign.... Verily, Allah has annulled the sounding of the Christian bell and the Jewish [ram's] horn and has replaced them with the call of monotheism and devotion. He has raised the sound of the word *Islam* as a sign of the true vocation so as to throw into obscurity the call of the infidel, and he has replaced the bell with the [Muslim] call to prayer...just as He has replaced the Satanic scriptures with the Koran....

"Humiliation and derision are to be the lot of those that disobey my word." The *dhimmis* are the most disobedient of His command and contrary to His word; consequently, it befits them to be humiliated by distinguishing them from the comportment of the Muslims whom Allah has exalted through their obedience to Him and His Prophet above those that have disobeyed Him.... That a distinctive sign [*ghiyar*] must be imposed upon them is clear from the Prophet's statement, "He of the people who resembles them [the *dhimmis*] shall be deemed of their number." ... Moreover the distinctive dress serves other purposes. He [the Muslim] will thereby know that he is not to go to meet him, he is not to seat him among Muslim company, he is not to kiss his hand, he is not to stand up for him, he is not to address him with the terms brother or master, he is not to wish him success or honor as is customary toward a Muslim, he is not to give him Muslim charity, he is not to call him as a witness, either for accusation or defence...[64]

The jihad to impose these and other humiliations upon Christians and Jews in Europe was soon to resume and make immense gains. However, if the Crusades had never been attempted at all, it is quite possible that the warriors of jihad would have overrun all of Europe, and the subsequent history of the world would have taken a drastically different course. Instead, Europe experienced the High Middle Ages, the Reformation, and the Enlightenment, and the foundations of modern society were laid. It would not be until the twenty-first century that the free societies created out of this intellectual ferment would again be seriously imperiled by the forces of jihad.

II. THE RECONQUISTA GAINS GROUND

The Almohads

In the early twelfth century, a Berber Muslim scholar named Abu Abdallah Muhammad ibn Tumart began to preach that the ruling Almoravids had strayed from the pure religion of Muhammad, and that the Muslims in its domains needed to return to full implementation of the teachings of the Qur'an and Sunnah. His message found a ready audience among Muslims who had imbibed the Qur'anic notion that Allah bestowed or withheld his blessings to a society in direct correlation to how obedient it was to his commands. In 1121, his followers proclaimed him the Mahdi, the savior figure who was to return before Judgment Day in order to prepare and purify the believers. His followers, according to a contemporary chronicler, "swore that they would fight for him and dedicate their lives to his service."[65]

Ibn Tumart died around 1130, but the movement he began lived on. The rigorists, who called themselves Almohads (monotheists), rapidly gained ground, and in 1147 were able to overthrow the Almoravids in North Africa; the Almohad leader, Abd al-Mu'min al-Gumi, declared himself caliph. Over the next twenty-five years, the Almohads gained control over all the remaining Muslim domains of al-Andalus.

Life was not pleasant for non-Muslims in Almohad Spain. The Muslim historian Ibn Baydhaq detailed how the Almohads treated the Jews as they advanced:

> Abd al-Mumin...the leader of the Almohads after the death of Muhammad ibn Tumart the Mahdi...captured Tlemcen [in the Maghreb] and killed all those who were in

it, including the Jews, except those who embraced Islam.…
[In Sijilmasa] one hundred and fifty persons were killed for
clinging to their [Jewish] faith.… All the cities in the Almoravid state were conquered by the Almohads. One hundred thousand persons were killed in Fez on that occasion,
and 120,000 in Marrakesh. The Jews in all [Maghreb] lo-
calities [conquered]…groaned under the heavy yoke of the
Almohads; many had been killed, many others converted;
none were able to appear in public as Jews.[66]

The renowned Jewish philosopher Moses ben Maimon, Maimonides,
was born in Córdoba but fled the supposedly tolerant and pluralistic
Muslim Spain in the 1160s. He later remarked:

You know, my brethren, that on account of our sins God has
cast us into the midst of this people, the nation of Ishmael,
who persecute us severely, and who devise ways to harm us
and to debase us.… No nation has ever done more harm to
Israel. None has matched it in debasing and humiliating us.
None has been able to reduce us as they have.… We have
borne their imposed degradation, their lies, and absurdities,
which are beyond human power to bear. We have become as
in the words of the psalmist, "But I am as a deaf man, I hear
not, and I am as a dumb man that opens not his mouth"
(Ps. 38:14). We have done as our sages of blessed memory
have instructed us, bearing the lies and absurdities of Ishmael. We listen but remain silent.… In spite of all this, we
are not spared from the ferocity of their wickedness and
their outbursts at any time. On the contrary, the more we
suffer and choose to conciliate them, the more they choose
to act belligerently toward us. Thus David has depicted our
plight: "I am at peace, but when I speak, they are for war!"
(Ps. 120:7).[67]

The Almohads meant to revive the spirit of jihad among the Muslims
of Spain and expand those domains. Driven by a revivalist fervor rival-
ing that of the jihadis of earlier centuries, the Almohads won a series

of victories over the Christians, capturing Alcácer do Sal, the gateway
to Lisbon, in 1191. Four years later, they declared a new jihad against
the Christians of Spain and decisively defeated King Alfonso VIII of
Castile in 1195—the most disastrous defeat the Christians of Spain
had suffered since the debacle at Sagrajas 109 years before. In 1197,
they besieged Madrid.

In line with their rigorist origins, the Almohads made sure to enforce
the humiliation of the *dhimmis* in their domains. The thirteenth-century
Muslim historian al-Marrakushi noted that in 1198, Abu Yusuf, the Almohad ruler in Spain,

> ordered the Jewish inhabitants of the Maghreb to make
> themselves conspicuous among the rest of the population
> by assuming a special attire consisting of dark blue gar-
> ments, the sleeves of which were so wide as to reach to their
> feet and—instead of a turban—to hang over their ears a cap
> whose form was so ill-conceived as to be easily mistaken for
> a pack-saddle. This apparel became the costume of all the
> Jews of the Maghreb and remained obligatory until the end
> of the prince's reign and the beginning of that of his son
> Abu Abd Allah [Abu Muhammad Abd Allah al-Adil, the
> Just, 1224–1227].[68]

Abu Abd Allah, however, was not offering actual justice or equitable
treatment:

> The latter made a concession only after appeals of all kinds
> had been made by the Jews, who had entreated all those
> whom they thought might be helpful to intercede on their
> behalf. Abu Abd Allah obliged them to wear yellow gar-
> ments and turbans, the very costume they still wear in the
> present year 621 [1224]. Abu Yusuf's misgivings as to the
> sincerity of their conversion to Islam prompted him to take
> this measure and impose upon them a specific dress. "If I
> were sure," said he, "that they really had become Muslims,
> I would let them assimilate through marriage and other
> means; on the other hand, had I evidence that they had re-

mained infidels I would have them massacred, reduce their children to slavery and confiscate their belongings for the benefit of the believers."[69]

Meanwhile, with Saladin's defeat of the Crusaders at Hattin and Jerusalem in 1187, just a few years before these reversals in Spain, the Christian losses in the Holy Land and in Spain made it appear as if Christendom was beset by an implacable foe with a global reach. And, indeed it was. In February 1210, Pope Innocent III wrote to Archbishop Rodrigo of Toledo, urging the Christians of Spain not to make the same mistakes that had led to so many defeats at the hands of the Muslims in the Holy Land—chiefly disunity and impiety.[70] His warning appeared all the more urgent the following year, when the Almohads under the leadership of their caliph, Muhammad al-Nasir, invaded Spain with a huge army of jihadis and began advancing again. Innocent, aware of the urgency of the situation, sent new letters calling for unity and renewed religious fervor to other Christian leaders, both spiritual and temporal, culminating in letters in 1212 to the bishops of France, informing them of the gravity of the jihad threat and calling for spiritual and material aid for Alfonso and the other Christian rulers who were preparing to confront the Almohads.[71]

Innocent also wrote to Alfonso, urging him to humble himself before the Lord, and not to try to engage the Almohads if he was not confident of victory, but to seek a truce if necessary.[72] Then he called for a general fast among the people of Rome and a procession in the city to pray for the peace of the Church and the favor of God in the battle with the Muslims in Spain.[73]

On July 16, 1212, the Christians won a massive victory over the Almohads at Las Navas de Tolosa in the southern Spanish province of Jaén. The caliph Muhammad, in imminent danger of being captured, fled in a panic, leaving behind his standard, which the Christians recovered and sent to the house of a religious order near Burgos, where it remains to this day. King Alfonso VIII wrote happily to Pope Innocent III:

> In order to show how immense were the numbers of the enemy, when our army rested after the battle for two days in the enemy camp, for all the fires which were needed to cook

food and make bread and other things, no other wood was
needed than that of the enemy arrows and spears which were
lying about, and even then we burned scarcely half of them.[74]

Innocent received the news as an answer to his prayers. The power of the
jihad in Spain was definitively broken, not to be revived until centuries
later. From 1212 on, the Christians in Spain made steady gains. Not
only the jihad that the Almohads had called in 1195, but the jihad that
began when Tariq ibn Ziyad burned his boats and declared to his men
that they were going to conquer or die, was now a spent force, although
it would still be nearly three hundred years before Islamic rule in Spain
ended completely.

In 1236, the Christians captured Córdoba; in 1243, they took Valencia; and in 1248, Seville. By 1249, the emirate of Granada was all
that was left of Islamic al-Andalus. In 1280, however, the Muslims of
Granada defeated an invading Christian force, and the Reconquista was
stymied for a time. By that point, however, the Muslims of Spain were
directing their energies solely to holding on to the territories they had,
not to winning more.

Elsewhere, however, the jihad met with greater success.

III. THE JIHAD RESUMES IN INDIA

If Innocent III had been aware of the larger global picture and had
a comprehensive understanding of how not just Christians but all
non-Muslim states and individuals are threatened by the jihad imperative, he might have been just as alarmed by the news out of India as he
was by the tidings from the Holy Land and Spain. For just as Saladin
was reviving the fortunes of the jihad in the Holy Land, another Muslim commander, Mu'izz ad-Din Muhammad Ghori, was reviving the
jihad in India.

In 1191 and 1192, Muhammad Ghori twice defeated a force of
Rajputs led by the Hindu commander Prithviraj Chauhan in northern
India. The thirteenth-century Muslim historian Hasan Nizami revealed
his contempt for the Hindus as he noted that a primary objective of the
jihad remained the destruction of Hindu "idolatry":

The victorious army on the right and on the left departed towards Ajmer.... When the crow-faced Hindus began to sound their white shells on the backs of the elephants, you would have said that a river of pitch was flowing impetuously down the face of a mountain of blue.... The army of Islam was completely victorious, and a hundred thousand groveling Hindus swiftly departed to the fire of hell.... He destroyed [at Ajmer] the pillars and foundations of the idol temples, and built in their stead mosques and colleges, and the precepts of Islam, and the customs of the law were divulged and established."[75]

At Aligarh, the Muslims put down a Hindu uprising and, said Hasan Nizami, raised "three bastions as high as heaven with their heads, and their carcasses became food for beasts of prey." As was so often the case in jihad warfare, brutality mixed with piety: "The tract was freed from idols and idol-worship and the foundations of infidelism were destroyed."[76]

The following year, Muhammad Ghori defeated the Indian king Jayachandra of Kanauj and plundered the Hindu treasures at Asni and Varanasi. The contemporary Muslim historian Ibn Asir recounted: "The slaughter of Hindus [at Varanasi] was immense; none were spared except women and children, and the carnage of men went on until the earth was weary."[77] The women and children were, of course, enslaved. The warriors of jihad then set out to seal the triumph of Islam: according to Hasan Nizami, "In Benares, which is the centre of the country of Hind, they destroyed one thousand temples and raised mosques on their foundations."[78] After a victory by the jihad commander Muhammad bin Bakhtiyar Khilji in another place, according to a thirteenth-century Muslim historian, "great plunder fell into the hands of the victors. Most of the inhabitants were Brahmins with shaven heads. They were put to death. Large numbers of books were found...but no one could explain their contents as all the men had been killed."[79]

At Delhi, the Muslims destroyed twenty-seven Hindu temples and built a grand mosque. They were under the command of Qutbuddin Aibak, a slave soldier who succeeded Muhammad Ghori and founded the Mamluk sultanate. Nizami recounts that the Muslims decorated the new mosque "with the stones and gold obtained from the temples which had been demolished by elephants."[80] In 1196, Aibak and his jihadis attacked Anahilwar Patan, the capital of Gujarat. According to Nizami, "Fifty thousand infidels were dispatched to hell by the sword" and "more than twenty thousand slaves, and cattle beyond all calculation fell into the hands of the victors."[81] After Aibak's conquest of Kalinjar in 1202, said Nizami, "the temples were converted into mosques.... Fifty thousand men came under the collar of slavery and the plain became black as pitch with Hindus."[82]

Nizami summarized Muhammad Ghori's reign as a triumph for Islam: "He purged by his sword the land of Hind from the filth of infidelity and vice and freed the whole of that country from the thorn of God-plurality and the impurity of idol-worship, and by his royal vigour and intrepidity left not one temple standing."[83]

The jihad continued relentlessly. In 1234, Aibak's successor, Shamsuddin Iltutmish, invaded Malwa in west-central India and destroyed an ancient Hindu temple at Vidisha. The sixteenth-century Muslim historian Abdul Qadir Badauni recounted that Shamsuddin imitated Mahmoud of Ghazni in using the destruction of the Hindu idols to portray the victory of Allah and Islam: "Having destroyed the idol temple of Ujjain which had been built six hundred years previously, and was called Mahakal, he leveled it to its foundations, and threw down the image of Rai Vikramajit from whom the Hindus reckon their era, and brought certain images of cast molten brass and placed them on the ground in front of the doors of mosques of old Delhi and ordered the people to trample them under foot."[84]

The Hindus resisted wherever they could, but the Muslim response to such effrontery was ruthless. In 1254, the Mamluk sultan Ghiyasuddin Balban left Delhi and crossed the Ganges with a jihad force. Badauni stated that "in two days after leaving Delhi, he arrived in the midst of the territory of Katihar and put to death every male, even those of eight years of age, and bound the women."[85]

In the same year that his fellow jihadis were destroying the last of the Crusader states, 1291, the Muslim warrior Jalaluddin Khalji, who established the Khalji sultanate in Delhi, led a jihad foray to Ranthambhor, destroying Hindu temples along the way. Emulating other jihad leaders in India, he ordered that the broken pieces of the Hindu idols be sent to Delhi, where they were to be placed, in what was by now a time-honored Islamic practice, at the entrance of the Jama mosque, so that the faithful would trample them on their way into the mosque to pray, and again on the way out.[86]

The following year, Jalaluddin's nephew Alauddin, who was to succeed him, led a jihad force to Vidisha. Badauni said that Alauddin "brought much booty to the Sultan and the idol which was the object of worship of the Hindus, he caused to be cast in front of the Badaun gate to be trampled upon by the people." Jihad and humiliating the Hindus were profitable for Alauddin personally: "The services of Alauddin were highly appreciated, the jagir of Oudh also was added to his other estates."[87]

The Islamic state in India

Despite these powerful appeals to embrace Islam, however, many Hindus still resisted, and the jihad went on. The Hindus had good reason to resist, as the society that the Muslim overlords established was hardly a pleasant one for them. Muhammad ibn Qasim's granting of People of the Book status to the Hindus alleviated the misery of the conquered people to some degree, but only marginally. Around the turn of the fourteenth century, the sultan Alauddin Khalji asked the Islamic scholar Qazi Mughisuddin about the legal status of the Hindus within his domains and the permissibility of conferring *dhimmi* status upon them. The *qazi* answered:

> These are called payers of tribute, and when the revenue officer demands silver from them, they should without question, and with all humility and respect, tender gold. If the officer throws dirt in their mouths, they must without reluctance open their mouths wide to receive it.... The due subordination of the Dhimmi is exhibited in this humble payment, and by this throwing of dirt in their mouths. The glorification of Islam is a duty, and contempt for religion is vain. God holds them in contempt, for he says, "Keep

them in subjection." To keep the Hindus in abasement is especially a religious duty, because they are the most inveterate enemies of the Prophet, and because the Prophet has commanded us to slay them, plunder them, and make them captive, saying, "Convert them to Islam or kill them, and make them slaves, and spoil their wealth and property." No doctor but the great doctor [Hanifah], to whose school we belong, has assented to the imposition of jizya on Hindus; doctors of other schools allow no other alternative but "Death or Islam."[88]

The Hanifah was one of the four principal Sunni schools of Islamic law. The *qazi's* ruling was in accord with a manual of Islamic law that directed that "the main object in levying the tax is the subjection of infidels to humiliation...and...during the process of payment, the *Zimmi* is seized by the collar and vigorously shaken and pulled about in order to show him his degradation."[89]

The fourteenth-century Muslim political theorist Ziauddin Barani, a high official in the Delhi sultanate, directed that even Hindus who converted to Islam were not to be accepted as equals, but to be treated with continued contempt: "Teachers are to be sternly ordered not to thrust precious stones [scriptures] down the throats of dogs [converts]. To shopkeepers and the low born they are to teach nothing more than the rules about prayer, fasting, religious charity and the Hajj pilgrimage along with some chapters of the Quran...they are to be instructed in nothing more.... The low born are capable of only vices."[90] The power of the Muslim state was the military, which was made up of Muslims. Even Muslims from other lands, including those who were illiterate or otherwise incompetent, received preferential treatment over Hindus for government positions, and here, as in Muslim Spain, the placement of a *dhimmi* in a position of authority and responsibility was viewed inconsistent with the state of humiliation in which he was supposed to be living.[91]

The fourteenth-century Sufi scholar and poet Amir Khusrau looked around at the society thus created and liked what he saw. "Happy Hindustan," he exclaimed, "the splendor of Religion, where the Law finds perfect honour and security. The whole country, by means of the sword of our holy warriors, has become like a forest denuded of its thorns by fire…. Islam is triumphant, idolatry is subdued. Had not the Law granted exemption from death by the payment of poll-tax, the very name of Hind, root and branch, would have been extinguished."[92] That the name remained he regarded as an example of Islamic tolerance; the Hindus under the rule of the Muslims had a different view.

THE JIHAD ADVANCES INTO EUROPE

Jihad in the Fourteenth and Fifteenth Centuries

I. THE DECLINE AND FALL OF THE BYZANTINE EMPIRE

The Coming of the Ottomans

No sooner had the last Crusader state in the Holy Land been extinguished than the Muslims began to move toward realizing Saladin's aspiration to take the jihad back to the homes of the Crusaders. The Seljuk sultanate of Rum had been weakened by the Crusades and a Mongol invasion, and ultimately dissolved into a group of smaller Turkish states in Asia Minor. The chieftain of one of these, a warrior named Osman, began conducting jihad raids into Byzantine territory. Osman was a fiercely pious Muslim. Legend had it that after he spent one night devoutly reading the Qur'an instead of sleeping, an angel came to him with a message from Allah: "Since thou hast read my eternal word with so great respect, thy children and the children of thy children shall be honoured from generation to generation."[1]

Osman began to win those honors in 1301, just ten years after the Muslim conquest of the last of the Crusader states, when his jihadis routed a Byzantine force at Bapheus, near Nicaea. Osman, motivated by the Islamic doctrine that land once ruled by Muslims belonged by right to Islam forever (succinctly stated in the Qur'an in the command "drive them out from where they drove you out," 2:191), was determined to recapture Nicaea itself, which had been the capital of the sultanate of Rum but had been retaken by the Byzantines in 1147.[2]

The great warrior did not, however, realize that aspiration before he died in 1324. His successor, Orkhan, succeeded in conquering Nicaea in 1331, and continued Osman's work of consolidating the Turkish states of Asia Minor under his rule. The resulting sultanate and future caliphate and empire bore the name of its first leader, Osman, and became known in English as the Ottoman Empire. The Ottomans were able to gain control over the other small Turkish states of the region because, it was said, of their indefatigable commitment to jihad.[3] Their rigor was reinforced by Islamic scholars of the day such as Ibn Taymiyya (1263–1328), who declared that a Muslim ruler who did not enforce all the precepts of Sharia forfeited his right to rule.[4] The Ottomans scrupulously avoided such challenges to their authority.

Disunity

In 1332, when King Philip VI of France was considering mounting a new Crusade, a German priest named Brocardus wrote to warn him about the Assassins:

> The Assassins...are to be cursed and fled. They sell themselves, are thirsty for human blood, kill the innocent for a price, and care nothing for either life or salvation. Like the devil, they transfigure themselves into angels of light, by imitating the gestures, garments, languages, customs and acts of various nations and peoples; thus, hidden in sheep's clothing, they suffer death as soon as they are recognized.... So execrable is their profession, and so abominated by all, that they conceal their own names as much as they can. I therefore know only one single remedy for the safeguarding and protection of the king, that in all the royal household, for whatever service, however small or

brief or mean, none should be admitted, save those whose country, place, lineage, condition and person are certainly, fully and clearly known.[5]

But a much greater threat to the Christians came from within. The Muslims were aided in their jihad, as jihadis so often were throughout the history of Islam, by shortsighted Christians. Then, as now, business considerations frequently overrode concern among Christians about what the jihadis were doing. In 1335, the Republic of Ragusa concluded a commercial treaty with the Ottomans, giving the people of Ragusa the right to market their wares within Ottoman domains and to sail the seas without worrying about Ottoman pirates. The Sultan could not write, so he marked the treaty with his thumbprint.[6] Four years later, the Byzantine emperor Andronicus III Paleologus sent the monk Barlaam, who had been born in Italy, to Avignon to meet Pope Benedict XII and appeal to him for an ecumenical council to heal the schism between the churches, and for a new Crusade against the Ottomans.

"Most holy father," said Barlaam to Benedict, "the emperor is not less desirous than yourself of a union between the two churches: but in this delicate transaction, he is obliged to respect his own dignity and the prejudices of his subjects. The ways of union are twofold; force and persuasion." Force, he said, had been tried when the Latins "subdued the empire, without subduing the minds, of the Greeks," and at the supposed reunion Council of Lyons in 1274, where the Byzantines had not had a say. Barlaam advised that "a well-chosen legate should be sent into Greece, to convene the patriarchs of Constantinople, Alexandria, Antioch, and Jerusalem; and, with their aid, to prepare a free and universal synod." He reminded the pope that "the empire is assaulted and endangered by the Turks, who have occupied four of the greatest cities of Anatolia. The Christian inhabitants have expressed a wish of returning to their allegiance and religion; but the forces and revenues of the emperor are insufficient for their deliverance: and the Roman legate must be accompanied, or preceded, by an army of Franks, to expel the infidels, and open a way to the holy sepulchre."[7]

Pope Benedict was unmoved. He sent back a haughty refusal, insultingly addressing the emperor of the Romans as the "moderator of the Greeks," and the Eastern patriarchs as "the persons who style themselves the patriarchs of the Eastern churches."[8] He appeared thoroughly untroubled by the prospect of the destruction of the Byzantine Empire and the advance of the jihad into Europe. Not until the days of Pope Francis would the See of Rome have an occupant more useful to the jihad force than Benedict XII.

There was never any shortage of blinkered Christians. In the early fourteenth century, the Byzantine emperor Andronicus II hired a corps of Catalan mercenaries; the Byzantines had engaged mercenaries for centuries, with varying degrees of success. This time, it was an unmitigated disaster: the Catalan mercenaries quarreled with their Byzantine employers, caused unrest in Constantinople, and finally turned openly against them, asking the Turks—the people they had come to fight—for help in creating their own state at Gallipoli, on the European side of the Hellespont.[9]

The Ottomans, of course, were only too happy to help the ostensibly Christian Catalans and quickly established substantial forces in Thrace and Macedonia. The leader of this detachment, Halil, agreed to withdraw, but then reneged when the Byzantines demanded that his forces surrender the booty they had seized in Thrace. In an initial clash, Halil and his jihadis soundly defeated the forces of Byzantine emperor Michael IX Paleologus, who had to flee for his life, leaving behind his imperial helmet, which Halil promptly donned to mock the great emperor of the Romans.[10] Finally Michael was able to summon a force of Serbians that drove Halil and his men from Europe, only to have one of his successors invite the Turks back several decades later.

Allying with the Jihad

In 1345, the Byzantine emperor John VI Cantacuzenus asked for help from the Turks amid a dynastic dispute that had escalated into a full-scale civil war. Orkhan agreed to help if John gave him his daughter, Theodora, in marriage. Expediency swept away all considerations of outraged pride and of the travesty of a Christian princess' being given in marriage to a non-Christian sovereign; John either had to agree or give up his claim to the imperial throne, and he wasn't about to do that.

Gibbon described the bizarre scene as the daughter of the Christian emperor was given in marriage to a warrior king whose coreligionists had been trying to destroy that Christian empire for nearly seven hundred years:

> A body of Turkish cavalry attended the ambassadors, who disembarked from thirty vessels, before his camp of Selybria. A stately pavilion was erected, in which the empress Irene passed the night with her daughters. In the morning, Theodora ascended a throne, which was surrounded with curtains of silk and gold: the troops were under arms; but the emperor alone was on horseback. At a signal the curtains were suddenly withdrawn to disclose the bride, or the victim, encircled by kneeling eunuchs and hymeneal torches: the sound of flutes and trumpets proclaimed the joyful event; and her pretended happiness was the theme of the nuptial song, which was chanted by such poets as the age could produce.
>
> Without the rites of the church, Theodora was delivered to her barbarous lord: but it had been stipulated, that she should preserve her religion in the harem of Bursa; and her father celebrates her charity and devotion in this ambiguous situation.
>
> After his peaceful establishment on the throne of Constantinople, the Greek emperor visited his Turkish ally, who with four sons, by various wives, expected him at Scutari, on the Asiatic shore. The two princes partook, with seeming cordiality, of the pleasures of the banquet and the chase; and Theodora was permitted to repass the Bosphorus, and to enjoy some days in the society of her mother.[11]

Belying this pleasant scene, Orkhan had insisted that his treaty with the Byzantines should allow him to sell his prisoners of war as slaves in Constantinople. Gibbon recounted: "A naked crowd of Christians of both sexes and every age, of priests and monks, of matrons and virgins, was exposed in the public market; the whip was frequently used to quicken the charity of redemption; and the indigent Greeks deplored the fate of their brethren, who were led away to the worst evils of temporal and spiritual bondage."[12]

Their fate was a more reliable indication of what John VI Cantacuzenus had gotten into than the wedding banquet. Ottoman warriors of jihad soon arrived in Europe to help John, crossing over the Dardanelles in 1348 and occupying Gallipoli in 1354. But how much the cordial scene at the wedding ran contrary to reality quickly became apparent. When Genoa went to war with the Byzantines soon after the treaty between John and Orkhan was concluded, Orkhan switched sides without hesitation and aided the Genoese against the Byzantines.[13] The warriors of jihad, after all, had been trying to conquer the Byzantine empire since 711; if the Genoese were working to weaken the Byzantines, the jihadis could count them as friends.

The Genoese and Venetians concluded treaties with the Byzantines in 1355. The treaties included the promise that they would defend the Christian empire against its enemies, but specifically exempted "Morat Bey and his Turks," that is, Murad, Orkhan's son and the effective ruler of the sultanate during his father's dotage.[14] Genoa and Venice had business interests with the Ottomans that precluded their going to war with them. Genoa even entered into a pact of friendship with "the magnificent and powerful lord of lords, Moratibei."[15] Yet consistency was not the Genoese's strong suit. Both Genoa and Venice tried to play both sides against each other; in 1356, they joined an alliance "against that Turk, son of unrighteousness and evil, and enemy of the Holy Cross, Morat Bey and his sect, who are attempting so grievously to attack the Christian race."[16]

It was rare for the Christians of the West to express such concerns. Nor did they do much to stop Murad from attacking "the Christian race." In 1357, jihadis under Murad's command captured the imposing Byzantine fortress of Adrianople, the third most important city in the Byzantine Empire, after Constantinople and Thessalonica.

That same year, pirates kidnapped the son of Orkhan and Theodora. Demonstrating his power over the Byzantines, Orkhan ordered the emperor John V Paleologus to rescue him personally. John duly besieged

Phocaea on the west coast of Asia Minor, where the pirates were holding the young man, but ultimately the troops under John's command refused to continue the siege, and the emperor had to report shamefacedly to Orkhan that he could not complete the task he had been ordered to do.[17]

The Janissaries

With the Ottomans now ruling over a substantial population of Christians, in 1359, Murad founded the janissary corps, a crack force of young men who were seized as boys from their Christian families, enslaved, and forcibly converted to Islam. This was the seizure and enslavement of twenty percent of the Christian children from predominantly Christian areas of the Ottoman Empire. These boys, once seized from their families, were given the choice of Islam or death. Those who chose Islam were, after rigorous training, enrolled in the janissary corps, the emperor's crack troops.

All of this was in accord with Islamic law. It was Murad's vizier, or chief minister, who reminded him that the Qur'an entitled him to take twenty percent of the spoils of war that the Muslims had won: "And know that anything you obtain of war booty, then indeed, for Allah is one fifth of it and for the Messenger and for near relatives and the orphans, the needy, and the traveler, if you have believed in Allah and in that which We sent down to Our Servant on the day of criterion, the day when the two armies met. And Allah, over all things, is competent." (8:41) Who stood in the place of Allah and his Messenger but the caliph? And the twenty percent of the spoils meant that Murad and the Muslims were entitled to the labors of twenty percent of the young Christian boys in the lands they had conquered.

Gibbon recorded that the vizier suggested that "the duty might easily be levied, if vigilant officers were stationed in Gallipoli, to watch the passage, and to select for his use the stoutest and most beautiful of the Christian youth."[18] Murad liked the idea. "The advice was followed: the edict was proclaimed; many thousands of the European captives were educated in religion and arms; and the new militia was consecrated and named by a celebrated dervish. Standing in the front of their ranks, he stretched the sleeve of his gown over the head of the foremost soldier, and his blessing was delivered in these words: 'Let them be called [*Yengi cheri*, or new soldiers]; may their countenance be ever bright! their hand victorious! their sword keen! may their spear always hang over the heads of their enemies! and wheresoever they go, may they return with a *white face!*'"[19] "*Yengi cheri*" became "janissaries" in the West.

Some Christian families actually welcomed the seizure of their children, for this at least was a way out of the miserable life of the *dhimmi* and a chance to advance in Ottoman society. Nevertheless, Godfrey Goodwin, historian of the janissary corps, painted a romanticized but still inescapably grim picture of the recruitment of these young Christians:

> Whatever ambitions families might or might not have, it was an unhappy day when the troops trudged into the village, hungry and thirsty. The priest was ready with his baptismal rolls and so were the boys with their fathers; in theory mothers and sisters were left to weep at home. Then each of the recruits had to be examined both physically and mentally.... Once the selection process was completed, the roll was drawn up in duplicate.... Now was the time for tears and some farewells must have been poignant but the boys tramped the dusty roads side by side with friends and all had the excitement of starting out on an adventure. They could dream of promotion and fortune while the peasants returned to their fields, doubtless to weep longer than their sons.[20]

Gibbon noted what a terrifying force was thereby created:

> Such was the origin of these haughty troops, the terror of the nations, and sometimes of the sultans themselves. Their valour has declined, their discipline is relaxed, and their tumultuary array is incapable of contending with the order and weapons of modern tactics; but at the time of their institution, they possessed a decisive superiority in war; since a regular body of infantry, in constant exercise and pay, was not maintained by any of the princes of Christendom.[21]

At first these boys were torn from their homes and families only at irregular intervals—sometimes every seven years and sometimes every four—but after some time, the *devshirme* became an annual event.[22] By the time it ended, in the late seventeenth century, around two hundred thousand boys had been enslaved in this manner.[23]

The janissaries became the Ottoman Empire's most formidable warriors against Christianity. The collection of boys for this corps in some places became an annual event: Christian fathers were forced to appear in the town squares with their sons; the Muslims took the strongest and brightest young men, who never saw their homes again unless they happened to be part of a Muslim fighting force sent to that area.

The Christians in the West, if they knew about this at all, were unmoved either by the *devshirme* or by the ongoing plight of the Christians in the East. For all too many, the Great Schism overrode all other considerations and militated against a sense of perspective. Even the great Renaissance scholar and poet Petrarch wrote in the 1360s to Pope Urban V: "The Osmanlis are merely enemies, but the schismatic Greeks are worse than enemies."[24]

And so the Muslims were in Europe to stay, and they continued their jihad to expand their European domains. With Europe disunited and distracted, and the Byzantines essentially their vassals, they were able to seize ever-larger tracts of European land: Greece, Bulgaria, Serbia, Macedonia, Albania, Croatia, and more.

The Vassal Byzantine Emperors

In 1362 in Adrianople, which he renamed Edirne, Murad proclaimed himself the caliph of all the Muslims. It would take over a century for this claim to gain significant traction, but ultimately the Ottoman caliphate would be the last one to command the allegiance of a significant percentage of Muslims worldwide.

Like Orkhan before him, Murad delighted in reminding John V Paleologus of his vassal status. When John's son Andronicus formed an alliance with Murad's son Sauzes (Gibbon said they had "an intimate and guilty friendship") and both rebelled against their fathers, Murad unhesitatingly had Sauzes blinded and demanded that John do the same with Andronicus.[25] The emperor, said Gibbon, "trembled and obeyed," but ensured that the operation was performed so ineptly that Andronicus ended up blind in only one eye.[26]

On June 15, 1389, the jihadis engaged Christian forces in battle at Kosovo. As in the early days of jihad, the Muslims prevailed against a stronger, larger force of Serbs and Bulgarians, burning June 15 into the Serbian national consciousness as a day of mourning forever after. The jihad force was composed largely of janissaries. Said Gibbon:

> The Janizaries fought with the zeal of proselytes against their idolatrous countrymen; and in the battle of Cossova [Kosovo], the league and independence of the Sclavonian tribes was finally crushed. As the conqueror walked over the field, he observed that the greatest part of the slain consisted of beardless youths; and listened to the flattering reply of his vizier, that age and wisdom would have taught them not to oppose his irresistible arms.[27]

The fulsome praise was premature. As Murad traversed the bloody battleground, stepping over the corpses, a Serbian soldier suddenly appeared and stabbed him before his men could react. At the moment of his great triumph, he was dead.

But, of course, the jihad in Eastern Europe and against the Byzantines continued. Perhaps anticipating further inroads against the Byzantines, Murad's successor, Bayezid I, bestowed upon himself the title Sultan of Rum, that is, of the Roman Empire, and played the various claimants to the Byzantine imperial crown against each other, seeking always to weaken them all, and ultimately to subvert the small remnants of the Christian empire altogether.[28] To remind the Byzantines that they were vassals of the sultan, Bayezid demanded that John V Paleologus' son Manuel live at his court. John had to comply, and at the sultan's court, Manuel was subjected to regular mockery and humiliation.[29] When John began work to strengthen the walls of Constantinople, Bayezid forced him to stop almost immediately by threatening to have Manuel blinded.[30]

When John V Paleologus died in 1390, which some attributed to the constant humiliations to which Bayezid had subjected him, Manuel managed to escape from the sultan's court and take his place as Emperor Manuel II Paleologus. Bayezid continued to taunt him from afar, reminding him that by this time his "imperial" holdings consisted of little more than the city of Constantinople itself. He forced Manuel to set up an area in Constantinople where Turkish merchants could hawk their wares, as well as, more ominously, erect a mosque staffed by a *cadi*, a judge of Islamic law.[31] He even demanded, and received, Manuel's agreement to set aside a quarter of the city to be settled by Muslims.[32]

In 1391, he forced Manuel, as his vassal, to march with him into central Asia Minor in order to fight the Isfendiyarids, another Muslim dynasty that controlled part of the territory south of the Black Sea. Manuel wrote from this desolate area and revealed his own desolation:

> Certainly the Romans had a name for the small plain where we are now when they lived and ruled here…. There are many cities here, but they lack what constitutes the true splendor of a city…that is, human beings. Most now lie in ruins…not even the names have survived…. I cannot tell you exactly where we are…. It is hard to bear all this…the scarcity of supplies, the severity of winter and the sickness which has struck down many of our men…[have] greatly depressed me…. It is unbearable…to be unable to see anything, hear anything, do anything during all this time which could somehow…lift our spirit…. The blame lies with the present state of affairs, not to mention the individual [i.e. Bayezid] whose fault they are.[33]

To forestall help coming to the Byzantines from Hungary or others in Europe, Bayezid worked to strengthen the Ottoman position in southeastern Europe, conquering Thessaly and Bulgaria in 1393. In 1394 he began a new siege of Constantinople, which turned out to be the longest ever, lasting eight years. Bayezid summoned Manuel and some key members of the Byzantine imperial court to his presence, planning to kill them all; most of them, however, managed to get out alive, including the emperor himself, who thereafter ignored all of the sultan's summonses to appear.[34]

At Nicopolis in western Greece in 1396, Bayezid defeated a force of a hundred thousand Christian Crusaders that had been gathered by

King Sigismund of Hungary. Flush with victory, Bayezid boasted that he would soon lay siege to Buda in Hungary, and then move on to conquer Germany and Italy for Allah, finally putting a cap to it all by feeding his horse with a bushel of oats placed on the altar of St. Peter's in the Vatican.[35] But instead, the would-be conqueror of Europe suffered an attack of gout and had to return home.

Tamerlane versus Bayezid

Manuel tried to get help from everywhere he possibly could. A hundred years earlier, there had been talk of a Christian alliance with the Mongols against the Muslims; nothing had come of it, but maybe it wasn't too late: in 1399, Manuel appealed to Timur the Lame, or Tamerlane, the Mongol conqueror of Central Asia.[36] The Mongols had converted to Islam in the early fourteenth century, and Tamerlane was a zealous jihadi. However, he had not hesitated to fight against the Tughlaq sultanate of Delhi, and he regarded the Ottomans in the same way, writing with stinging contempt to Bayezid:

> Dost thou not know, that the greatest part of Asia is subject to our arms and our laws? That our invincible forces extend from one sea to the other? That the potentates of the earth form a line before our gate? And that we have compelled Fortune herself to watch over the prosperity of our empire. What is the foundation of thy insolence and folly? Thou hast fought some battles in the woods of Anatolia; contemptible trophies! Thou hast obtained some victories over the Christians of Europe; thy sword was blessed by the apostle of God; and thy obedience to the precept of the Koran, in waging war against the infidels, is the sole consideration that prevents us from destroying thy country, the frontier and bulwark of the Moslem world. Be wise in time; reflect; repent; and avert the thunder of our vengeance, which is yet suspended over thy head. Thou art no more than a pismire; why wilt thou seek to provoke the elephants? Alas! They will trample thee under their feet.[37]

Bayezid was used to terrorizing and lording it over the emperors of the Romans; he wasn't used to being addressed the way he addressed them. He wrote back to Tamerlane with his own boasts:

> Thy armies are innumerable: be they so; but what are the arrows of the flying Tartar against the cimeters [scimitars] and battle-axes of my firm and invincible Janizaries? I will guard the princes who have implored my protection: seek them in my tents. The cities of Arzingan and Erzeroum are mine; and unless the tribute be duly paid, I will demand the arrears under the walls of Tauris and Sultania.[38]

In his rage and wounded pride, Bayezid could not resist adding a personal insult:

> If I fly from thy arms, may *my* wives be thrice divorced from my bed: but if thou hast not courage to meet me in the field, mayest thou again receive *thy* wives after they have thrice endured the embraces of a stranger.[39]

It was the ultimate insult one jihad warrior could give to another: the implication that he was not man enough either to fight or to hold on to his wives. Tamerlane answered on the battlefield, invading Asia Minor and soundly defeating Bayezid at Ankara in 1402.[40]

Tamerlane then granted clemency to his beaten rival, even as (in another move characteristic of jihadis throughout history) he blamed him for the conflict:

> Alas! The decree of fate is now accomplished by your own fault; it is the web which you have woven, the thorns of the tree which yourself have planted. I wished to spare, and even to assist, the champion of the Moslems; you braved our threats; you despised our friendship; you forced us to enter your kingdom with our invincible armies. Behold the event. Had you vanquished, I am not ignorant of the fate which you reserved for myself and my troops. But I disdain to retaliate: your life and honour are secure; and I shall express my gratitude to God by my clemency to man.[41]

Tamerlane's clemency to Bayezid was more proclaimed than actual. Out-doing Bayezid's own humiliation of the Byzantine emperors, Tamerlane had Bayezid displayed in an iron cage, and used the Ottoman sultan as an ottoman, as well as a mounting block when he got on his horse. He commandeered Bayezid's harem, and perhaps remembering Bayezid's boast about his wives, forced one of the sultan's wives to serve at his table while naked. After enduring eight months of this, Bayezid died.[42]

When Bayezid died, Tamerlane was in Asia, on his way to bring the jihad to China. Given the news that Bayezid had died, he wept and claimed that he had planned to restore Bayezid to the throne, with great-er grandeur than ever.[43]

Last-ditch Attempts to Save the Byzantine Empire

The claim was easy to make when Bayezid was dead. In any case, Tamer-lane's desire to destroy all rival Muslim leaders won for the Byzantine Empire a bit of much-needed time, although Tamerlane ensured that no one would think he was allying with the Christians when he also besieged and conquered Smyrna, defeating a force of Christian Knights Hospitaller. Ships arrived to reinforce the knights after Tamerlane had already entered the city and laid waste; the great commander ordered that his catapults be fitted with the bloody severed heads of the knights the jihadis had killed inside Smyrna. After a barrage of these heads filled the sky and hit the men on the ships, the reinforcing vessels turned back in horror and disarray.[44]

Emperor Manuel had in 1399 embarked upon an extensive four-year tour of Western Europe, meeting with the pope and with the crowned kings of England, France, and elsewhere. Lofty promises were made, but little actual help was forthcoming, in part because the Western Europe-ans were keen for Manuel to accept the authority of the pope, which the emperor could not do without alienating a substantial number of his own people. Manuel said this of the Ottomans to his chamberlain Phranzes:

> Our last resource is their fear of our union with the Latins,
> of the warlike nations of the West, who may arm for our

relief and for their destruction. As often as you are threatened by the miscreants, present this danger before their
eyes. Propose a council; consult on the means; but ever delay and avoid the convocation of an assembly, which cannot
tend either to our spiritual or temporal emolument. The
Latins are proud; the Greeks are obstinate; neither party
will recede or retract; and the attempt of a perfect union
will confirm the schism, alienate the churches, and leave us,
without hope or defence, at the mercy of the Barbarians.[45]

Yet Manuel kept trying. In 1424, when he was seventy-four years old,
he yet again sought help from the Hungarians against the Turks and
was, once again, unsuccessful. The Ottomans forced him to agree to pay
tribute to the sultan, reinforcing the status of the Byzantine Empire as a
mere vassal of the Ottoman sultanate.

Manuel II Paleologus Becomes Notorious

Manuel II Paleologus, little remembered after his death, shot to fame
nearly six hundred years later, when on September 12, 2006, in Regensburg, Germany, Pope Benedict XVI dared to enunciate some truths
about Islam that proved to be unpopular and unwelcome among Muslims worldwide. Most notoriously, the pope quoted Manuel on Islam:
"Show me just what Muhammad brought that was new, and there you
will find things only evil and inhuman, such as his command to spread
by the sword the faith he preached."[46]

Manuel was not speaking of an abstract threat he had read about in
books. Every day of his life, he was confronted by the ever-advancing
and implacable menace of jihad. All his life, he had experienced Islam
and jihad firsthand, as well as the contempt that Islam mandated for
non-Muslims: "Muhammad is the apostle of Allah. Those who follow
him are merciful to one another, harsh to unbelievers" (Qur'an 48:29).
His life was many times in imminent danger from the warriors of jihad.
He no doubt heard of the misery of many Christians who, because
of the Ottoman conquests, found themselves subject to harsh rulers
who believed they had a divine mandate to subjugate the Christians
and relegate them to second-class status in society, if not death. In the

twenty-first century, Manuel's words were denounced as "Islamophobic"; yet, no one among his contemporaries would assert something so naïve and unrealistic.

Pope Benedict also quoted Manuel saying: "God is not pleased by blood—and not acting reasonably is contrary to God's nature. Faith is born of the soul, not the body. Whoever would lead someone to faith needs the ability to speak well and to reason properly, without violence and threats.... To convince a reasonable soul, one does not need a strong arm, or weapons of any kind, or any other means of threatening a person with death."[47]

Benedict's quotations of the long-dead emperor were not received by reasonable souls, at least among the descendants of those who had menaced Manuel II Paleologus and his people throughout that unfortunate emperor's lifetime. Muslims rioted and, in several countries, murdered Christians who had, of course, nothing whatsoever to do with what Pope Benedict had said. Several days after the Regensburg address, a group of Muslim clerics in Gaza issued an invitation to the pope to convert to Islam, or else: "We want to use the words of the Prophet Muhammad and tell the pope: '*Aslim Taslam*'"—that is, embrace Islam and you will be safe.[48] The implication, of course, was that the one to whom this "invitation" was addressed would *not* be safe if he declined to convert.

Many Christians in Eastern Europe would receive that "invitation" in the years following Tamerlane's siege of Smyrna. But the Byzantines made one more attempt to stave off the inevitable when they agreed to travel to Italy for another attempt at reunion with the Latin Church. The council convened in Ferrara in April 1438, with the emperor John VIII Paleologus and the patriarch Joseph II of Constantinople present, heading up a large Byzantine delegation. Their appearance was impressive, but the Byzantines were in desperate straits and had no bargaining position at all. As the council's deliberations went on, transferred to Florence in January 1439 to avoid the Black Plague, the Byzantine delegation gave in on every one of the theological issues that had formally divided the two Churches since the Great Schism of 1054. Finally they agreed to a reunion with the Latin Church based essentially on acceptance of all the Western Church's doctrines.

One Byzantine bishop present, Mark of Ephesus, refused to go along and argued strenuously against the council's conclusions; he proved to be an apt representative of the popular feeling about the council back in Constantinople, where it was generally considered illegitimate and never gained significant support among the people. Lukas Notaras, megadux of the Byzantine Empire—that is, commander-in-chief of the imperial navy and de facto prime minister—summed up a widespread opinion with the succinct phrase "Better the turban of the Sultan than the tiara of the Pope."[49]

It may seem incredible considering the carnage that followed the Muslim conquest that anyone could have seriously held such a view, but Lukas Notaras said this *before* the Muslim conquest of Constantinople. The Crusader sacking of Constantinople in 1204 was still a fresh memory for many Byzantines, and the subsequent establishment of a Latin patriarchate, combined with the intransigence of the Latins at Florence, led many Byzantines to believe that the sultan would at least allow them to maintain their religion and culture, while the pope would not—a not unreasonable surmise. Many Byzantine emperors had made accords with the Ottomans. No doubt many believed that the jihadis were a problem that had been managed in the past and could continue to be managed, while the pope's demands were absolute.

And so the reunion that was concluded at the Council of Florence, although officially proclaimed, never gained significant traction in the East. Nor did the expected military help make any difference. Pope Eugenius IV did call a new Crusade, but there was no enthusiasm for it in Western Europe. The Eastern European states of Poland, Wallachia, and Hungary did manage to assemble a Crusader army of thirty thousand men, only to see it crushed by Murad II and his jihadis at Varna in Hungary in November 1444. King Ladislas of Hungary was killed in the battle; his head was sent back to Bursa, the Asia Minor city that had served as the first capital of the Ottoman sultanate, where it was carried through the streets as a trophy of the Muslims' victory over the Crusaders.[50]

The Fall of Constantinople

In 1451, Murad II's son succeeded his father as the sultan Mehmet II and brought to the sultanate his intense desire to be the conqueror of Constantinople. It wasn't long before he got his wish. After over seven hundred years of trying, the warriors of jihad finally entered the great city on May 29, 1453. When they did, they made the streets run with rivers of blood. Historian Steven Runciman notes that the Muslims "slew everyone that they met in the streets, men, women, and children without discrimination. The blood ran in rivers down the steep streets from the heights of Petra toward the Golden Horn. But soon the lust for slaughter was assuaged. The soldiers realized that captives and precious objects would bring them greater profit."[51]

Muslims raided monasteries and convents, emptying them of their inhabitants, and plundered private houses. They entered the Hagia Sophia, which for nearly a thousand years had been the grandest church in Christendom. The faithful had gathered within its hallowed walls to pray during the city's last agony. The Muslims halted the celebration of *Orthros* (morning prayer), while the priests, according to legend, took the sacred vessels and disappeared into the cathedral's eastern wall, through which they shall return to complete the divine service one day. The Muslims then killed the elderly and weak and led the rest off into slavery.

The Byzantine scholar Bessarion wrote to the Doge of Venice in July 1453, saying that Constantinople had been

> ...sacked by the most inhuman barbarians and the most savage enemies of the Christian faith, by the fiercest of wild beasts. The public treasure has been consumed, private wealth has been destroyed, the temples have been stripped of gold, silver, jewels, the relics of the saints, and other most precious ornaments. Men have been butchered like cattle, women abducted, virgins ravished, and children snatched from the arms of their parents.[52]

Islamic tradition held that Muhammad himself had prophesied the Muslim conquest of Constantinople, as well as of Rome itself, which remains an object of jihadi desire to this day. The modern-day Sheikh

Yusuf al-Qaradawi, in writing about "signs of the victory of Islam," referred to a *hadith*:

> The Prophet Muhammad was asked: "What city will be conquered first, Constantinople or Romiyya [Rome]?" He answered: "The city of Hirqil [ruled by the Byzantine emperor Heraclius] will be conquered first"—that is, Constantinople—Romiyya is the city called today 'Rome,' the capital of Italy. The city of Hirqil [that is, Constantinople] was conquered by the young 23-year-old Ottoman Muhammad bin Morad, known in history as Muhammad the Conqueror, in 1453. The other city, Romiyya, remains, and we hope and believe [that it too will be conquered]. This means that Islam will return to Europe as a conqueror and victor, after being expelled from it twice—once from the South, from Andalusia, and a second time from the East, when it knocked several times on the door of Athens."[53]

When the slaughter and pillage was finished, Mehmet II ordered an Islamic scholar to mount the high pulpit of the Hagia Sophia and declare that there was no God but Allah, and Muhammad was his prophet. The magnificent old church was turned into a mosque; hundreds of other churches in Constantinople and elsewhere suffered the same fate. Millions of Christians joined the ranks of the *dhimmis*; others were enslaved, and many were killed. Mehmet went from the great cathedral-turned-mosque to the Sacred Palace, which had been considerably damaged and looted. As he walked through the ruined building, he recited a line from a Persian poem: "The spider weaves the curtains in the palace of the Caesars; the owl calls the watches in Afrasiab's towers."[54]

While the conquered city was still smoldering, Mehmet turned his mind away from war and looked for some relaxation. He sent a eunuch to the home of Lukas Notaras' home, demanding that the megadux send him his fourteen-year-old son, renowned for his appearance, for the Sultan's delectation. Notaras refused, whereupon the sultan, his evening spoiled, furiously ordered the boy killed, along with his brother-in-law and father. Notaras asked that the two young men be killed first, so that they wouldn't lose heart seeing him killed and give in to the sultan's immoral desires. Mehmet obliged him. Once all three were beheaded, Mehmet ordered that their heads be placed on his banquet table.[55]

Jihad causes the Renaissance

One consequence of the fall of Constantinople was the emigration of Greek intellectuals to Western Europe. Muslim territorial expansion at Byzantine expense led so many Greeks to seek refuge in the West that Western universities became filled with Platonists and Aristotelians to an unprecedented extent. This led to the rediscovery of classical philosophy and literature and to an intellectual and cultural flowering the like of which the world had never seen (and still hasn't).

The Jihad in Eastern Europe

If the jihadis had had their way, however, those Greek refugees would not have been safe even in their new homes. Once Constantinople and the Byzantine Empire had fallen, the jihadis turned their sights again to the rest of Europe. First Mehmet cleared Asia Minor of any resistance to his rule. When his own mother, a Syrian Christian slave, pleaded with him not to attack the city of Trebizond, which had become a center of opposition to the Ottomans, Mehmet replied: "Mother, the sword of Islam is in my hand."[56]

The rulers of Europe knew this. Even though it had been a very long time coming, the fall of Constantinople was a profound shock to Western Europe. There were immediate calls for a new Crusade to wrest the great city from the warriors of jihad. In 1455, the new pope, Calixtus III, took a solemn oath at his consecration:

> I, Pope Calixtus III, promise and vow to the Holy Trinity, Father, Son, and Holy Spirit, to the Ever-Virgin Mother of God, to the Holy Apostles Peter and Paul, and to all the heavenly host, that I will do everything in my power, even if need be with the sacrifice of my life, aided by the counsel of my worthy brethren, to reconquer Constantinople, which in

punishment for the sin of man has been taken and ruined by Mahomet II, the son of the devil and the enemy of our Crucified Redeemer.

Further, I vow to deliver the Christians languishing in slavery, to exalt the true Faith, and to extirpate the diabolical sect of the reprobate and faithless Mahomet in the East. For there the light of faith is almost completely extinguished. If I forget thee, O Jerusalem, let my right hand be forgotten. Let my tongue cleave to my jaws, if I do not remember thee. If I make not Jerusalem the beginning of my joy, God and His holy Gospel help me. Amen.[57]

A Crusader force assembled and defeated the jihadis at Belgrade in 1456, but that was as far as it was able to get. Constantinople was securely in the hands of Islam, and the warriors of jihad were advancing. In 1461, Mehmet brought the sword of Islam against the Wallachian prince Vlad Dracula, whose surname meant "son of the dragon," after his father, who was known as The Dragon, or Dracul.

At one point, Dracula's forces invaded Ottoman territory and then retreated; when Mehmet's forces entered the area in Targoviste in modern-day Romania, they encountered the horrifying sight of twenty thousand corpses impaled on stakes, Vlad Dracula's favorite method of execution—which earned him the name Vlad the Impaler. Mehmet, appalled, pursued Dracula and finally drove him into exile; upon this victory, Mehmet's commanders presented him with the gift of two thousand heads of Dracula's men.[58]

The jihadis proceeded on to Bosnia. King Stephen of Bosnia wrote to Pope Pius II that the sultan's "insatiable thirst for domination knows no limits." Mehmet, said Stephen, wanted not just Bosnia but Hungary and Venice, adding, "He also speaks frequently of Rome, which he dreams of attaining."[59] The renowned warrior Skanderbeg held out fiercely in Albania, such that when he died in 1467, Mehmet exulted: "At last Europe and Asia belong to me! Unhappy Christianity. It has lost both its sword and its buckler."[60]

Mehmet's joy was a trifle premature. Venice fought fiercely against the Ottomans and dashed the sultan's hopes of jihad conquest of Europe.

He never got an opportunity to besiege Rome. But the warriors of jihad were patient.

Before he died in 1481, only forty-nine years old, Mehmet enacted a law designed to ensure the ongoing stability of his domains: "For the welfare of the state, the one of my sons to whom God grants the Sultanate may lawfully put his brothers to death. This has the approval of a majority of jurists."[61]

II. *DHIMMI* OPPRESSION IN EGYPT AND NORTH AFRICA

Egypt was outside Ottoman domains during this period, ruled by the Mamluks, a class of slave warriors, from around 1250. The Mamluks were determined to reassert the humiliations of the *dhimma* over the non-Muslims in their domains. The fourteenth-century Muslim historian Ibn Naqqash recorded that in 1301, the vizier of Gharb in North Africa undertook the pilgrimage to Mecca, and on his way stopped in Cairo to visit the Mamluk sultan al-Malik an-Nasir and several other high dignitaries, including the emir Rukn ad-Din Baybar al-Jashangir, "who offered him magnificent presents and received him with the greatest distinction."[62]

But amid all the pleasantness of the visit, the vizier had a complaint. He was not happy with what he had seen in Egypt, where the *dhimmi* Jews and Christians were "attired in the most elegant clothes" and "rode on mules, mares, and expensive horses."[63] Even worse, they were "considered worthy of being employed in the most important offices, thus gaining authority over the Muslims."[64]

In Gharb, by contrast, the Jews and Christians were "maintained with constraints of humiliation and degradation. Thus they were not permitted to ride on horseback, nor to be employed in the public administration."[65]

The emir Rukn and several others were impressed, and "unanimously declared," according to Ibn Naqqash, "that if similar conditions were to prevail in Egypt this would greatly enhance the [Muslim] religion. Consequently, they assembled the Christians and Jews on Thursday, 20 Rajab, and informed them that they would no longer be employed either in the public administration or in the service of the emirs. They were to change their turbans: blue ones for the Christians, who were moreover to wear a special belt [*zunnar*] around their waists; and yellow turbans for the Jews."[66]

The Jewish and Christian leaders appealed and even offered substantial sums for the rescinding of these new decrees, but to no avail. And there was more. Ibn Naqqash continued: "The churches of *Misr* [old Cairo] and Cairo were closed and their portals were sealed after having been nailed up."[67] The new rules were swiftly enforced: "By the twenty-second of Rajab all the Jews were wearing yellow turbans and the Christians blue ones; and if they rode on horseback, they were obliged to ride with one of their legs bent under them. Next, the *dhimmis* were dismissed from the public administration and the functions that they occupied in the service of the emirs. They were then prohibited to ride horses or mules. Consequently, many of them were converted to Islam."[68]

The sultan extended some of these rules to all of his domains. According to Ibn Naqqash, "The Sultan gave orders to all the provinces recently added to his states and in which there were houses owned by Jews and Christians, in order that all those that were higher than the surrounding Muslim abodes should be demolished to their height. Furthermore all the *dhimmis* who owned a shop near that of a Muslim, should lower their *mastaba* [ground floor] so that those of the Muslims would be higher. Moreover, he recommended vigilance in the observance of the distinctive badges [*ghiyar*] in accordance with ancient custom."[69]

As time went by, however, these laws were once again relaxed, as the complex realities of human relationships were always in tension with the cold statute. But since they were part of Islamic law, they could be reasserted more easily than they could be relaxed. In 1419, the Egyptian Mamluk sultan Malik Safyad-din summoned the Coptic pope Gabriel V to his presence. "While remaining standing," recounted the fifteenth-century Muslim historian Ibn Taghribirdi, Gabriel "received reproaches and blows and was berated by the sultan on account of the humiliations to which the Muslims had been subjected by the prince of the Abyssinians," although it was wildly implausible that a subjugated people would have dared to subject their overlords to such treatment. Nonetheless, Gabriel was "even threatened with death."

The real problem was that the Christians were no longer observing the *dhimmi* restrictions. Malik summoned the chief of the Cairo police and reprimanded him for the "contempt" the Christians had toward the laws requiring that they wear distinctive dress. But attire was the least of the Christians' problems. Ibn Taghribirdi continued:

> After a long discussion between the doctors of the Law and the sultan on this subject, it was decided that none of these infidels would be employed in government offices, nor by the emirs; neither would they escape the measures taken to maintain them in a state of humiliation. There-upon the sultan summoned Al-Akram Fada'il, the Christian, the vizier's secretary, who had been imprisoned for several days; he was beaten, stripped of his clothes, and ignominiously paraded through the streets of Cairo in the company of the chief of police, who proclaimed, "This is the reward for Christians employed in government of-fices!" After all this, he was thrown back into prison.
>
> So thoroughly did the sultan carry out these measures, that nowhere in Egypt was a Christian to be found em-ployed in the administration. These infidels, as well as the Jews, were obliged to remain at home, decrease the volume of their turbans, and shorten their sleeves. All were prevent-ed from riding on donkeys, with the result that when the [common] people saw a mounted Christian, they attacked him and confiscated his donkey and all that he had....
>
> Thus the edict issued by this prince is tantamount to a second conquest of Egypt; in this manner was Islam exalted and infidelity humiliated, and nothing is more praiseworthy in the eyes of Allah.[70]

The humiliation was most vividly enforced during the payment of the *jizya*. In the latter half of the fifteenth century, the Berber Islamic schol-ar Muhammad al-Maghili, who was responsible for the expulsion of the Jews from the city of Tlemcen and the destruction of the synagogue there, reiterated the manner in which the *dhimmis* were to make their payments:

On the day of payment they shall be assembled in a public place like the *suq*. They should be standing there waiting in the lowest and dirtiest place. The acting officials representing the Law shall be placed above them and shall adopt a threatening attitude so that it seems to them, as well as to the others, that our object is to degrade them by pretending to take their possessions. They will realize that we are doing them a favor [again] in accepting from them the *jizya* and letting them [thus] go free. Then they shall be dragged one by one [to the official responsible] for the exacting of payment. When paying, the *dhimmi* will receive a blow and will be thrust aside so that he will think that he has escaped the sword through this [insult]. This is the way that the friends of the Lord, of the first and last generations will act toward their infidel enemies, for might belongs to Allah, to His Prophet, and to the Believers.[71]

Thus it was throughout history in the various Islamic domains: periods of relaxation of the *dhimmi* laws would be followed by periods of their reassertion, often in the context of revivalist movements that blamed the troubles of the Muslims on the prosperity of the *dhimmis*, and on Allah's anger that they had not been put in their place.

III. THE RAVAGING OF INDIA

Despoiling India for the Abbasids

By the dawn of the fourteenth century, the warriors of jihad had managed to destroy virtually all of the renowned Hindu temples within their domains in India and had plundered the treasures of those temples for their own personal enrichment and the endowment of the mosques they constructed.[72] Taxes were high and raids frequent. Consequently, the Muslim rulers of India had at their disposal almost unimaginable wealth. In 1343, therefore, when the Delhi sultan Muhammad ibn Tughlaq attempted to shore up the legitimacy of his rule by attaching it to the authority of the Abbasid caliphate—even though by this time the Abbasid caliph al-Hakim was almost powerless, exiled from Baghdad, and residing in virtual impotence in Cairo—he was able to send al-Hakim extraordinary gifts. The Muslim court historian Ziyauddin Barani remarked drily: "So great was the faith of the Sultan in the Abbasid Khalifas that he would have sent all his treasures in Delhi to Egypt, had it not been for the fear of robbers."[73]

When an emissary of the Abbasids visited Delhi, Muhammad ibn Tughlaq showered him with gifts as well, including a million tankahs, which was equivalent to four hundred thousand dinars, as well as land, gold, silver, sex slaves, and robes that had in place of buttons "pearls as large as big hazel nuts."[74] The emissary was able to witness the brutal efficiency of the Delhi sultan's rule, for executions were carried out right in front of the palace, and were so frequent that the entrances to the palaces were often blocked by corpses.[75]

Muhammad ibn Tughlaq amassed all of this wealth at the expense of his Hindu subjects. At one point, recounts a contemporary historian, Muhammad ibn Tughlaq "led forth his army to ravage Hindostan. He laid the country waste from Kanauj to Dalmau [on the Ganges, in the Rai Baréli District, Oudh], and every person that fell into his hands he slew. Many of the inhabitants fled and took refuge in the jungles, but the Sultan had the jungles surrounded, and every individual that was captured was killed."[76]

Muhammad's successor, Firuz Shah Tughlaq, exulted that "the greatest and best of honours that I obtained through God's mercy was, that by my obedience and piety, and friendliness and submission to the Khalifa, the representative of the holy Prophet, my authority was confirmed, for it is by his [the caliph's] sanction that the power of the kings is assured, and no king is secure until he has submitted himself to the Khalifa, and has received a confirmation from the sacred throne."[77]

Bringing Islam to the Hindus

Secure in this legitimacy, Firuz Shah Tughlaq resumed the jihad against the Hindus, targeting in 1360 one of the few remaining grand Hindu temples, the temple of Jagannath at Puri in southeastern India. According to Barani's *Tarikh-e Firuz Shahi* (*History of Firuz Shah*):

Allah who is the only true God and has no other emanation, endowed the king of Islam with the strength to destroy this ancient shrine on the eastern sea-coast and to plunge it into he sea, and after its destruction he [Firuz Shah] ordered the image of Jagannath to be perforated, and disgraced it by casting it down on the ground. They dug out other idols which were worshipped by the polytheists in the kingdom of Jajnagar and overthrew them as they did the image of Jagannath, for being laid in front of the mosques along the path of the Sunnis and the way of the *musallis* [Muslim congregation for *namaz* (prayers)] and stretched them in front of the portals of every mosque, so that the body and sides of the images might be trampled at the time of ascent and descent, entrance and exit, by the shoes on the feet of the Muslims.[78]

The jihadis were merciless. After this, Barani recounted, they proceeded to a nearby island, where "nearly 100,000 men of Jajnagar had taken refuge with their women, children, kinsmen and relations."[79] But the Muslims transformed "the island into a basin of blood by the massacre of the unbelievers.... Women with babies and pregnant ladies were haltered, manacled, fettered and enchained, and pressed as slaves into service at the house of every soldier."[80] At Nagarkot, Firuz Shah Tughlaq "broke the idols of Jvalamukhi, mixed their fragments with the flesh of cows and hung them in nosebags round the necks of the Brahmins. He sent the principal idol as trophy to Medina."[81]

Firuz Shah, said Barani, "made the laws of the Prophet his guide."[82] Accordingly, when the sultan discovered that Hindus were not passively accepting the destruction of their temples, but were building new ones, he was enraged. "Under divine guidance," he recalled later, "I destroyed these edifices, and I killed those leaders of infidelity who seduced others into error, and the lower orders I subjected to stripes and chastisement, until this abuse was entirely abolished."[83] At Kohana, he had some Hindus who had dared to construct a new temple executed in public, "as a warning that no *zimmi* could follow such wicked practices in a Musalman country."[84] He treated a Hindu sect with similar harshness: "I cut off the heads of the elders of this sect, and imprisoned and banished the rest, so that their abominable practices were put an end to."[85] After discovering that the Brahmins had been exempted from paying the jizya by previous Muslim rulers, he commanded that they pay, and held firm even through a Brahmin hunger strike.[86]

At Maluh, near Delhi, he discovered that even some "graceless" Muslims were attending a Hindu religious festival. "I ordered that the leaders of these people and the promoters of this abomination should be put to death. I forbade the infliction of any severe punishment on the Hindus in general, but I destroyed their idol temples and instead thereof raised mosques."[87]

Firuz Shah was likewise zealous for Sunni Islam, recounting that "the sect of Shias, also called Rawdfiz, had endeavoured to make proselytes."[88] The Delhi sultan began a jihad against them: "I seized them all and I convicted them of their errors and perversions. On the most zealous I inflicted capital punishment [siyasat], and the rest I visited with censure [tazir], and threats of public punishment. Their books I burnt in public and by the grace of God the influence of this sect was entirely suppressed."[89] Upon discovering that a Muslim was claiming to be the Mahdi, he demanded that the "doctors learned in the holy Law" kill him forthwith; they complied. "For this good action," said Firuz Shah piously, "I hope to receive future reward."[90]

Under the pressure of the relentless persecution they suffered, many Hindus converted to Islam, as Firuz Shah later recalled with satisfaction: "I encouraged my infidel subjects to embrace the religion of the prophet, and I proclaimed that every one who repeated the creed and became a Musalman should be exempt from the jizya or poll-tax. Information of this came to the ears of the people at large, and great numbers of Hindus presented themselves, and were admitted to the honour of Islam. Thus they came forward day by day from every quarter, and, adopting the faith, were exonerated from the jizya, and were favoured with presents and honours."[91]

Meanwhile, there was no mercy to be accorded to the captive people. In 1391, the Muslims of Gujarat complained to Muhammad Shah, the son and second successor of Firuz Shah as Tughlaq sultan of Delhi, about a local governor. His crime? Being too lenient with the Hindus. Muhammad Shah immediately removed the wayward governor from office and replaced him with Muzaffar Khan, a man who was less likely to be pliant.[92] According to the *Tabqat i-Akbari*, a sixteenth-century history of India written by the Muslim historian Nizamuddin Ahmed, the Hindus of the Kingdom of Idar began a full-scale revolt, whereupon "the armies of Zafar Khan occupied the Kingdom of Idar and started plundering and destroying it. They levelled with the ground whatever temple they found."[93] Pursuing the fleeing Raja of Idar to the fortress of Bijanagar, "in the morning Zafar Khan entered the fort and, after expressing his gratefulness to Allah, and destroying the temples, he appointed officers in the fort."[94]

Anointing himself Muzaffar Shah, Sultan of Gujarat, independent of the Tughlaqs in Delhi, he proceeded to Somnath in 1395, where the Hindus had rebuilt the temple that Muslims had previously destroyed.[95] "On the way," according to the *Tabqat i-Akbari*, "he made Rajputs food for his sword and demolished whatever temple he saw at any place. When he arrived at Somnat, he got the temple burnt and the idol of Somnat broken. He made a slaughter of the infidels and laid waste the city."[96] Enraged at what he called the "impudence" of the Hindus, he killed many of them, had a mosque built on the site of the temple, and appointed officials to enforce the Sharia.[97]

In 1401, when the Hindus had the temerity to build a temple there again, he returned and once again tore down the temple and had a mosque built.[98] Some Hindus resisted; according to Nizamuddin Ahmed, the Muslim warrior Azam Humayun "reached that place speedily and he slaughtered that group. Those who survived took shelter in the fort of the port at Dip [Diu]. After some time, he conquered that place as well, slaughtered that group also, and got their leaders trampled under the feet of elephants. He got the temples demolished and a Jami Masjid constructed"—that is, the main mosque for the area. "Having appointed a qazi, mufti and other guardians of Shariah, he returned to the capital."[99]

Tamerlane in India

Meanwhile, the Mongols had designs upon India as well. In 1398, Tamerlane, heedless of the authority that the Abbasid caliphs had bestowed upon the Tughlaqs, invaded the Indian subcontinent. His object was not, at least initially, to challenge the power of the Delhi sultanate. An erudite man, Tamerlane is unusual among the great Muslim warriors of jihad in leaving behind an autobiography. In it he made clear, as had other jihad leaders in India before him, that the invasion was all about Islam. He quoted the Qur'an: "O Prophet, fight against the disbelievers and the hypocrites and be harsh upon them." (9:73) Then he explained his own motives:

> My object in the invasion of Hindustan is to lead a cam-
> paign against the infidels, to convert them to the true faith
> according to the command of the Prophet (on whom be the
> blessing of God!), to purify the land from the defilement of
> [misbelief] and polytheism, and overthrow the temples and
> idols, whereby we shall be *Ghazis* [raiders] and *Mujahids* [ji-
> hadis], champions and soldiers of the Faith before God.[100]

Sharaf ad-Din Ali Yazdi, a fifteenth-century Persian who wrote a bi-ography of Tamerlane, observed that "the Alcoran [Qur'an] says the highest dignity man can attain is that of making war in person against the enemies of his religion. Mahomet [Muhammad] advises the same thing, according to the tradition of the mussulman [Muslim] doctors: wherefore the great Temur always strove to exterminate the infidels, as much to acquire that glory, as to signalise himself by the greatness of his conquests."[101]

Tamerlane also expressed the hope that "the army of Islam might gain something by plundering the wealth and valuables of the Hin-dus."[102] At the fortress of Kator on the Kashmir, he recounted with sat-isfaction, Tamerlane ordered the warriors of jihad to "kill all the men, to make prisoners of the women and children, and to plunder and lay waste all their property."[103] Then he "directed towers to be built on the moun-tain of the skulls of those obstinate unbelievers."[104]

At Bhatnir, he "made great slaughter," as the Qur'an directs (8:67), at a Rajput fortress. He wrote in his autobiography: "In a short space of time all the people in the fort were put to the sword, and in the course of one hour the heads of 10,000 infidels were cut off. The sword of Islam was washed in the blood of the infidels, and all the goods and effects, the treasure and the grain which for many a long year had been stored in the fort became the spoil of my soldiers. They set fire to the houses and reduced them to ashes, and they razed the buildings and the fort to the ground."[105]

Tamerlane clearly relished all of this bloodshed and thought of himself as the executor of the wrath of Allah, as commanded in the Qur'an: "Fight them; Allah will punish them by your hands." (9:14) At Sarsuti, he recounted, "all these infidel Hindus were slain, their wives and children were made prisoners and their property and their goods became the spoils of the victors."[106] At Haryana, he told his men to "plunder and destroy and kill every one whom they met."[107] The jihadis obeyed; they "plundered every village, killed the men, and carried a number of Hindu prisoners, both male and female."[108] At Delhi, the warriors of jihad took some Muslim prisoners, which was understandable, since the city was the capital of the Tughlaq's Delhi sultanate.

Tamerlane commanded that the Muslim prisoners "should be separated and saved, but the infidels should all be dispatched to hell with the proselytizing sword."[109]

Even when those prisoners had been killed, however, the immense success of Tamerlane's jihad presented him with a problem: he had a hundred thousand Hindu prisoners. As he prepared to face an army of the Tughlaqs in an internecine jihad battle, his advisors told him "that on the great day of battle these 100,000 prisoners could not be left with the baggage, and that it would be entirely opposed to the rules of war to set these idolaters and enemies of Islam at liberty."[110] Thus, "no other course remained but that of making them all food for the sword."[111] Tamerlane recalls: "I proclaimed throughout the camp that every man who had infidel prisoners should put them to death, and whoever neglected to do so should himself be executed and his property given to the informer. When this order became known to the ghazis of Islam, they drew their swords and put their prisoners to death. One hundred thousand infidels, impious idolaters, were on that day slain. Maulana Nasiruddin Umar, a counselor and man of learning who, in all his life, had never killed a sparrow, now, in execution of my order, slew with his sword fifteen idolatrous Hindus, who were his captives."[112]

Tamerlane's warriors defeated the Tughlaqs and found in Delhi that "a great number of Hindus with their wives and children, and goods and valuables, had come into the city from all the country round."[113] He ordered them to be taken captive, and their property given to the Muslims.

> Many of them [Hindus] drew their swords and resisted.... The flames of strife were thus lighted and spread through the whole city from Jahanpanah and Siri to Old Delhi, burning up all it reached. The Hindus set fire to their houses with their own hands, burned their wives and children in them and rushed into the fight and were killed.... On that day, Thursday, and all the night of Friday, nearly 15,000 Turks were engaged in slaying, plundering and destroying. When morning broke on Friday, all my army...went off to the city and thought of nothing but killing, plundering and making prisoners.... The following day, Saturday the 17th, all passed in the same way, and the spoil was so great that each man secured from fifty to a hundred prisoners, men, women, and children. There was no man who took less than twenty. The other booty was immense in rubies, diamonds, garnets, pearls, and other gems and jewels; *ashrafis*, tankas of gold and silver of the celebrated Alai coinage: vessels and silver ornaments of Hindu women were obtained in such quantities as to exceed all account. Excepting the quarter of the Sayids, the ulama and other Musulmans, the whole city was sacked.[114]

The Jihad Against China

In 1404, Tamerlane resolved to take the jihad to China, even though he had been warned by one of his envoys who had gone to Beijing that "the Emperor of China was lord of so many warriors that when his host went forth to wage war beyond the limits of his Empire, without counting those who marched with him he could leave four hundred thousand horsemen behind to guard his realm together with numerous regiments of footguards."[115]

Tamerlane was undeterred. On his way to China, he decided to subdue for Islam the Kingdom of Georgia, which he had left alone many times as he passed to and from India. His warriors found a way into the fortress of Kurtin, where, shouting *"Allahu akbar,"* they surprised and overwhelmed the Georgians. Delighted, Tamerlane rewarded these jihadis with gorgeous robes, weapons, horses, land, and a large number of sex slaves.[116]

As Tamerlane advanced in Georgia, according to a contemporary chronicler, "he plundered seven hundred towns and villages, laying waste the cultivated lands, ruining the monasteries of the Christians and razing the churches to the very foundations."[117] He continued his destruction of churches and the countryside, killing so many people that the piles of skulls became the tallest feature of the landscape. When the king of Georgia agreed to pay the *jizya*, however, it was time to move on to China.[118]

Tamerlane's biographer Yazdi compared the advance of the jihadis to the progress of medicine in the human body.

> In the same manner, God, who was pleased to purge the world, made use of a medicine which was both sweet and bitter, to wit the clemency and the wrath of the incomparable Temur; and to that effect inspired in him an ambition to conquer all Asia and to expel the several tyrants thereof. He established peace and security in this part of the world so that a single man might carry a silver basin filled with gold from the east of Asia to the west. But yet he could not accomplish this great affair without bringing in some measure upon the places he conquered destruction, captivity and plunder, which are the concomitants of victory.[119]

Tamerlane's desire for cleansing destruction, captivity, and plunder was stymied by the savage Central Asian winter, which was so severe, said Yazdi, that "several men and horses perished in the road, some losing their hands and feet, others their ears and noses."[120] The ground was blanketed with snow so thick that the warriors of jihad made their way only with great difficulty. But Tamerlane was undeterred. The march to China would continue.

The Muslim historian Ahmed ibn Arabshah, a contemporary of Tamerlane, noted the warlord's determination not to let the weather stop him. But the onslaught was relentless. "But winter dealt damage to him, breaking on him from the flanks with every wind kindled and raging against his army with all winds blowing aslant, most violent, and smote the shoot of the army with its intense cold."[121]

Still Tamerlane would not call off the march, even as the warriors of jihad began to succumb to the inhuman conditions. "On all sides," said Arabshah with a fine poetic flair, "with the snow that fell from above the whole earth became like the plain of the last judgment or a sea which God forged out of silver. When the sun rose and the frost glittered, the sight was wonderful, the sky of Turkish gems and the earth of crystal, specks of gold filling the space between."[122]

Beautiful, but deadly. By the middle of January 1405, the jihadis had gotten only as far as Otrar in Kazakhstan. Everywhere the snow was so deep as to be impassible. Soon the great warrior, by now sixty-eight years old, caught a cold. His condition rapidly worsened, no doubt in part because one of the treatments tried on him involved covering his chest with ice. He asked those attending him to say *"Allahu akbar"* and recite the Fatiha, the first chapter of the Qur'an, to comfort him. Before long, he was dead. China was saved from the sword of jihad by the deep snow, the bitter cold, and the freezing wind.

India: The Long Persecution

The jihad in India found more favorable weather. In 1414, the Gujarat sultan Ahmed Shah appointed an official whose sole task was to ensure the destruction of all the temples in Gujarat. The following year, he invaded Sidhpur and converted the temple at Rudramahalaya into a mosque.[123] In 1419, according to the *Tabqat i-Akbari*, Ahmed Shah "encamped near Champaner" and "destroyed temples wherever he found them."[124]

Muslim rulers in other parts of India behaved in the same way. Sultan Mahmud Khalji of the Marwa sultanate in central India, who reigned in the middle of the fifteenth century, once approached a fort near Kumbhalmir that was, said Nizamuddin Ahmed, "a very big fort of that province, and well-known for its strength all over Hindustan." The Muslims quickly saw that "a magnificent temple had been erected in front of that fort and surrounded by ramparts on all sides. That temple had been filled with weapons of war and other stores."[125]

The Muslims were victorious, whereupon "a large number of Rajputs were made prisoners and slaughtered. About the edifices of the temple, he ordered that they should be stocked with wood and fired, and water and vinegar was sprinkled on the walls. That magnificent mansion which it had taken many years to raise, was destroyed in a few moments. He got the idols broken and they were handed over to the butchers for being used as weights while selling meat. The biggest idol which had the form of a ram was reduced to powder which was put in betel-leaves to be given to the Rajputs so that they could eat their god."[126]

At Mandalgadh in 1456, Mahmud Khalji "issued orders that trees should be uprooted, houses demolished and no trace should be left of human habitation." When the Muslims defeated the Hindus, "Sultan Mahmud offered thanks to Allah in all humility. Next day, he entered the fort. He got the temples demolished and their materials used in the construction of a Jami Masjid. He appointed there a qazi, a mufti, a muhtasib, a khatib and a muezzin, and established order in that place."[127] He also led jihadi warriors into Nepal, where they destroyed the temple of Svayambhunath in Katmandu.[128]

Islamic piety always underlay the jihad. A Hindu ruler, the Mandalika of Junagadh, was paying tribute to the Gujarat sultan Mahmud Bigarha, but in 1469 Mahmud invaded Junagadh anyway. The Mandalika, dismayed, reminded the sultan that he had always been prompt and regular with his payments. Mahmud was unmoved, explaining to the Mandalika that he wasn't interested in money as much as he was in spreading Islam. He forced the Mandalika to convert and renamed Junagadh Mustafabad.[129] Mahmud also offered conversion to the Hindu ruler of Champaner, Raja Jayasingh, but Raja refused and was duly murdered. Mahmud renamed Champaner after himself, Mahmudabad.[130]

The Bahmani sultan Muhammad Shah was just as pious. The sixteenth-century Persian historian Firishta recounted that at Kondapalli in 1481, "the King, having gone to view the fort, broke down an idolatrous temple and killed some brahmans who officiated at it, with his own hands, as a point of religion. He then gave orders for a mosque to be erected on the foundations of the temple, and ascending the pulpit, repeated a few prayers, distributed alms, and commanded the Khutba [Friday sermon] to be read in his name. Khwaja Mahmud Gawan now represented that as his Majesty had slain some infidels with his own hands, he might fairly assume the title of Ghazi [warrior for Islam], an appellation of which he was very proud. Muhammad Shah was the first of his race who had slain a brahman."[131]

At Kondapelli, the jihadis learned that there was still more glory to be had. Firishta wrote that while he was there, Muhammad Shah was "informed by the country people that at the distance of ten days' journey was the temple of Kanchi, the walls and roof of which were covered with plates of gold and ornamented with precious stones, but that no Muhammadan monarch had as yet seen it or even heard of its name. Muhammad Shah accordingly selected six thousand of his best cavalry, and leaving the rest of his army at Kondapalli, proceeded by forced marches to Kanchi. He moved so rapidly on the last day, according to the historians of the time, that only forty troopers kept up with him."[132] Muhammad Shah prevailed over two Hindus in hand-to-hand combat, but then "swarms of people, like bees, now issued from within and ranged themselves under its walls to defend it. At length, the rest of the King's force coming up, the temple was attacked and carried by storm with great slaughter. An immense booty fell to the share of the victors, who took away nothing but gold, jewels, and silver, which were abundant. The King then [March 12, 1481] sacked the city of Kanchi, and, after remaining there for a week, he returned to his army."[133]

Outdoing even Mahmud Bigarha and Muhammad Shah in devotion to Islam was the Delhi sultan Sikandar Lodi, who came to power in 1489. He adhered strictly to Sharia and was consequently extraordinarily antagonistic to Hinduism.[134] According to the seventeenth-century *Tarikh-i-Khan Jahan Lodi*, by the Muslim court historian Niamatullah, "Sultan Sikandar was yet a young boy when he heard about a tank [pool of holy water] in Thanesar which the Hindus regarded as sacred and went for bathing in it. He asked the theologians about the prescription of the Shariah on this subject. They replied that it was permitted to demolish the ancient temples and idol-houses of the infidels, but it was not proper for him to stop them from going to an ancient tank. Hearing this reply, the prince drew out his sword and thought of beheading the theologian concerned, saying that he [the theologian] was siding with the infidels."[135]

The sixteenth-century Muslim historian Ahmad Yadgar recounted that "Sultan Sikandar led a very pious life. Islam was regarded very highly in his reign. The infidels could not muster the courage to worship idols or bathe in the [sacred] streams. During his holy reign, idols were hidden underground. The stone [idol] of Nagarkot, which had misled the [whole] world, was brought and handed over to butchers so that they might weigh meat with it."[136]

Another sixteenth-century Muslim historian, Shaikh Rizqullah Mushtaqi, provided more detail about that stone: "Khawas Khan…having been ordered by the Sultan to march towards Nagarkot, in order to bring the hill country under subjection, succeeded in conquering it, and having sacked the infidels temple of Debi Shankar, brought away the stone which they worshipped, together with a copper umbrella, which was placed over it, and on which a date was engraved in Hindu characters, representing it to be two thousand years old. When the stone was sent to the King, it was given over to the butchers to make weights out of it for the purpose of weighing meat. From the copper of the umbrella, several pots were made, in which water might be warmed, and which were placed in the *masjids* and the King's own palace, so that everyone might wash his hands, feet and face in them and perform his purifications before prayers."[137]

The jihad in India, and the wholesale destruction of the idols, would continue into the sixteenth century, courtesy of Sikandar Lodi and a host of other Muslim leaders.

IV. THE FALL OF AL-ANDALUS

Meanwhile, toward the end of the fifteenth century came the culmination of what is to date the largest-scale resistance to jihad that has ever been successfully undertaken. In 1469 King Ferdinand of Aragon married Queen Isabella of Castile. Their combined forces began to confront the last remaining Islamic strongholds in Spain. In 1492, after ten years of war, they defeated the Emirate of Granada, the last bastion of al-Andalus on the Iberian Peninsula. Seven hundred eighty-one years after Tariq ibn Ziyad's boats (the gift of the Christian Count Julian) landed in Spain, with the Muslim commander determined to take the land or die there, the Christians had fully driven the warriors of jihad from Spain.

To this day, Spain remains one of the few places once ruled by Islam but no longer; usually what the jihadis have conquered, they've kept. Because of the Qur'anic command to "drive them out from where they drove you out" (2:191), Spain remains high on the list of countries that contemporary jihad groups hope to reconquer for Islam. The Christian Reconquista may not be the last one Spain ever sees.

Also in 1492, Christopher Columbus sailed west, commissioned by Ferdinand and Isabella to search for a new, westward sea route to Asia. He was on this search because the fall of Constantinople to the Muslims in 1453 effectively closed the trade routes to the East, making them too hazardous to traverse by non-Muslim tradesmen, who risked kidnapping, enslavement, and death by doing so. This was devastating for Europe, as European traders had until then traveled to Asia for spices and other goods by land. Columbus' voyage was an attempt to ease the plight of these merchants by bypassing the Muslims altogether and making it possible for Europeans to reach India by sea, without being attacked by jihadis.

He was, of course, to make a momentous discovery that would, as the years sped by, ultimately provide an entirely new field of operations for the warriors of jihad.

CHAPTER SEVEN

THE OTTOMANS AND MUGHALS IN ASCENDANCE

Jihad in the Sixteenth and Seventeenth Centuries

I. THE JIHAD IN EUROPE

The Ottomans continued their ascent. The Safavid Persians, who had just adopted Shi'ism in 1501, were a new and potent force confronting the Ottoman sultanate in eastern Asia Minor; as the Ottomans grew in power and confidence, a confrontation was inevitable.

There was, however, one obstacle: the Qur'an forbids Muslims to kill fellow Muslims (4:92), and so these Shi'a had to be declared non-Muslim. A decree therefore went out that "according to the precepts of the holy law," the Safavid Shah Ismail and his followers were "unbelievers and heretics. Any who sympathize and accept their false religion or assist them are also unbelievers and heretics. It is a necessity and a divine obligation that they be massacred and their communities be dispersed."[1]

The Ottoman sultan Selim then wrote to Shah Ismail: "You have subjected the upright community of Muhammad…to your devious will [and] undermined the firm foundation of the faith; you have unfurled the banner of oppression in the cause of aggression [and] no longer uphold the commandments and prohibitions of the Divine Law; you have incited your abominable Shii faction to unsanctified sexual union and the shedding of innocent blood."[2]

The jihad against the Shi'ites thus justified, the Ottomans defeated them in 1514, and drove them from the eastern regions of Asia Minor.

Two years later, the Ottomans defeated the Mamluks and gained control of Syria and the Holy Land and defeated them again to win Egypt shortly thereafter. Their preeminence in the Islamic world, outside of Persia and India, was now secured, and then cemented in 1517 when the last Abbasid caliph, al-Mutawakkil III, surrendered his authority to the Ottoman caliph Selim I.[3]

Although the Holy Land had been occupied by Muslims since 1291, the Ottoman presence there was alarming to the crowned heads of Europe, who had long had an opportunity to see the Ottomans up close, far closer than they would have preferred. Pope Leo X tried to organize a new Crusade, and in 1518 called upon the leaders of Europe to stop their infighting and unite against the jihadis, but it was that very infighting that prevented any concerted European effort against the Ottomans.

The Ottomans even became a rhetorical weapon in that infighting. In response to Pope Leo X's efforts toward a new Crusade, the pioneering reformer Martin Luther declared that "to fight against the Turk is the same thing as resisting God, who visits our sin upon us with this rod."[4] In polemicizing against the Roman Church, Luther even charged that the papacy was worse than the Ottoman caliphate, thus making a Crusade against the Ottomans in alliance with the pope anathema to many Protestants:

> The Pope, with his followers, commits a greater sin than the Turk and all the Heathen…. The Turk forces no one to deny Christ and to adhere to his faith…. Though he rages most intensely by murdering Christians in the body—he, after all, does nothing by this but fill heaven with saints…. The Pope does not want to be either enemy or Turk…. He fills hell with nothing but "Christians"…. This is committing real spiritual murder and is every bit as bad as the teaching and blasphemy of Mohammed and the Turks. But whenever men do not allow him to practice this infernal diabolical seduction—he adopts the way of the Turk, and commits bodily murder too…. The Turk is an avowed enemy of Christ. But the Pope is not. He is a secret enemy and persecutor, a false friend. For this reason, he is all the worse![5]

Luther's broadside was one of the earliest examples of what was to become a near-universal tendency in the West: the downplaying of jihad atrocities and their use in arguments between Westerners to make one side look worse.

No Crusade was forthcoming. And so, with their rivals defeated or at bay, the now undisputed Ottoman caliphate could turn its attention once again to Europe. The janissaries were the spearhead of this new jihad effort. As converted Christians, they were more trustworthy as slaves of the sultan than Muslims would have been, as it was widely believed that the Muslims would use their position to favor their relatives and home regions.

But the janissaries, cut off from their families and homelands, aroused no such concerns. A contemporary observer explained: "If Christian children accept Islam, they become zealous in the faith and enemies of their relatives."[6] This was so widely accepted as axiomatic that a Christian visitor, Baron Wenceslas Wradislaw, noted: "Never... did I hear it said of any pasha, or observe either in Constantinople or in the whole land of Turkey, that any pasha was a natural born Turk; on the contrary, kidnapped, or captured, or turned Turk."[7]

Commanding this force of zealous converts from 1520 to 1566 was the sultan who came to be known as Suleiman the Magnificent, who took the Ottoman caliphate to the height of its power. His jihadis defeated the Knights Hospitallers of the Order of St. John of Jerusalem, whom the Ottomans regarded (in the words of an official of the sultanate) as "professional cutthroats and pirates," taking the island of Rhodes after a 145-day siege in 1522.[8]

Ottoman power over the eastern Mediterranean was near total, with only Cyprus and Crete remaining outside the domains of the caliphate. But the Ottomans generally neglected Rhodes, to the degree that the Venetian envoy Pietro Zeno asserted the year after its conquest that "the Sultan has no use for Rhodes."[9] Zeno may not have realized that the Ottomans had not taken Rhodes to put it to any particular use, but simply because the jihad imperative was universal and absolute.

In 1526, the sultan ordered his jihad warriors to take Vienna. The armies were under the supervision of Ibrahim Pasha, Suleiman's grand vizier, a Greek Christian who had been captured, enslaved, and converted to Islam as a boy, and who had then risen high in the Ottoman court after befriending Suleiman. When the jihadis arrived at Belgrade on their way to Austria, Suleiman ordered Ibrahim to take it, recounting later in his diary that he told him "it will be but a bite to last him till breakfast at Vienna."[10] Once Belgrade was taken, Suleiman noted with satisfaction that "the Grand Vezir has 500 soldiers of the garrison beheaded; 300 others are taken away into slavery."[11]

The jihadis moved into Hungary, where they soundly defeated a massive Hungarian force at Mohacs. On August 31, 1526, Suleiman recorded in his diary, speaking of himself in the third person: "The Sultan, seated on a golden throne, receives the homage of the viziers and the beys; massacre of 2,000 prisoners; the rain falls in torrents."[12] He ordered Mohacs to be burned. Its site came to be known among Hungarians as "the tomb of the Hungarian nation."[13]

Four days later, the jihadis took Buda. Suleiman recorded the details: "Sept. 4. Order to massacre all peasants in the camp. Women alone exempted. *Akinjis* forbidden to plunder."[14] The *akinjis* were the Ottoman cavalry and advance troops. They ignored the antiplunder order, and Suleiman did not punish them for doing so.[15] The jihadis burned Buda and seized the treasures of its renowned library and much of its great art, including statues of Hercules, Diana, and Apollo, for shipment back to Constantinople.[16] Suleiman took the most satisfaction in seizing two immense cannons that Mehmet II was forced to leave behind after one of his campaigns. The Hungarians had put them on display as trophies signifying their defeat of the Ottomans; there was to be no more of that.[17]

Suleiman lingered awhile in Hungary, but unexpectedly, he did not make it part of the Ottoman Empire. The historian Kemal Pasha Zadeh, a contemporary of Suleiman, wrote: "The time when this province should be annexed to the possession of Islam had not yet arrived.... The matter was therefore postponed to a more suitable occasion."[18] He instead chose the next Hungarian king, John Zapolya, and made him his vassal.

Apparently, the sultan did not think that the territory could be held securely or governed effectively from Constantinople at that time, and this was reinforced when he set out again in May 1529 and his armies, stymied by heavy rains, took almost four months to return to Buda.[19]

Once there, Suleiman crowned his vassal Hungarian king and embarked for Vienna. When they arrived in September 1529, the Muslims plundered and set fire to the villages surrounding the city, and then laid siege to the city itself.

This time Luther green-lighted the defense of Christendom against the Turks, and a combined force of Catholics and Protestants, some of whom had just arrived three days before the Ottomans, were inside Vienna ready to defend it against the jihadi onslaught. The bad weather forced Suleiman to leave behind some of his key equipment at Buda, and this hampered the assault by the Muslims, yet they still had a considerable force to throw at the city, and they did.

The Christians held firm. Suleiman abandoned the siege in mid-October, burning to death all of his prisoners except those who would be useful as slaves, and set out for Constantinople. Back at Buda, John Zapolya lavished flattery upon his master, congratulating Suleiman for his "successful campaign."[20]

Suleiman tried again in 1532 to take Vienna but wasn't even able to get into Austria; Archduke Ferdinand of Austria stopped the jihadis in Hungary. However, the sultan did not forget Vienna.

He had better luck against the Shi'ite Safavids, from whom he took Baghdad in 1534. On a fortress in Bessarabia (modern-day Moldova), Suleiman inscribed a boast proclaiming himself the master of the Safavids, Byzantines, and Mamluks: "In Baghdad I am the shah, in Byzantine realms the Caesar, and in Egypt the sultan."[21] The Safavids and Mamluks were not entirely subdued, but he had beaten them both enough to give substance to the boast. Egypt became a valued source for slaves captured from sub-Saharan Africa: at the Turkish port of Antalya, a customs official in 1559 noted the arrival of cargo from Egypt, among which "black slaves, both male and female, constituted the bulk of the traffic. Many ships carried slaves exclusively."[22]

Mindful of his Islamic responsibility, Suleiman oversaw extensive renovations at Mecca, ensuring a pure water supply for pilgrims and opening schools of Islamic theology. In Jerusalem, he had the Dome of the Rock redecorated in the Ottoman style. He was careful always to keep the *dhimmis* in their place. In 1548, the French ambassador to the Ottoman Empire, M. d'Aramon, visited the Holy Land and reported:

"Jerusalem has been enclosed by city walls built by the Turks, but there are neither ramparts nor a ditch. The town is medium-sized and not much populated, the streets are narrow and unpaved.... The so-called temple of Solomon is at the base of the city...round and with a lead-covered dome; around its core are chapels as in our churches, which is all one can surmise because no Christian is permitted to enter the area without threat of death or having to become a [Muslim]."[23]

As he grew older, Suleiman's zealousness for jihad waned. His campaigns against Christian Europe became a distant memory. For some of those around him, this was an indictment. In 1566, when Suleiman was seventy-one years old and had not led an expedition into Europe for twenty-three years, his daughter Mihrimah Sultan reproached the caliph for neglecting his Islamic obligation to lead the armies of Islam in jihad warfare against non-Muslims.[24]

Suleiman was stung by the criticism, particularly from a woman, and found no better retort than to get back on his horse. Several months later, outside the fortress of Szigetvar in Hungary, which the jihadis were besieging, the old warrior died in his tent.[25] To avoid demoralizing the troops, his death was not announced for forty-eight days; a page who slightly resembled him was dressed in his clothes and carried in his litter on the journey home, but most onlookers saw through the ruse.[26]

The real Suleiman's heart, liver, and some other organs were buried in a tomb there that became a popular pilgrimage site for Ottoman Muslims; the rest of his remains were taken back to Constantinople—which the Ottomans often referred to as Istanbul ("to the city" in Greek) or, using the Turkish cognate, Konstantiniyye—and buried there.[27]

Russia and a Canal

Suleiman's successor as sultan and caliph, Selim II, immediately faced new challenges. In 1552, the Russian czar Ivan the Terrible annexed the Central Asian Tatar khanate of Kazan; in 1556 he likewise incorporated the Astrakhan khanate into his domains. A large number of Muslims came under Russian rule. In 1567, he built a fort on the River Terek in the Caucasus. Muslims in the area appealed to Selim for help, claiming that because the Russians controlled Astrakhan, they could not safely make the pilgrimage to Mecca, as the route now required they pass through Russian domains.[28] In 1571, the Tatars raided Moscow, yet failed to repeat that victory the following year, and had to give up hope of reconquering the area.[29]

Searching for a way to enable the Muslims of the Caucasus and Central Asia to make the pilgrimage to Mecca without running afoul of the Russians, an Ottoman imperial official sent this order to the governor of Egypt:

> Because the accursed Portuguese are everywhere, owing to their hostilities against India, and the routes by which Muslims come to the Holy Places are obstructed and, moreover, it is not considered lawful for people of Islam to live under the power of miserable infidels…you are to gather together all the expert architects and engineers of that place…and investigate the land between the Mediterranean and Red Seas and…report where it is possible to make a canal in that desert place and how long it would be and how many boats could pass side-by-side.[30]

The canal was not built. But the idea of one remained alive.

Cyprus and a Treaty

Selim II was known to have a fondness for wine—so much fondness, in fact, that he has gone down in history as Selim the Sot. His favorite wine came from the island of Cyprus, which was under the control of the Republic of Venice.[31] And so in 1571, the Ottomans accused the Venetians of aiding pirates from Cyprus that attacked Ottoman vessels and seized the island. This was in violation of a peace treaty that Selim had concluded with the Venetians, but a Muslim cleric issued a fatwa for Selim, explaining that a peace treaty with infidels could be set aside for the greater good of Islam.

> A land was previously in the realm of Islam. After a while the abject infidels overran it, destroyed the colleges and mosques, and left them vacant. They filled the pulpits and

galleries with the tokens of infidelity and error, intending to insult the religion of Islam with all kinds of vile deeds, and by spreading their ugly acts to all corners of the earth.... When peace was previously concluded with other lands in possession of the said infidels, the aforenamed land was included. An explanation is sought as to whether, in accordance with the [sacred law], this is an impediment to the Sultan's determining to break the treaty.

ANSWER:

There is no possibility that it could ever be an impediment. For the Sultan of the people of Islam (may God glorify his victories) to make peace with the infidels is legal only where there is benefit to all Muslims. When there is no benefit, peace is never legal. When a benefit has been seen, and it is then observed to be more beneficial to break it, then to break it becomes absolutely obligatory and binding.[32]

Lepanto

The Sublime Porte (as the Ottoman central government was known) financed the Cyprus campaign by selling monasteries and churches out from under the Christians who owned them.[33] But Selim the Sot was to pay a heavy price for his Cyprus wine: in response to the Ottoman action in Cyprus, Pope Pius V called another Crusade and formed the Holy League, which consisted of the Papal States, Spain, the Republic of Venice, the Republic of Genoa, the Knights of Malta, the Duchy of Savoy, and several Italian duchies, and was intent upon destroying the Ottoman Empire as a maritime power.

On October 7, 1571, the Holy League and the Ottomans, both with over two hundred ships, met in what was until then the largest sea battle ever at Lepanto, in the caliphate's domains in Greece. The commander of the Christian forces, Don John of Austria, told his men just before the battle: "My children, we are here to conquer or to die as Heaven may determine. Do not let our impious foe ask us, 'Where is your God?' Fight in His holy name and in death or in victory you will win immortality."[34]

It was to be in victory. The Christian triumph was total: the Ottoman fleet was completely destroyed, and as many as forty thousand jihadis were killed. Eyewitnesses recalled that the sea was red with blood.[35]

For the first time in a major battle, the Christian Europeans had defeated the Ottomans, and there was rejoicing throughout Europe. Miguel de Cervantes Saavedra, the author of *Don Quixote*, lost his left hand at Lepanto and was known thereafter as El Manco de Lepanto, that is, the One-Handed One of Lepanto. Referring to his own injury, and himself in the third person, Cervantes said: "Although it looks ugly, he holds it for lovely, because he received it on the most memorable and lofty occasion which past centuries have beheld—nor do those [centuries] to come hope to see the like."[36] He recalled the Battle of Lepanto as "that day so fortunate to Christendom when all nations were undeceived of their error in believing that the Turks were invincible."[37] When Pope Pius V heard the news, he thought of Don John of Austria and murmured words from the New Testament: "There was a man sent from God, whose name was John."[38]

When he learned of the catastrophic defeat, Selim was enraged, and declared that he was going to order that all the Christians in his domains be executed.[39] But cooler heads prevailed, and this order was not issued. By the time the grand vizier Mehmed Sokullu met with Barbaro, the ambassador from the Republic of Venice to the sultanate, in Constantinople a few days after the battle, the Ottomans were determinedly downplaying the significance of the battle. "You come to see how we bear our misfortune," said Sokullu to Barbaro. "But I would have you know the difference between your loss and ours. In wresting Cyprus from you, we deprived you of an arm; in defeating our fleet, you have only shaved our beard. An arm when cut off cannot grow again; but a shorn beard will grow all the better for the razor."[40]

The Ottomans did indeed rebuild their fleet, and the Holy League was not able to follow up on this victory with further effective strikes against the caliphate. The shorn beard did indeed grow back. Nonetheless, Lepanto became a celebrated name throughout Europe and was clear proof that the Ottomans could, after all, be beaten.

The last casualty of Selim the Sot's seizure of Cyprus was Selim himself. In 1574 he visited a Turkish bath, where he drank a whole bottle of his prized wine from Cyprus. Soon after, he slipped on the marble floor and cracked his skull, dying at age fifty.[41] His successor, Murad III, was enamored of women as much as Selim was of wine, to the degree that the price for sex slaves in the slave markets of Constantinople doubled as the demand from the imperial court alone began to exceed the supply. Murad was the father of over a hundred children.[42]

Murad was also mindful of jihad, launching an attack against Shi'ite Persia in 1578 that included the Ottoman seizure of Christian Georgia, where the Muslims quickly converted the churches into mosques.[43] In 1587, Murad seized the Church of the Pammakristos in Konstantiniyye, which had been the seat of the patriarchate of Constantinople since the fall of the city in 1453, and converted it into the Mosque of Victory (Fethiye Camii).[44]

The jihad against Europe also continued, when it was possible to continue it amid increasing political instability. At Keresztes in northern Hungary in 1596, the Ottomans under Sultan Mehmet III, bearing the standard of Muhammad, the Prophet of Islam, decisively defeated a Christian force of thirty thousand men.[45] Ten years later, however, the Ottomans concluded a treaty with Habsburg Austria that demonstrated how weak the sultanate had become. In the past, when temporary truces had been concluded between the Ottomans and Austria, they had been contemptuously headed "Graciously accorded by the Sultan, ever victorious, to the infidel King of Vienna, ever vanquished."[46] This new treaty, however, treated the Ottoman sultan and the Austrian emperor as equals.

And the decline continued. In 1621, the seventeen-year-old Osman II, who had become sultan upon the deposition of his uncle Mustafa the Mad (whose nickname reveals the reason for the deposition), led a jihad force against Poland, but was so ignominiously defeated that the janissaries deposed him as well. He was murdered soon afterward.[47]

New Rigor

After a period of lax enforcement, in 1631 the sultan Murad IV attempted to ensure that the Ottoman decline was not a result of incurring the divine wrath by lax enforcement of the Sharia. He issued a decree restating the dress restrictions for *dhimmis*, to ensure that they would "feel themselves subdued" (Qur'an 9:29):

> Insult and humiliate infidels in garment, clothing and manner of dress according to Muslim law and imperial statute. Henceforth, do not allow them to mount a horse, wear sable fur, sable fur caps, satin and silk velvet. Do not allow their women to wear mohair caps wrapped in cloth and "Paris" cloth. Do not allow infidels and Jews to go about in Muslim manner and garment. Hinder and remove these kinds. Do not lose a minute in executing the order that I have proclaimed in this manner.[48]

Murad may have believed that this had worked in 1638 when he defeated the Safavids and took Baghdad (which the Persians had seized back from the Ottomans in 1623). And indeed, the fortunes of the empire began to turn, if ever so slightly. His successor, the sultan Ibrahim, in 1645 took the jihad back to Christian Europe once again, after pirates operating from Malta captured a Turkish ship on which was one of his favorite sex slaves.[49] Ibrahim, in a wild fury, ordered the killing of all the Christians in Ottoman domains. Once his noblemen talked him out of that, he ordered that all Christian ambassadors to the Ottoman Empire be imprisoned, and upon learning that the Maltese pirates were French, contemplated jihad against France. France, however, was far away; Crete, a possession of the Republic of Venice, was closer. Ibrahim decided to seize it, but in the end, it took the Ottomans twenty-four years to do so.[50]

Worries about the divine wrath returned in 1660, when a fire destroyed much of Constantinople. The Ottomans blamed the city's Jews and expelled them from the city. Inscribed in the royal mosque in the city was a reference to Muhammad's expulsion of the Jews from Medina; the mosque's endowment deed includes a reference to "the Jews who are the enemy of Islam."[51] Allah's wrath, presumably, was averted once again.

Sobieski to the Rescue

With the jihad for Crete finally concluded successfully, the Ottomans again moved against Poland, this time more successfully than before. In 1672, the sultan Mehmet IV defeated a substantial Polish force and won significant territorial concessions north of the Black Sea. The Polish king Jan Sobieski would not, however, accept this, and went to war with the Ottomans again four years later. Again the sultanate was victorious, winning even more territory than it had before.[52]

Jan Sobieski, although forced in 1676 to accept the terms of a humiliating peace treaty, was still not willing to accept this as a result. He would be heard from again. His third chance came in the late summer of 1683, when Mehmet IV assembled a large force of jihad warriors and set forth once more into Europe, intent upon succeeding in bringing it to heel where his illustrious forbears had failed. At Osijek in the Ottoman domains of Croatia, the forces of the Hungarian anti-Habsburg count Emmerich Tekeli joined the Ottomans. Tekeli was the sultan's vassal king of western Hungary, set up to challenge and harass the Habsburgs. Tekeli's troops carried a standard inscribed "For God and Country" and "*Kruczes*," or "men of the cross," thereby earning Tekeli a place among the long list of Christian servants of the jihad, going back to Count Julian and continuing to Pope Francis.[53]

Mehmet's grand vizier, Kara Mustafa, urged him to try again to take Vienna, arguing that it was the key to the conquest of Europe and that if he conquered it, "all the Christians would obey the Ottomans."[54] The jihadis duly placed Vienna under siege once again but did not count on Jan Sobieski, who hurried to the city with a relief force. Approaching Vienna, Sobieski saw the arrangement of the sultan's forces around the city and remarked, "This man is badly encamped. He knows nothing of war, we shall certainly defeat him."[55]

In the dawn hours of September 12, he did. His forces descended upon the surprised jihadis with fury, with Jan Sobieski himself leading the charge. As the Polish king approached the very heart of the Muslim camp, the Tatar khan, another vassal of Mehmet IV, saw him and exclaimed in shock and horror: "By Allah! The King really is among us!"[56]

The Ottoman siege was decisively broken, and Christendom once again saved. The warriors of jihad fled in confusion.

Four years later, the Ottomans made one last stand in Central Europe, facing the Austrians at Mohacs, where they had won such a decisive victory in 1526. But these were no longer the days of Suleiman the Magnificent. The warriors of jihad were beaten so badly that Austria established control over much of Hungary and threatened Ottoman holdings in the Balkans.

The jihadis would not return to the heart of Europe for several centuries. When they did once more strike the West, it was in the New World metropolises of New York and Washington. The day of that strike was September 11, 2001. Many have speculated that the mastermind of that jihad decided to set it on the anniversary of the high-water mark of the jihadi advance into Europe, the day before the defeat of the jihadis and the acceleration of the Ottoman decline set in motion the chain of events that would lead to the jihad's becoming a dim memory in the West.

In any case, after Vienna, Europe would, for a considerable time, get a respite.

II. THE BARBARY STATES

That respite was to be from large-scale jihad attacks. North African pirates, however, continued to harass European states with audacious jihad raids, during which the primary goal was to seize Europeans for service as slaves. This won them considerable renown among their peers; the Muslim chronicler al-Magiri reported: "They lived in Salé, and their sea-borne jihad is now famous. They fortified Salé and built in it palaces, houses and bathhouses."[57]

Non-Muslim slaves did the bulk of this work. In 1611, a slave from Timbuktu named Ahmed Baba, who had been enslaved by the Moroccans in 1591 and was learned in Islam, wrote to the Moroccan sultan Zidan Abu Maali protesting his enslavement on the grounds that he was a Muslim. "The reason for enslavement," he explained, "is disbelief. The position of unbelieving Negroes is the same as that of other unbelievers, Christians, Jews, Persians, Turks, etc."[58] He repeated the classic Islamic formulation that unbelievers should be first invited to accept Islam or *dhimmi* status, with jihad being waged against those who refused both.

Captives taken in these jihad battles, if they were non-Muslim, could legitimately be enslaved.

This was indeed the general practice in Morocco. Many of the slaves in Morocco had been taken in raids on European Christian states. In July 1625, a twenty-ship contingent of pirates from Morocco arrived in Mount's Bay in southern England. Bursting into the local parish church during a service, they captured sixty men, women, and children from the terrified congregation and took them back to Morocco, to live a life of slavery. At Looe, they took eighty more and set the town ablaze. In a series of similar raids, they took two hundred people as slaves and seized twenty-seven British ships as well.[59]

During another raid soon after that, they seized Lundy Island and made it their base, raising the flag of Islam. More slave raids followed. The English could do little in response; as Francis Stuart, a veteran mariner whom the Duke of Buckingham had sent to get rid of the pirates, said of his foes, "They are better sailers than the English ships."[60] By the end of 1625, the English had lost a thousand ships to the pirates, and the warriors of jihad from Morocco had gained a thousand English slaves.

One of these slaves, Robert Adams, who was ransomed and returned to England, recounted that as a slave in Morocco he had been given only "a littell coarse bread and water," and lived in "a dungion under ground, wher some 150 or 200 of us lay, altogether, having no comforte of the light, but a littell hole." Adams recounted that he was "every day beaten to make me turn Turk," that is, convert to Islam.[61]

Despite efforts to conclude a truce and end the raids, they continued for years; in May 1635 alone, the Muslims seized and enslaved 150 more English people.[62] In 1643, Parliament ordered English churches to begin taking up collections to pay ransom to the Muslims and buy back the English slaves.[63] In the 1660s, the Moroccans began targeting American colonial ships and enslaving those upon them as well.[64]

All of this was in full accord with Islamic law, which envisions Muslims taking non-Muslims captive in jihad attacks and, if it is deemed beneficial to the Muslims, enslaving them. A manual of Islamic law stipulates that "when an adult male is taken captive, the caliph considers the interests…[of Islam and the Muslims] and decides between the prisoner's death, slavery, release without paying anything, or ransoming himself in exchange for money or for a Muslim captive held by the enemy."[65]

A revered Islamic jurist from the eleventh century, Al-Mawardi, agreed: "As for the captives, the amir has the choice of taking the most beneficial action of four possibilities: the first, to put them to death by cutting their necks; the second, to enslave them and apply the laws of slavery regarding their sale or manumission; the third, to ransom them in exchange for goods or prisoners; and fourth, to show favor to them and pardon them."[66]

The piracy and slave raids would continue, despite European efforts to end them by force or persuasion.

III. THE JIHAD IN INDIA

Sikandar Lodi and Babur

In 1501, the Delhi sultan Sikandar Lodi marched upon Dhulpur, where he was able to occupy a Hindu fort. Upon entering the fort, Sikandar demonstrated what to modern-day non-Muslims is the paradox of jihad activity. He immediately fell to his knees and gave thanks to Allah for the victory. At that same moment, according to Niamatullah, "the whole army was employed in plundering and the groves which spread shade for seven *kos* around Bayana were torn up from the roots."[67]

For Sikandar Lodi and his jihadis, prayers juxtaposed with plunder was not odd at all. Allah had granted the Muslims victory, and by the dictates of Allah's own law, that victory entitled them to the possessions of the vanquished.

Three years later, during Ramadan, the month of jihad, in which Muslims were to struggle to show their devotion to Allah, Sikandar, according to Niamatullah, "raised the standard of war for the reduction of the fort of Mandrail; but the garrison capitulating, and delivering up the citadel, the Sultan ordered the temples and idols to be demolished, and mosques to be constructed." Then he "moved out on a plundering expedition into the surrounding country, where he butchered many people, took many prisoners, and devoted to utter destruction all the groves and habitations; and after gratifying and honouring himself by this exhibition of holy zeal he returned to his capital Bayana."

At Mandrail, said Nizamuddin Ahmed, Sikandar "got the temples demolished and mosques erected in their stead."[68] Finding churches in the same city, he had them destroyed as well.[69] Sikandar amplified his contempt for Hinduism by persecuting the Hindus in his domains. Niamatullah noted that "the Islamic sentiment [in him] was so strong that he demolished all temples in his kingdom and left no trace of them. He constructed *sarais, bazars, madrasas* and mosques in Mathura, which is a holy place of the Hindus and where they go for bathing. He appointed government officials in order to make sure that no Hindu could bathe in Mathura. No barber was permitted to shave the head of any Hindu with his razor. That is how he completely curtailed the public celebration of infidel customs."[70] Mushtaqi added: "If a Hindu went there for bathing even by mistake, he was made to lose his limbs and punished severely. No Hindu could get shaved at that place. No barber would go near a Hindu, whatever be the payment offered."[71] This was because of the Qur'anic dictum that the idolaters were "unclean." (9:28)

Sikandar Lodi died in 1517, but the Hindus had no respite. Sikandar's son Ibrahim Lodi succeeded him as sultan. According to Niamatullah, Ibrahim Lodi sent jihad warriors to Gwalior, where they "captured from the infidels the statue of a bull which was made of metals such as copper and brass, which was outside the gate of the fort and which the Hindus used to worship. They brought it to the Sultan. The Sultan was highly pleased and ordered that it should be taken to Delhi and placed outside the Red Gate which was known as the Baghdad Gate in those days."[72] Later, however, the Mughal emperor Akbar the Great ordered the bull to be melted down and the metal used for cannons and other weapons.[73]

Nor did the Hindus find any relief when the Mughal Babur defeated Ibrahim Lodi in the First Battle of Panipat in 1526. The Mughal Empire at its zenith covered most of the Indian subcontinent, as well as Afghanistan, and continued the relentless jihad against the Hindus. Babur, like Tamerlane, left behind a memoir, in which he recounted his exploits with relish. "In AH 934 [AD 1528]," he wrote, "I attacked Chanderi and, by the grace of Allah, captured it in a few hours. We got the infidels slaughtered and the place which had been a *daru l-harb* [house of war] for years, was made into a *daru l-Islam* [house of Islam]."[74]

At Urwa, Babur noted, "people have carved statues in stone. They are in all sizes, small and big. A very big statue, which is on the southern side, is perhaps 20 yards high. These statues are altogether naked and even their private parts are not covered. Urwa is not a bad place. It is an enclosed space. Its biggest blemish is its statues. I ordered that they should be destroyed."[75]

After battles with Hindu forces, Babur delighted in sitting by and watching as the heads of the Hindus were piled up together, and the pile grew higher and higher.[76] Sher Shah Suri, who took over the Mughal Empire in 1540, was not as zealous for the deaths of infidels, but he did his Islamic duty. In 1543, according to Shaykh Nurul Haq's contemporary history *Zubdat ut-Tawarikh*, the Hindu Puranmal "held occupation of the fort of Raisen.... He had 1000 women in his harem... and amongst them several Musulmanis whom he made to dance before him."[77] That was intolerable. Sher Shah Suri thus resolved to take the fort. "After he had been some time engaged in investing it, an accommodation was proposed...and it was finally agreed that Puranmal with his family and children and 4000 Rajputs of note should be allowed to leave the fort unmolested."[78]

That, too, was intolerable. "Several men learned in the law [of Islam] gave it as their opinion that they should all be slain, notwithstanding the solemn engagement which had been entered into. Consequently, the whole army, with the elephants, surrounded Puranmal's encampment. The Rajputs fought with desperate bravery and after killing their women and children and burning them, they rushed to battle and were annihilated to a man."[79]

The End of the Vijayanagara Empire

The Hindu resistance was seldom strong or well-organized. The Muslims had superior firepower, better organization, and in most cases, unity. Although there was always considerable internecine jihad between rival Muslim factions, the warring groups could usually unite against the infidels. In 1564, the sultans of Bijapur, Bidar, Ahmadnagar, and

Golkonda formed such an alliance against the Hindu Vijayanagara Empire, which ruled southern India. The following January, Rama Raya, the de facto Vijayanagara ruler, met the forces of the Muslim alliance near a Vijayanagara fortress, Talikota, with a mixed force of Hindus and Muslims. The Hindus were winning the battle when two Muslim generals fighting for Vijayanagara deserted and joined the jihadi alliance. The Hindu line was broken, and Rama Raya was almost immediately captured and beheaded.[80]

The Muslims quickly stuffed his head with straw and mounted it on a pike for display. That was the turning point in the battle: the Hindus fled in shock and confusion. Noted Firishta: "The Hindus, according to custom, when they saw their chief destroyed, fled in the utmost disorder from the field, and were pursued by the allies with such success that the river was dyed red with their blood. It is computed by the best authorities that above one hundred thousand infidels were slain during the action and the pursuit."[81]

To the victors went, as always, the spoils, as the Muslims entered the city of Vijayanagar, the seat of the empire. In 1522, the Portuguese traveler Domingos Paes had visited Vijayanagar, and reported that it was comparable in size to Rome, with a population of five hundred thousand. He called Vijayanagar "the best provided city in the world...for the state of this city is not like that of other cities, which often fail of supplies and provisions, for in this one everything abounds." Inside the palace, he saw a room "all of ivory, as well the chamber as the walls from top to bottom, and the pillars of the cross-timbers at the top had roses and flowers of lotuses all of ivory, and all well executed, so that there could not be better—it is so rich and beautiful that you would hardly find anywhere another such."[82]

It was in this grand city that the warriors of jihad now went to work. "The plunder was so great," said Firishta, "that every private man in the allied army became rich in gold, jewels, effects, tents, arms, horses, and slaves; as the sultans left every person in possession of what he had acquired, only taking elephants for their own use."[83] They slaughtered as many people as they could and entered the temples in order destroy the statues. After smashing the statues in the temple of Vitthalaswami, they set fire to it.[84]

Akbar the Great

The Mughal emperor Akbar the Great in 1568 besieged the fort at Chittor and ordered, after taking it, that everyone inside be killed. Abul Fazl, Akbar's official court historian, recorded that "there were 8,000 fighting Rajputs collected in the fortress, but there were more than 40,000 peasants who took part in watching and serving. From early dawn till midday the bodies of those ill-starred men were consumed by the majesty of the great warrior. Nearly 30,000 men were killed.... When Sultan Alauddin [Khalji] took the fort after six months and seven days, the peasantry were not put to death as they had not engaged in fighting. But on this occasion they had shown great zeal and activity. Their excuses after the emergence of the victory were of no avail, and orders were given for a general massacre."[85] Akbar himself gave effusive thanks to Allah for the victory and issued a proclamation explaining with profuse quotations from the Qur'an that everything he had done had been in accord with Islamic law.[86]

Akbar was not, however, a doctrinaire jihad warrior, and began to manifest a growing disenchantment with Islam itself. He even abolished the *jizya*, an extraordinary departure from Sharia mandates that made him extraordinarily popular among the Hindus within his domains.[87] In 1579, he made contact with the Portuguese at Goa and asked them for information about Christianity.[88] He began in that same year to preach his own sermons at the mosque, and the following year even banned the mention of Muhammad in public prayers.[89] He favored the exclamation *"Allahu akbar,"* but this was not a sign that he retained some belief in orthodox Islam: since his name was Akbar, the phrase took on a thrilling double meaning, not only "Allah is greater" but also "Akbar is Allah."[90]

In 1582, he finally made his break with Islam official, proclaiming his new Divine Religion (Din Ilahi), which rejected Muhammad as a prophet, essentially replacing him with Akbar himself. He began to introduce practices derived from Hinduism, Zoroastrianism, Jainism, and Christianity.[91] He forbade the consumption of beef and the naming of children Muhammad. Echoing Sharia laws for *dhimmis*, he forbade Muslims to build new mosques or repair old ones. No one was to make prostrations except to Akbar himself.[92]

Understandably, Akbar's apostasy caused considerable consternation among Muslims, and the cadi of Jaunpur declared the emperor an apostate, which meant that he could lawfully be deposed and killed. Akbar, however, was superior to the rebels both in military might and ruthlessness, and he was able not only to crush the rebellions but to expand Mughal domains considerably in a series of wars with neighboring Muslim kingdoms.

Other Muslims continued to wage jihad. In 1582, involving the Turcoman Muslim commander Husain Quli Khan, the *Tabqat i-Akbari* described how "the fortress [*hissar*] of Bhim, which is an idol temple of Mahamai, and in which none but her servants dwelt, was taken by the valour of the assailants at the first assault. A party of Rajputs, who had resolved to die, fought most desperately till they were all cut down. A number of Brahmans who for many years had served the temple, never gave one thought to flight, and were killed. Nearly 200 black cows belonging to Hindus had, during the struggle, crowded together for shelter in the temple. Some savage Turks, while the arrows and bullets were falling like rain, killed those cows. They then took off their boots and filled them with the blood and cast it upon the roof and walls of the temple."[93]

Akbar, however, was more concerned with expanding his domains. When he died in 1605, his new religion died with him. It may have died before that, as his son and his successor, Jahangir, who had revolted against his father but managed to survive and succeed him, said that before he died, Akbar began "returning again a little into the right way" and showed that he was "once more an orthodox believer."[94]

Jahangir himself was a rigid Muslim. In fact, Jahangir had the man he blamed for his father's discarding Islam killed, a man named Abul Fazzel. It was he, said Jahangir, who had convinced Akbar that Muhammad was not a prophet but just a well-spoken con artist. "For towards the close of my father's reign," Jahangir explained, "availing himself of the influence which by some means or other he had acquired, he so wrought upon the mind of his master [that is, Akbar], as to instil into him the belief that the seal and asylum of prophecy, to whom the devotion of a thousand lives such as mine would be a sacrifice too inadequate to speak of, was no more to be thought of than as an Arab of singular eloquence, and that the sacred inspirations recorded in the Koran were nothing else but fabrications invented by the ever-blessed Mahommed." Jahangir gives his story a happy ending: "Actuated by these reasons it was that I employed the man who killed Abul Fazzel and brought his head to me, and for this it was that I incurred my father's deep displeasure."[95]

His father was enraged and arranged for Jahangir to be passed over in the imperial succession, arranging for Jahangir's son to become emperor after him. Akbar, however, died without ensuring that his wishes would be implemented. Jahangir became emperor, and the jihad in India resumed. It is noteworthy in any case that it took an emperor's departure from Islam to give the Hindus of India any respite from the jihadi onslaught.

Jahangir Returns India to Islam

Jahangir began his reign in 1606 by having the leader of the Sikhs, Guru Arjan, tortured and killed. Some ascribed this to Arjan's aiding of a rebel prince, not to a determination to persecute the Sikhs.[96] However, Jahangir himself wrote contemptuously of Arjan: "A Hindu named Arjun lived in Govindwal on the bank of river Beas in the garb of a saint and in ostentation. From all sides cowboys and idiots became his fast followers. The business had flourished for three or four generations. For a long time it had been in my mind to put a stop to this *dukan-e-batil* [market of falsehood] or to bring him into the fold of Islam."[97] Jahangir was also said to have demanded that Arjan include passages from the Qur'an in Adi Granth, the Sikh scripture.[98]

A contemporary court historian recounted that Jahangir also moved against the Jains: "One day at Ahmadabad it was reported that many of the infidel and superstitious sect of the *Seoras* [Jains] of Gujarat had made several very great and splendid temples, and having placed in them their false gods, had managed to secure a large degree of respect for themselves and that the women who went for worship in those temples were polluted by them and other people. The Emperor Jahangir ordered them banished from the country, and their temples to be demolished."[99] Again following the practice of previous jihad rulers, Jahangir ordered contempt to be shown to the gods of the conquered people: "Their idol was thrown down on the uppermost step of the mosque, that it might be trodden upon by those who came to say their daily prayers there. By this order of the Emperor, the infidels were exceedingly disgraced, and Islam exalted."[100]

Exalting Islam was Jahangir's priority. Another contemporary historian noted Jahangir's zealousness for the religion: "The Emperor by the divine guidance, had always in view to extirpate all the rebels in his dominions, to destroy all infidels root and branch, and to raze all Pagan temples level to the ground. Endowed with a heavenly power, he devoted all his exertions to the promulgation of the Muhammadan religion; and through the aid of the Almighty God, and by the strength of his sword, he used all his endeavours to enlarge his dominions and promote the religion of Muhammad."[101]

Jahangir also manifested his Islamic piety in his memoirs:

> On the 7th Azar I went to see and shoot on the tank [holy water pool] of Pushkar, which is one of the established praying-places of the Hindus, with regard to the perfection of which they give [excellent] accounts that are incredible to any intelligence, and which is situated at a distance of three kos from Ajmir. For two or three days I shot water-fowl on that tank and returned to Ajmir. Old and new temples which, in the language of the infidels, they call Deo-hara are to be seen around this tank. Among them Rana Shankar, who is the uncle of the rebel Amar, and in my kingdom is among the high nobles, had built a Deohara of great magnificence, on which 100,000 rupees had been spent. I went to see that temple. I found a form cut out of black stone, which from the neck above was in the shape of a pig's head, and the rest of the body was like that of a man. The worthless religion of the Hindus is this, that once on a time for some particular object the Supreme Ruler thought it necessary to show himself in this shape; on this account they hold it dear and worship it. I ordered them to break that hideous form and throw it into the tank. After looking at this building there appeared a white dome on the top of a hill, to which men were coming from all quarters. When I asked about this they said that a Jogi lived there, and when

the simpletons come to see him he places in their hands a handful of flour, which they put into their mouths and imitate the cry of an animal which these fools have at some time injured, in order that by this act their sins may be blotted out. I ordered them to break down that place and turn the Jogi out of it, as well as to destroy the form of an idol there was in the dome.[102]

Jahangir was proud of his efforts to extirpate Hinduism, and had plenty of them to relate:

I am here led to relate that at the city of Banaras a temple had been erected by Rajah Maun Singh, which cost him the sum of nearly thirty-six laks of five methkaly ashrefies [a considerable sum]. The principal idol in this temple had on its head a tiara or cap, enriched with jewels to the amount of three laks ashrefies. He had placed in this temple moreover, as the associates and ministering servants of the principal idol, four other images of solid gold, each crowned with a tiara, in the like manner enriched with precious stones. It was the belief of these Jehennemites that a dead Hindu, provided when alive he had been a worshipper, when laid before this idol would be restored to life. As I could not possibly give credit to such a pretence, I employed a confidential person to ascertain the truth; and, as I justly supposed, the whole was detected to be an impudent imposture. Of this discovery I availed myself, and I made it my plea for throwing down the temple which was the scene of this imposture and on the spot, with the very same materials, I erected the great mosque, because the very name of Islam was proscribed at Banaras, and with God's blessing it is my design, if I live, to fill it full with true believers.[103]

Immediately after relating this story of jihad and persecution with pride, Jahangir recounted his heretical father Akbar the Great's answer when Jahangir asked him why he didn't persecute the Hindus:

"My dear child," said he, "I find myself a puissant monarch, the shadow of God upon earth. I have seen that he bestows the blessings of his gracious providence upon all his creatures without distinction. Should I discharge the duties of my exalted station, were I to withhold my compassion and indulgence from any of those entrusted to my charge? With all of the human race, with all of God's creatures, I am at peace: why then should I permit myself under any consideration, to be the cause of molestation or aggression to any one? Besides, are not five parts in six of mankind either Hindus or aliens to the faith; and were I to be governed by motives of the kind suggested in your inquiry, what alternative can I have but to put them all to death! I have thought it therefore my wisest plan to let these men alone. Neither is it to be forgotten, that the class of whom we are speaking, in common with the other inhabitants of Agrah, are usefully engaged, either in the pursuits of science or the arts, or of improvements for the benefit of mankind, and have in numerous instances arrived at the highest distinctions in the state, there being, indeed, to be found in this city men of every description, and of every religion on the face of the earth."[104]

Jahangir passed on this sage advice without comment. Since he juxtaposed it in his memoirs with his account of how he destroyed the temple and built the mosque at Banaras, he apparently intended this quotation to stand as a subtle rebuke of his father, and an indication of how he had eschewed his heresy and returned to Islamic orthodoxy.

During Jahangir's reign, the perilous existence that the Hindus had endured before Akbar the Great abandoned Islam returned. The Dutch merchant Francisco Pelsaert, in India while Jahangir was emperor, recounted that the Hindus were not safe even when Sunnis and Shi'a fought among themselves. He wrote that during Muharram, when the Shi'a mourn publicly the death of Husayn at Karbala, the Sunnis and Shi'a would battle, and Hindus could all too easily get caught in the middle: "The outcry [of mourning] lasts till the first quarter of the day; the coffins [*tazias*] are brought to the river, and if the two parties meet carrying their biers [it is worse on that day], and one will not give place to the other, then if they are evenly matched, they may kill each other as if they were enemies at open war, for they run with naked swords like madmen. No Hindu can venture into the streets before midday, for even if they should escape with their life, at the least their arms and legs would be broken to pieces."[105]

The English merchant William Finch, also in India around the same time, stated that Jahangir and his noblemen also used Hindu peasants for sport, and traded for horses and dogs. They played a game called *Kamargha* (human circle), which consisted of having guards surround a tract of wooded land. Inside the enclosed space, everything alive was prey. "Whatever is taken in this enclosure," Finch related, "is called the King's *shikar* or game, whether men or beasts.... The beasts taken, if men's meat, are sold...if men, they remain the King's slaves, which he sends yearly to Kabul to barter for horses and dogs: these being poor, miserable, thievish people, that live in woods and deserts, little differing from beasts."[106] Some of those Hindus who lived in woods and deserts may have been there in order to escape the persecution of the Muslims. In any case, Jahangir's rejection of his father's words—"With all of the human race, with all of God's creatures, I am at peace: why then should I permit myself under any consideration, to be the cause of molestation or aggression to any one?"—could not have been more complete.

Shah Jahan

Jahangir died in 1627. His successor, Shah Jahan, continued his persecution of the Hindus. Shah Jahan's court historian Abdul Hamid Lahori recorded in his *Padshahnama* (*Chronicle of the Emperor*) the emperor's swift action in 1633 against Hindus who tried to build new temples to replace the many that Muslims had destroyed: "It had been brought to the notice of His Majesty that during the late reign many idol temples had been begun, but remained unfinished at Benares, the great stronghold of infidelism. The infidels were now desirous of completing them. His Majesty, the defender of the faith, gave orders that at Benares, and throughout all his dominions at every place, all temples that had been begun should be cast down. It was now reported from the province of Allahabad that 76 temples had been destroyed in the district of Benares."[107]

That same year, according to Lahori, "400 Christian prisoners, male and female, young and old, with the idols of their worship" were brought "to the presence of the faith-defending Emperor. He ordered that the principles of the Muhammadan religion should be explained to them, and that they should be called upon to adopt it. A few appreciated the honour offered to them and embraced the faith: they experienced the kindness of the Emperor. But the majority in perversity and wilfulness rejected the proposal. These were distributed among the *amirs*, who were directed to keep these despicable wretches in rigorous confinement. When any one of them accepted the true faith, a report was to be made to the Emperor, so that provision might be made for him. Those who refused were to be kept in continual confinement. So it came to pass that many of them passed from prison to hell. Such of their idols as were likenesses of the prophets were thrown into the Jumna [river], the rest were broken to pieces."[108]

Two years later, Shah Jahan's jihadis overran Bundela, the Rajput kingdom in central India. The jihadis seized the wives of Jajhar Singh, the Bundela king, and presented them to Shah Jahan, who, heedless of their status, made them sex slaves. To head off the possibility of future rebellions, Shah Jahan had Jajhar's son and grandson forcibly converted to Islam.[109] In Orchha, the capital of the Bundela kingdom, Shah Jahan had the majestic temple of Bir Singh Dev demolished and a mosque built where it had stood.[110]

Aurangzeb

This continued when Shah Jahan became seriously ill in 1657, for his son and heir apparent, Dara Shikoh, was a man in the mold of his great-grandfather, Akbar the Great: he was deeply influenced by Sufism and so admired Hinduism that he declared the Upanishads to be a divine revelation that predated the Qur'an. He was also so friendly with the Portuguese Jesuits that he was rumored to be on the verge of converting to Christianity. All of this made the prospect of his becoming Mughal emperor abominable to his younger brother, Aurangzeb, a devout and committed Muslim.[111] Aurangzeb defeated his brother in battle and had him beheaded; when the head was presented to him, Aurangzeb was said to have shed tears.[112] He had Shah Jahan placed under house arrest, and dedicated himself to outdoing all his predecessors in persecuting and waging jihad against the Hindus.

The contemporary historian Mirza Muhammad Kazim recounted that Aurangzeb undertook this task with relish: "In 1661 Aurangzeb in his zeal to uphold the law of Islam sent orders to his Viceroy of Bihar, Daud Khan, to conquer Palamau. In the military operations that followed many temples were destroyed.... Towards the end of the same year, when Mir Jumla made a war on the Raja of Kuch Bihar, the Mughals destroyed many temples during the course of their operations. Idols were broken and some temples were converted into mosques."[113]

Another Muslim historian, Saqa Mustad Khan, writing just after Aurangzeb died in 1707, compiled a detailed record of Aurangzeb's jihad activity from the emperor's state archives. In 1669, "the Lord Cherisher of the Faith," Khan wrote, "learnt that in the provinces of Tatta, Multan, and especially at Benares, the Brahman misbelievers used to teach their false books in their established schools, and that admirers and students both Hindu and Muslim, used to come from great distances to these misguided men in order to acquire this vile learning. His Majesty, eager to establish Islam, issued orders to the governors of all the provinces to demolish the schools and temples of the infidels and with the utmost urgency put down the teaching and the public practice of the religion of these misbelievers."[114]

Khan recorded with obvious pride how, in 1670, the present capital of Pakistan got its name:

> During this month of Ramzan [Ramadan] abounding in miracles, the Emperor as the promoter of justice and over-thrower of mischief, as a knower of truth and destroyer of oppression, as the zephyr of the garden of victory and the reviver of the faith of the Prophet, issued orders for the demolition of the temple situated in Mathura, famous as the Dehra of Kesho Rai. In a short time, by the great exertions of his officers, the destruction of this strong foundation of infidelity was accomplished, and on its site a lofty mosque

was built at the expenditure of a large sum. Praised be the august God of the faith of Islam, that in the auspicious reign of this destroyer of infidelity and turbulence, such a wonderful and seemingly impossible work was successfully accomplished. On seeing this instance of the strength of the Emperor's faith and the grandeur of his devotion to God, the proud Rajas were stifled and in amazement they stood like images facing the wall. The idols, large and small, set with costly jewels which had been set up in the temple were brought to Agra, and buried under the steps of the mosque of the Begam Sahib, in order to be continually trodden upon. The name of Mathura was changed to Islamabad.[115]

That same year, Aurangzeb also issued this sweeping decree: "Every idol-house built during the last 10 or 12 years, whether with brick or clay, should be demolished without delay. Also, do not allow the crushed Hindus and despicable infidels to repair their old temples. Reports of the destruction of temples should be sent to the Court under the seal of the qazis and attested by pious Shaikhs."[116]

Aurangzeb also had the temple Viswanath at Kashi destroyed.[117] At Khandela in 1679, his jihadis demolished the temple and killed the three hundred Hindus who were defending it. Aurangzeb's commander followed the familiar practice: "Khan Jahan Bahadur came from Jodhpur, after demolishing the temples and bringing with himself some cartloads of idols, and had audience of the Emperor, who highly praised him and ordered that the idols, which were mostly jewelled, golden, silvery, bronze, copper or stone, should be cast in the yard [jilaukhanah] of the Court and under the steps of the Jama mosque, to be trodden on. They remained so for some time and at last their very names were lost."[118]

And on and on. Saqa Mustad Khan reported that in January 1680, "the Emperor went to view lake Udaisagar, constructed by the Rana, and ordered all the three temples on its banks to be demolished." The following day, "Hasan Ali Khan brought to the Emperor twenty camel-loads of tents and other things captured from the Rana's palace and reported that one hundred and seventy-two other temples in the environs of Udaipur had been destroyed."[119] Later that year, "Abu Turab, who had been sent to demolish the temples of Amber, returned to Court…and reported that he had pulled down sixty-six temples."[120]

Aurangzeb rewarded the destroyers of temples. Hasan Ali Khan "received the title of Bahadur Alamgirshahi."[121] And Hamiduddin Khan Bahadur, "who had gone to demolish a temple and build a mosque [in its place] in Bijapur, having excellently carried out his orders, came to Court and gained praise and the post of darogha of gusalkhanah, which brought him near the Emperor's person."[122]

Aurangzeb personally issued orders for the destruction of temples. "The temple of Somnath," he wrote, "was demolished early in my reign and idol worship [there] put down. It is not known what the state of things there is at present. If the idolaters have again taken to the worship of images at the place, then destroy the temple in such a way that no trace of the building may be left, and also expel them [the worshippers] from the place."[123]

On another occasion, he issued this order: "The houses of this country [Maharashtra] are exceedingly strong and built solely of stone and iron. The hatchet-men of the government in the course of my marching do not get sufficient strength and power [that is, time] to destroy and raze the temples of the infidels that meet the eye on the way. You should appoint an orthodox inspector [darogha] who may afterwards destroy them at leisure and dig up their foundations."[124] Aurangzeb had Sikh as well as Hindu temples demolished, and mosques built in their place.[125] He observed: "The demolition of a temple is possible at any time, as it cannot walk away from its place."[126]

The Ganj i-Arshadi, another contemporary Muslim account of Aurangzeb's reign, related an instance of Hindu resistance that resulted in the emperor's undertaking even harsher measures:

> The infidels demolished a mosque that was under construction and wounded the artisans. When the news reached Shah Yasin [one of Aurangzeb's commanders], he came to Banaras from Mandyawa and collecting the Muslim weavers, demolished the big temple. A Sayyid who was an artisan by profession agreed with one Abdul Rasul to build a mosque at Banaras, and accordingly the foundation was laid. Near the place there was a temple and many hous-

es belonging to it were in the occupation of the Rajputs. The infidels decided that the construction of a mosque in the locality was not proper and that it should be razed to the ground. At night, the walls of the mosque were found demolished. Next day, the wall was rebuilt but it was again destroyed. This happened three or four times.[127]

Finally Shah Yasin "determined to vindicate the cause of Islam." He and his jihadis "demolished about 500 temples. They desired to destroy the temple of Beni Madho, but as lanes were barricaded, they desisted from going further."[128]

According to the eighteenth-century Muslim history *Kanzu i-Mahfuz*, there was in the city of Agra a temple that was a popular pilgrimage site. The Mughal rulers had for years collected a fee from the pilgrims, thereby considerably augmenting the royal treasury. When he found out about it, however, Aurangzeb was furious and forbade pilgrimages to the temple. His noblemen tried to reason with him, explaining that there would be a great loss of revenue for the government if these pilgrimages were forbidden. Aurangzeb replied: "What you say is right, but I have considered well on the subject, and have reflected on it deeply; but if you wish to augment the revenue, there is a better plan for attaining the object by exacting the *jizya*. By this means, idolatry will be suppressed, the Muhammadan religion and the true faith will be honoured, our proper duty will be performed, the finances of the state will be increased, and the infidels will be disgraced." The noblemen were pleased with this solution, and Aurangzeb ordered the Agra temple destroyed.[129]

Aurangzeb did not reintroduce the *jizya* only for the Hindus of Agra, but in 1679 for all the Hindus in his domains, in order to, so said the decree, "spread Islam and put down the practice of infidelism."[130] A delegation of Hindus appealed to Aurangzeb to reconsider. They reminded him that Akbar the Great, as well as Jahangir and Shah Jahan, had not collected the *jizya*, and their domains had prospered:

> Such were the benevolent intentions of your ancestors. Whilst they pursued these great and generous principles, wheresoever they directed their steps, conquest and prosperity went before them, and then they reduced many

countries and fortresses to their obedience. During your majesty's reign, many have been alienated from the empire, and further loss of territory must necessarily follow, since devastation and rapine now universally prevail without restraint. Your subjects are trampled under foot, and every province of your empire is impoverished, depopulation spreads, and difficulties accumulate.

If Your Majesty places any faith in those books by distinction called divine, you will there be instructed that God is the God of all mankind, not the God of Muhammadans alone. The Pagan and the Musalman are equally in His presence. Distinctions of colour are of his ordination. It is He who gives existence. In your temples, to His name the voice is raised in prayer; in a house of images, when the bell is shaken, still He is the object of adoration. To vilify the religion or customs of other men is to set at naught the pleasure of the Almighty. When we deface a picture we naturally incur the resentment of the painter; and justly has the poet said, "Presume not to arraign or scrutinize the various works of power divine." In fine, the tribute you demand from the Hindus is repugnant to justice; it is equally foreign from good policy, as it must impoverish the country; moreover, it is an innovation and an infringement of the laws of Hindostan.[131]

Aurangzeb was as unmoved by this as Jahangir was by Akbar the Great's explanation of why he didn't persecute the Hindus. The *jizya* was reimposed, and Aurangzeb persecuted the Sikhs as well. The historian Khafi Khan, a contemporary of Aurangzeb, noted that he also "ordered the temples of the Sikhs to be destroyed and the guru's agents [*masands*] for collecting the tithes and presents of the faithful to be expelled from the cities."[132]

Saqa Mustad Khan found much to admire in Aurangzeb because of all this:

As his blessed nature dictated, he was characterized by perfect devotion to the rites of the Faith; he followed the teaching of the great Imam, Abu Hanifa (God be pleased with him!), and established and enforced to the best of his power the five foundations of Islam. Through the auspices of his hearty endeavour, the Hanafi creed [that is, the Orthodox Sunni faith)] has gained such strength and currency in the great country of Hindustan as was never seen in the times of any of the preceding sovereigns. By one stroke of the pen, the Hindu clerks [writers] were dismissed from the public employment. Large numbers of the places of worship of the infidels and great temples of these wicked people have been thrown down and desolated. Men who can see only the outside of things are filled with wonder at the successful accomplishment of such a seemingly difficult task. And on the sites of the temples, lofty mosques have been built.[133]

Bakhtawar Khan, a nobleman during Aurangzeb's reign, was also pleased, noting that "Hindu writers have been entirely excluded from holding public offices, and all the worshipping places of the infidels and great temples of these infamous people have been thrown down and destroyed in a manner which excites astonishment at the successful completion of so difficult a task. His Majesty personally teaches the sacred kalima [fundamentals of the Islamic faith] to many infidels with success. All the mosques in the empire are repaired at public expense. Imams, criers to the daily prayers, and readers of the khutba [sermon] have been appointed to each of them, so that a large sum of money has been and is still laid out in these disbursements."[134]

By the time of Aurangzeb's death in 1707, he was so hated for his harshness, and not just toward the Hindus and Sikhs, that the Mughals faced numerous rebellions. But the jihad, as always, would go on.

CHAPTER EIGHT

DÉGRINGOLADE

Jihad in the Eighteenth and Nineteenth Centuries

I. THE OTTOMANS IN DECLINE

Wars with Russia and Austria

The Ottoman Empire for much of its existence conducted its affairs in much the same way European states did, declaring war and concluding treaties. Underlying all of its activity, however, was the jihad imperative, which ensured that its foreign policy remained imperialistic and expansionist. Yet this expansion, as the empire declined, was often more a matter of theory than of practice.

When King Charles XII of Sweden fled to the Sublime Porte after being defeated by Czar Peter the Great in 1709, the Ottomans, who had a treaty with the Russians, nonetheless refused to turn Charles over to them; they saw a chance to expand their domains north of the Black Sea at the Russians' expense.

Charles spent his time in Constantinople trying to gain support for an Ottoman attack on the Russians, which the Tatar Ottoman clients in the Crimea very much wanted as well. After much intrigue, in October 1712, the Ottoman Empire declared war on Russia.[1] The Ottomans, victorious, forced Peter the Great to give up Azov on the Don River, east of the Crimea, along with other territories, as well as to provide a safe conduct for Charles XII to get back to Sweden and to promise to withdraw Russian armies from Poland. Peter, in a deep depression, lamented: "The Lord God drove me out of this place, like Adam out of paradise."[2]

Peter the Great was being a trifle overdramatic. The Russian losses were not actually very great. In fact, Charles of Sweden was enraged that the Ottomans did not pursue and destroy utterly the retreating Russian army. By this time, however, the sultanate had neither the will nor the resources to take the jihad to the Russian infidels in a major and concerted effort to win and hold more territory; its posture toward the Russians remained primarily defensive, even as it declared war in 1712.

The Ottomans had at the same time lowered their sights in Europe. In 1715 they seized Morea from the Republic of Venice, which, like the Ottoman Empire, had seen better days. But they were not able to enjoy their victory for long, as the Habsburg emperor Charles VI, who was allied with the Venetians, saw the capture of Morea as an act of war. The Austrians advanced upon Belgrade, defeating the Ottomans in 1716, taking from them by a subsequent treaty most of their Balkan territories.[3]

The days of Ottoman jihadis threatening the very survival of Christian Europe were at an end. The states of Europe began to look for opportunities to strengthen their domains against the Ottomans. The eighteenth-century Muslim historian Umar Busnavi recounted what led the Russians to declare war against the Ottomans in 1735, and the Austrians to join two years later, ascribing it all to the perception of Ottoman weakness. Busnavi's language also shows that even if the Ottoman ability to pursue jihad had waned, the Ottomans still tended to see the world in terms of Islam's uncompromising believer/unbeliever division:

> It was owing to the perfidious Muscovite infidels having violated their engagements with the Porte, that five thousand chosen men, standard-bearers, surgeons, and a number of brave officers, had been sent to the Russian frontiers, for the purpose of aiding the army of the faithful against the aggressions of the infidels. This circumstance left the kingdom of Bosnia in a great measure exposed, and also afforded an occasion to the infidel Germans to believe, that the country was in such a defenceless state, that they also were induced to violate the peace. Both Germans and Muscovites had formed, long before this, schemes against the peace and tranquillity of the empire; and now both began

to put their wicked designs into execution. Owing to the disasters which had befallen the empire in the east, these hateful wretches, the Germans, were led to think, when they perceived that Bosnia and the adjacent provinces were in a defenceless state in consequence of the war with the Muscovites, that the exalted Mohammedan power had become lax and feeble. They became inflamed with prospects of success, and wickedly resolved on attacking the Ottoman empire in various quarters.[4]

This time, however, the Ottomans were victorious, and won back all the territory the empire had lost twenty years before in Serbia, Bosnia, and Wallachia. Busnavi attributed this in large part to the valor of the Bosnian Muslims, Europeans who had embraced Islam rather than the sufferings that dhimmitude entailed. He explained that "by reason of this country's vicinity to the infidel nations, such as the deceitful Germans, Hungarians, Serbs [Sclavonians], the tribes of Croats, and the Venetians, strong and powerful, and furnished with abundance of cannon, muskets, and other weapons of destruction, it has had to carry on fierce war from time to time with one or other, or more, of these deceitful enemies—enemies accustomed to mischief, inured to deeds of violence, resembling wild mountaineers in asperity, and inflamed with the rage of seeking opportunities of putting their machinations into practice." The Bosnians, said Busnavi, "know this," and were in response "strong, courageous, ardent, lion-hearted, professionally fond of war, and revengeful."[5] Europe would see more of these aggressive and warlike qualities in the late twentieth century.

The Wahhabi Revolt

Even as the Ottomans remained, for people such as Busnavi, guardians and foremost exponents of Islam, they presently faced a challenge from other Muslims on precisely those grounds. In the 1740s, a Muslim preacher in Arabia named Muhammad ibn Abdul Wahhab began to preach against "ignorance, *shirk*, and innovation."[6] *Shirk* is worshipping others along with or aside from Allah, and is the foremost sin in Islam; innovation (*bid'ah*) is the adoption of practices that neither the Qur'an nor Muhammad mandate. Wahhab demanded that all *shirk* and *bid'ah* be swept away, and that Muslims return to strict observance solely of what was taught in the Qur'an and Sunnah. Wahhab's teachings were so simple that one of his publications, *The Book of Monotheism* (*Kitab al-Tauhid*), consisted of nothing but *ahadith*, traditional reports of Muhammad's words and deeds, without a single word of comment or explanation from Wahhab at all.[7]

But Wahhab's message was as powerful as it was crude. He wrote to the people of Qasim in Arabia:

> I assert that *jihad* will always be valid under the *Imam*'s leadership, whether [he is] righteous or sinner; praying behind [sinner] *imams* is also permissible.
>
> *Jihad* cannot be stopped by the injustice of the unjust or even the fairness of those who are just.
>
> I believe that hearing and obeying Muslim rulers is [mandatory (*wajib*)], whether they are righteous or sinners, as long as they do not enjoin Allah's disobedience.
>
> And he who becomes the Caliph and the people take him as such and agree to his leadership, or if he overpowers them by the word to capture the *Khilafah* [until he captures it, then obedience to him becomes a necessity and rising against him becomes *haram* (forbidden)].
>
> I believe the people of *bid'ah* should be boycotted and shunned until they repent.
>
> I judge people of *bid'ah* according to their outward conduct and refer knowledge of their inward [state of faith] to Allah...[8]

Despite these declarations that the Muslim ruler must be obeyed, Wahhab and his jihadis began to wage jihad against the local authorities in Arabia, coming ever closer to a direct challenge to Ottoman power. (Wahhab's statements about obeying Muslim rulers, however, would prove quite useful to the later Saudi state.) The Ottomans and other Muslims, he charged, had departed from this strict observance and were thus guilty of *bid'ah* and apostasy; they were no longer Muslims.

After gaining the loyalty of Uthman ibn Muammar, the emir of Uyayna in Arabia, Wahhab and his warriors began to gain notice by smashing the tomb of Zayd ibn al-Khattab, a companion of Muhammad, as Wahhab held that the tombs of the saints were idolatrous. Shortly thereafter, Wahhab personally stoned an accused adulteress to death, an act that won him great admiration; he began to gain followers in large numbers. "Thereafter," writes a modern-day Saudi biographer of Wahhab, "his cause flourished, his power increased, and true tauhid [monotheism] was everywhere disseminated, together with the enjoining of virtue and the prohibition of vice."[9]

Expelled under pressure from Uyayna, Wahhab moved on to Diriyya, cementing an alliance with the local emir that would have global consequences: the ruler's name was Muhammad ibn Saud.[10] Wahhab told Saud about his plans to wage jihad against all those who were not, in his view, implementing Islam properly, and Saud agreed to help. In 1746, they formally announced the beginning of this jihad, and began to plunder and pillage their way across Arabia. The Wahhabis soon conquered most of Najd, and then Riyadh in 1773.[11] According to the nineteenth-century French historian Louis Alexandre Olivier de Corancez, who wrote a history of the Wahhabis from their origins though 1809:

> At the moment when they were least expected, the Wahabis would arrive to confront the tribe they wished to subject, and a messenger from Abd al-Aziz ibn Saud would appear bearing a Koran in one hand and a sword in the other. His message was stark and simple: Abd el Aziz to the Arabs of the tribe of _____, hail! Your duty is to believe in the book I send you. Do not be like the idolatrous Turks, who give God a human intermediary. If you are true believers, you shall be saved; otherwise, I shall wage war upon you until death.[12]

The Ottomans, meanwhile, were too busy with the Russians to pay all of this much notice. The partition of Poland in 1764 by Catherine the Great of Russia and Frederick the Great of Prussia enraged the sultan Mustafa III, who was anxious for a new war with Russia. His advisors, noting the weakness of the empire by that point, counseled against it, but Mustafa was determined, telling them, "I will find some means of humbling these infidels."[13] The war came in 1768, and ended disastrously for the Ottomans in 1774, with the Muslims, not the infidels, ending up humbled. They lost, among other things, political sovereignty over the Tatar territories north of Black Sea, although the treaty recognized that the Ottoman sultan, as the caliph of Islam, would still have spiritual authority there. The Russian czar, in a reciprocal arrangement that displayed Ottoman weakness to the world, was acknowledged as the protector of the Christians in the Ottoman domains of Wallachia and Moldavia, with the right to intervene militarily on their behalf.[14]

Another war between the Ottoman Empire and Russia and Austria between 1787 and 1792 only confirmed the loss of the Crimea and other Black Sea territories, which had been formally annexed by Russia. The sultan Abdulhamid, mindful of Catherine the Great's designs on Constantinople, had Ottoman coins of this period labeled "Struck in Islambol," a name for the city meaning "Full of Islam" that was common among Ottoman Turks of the time, rather than "Struck in Constantinople" (although after the war, the Ottomans began using the name Constantinople again).[15] This both emphasized the Islamic character of the city and courted divine favor. The Islamic scholars of Islambol awarded Abdulhamid himself the title Warrior for the Faith.[16]

Enter Napoleon

But in the end, none of it helped. The Ottomans were so weak that they could not prevent Napoleon Bonaparte from invading Egypt in 1798. Napoleon professed his love for the Qur'an and Muhammad. To one imam he actually professed the Islamic faith, saying: "Glory to Allah! There is no other God but God; Mohammed is his prophet, and I am one of his friends.... The Koran delights my mind.... I love the prophet."[17] He told Egyptian imams that it was "the will of Mohammed" that the Egyptians ally with the French against the Mamluks.[18] He denounced the Russians to the Ottoman sultan, saying that they "abhor those who believe in the unity of God, because, according to their lies, they believe that there are three," an echo of the Qur'an's warning to Christians to "say not 'Three'" (4:171), that is, do not profess the faith in the Holy Trinity.[19] But when asked later if he had actually become Muslim, Napoleon laughed off that idea, saying: "Fighting is a soldier's religion; I never changed that. The other is the affair of women and priests. As for me, I always adopt the religion of the country I am in."[20]

The Egyptian people, however, were never convinced and never accepted his rule. The Egyptian historian Abd al-Rahman al-Jabarti, who lived through the French occupation of Egypt, gave one reason why Napoleon and his men were so unpopular: the French, he wrote, treated the *dhimmi* populations as equals; they allowed "the lowliest Copts, Syrian and Orthodox Christians, and Jews" to mount horses and bear arms, in blithe indifference to Sharia rules.[21]

The Ottoman sultan Selim III declared jihad against the French.[22] The French ventured into the Ottoman province of Syria in 1799 but were defeated, after which Napoleon returned to France, leaving his troops in Egypt under the command of General Jean-Baptiste Kléber, who quickly won several victories over the Ottomans and the Egyptians. The following year, however, Suleiman al-Halabi, a student at Cairo's venerable Islamic university, al-Azhar, stabbed Kléber to death. Al-Halabi was executed and, in a foreshadowing of the twenty-first-century tendency in the West to see all jihad activity as a manifestation of mental illness, his skull was sent to France, where for years it was displayed to enable students of phrenology to study its "bump of crime and fanaticism."[23]

Kléber's successor, Jacques François de Menou, took Napoleon's professed admiration for Islam one step farther, marrying an Egyptian woman and actually converting to Islam, taking the name Abdallah. But even this did not endear the French to the Egyptians, and gained Menou the contempt of his troops.[24] When the British arrived in 1801 to help the Ottomans against the French, they found Menou, who was not nearly as able a commander as Kléber (Napoleon called him "that fool Menou"), totally unprepared; the French withdrew from Egypt that same year.[25]

Egypt was not under direct Ottoman control (it was semiautonomous under the Mamluks), but the French had defeated the Ottomans more than once, and this invasion from a far-off Western European Christian state was yet another serious blow to the Ottoman self-image as tough, if no longer invincible, jihadis. The most memorable result of Napoleon's Egyptian venture is widely believed to be the loss of the

Sphinx's nose, shot off by French soldiers during target practice. This, however, is yet another piece of Islamic apologetic mythmaking; in reality, the nose had been removed centuries before the French got there, by the fourteenth-century Sufi Muslim leader Muhammad Sa'im al-Dahr. Al-Dahr had discovered that some of the Muslim peasants in Egypt, ignorant of their own faith's prohibitions against idolatry, were worshipping the Sphinx; he had the nose chipped off in order to show the impotence of this massive god statue.[26]

The Wahhabis in Mecca

Meanwhile, the Wahhabis continued advancing in Arabia. Saud died in 1766, and Wahhab in 1791, but the movement did not die with them. In 1801, the Wahhabis raided Karbala in Iraq, slaughtering about two thousand of the city's inhabitants, destroying the gravesite of Husayn and carrying off the jewels that had adorned his tomb, along with all the gold, silver, and other precious items they found in the city. They took Ta'if in Arabia in February 1803, killing two hundred people and burning all the books they found aside from the Qur'an and volumes of the *hadith*. Then, in April 1803, they entered Mecca and demanded the submission of the city's Islamic scholars; they were, however, driven out that summer. After seizing Medina in 1805, the Wahhabis returned to Mecca the following year, staying for six years this time, during which they destroyed many of the tombs it contained.

The Ottomans, as busy as they were with the Russians, could not ignore the Wahhabi occupation of the two holiest sites in Islam. Yet even they must have known that the Wahhabi/Saudi challenge to their power was in the tradition of many other such challenges throughout Islamic history. The Ottoman caliphate itself began as a challenge to the Abbasids. The Abbasids arose in revolt against the Umayyads. Muawiyya, the first Umayyad caliph, challenged the authority of Ali, the last "Rightly-Guided Caliph," and waged jihad against him. Wahhab was an Islamic revivalist in the mold of Ibn Tumart, who led the Almohad revolt against the Almoravids in Morocco in the early twelfth century. Ottoman officials had their own comparisons. The Ottoman admiral Eyüb Sabri Pasha compared the Wahhabis to the Qarmatians, the tenth-century thieves of the Black Stone of Mecca; other Ottoman officials likened them to the Khawarij, who in the beginning decades of Islam waged bloody jihad against all Muslims they considered sinful—that is, all other Muslims.[27]

In 1812, Muhammad Ali Pasha, the governor of Egypt, drove the Wahhabis from Medina and several months later from Mecca as well. Seven years later, he sacked the Wahhabi capital of Diriyya and executed two of Wahhab's grandsons. Abdullah ibn Saud, by this time the leader of the Wahhabis, was sent to Constantinople, where he was also executed.[28] But the Ottomans were too weak to keep Muhammad Ali Pasha's troops stationed in Arabia indefinitely and, once they left, the Wahhabis began a resurgence, establishing their new capital in Riyadh. In 1832, the Wahhabis invaded Oman and forced the sultan of Muscat to pay them tribute.[29]

In the middle of the nineteenth century, the British realized the Wahhabis' potential as a tool in their long-term plan to destroy the Ottoman Empire. In 1865, they put the Saud family on the imperial payroll; by 1917, the Saudis were receiving five thousand pounds from the British every month, just to keep up the pressure on the Ottomans.[30] Once again, the shortsighted calculations of non-Muslim politicians practicing realpolitik ended up aiding the global jihad.

Meanwhile, in the first decade of the nineteenth century, jihad raged with new intensity in sub-Saharan Africa, where Islam and its wars of conquest had been a presence since the fourteenth century. The Islamic scholar Usman dan Fodio declared jihad against the Hausa kingdoms of northern Nigeria and ultimately established the Sokoto Caliphate, with himself as caliph, in what is today Nigeria and Cameroon. Dan Fodio's success led to the creation of other Islamic states in Central and West Africa, which lasted until they were defeated by European colonialists. Dan Fodio's Sokoto Caliphate fell to the British in 1903.

Greek Independence

By the early nineteenth century, the Wahhabis were the least of the Ottomans' troubles. In 1804, the Serbs rose in rebellion against their Ottoman masters, who ruthlessly put the uprising down. The governor of Belgrade, Suleiman Pasha, had the rebels burned alive as they hung by their feet. Others he had castrated or bastinadoed (caning the soles of their feet). Still others he had impaled outside the city gates, their bodies serving as a warning to others who might have been contemplating rebellion.[31]

But revolution was in the air all over the world, and no Ottoman brutality could quench the thirst for independence among its subject Christian peoples. In 1821, it was the Greeks of the Morea. Thomas Gordon, a British army officer, published *The History of the Greek Revolution* in 1833, providing a vivid account of the Greek rage after centuries of oppression, and the brutality of the Ottoman response.

After the Greek independence fighters took Kalavryta, a small town that the Ottomans surrendered without a fight, the Greeks proceeded to Patras. After hearing what had happened at Kalavryta, the warriors of the Sultan were prepared to make a stand. According to Gordon, the Turks "commenced hostilities by setting fire to the house of a primate, named Papadiamandopoulos; but being attacked by a body of Ionians, that were prepared for the conflict, they fled to the castle, and opened a cannonade against the town. The Greek population immediately rose, and, amidst volleys of musketry, proclaimed with loud shouts the liberty of their country."[32]

The two sides, Gordon reported, "massacred each other without mercy."[33] Archbishop Germanos, the metropolitan of Patras, and, said Gordon, "the other Greek generals, Papadiamandopoulos, Londos, Zaimis, and Sotiri, primates of Patrass, Vostizza, and Kalavryta, set forth a proclamation containing merely these emphatic words—Peace to the Christians! Respect to the Consuls! Death to the Turks!"[34]

Chanting, "Not a Turk shall remain in the Morea," the Greeks, having endured centuries of brutal oppression, began a pitiless campaign against the Muslims, who were ready to respond in kind.[35] On the island of Crete, the janissaries killed the metropolitan of Candia and five bishops at the altar of their cathedral.[36] And in Patras on Palm Sunday, according to Gordon, "the Christians had prepared to celebrate with pomp a festival ushered in by inauspicious omens; first a smart shock of an earthquake, then a cannonade announcing the arrival of Yussuf Pasha, and lastly the appearance of an Ottoman brig of war, which saluted the fort, and cast anchor before the town."[37] That was the end of the Palm Sunday festivities. "The Mussulmans obtained a rich booty, and for several days the Pasha and his troops amused themselves at their leisure in impaling or beheading prisoners and circumcising Christian children."[38]

Determined to put down the rebellion, one week later the Ottomans arrested the patriarch of Constantinople, Gregory V, shortly after the conclusion of the Paschal Divine Liturgy on Easter Sunday. Although he had not worked with the rebels or said anything about the rebellion, Ottoman officials were determined to make an example of him, and told the patriarch that he was being dismissed from his office, as he was "unworthy of the patriarchal dignity and ungrateful to the Sublime Porte and a traitor."[39] He was stripped of his patriarchal robes, imprisoned, and tortured. His torturers told him that his misery could be ended simply by his conversion to Islam, but he replied, "Do your job. The patriarch of the Orthodox Christians dies as an Orthodox Christian."[40]

And so he did. The Ottomans hanged him in front of the gates of his patriarchate and left his body there, as a warning to others who might have been contemplating rebellion, for three days. Then, in keeping with their standard procedure of keeping the *dhimmi* communities antagonistic to one another, and to prevent them from uniting against their overlords, they prevailed upon some Jews of Constantinople to cut down the body and throw it into the sea.[41]

But the Ottomans could not crush the rebellion. The Greeks of the Morea won their independence. And more trouble was coming for the sultanate. The Albanian commander Mehmet Ali Pasha, appointed their wali (viceroy) in Egypt in 1805, began to pursue an independent course, ultimately challenging Ottoman control of Syria. The British and French Empires were ultimately the beneficiaries of this infighting, moving into Egypt and Syria, respectively. That would not be, however, for several more decades; and in the short term, the Ottomans needed British and French help in yet another war with the Russians over the Crimea.

Their help was going to come only at a price. Stratford Canning, the British ambassador to the Sublime Porte, in 1842 protested to the sultan Abdulmecid after seeing two Christians who had converted to Islam and then returned to Christianity executed in accord with Islam's death penalty for apostasy. He urged the caliph to "give his royal word that henceforward neither should Christianity be insulted in his dominions, nor should Christians be in any way persecuted for their religion."[42]

Needing British support, Abdulmecid agreed, for which Queen Victoria sent him congratulations. As the British and French allied with the Ottomans against Russia in the Crimean War, Canning used the increasing Ottoman dependence on the Western powers to continue to press the Ottomans for reform of the *dhimmi* laws. This culminated in the Hatt-i Humayun decree of 1856 that enacted what were known as the Tanzimat reforms, declaring that all Ottoman subjects were equal before the law, regardless of religion.

The Europeans added the Hatt-i Humayun decree to the Treaty of Paris that ended the Crimean War, and praised "the Sultan's generous intentions towards the Christian population of his Empire."[43] However, the British and French severely disappointed Canning by assuring the Ottomans and the world that they did not consider themselves to have any right "to interfere either collectively or individually in the relations of the Sultan with his subjects or in the internal administration of the Empire."[44]

Canning knew this would doom the reform: without Western pressure, the Ottomans would continue to enforce Islamic law, as the immutable law of Allah was more important and more binding than any treaty or decree. The Sublime Porte, Canning said, would "give way to its natural indolence and leave the firman [decree] of reform…a lifeless paper, valuable only as a record of sound principles."[45]

That is exactly what happened. The British consul James H. Skene wrote to another British official on March 31, 1859, that "the Christian subjects of the sultan at Aleppo still live in a state of terror." He attributed this to the trauma they had suffered nine years earlier, when

> …houses were plundered, men of distinction among them were murdered, and women violated.… They were not allowed to ride in the town, not even to walk in the gardens. Rich merchants were fain to dress in the humblest garb to

escape notice; when they failed in this they were often forced to sweep the streets or act as porters in order to give proofs of their patience and obedience; and they were never addressed by a Mussulman without expressions of contempt."[46]

Another British consul, James Brant, wrote in July 1860 about "the inability of the Sultans [sic] Government to protect its Christian subjects," referring to massacres of Christians by Muslim mobs in Ottoman domains.[47] Yet another British consul, James Finn, wrote at the same time that "oppression against Christians usually begins with the fanatic populace, but it is neither repressed nor punished by the Government."[48] This was because the "fanatic populace" was as aware of Islamic law as the government was, and was much more determined to enforce it.

Some Ottoman officials, on the other hand, realized that what the "fanatic populace" wanted was not always what was best for them. The grand vizier Ali Pasha gave the Sultan Abdulaziz a revolutionary reason why he should support these reforms: strict adherence to the Sharia was actually weakening the empire. Christians, being barred from military service, which was supposed to be one element of their subjugation, were getting rich devoting themselves to other pursuits, and the *jizya* was not enough to strip them of all this wealth:

> The [unequal] privileges enjoyed by different communities arise from inequalities in their obligations. This is a grave inconvenience. The Muslims are absorbed almost entirely in the service of government. Other people devote themselves to professions which bring wealth. In this way the latter establish an effective and fatal superiority over Your Majesty's Muslim subjects. In addition [only the Muslims serve in the army]. Under these circumstances the Muslim population, which decreases at a frightening rate, will be quickly absorbed and become nothing more than a tiny minority, growing weaker day by day.... What is a man good for when he returns to his village after spending the most vigorous part of his life in the army barracks or camps...? Muslims must, like the Christians, devote themselves to

[commercial] agriculture, trade, industry and crafts. Labour is the only durable capital. Let us put ourselves to work, Sire, that is the only way to safety for us. There is still time to liberate the Muslim population from obligations which benefit the Christians.... Let the Christians furnish soldiers, officers and government functionaries in proportion to their numbers.[49]

This was an extraordinary statement, and in a more devout age it might have cost Ali Pasha his head for implying that adherence to the law of Allah was disadvantageous in this world for the Turks, when Allah had promised that the believers would prosper in this world as well as in the next. Ali Pasha was presaging the subversive idea that Kemal Ataturk would make the basis of his secular Turkish government after World War I: the reason for Turkish failure was Islam, and the only path to its resuscitation required discarding Islam, at least as a political system.

Meanwhile, the Ottoman Empire continued its decline, although the sultan Abdulhamid II, who reigned from 1876 to 1909, declared that the caliphate was as powerful as it ever was and could be summoned by his word. He raised the prospect of jihad's being waged by Muslims who were living under the rule of the colonial powers:

As long as the unity of Islam continues, England, France, Russia and Holland are in my hands, because with a word [I] the caliph could unleash the *cihad* among their Muslim subjects and this would be a tragedy for the Christians.... One day [Muslims] will rise and shake off the infidel's yoke. Eighty-five million Muslims under [British] rule, 30 million in the colonies of the Dutch, 10 million in Russia... altogether 250 million Muslims are beseeching God for delivery from foreign rule. They have pinned their hopes on the caliph, the deputy of the Prophet Muhammad. We cannot [therefore] remain submissive in dealing with the great powers.[50]

But this was just empty bravado. In practice, Abdulhamid had little choice but to remain submissive in dealing with the great powers. At the

Conference of Berlin in 1878, his caliphate had little choice but to give up almost its European territories. Now Bosnia, Wallachia, Moravia, Bulgaria, and Serbia were all outside its domains. Without a shot, the Ottomans also handed over Cyprus, over which so much jihadi blood had been shed in the past, to the British.

Slavery in Tripoli, Dhimmitude in Morocco

In the North African lands formerly under Ottoman control, little changed with the waning of Ottoman power. In 1818, Captain G. F. Lyon of the British Navy traveled to Tripoli, where he noted that Muhammad al-Mukani of the Bey of Fezzan (in modern southwestern Libya) "waged war on all his defenceless neighbours and annually carried off 4000 or 5000 slaves. From one of these slave hunts into Kanem he had just returned to Tripoli, with a numerous body of captives and many camels, and was, in consequence, in the highest favour with the Bashaw," that is, the sultan of Tripoli, Yusuf Karamanli.[51] The sultan, noted Lyon, possessed "about fifty young women, all black and very comely…guarded by five eunuchs, who keep up their authority by occasionally beating them."[52]

Lyon witnessed the arrival of a shipment of slaves in Murzuq:

> At the end of the month [August 1819], a large *Kafflé* [caravan] of Arabs, Tripolines, and Tibboo, arrived from Bornou, bringing with them 1400 slaves of both sexes and all ages, the greater part being females…. We rode out to meet the great *kafflé*, and to see them enter the town—it was indeed a piteous spectacle! The poor oppressed beings were, many of them, so exhausted as to be scarcely able to walk; their legs and feet were much swelled, and by their enormous size, formed a striking contrast with their emaciated bodies. They were all borne down with loads of firewood; and even poor little children, worn to skeletons by fatigue and hardships, were obliged to bear the burthen, while many of their inhuman masters rode on camels, with the dreaded whip suspended from their wrists, with which they, from time to time, enforced obedience from these wretched

captives. Care was taken, however, that the hair of the fe-
males should be arranged in nice order, and that their bodies should be well oiled, whilst the males were closely shav-
en, to give them a good appearance on entering the town.
All the traders speak of the slaves as farmers do of cattle.[53]

In 1842, the British consul general in Morocco asked the Moroccan
sultan Abd al-Rahman what he was doing to restrict the slave trade.
Abd al-Rahman was incredulous, responding that "the traffic in slaves
is a matter on which all sects and nations have agreed from the time of
the sons of Adam...up to this day."[54] He said that he was "not aware of
its being prohibited by the laws of any sect" and that the very idea that
anyone would question its morality was absurd: "no one need ask this
question, the same being manifest to both high and low and requires
no more demonstration than the light of day."[55] From the beginnings
of Islam until the end of the eighteenth century, Muslim slave traders
who shared these views sent nearly ten million souls from sub-Saharan
Africa to the slave markets of the Islamic world, generally making sure
to enslave non-Muslims, not fellow Muslims.[56]

The *dhimmi* laws also remained in force in Morocco. A traveler to
that country in 1880 reported that "a deputation of Israelites, with a
grave and reverend rabbi at their head," asked the local Muslim ruler for
permission "for them to wear their shoes in the town. 'We are old, Bashador,' they said, 'and our limbs are weak; and our women, too, are del-
icately nurtured, and this law presses heavily upon us.'" As reasonable as
this request was, and as humane as it would have been for the bashador
to grant it, the traveler expressed relief that the Jews decided not to ask
after all. He "was glad they were dissuaded from pressing their request,
the granting of which would exasperate the populace, and might lead to
consequences too terrible to contemplate."[57]

Eight years later, the Anglo-Jewish Association pushed for the abolition of *dhimmi* laws in Morocco, under which Jews were required
to "live in the ghetto.... On leaving the ghetto they are compelled to
remove their footwear and remove their headcovering.... Jews are not
permitted to build their houses above a certain height.... Jews 'are not

allowed to drink from the public fountains in the Moorish quarter nor to take water therefrom' as the Jews are considered unclean."[58] The Anglo-Jewish Association appeal went nowhere.

The Armenian Genocide Begins

Meanwhile, more infidel blood was to be shed in another historic field of jihad, Asia Minor. In 1894, the Armenians rebelled at having to pay taxes both to Kurdish warlords in Anatolia and to the Ottoman state. The sultanate was in no mood to hear them out, and began massacring Armenians ruthlessly, committing mass rapes, killing even children, and burning Armenian villages.

The chief dragoman (Turkish interpreter) of the British Embassy wrote that those who committed these atrocities were "guided in their general action by the prescriptions of Sheri [Sharia] Law. That law prescribes that if the 'rayah' [subject] Christian attempts, by having recourse to foreign powers, to overstep the limits of privileges allowed to them by their Mussulman masters, and free themselves from their bondage, their lives and property are to be forfeited, and are at the mercy of the Mussulmans. To the Turkish mind, the Armenians had tried to overstep these limits by appealing to foreign powers, especially England. They, therefore, considered it their religious duty and a righteous thing to destroy and seize the lives and property of the Armenians."[59]

On August 18, 1894, the Ottoman authorities began a massacre of Armenians in the Sassoun region of eastern Asia Minor that lasted a full twenty-four days, until September 10. British vice consul Cecil M. Hallward investigated the massacre and reported to the British crown that "a large majority of the population of some twenty-five villages perished, and some of the villages were unusually large for this country."[60] At Bitlis, Ottoman soldiers "took eighty tins of petroleum…[which] was utilized for burning the houses, together with the inhabitants inside them."[61]

At Geliguzan, "a number of young men were bound hand and foot, laid out in a row, had brushwood piled on them, and were burned alive."[62] And "many other disgusting barbarities are said to have been committed, such as ripping open pregnant women, tearing children to pieces by main force."[63] At yet another Armenian village, "some sixty young women and girls were driven into a church, where some soldiers were ordered to do as they liked with them and afterwards kill them, which order was carried out."[64] Hallward noted that he collected these details largely from "soldiers who took part in the massacre."[65]

The jihad against the Armenians went on even in Constantinople, after Armenian revolutionaries seized the Bank Ottoman in 1894. In retaliation, Muslim mobs for two days bludgeoned Armenians to death with cudgels wherever they found them. The streets of the great city again ran red with blood, as they had on May 29, 1453, when Mehmet the Conqueror and his jihad warriors broke through the Byzantine defenses. The British *chargé* in Constantinople wrote that the "Turkish mob" was aided by "a large number of *softas* [student of Islamic theology] and other fanatics…individuals wearing turbans and long linen robes rarely seen in this part of the town. They mostly carried clubs which had evidently been carefully shaped after a uniform pattern; some had, instead of these, iron bars…there is nothing improbable in the stories current that the clubs and bars…were furnished by the municipal authorities."[66]

The French ambassador pointed to "the interminable series of events which exhaustively prove that it is the Sultan himself who arms these bludgeoners, exhorting them to go out and extirpate all that is Armenian. It is maintained that the police had given advance notice to all these rascals, distributing to them the cudgels, and deploying them at convenient spots."[67] The Austrian military attaché likewise charged that Ottoman authorities gave the mobs cudgels and sticks "fitted with a piece of iron" and told them "to start killing Armenians, irrespective of age and gender, for the duration of 48 hours…the method of killing involved the bludgeoning of the victims with blows on their heads. These horrible scenes repeated themselves before my eyes interminably."[68] The Russian Embassy dragoman Maximof indignantly carried one of the cudgels into the very palace of the sultan, declaring: "The Turks are killing in the streets the poor Armenians with these cudgels."[69]

The killing went on elsewhere in Ottoman domains as well. At Erzurum in 1895, the Ottomans massacred Christians indiscriminately and then buried three hundred of them in a mass grave. At Urfa in December 1895, the Armenians gathered in their cathedral and requested Ottoman government protection, which the officer in charge granted, surrounding the cathedral with troops. Then other Ottoman troops, along with local Muslim civilians, rampaged through the city, slaughtering Armenians and plundering their houses. A large group of young Armenians was taken to the local imam, who ordered them to be held down. An eyewitness said that the sheikh then recited some verses of the Qur'an and "cut their throats after the Mecca rite of sacrificing sheep."[70]

The French ambassador reported that in September 1896 in Egin, the Ottomans perpetrated "a terrible massacre" of "upwards of 2,000 Armenians," including "many women and children."[71] Here again, according to a British official on the scene, "an indirect order was sent from the Palace for the massacres in question to be carried out."[72] Another British official reported that at Malatya, "over 100 Armenians had gathered for safety" when Ottoman troops entered. The Armenians here received much the same treatment they had been given the previous year in Urfa: they "were circumcised, and afterwards killed as 'kurban,' i.e. thrown upon their backs and their throats cut, after the manner in which sheep are sacrificed."[73]

The German historian Johannes Lepsius visited the devastated areas at the time and chronicled the atrocities. He referred to the cover-up of these horrific events that had already begun:

> Are we then simply forbidden to speak of the Armenians as persecuted on account of their religious belief? If so, there have never been any religious persecutions in the world.... We have lists before us of 559 villages whose surviving inhabitants were converted to Islam with fire and sword; of 568 churches thoroughly pillaged, destroyed and razed to the ground; of 282 Christian churches transformed into mosques; of 21 Protestant preachers and 170 Gregorian [Armenian] priests who were, after enduring unspeakable tortures, murdered on their refusal to accept Islam. We repeat, however, that those figures express only the extent of our information,

and do not by a long way reach to the extent of the reality. Is this a religious persecution or is it not?[74]

Lepsius also reported that the Muslims had destroyed 2,500 Christian villages and 645 churches and monasteries, and that the number of those who had been forced to convert to Islam was fifteen thousand. Three hundred twenty-eight churches were converted into mosques, and 508 more were plundered.[75] One Ottoman soldier wrote home enthusiastically:

> My brother, if you want news from here we have killed 1,200 Armenians, all of them as food for the dogs.... Mother, I am safe and sound. Father, 20 days ago we made war on the Armenian unbelievers. Through God's grace no harm befell us.... There is a rumour afoot that our Batallion will be ordered to your part of the world—if so, we will kill all the Armenians there. Besides, 511 Armenians were wounded, one or two perish every day.[76]

In its dotage, the Ottoman sultanate was more savage than ever.

II. THE BARBARY WARS

The Barbary (Berber) states of Algiers, Tunis, and Tripoli, which were nominally Ottoman possessions but de facto independent, continued their jihad piracy and slave raids throughout the eighteenth century. They targeted American colonial vessels along with European ships, and when the United States of America declared its independence, they targeted its fleet as well. In 1784, pirates from neighboring Morocco captured the American ship *Betsey* and took its crew hostage, demanding that the new nation pay tribute to avoid future such incidents.[77]

The Americans, newly independent and having neither the resources nor the desire to get involved in a war with the Barbary states, paid the tribute. But once it had been established that the Americans would give in to the jihadi demands, those demands grew. In 1795, a payment to Algiers of nearly a million dollars comprised sixteen percent of federal revenue for that year.[78]

Even peace overtures came from a posture of bullying superiority: in June 1796, Pasha Hamouda, the bey of Tunis, offered to conclude a peace treaty with the United States, and stipulated that the Americans had six months to consider the offer, during which Tunisian pirates would not attack American ships. If they rejected the offer, the raids would resume, leaving the Americans no room to maneuver. Hamouda signed his treaty officer as "commander…of the frontier post of the Holy War," suggesting at once that the piracy was in service of a larger goal— jihad, conquest, and Islamization of the non-Muslim world—and that if the Americans rejected the offer, they would face war not just with Tunis but with the entire global forces of jihad.[79]

In the treaty that the United States concluded in 1797 with Tripoli, the payment of earlier tribute by the Americans was acknowledged, and the U.S. consul in Tripoli was directed to deliver to the ruler of Tripoli "twelve thousand Spanish dollars" as well as various supplies for the construction of ships.[80] That treaty also contained, in the English text only, a statement designated as Article 11, which appears to be designed to reassure the bey of Tripoli that the United States was not hostile to Islam; for reasons never explained, however, this article does not appear in the treaty's Arabic text.[81]

> As the government of the United States of America is not in any sense founded on the Christian Religion,—as it has in itself no character of enmity against the laws, religion or tranquility of Musselmen,—and as the said States never have entered into any war or act of hostility against any Mehomitan nation, it is declared by the parties that no pretext arising from religious opinions shall ever produce an interruption of the harmony existing between the two countries.[82]

The lack of hostility of any "Mehomitan nation" toward the United States, however, could not be assured. In 1786, Thomas Jefferson and John Adams met in London with Sidi Haji Abdrahaman, the *eyalet* (administrator) of Tripolitania's ambassador to London. Jefferson recounted to Congress what Abdrahaman's response was when he and Adams asked him "concerning the ground of the pretensions to make war upon nations who had done them no injury":

> The ambassador answered us that it was founded on the Laws of the Prophet, that it was written in their Koran, that all nations who should not have answered their authority were sinners, that it was their right and duty to make war upon them wherever they could be found, and to make slaves of all they could take as prisoners, and that every Mussulman who should be slain in battle was sure to go to Paradise.[83]

Thus it had been since the beginning of Islam, and thus it would remain. This particular eruption of the long hostility that Barbary piracy represented came to a head in 1801, when Yusuf Karamanli, the bashaw of Tripoli, increased his demands on an already cash-strapped republic, demanding two hundred and twenty thousand dollars up front and twenty-five thousand dollars each year from the United States.

The new president, Thomas Jefferson, opted to go to war rather than continue paying these increasingly exorbitant tributes. Emerging victorious against the Barbary states in 1805 and again in a second war in 1815, the Americans freed themselves from paying tribute and put an end to this long episode of jihad on the high seas. The Americans would, of course, hear again much later from those who believed, as did Sidi Haji Abdrahman, that "all nations who should not have answered their authority were sinners, that it was their right and duty to make war upon them wherever they could be found."

III. THE MUGHALS IN DECLINE

The British Raj and Jihad in Abeyance

The best days of the Mughal Empire, like those of the Ottoman Empire, were behind it by the beginning of the eighteenth century. But even as the power of their state diminished, the Mughals kept up the pressure on the Hindus as much as they could. In the 1720s, the nawab of Bengal,

Murshid Quli Khan, who was ostensibly under the authority of the Mughal emperor but operated independently, decided to attack the Hindu stronghold of Tipara.

An eighteenth-century Muslim historian, Azad al-Husaini, noted that "Tipara is a country extremely strong. The Raja is proud of his strength and the practice of conch-blowing and idol-worship prevailed there."[84] The Tipara soldiers fought valiantly to defend their fort at Udaipur but were defeated. As Murshid Quli's men entered the fort, they found the Hindu soldiers lying dead "in heaps."[85] The Muslims cried out "*Allahu akbar*" and repeated the Islamic profession of faith, "There is no god but Allah and Muhammad is his prophet."[86] They immediately destroyed the temple and had an Islamic sermon read out at its ruins in the name of the Mughal emperor Muhammad Shah. Azad al-Husaini concluded his account of this by writing: "The world-illuminating sun of the faith of Muhammad swept away the dark night of infidelity, and the bright day of Islam dawned."[87]

The world-illuminating faith of Muhammad, however, was not able to save the Mughals from the Hindu Maratha Empire, which steadily gained ground against the Mughals until it ruled most of India by the middle of the eighteenth century. The Mughals, by that time, ruled over little more than the capital of Delhi. When the Marathas moved into Punjab in 1758, however, they attracted the notice of Ahmad Shah Durrani, a military commander who had just staked out his own imperial realm in Afghanistan.

Durrani had invaded the Mughal Empire several times, but this time the issue was larger than the question of who would rule in a particular area: the Marathas, as Hindus, should not be ruling over Muslims. "The Marathas," Ahmad Shah told an allied leader, "are the thorn of Hindostan." Now "by one effort we get this thorn out of our sides for ever."[88] Both sides courted the allegiance of Shujau-d Daula, the ruler of Oudh in northern India, who, if he sided with the Marathas, could have impeded the passage of Ahmad Shah's forces into the heart of India. Shujau-d Daula, like the Marathas, was Indian, and Ahmad Shah Durrani and his forces were Afghan. But Shujau-d Daula was a Muslim, not a Hindu, and sided with Ahmad Shah.

Egging them on was the Indian Sufi Shah Wali Allah, a popular Islamic revivalist of the period who exhorted Muslims to take up the sword of jihad:

> It is the general authority to undertake the establishment of religion through the revival of religious sciences, the establishment of the pillars of Islam, the organization of *jihad* and its related functions of maintenance of armies, financing the soldiers, and allocation of their rightful portions from the spoils of war, administration of justice, enforcement of [the limits ordained by Allah, including the punishment for crimes (*hudud*)], elimination of injustice, and enjoining good and forbidding evil, to be exercised on behalf of the Prophet...[89]

Shah Wali Allah had an extremely elastic interpretation of the Qur'an's dictum that "there is no compulsion in religion" (2:256), arguing that forcing infidels to accept Islam was an act of mercy toward them:

> It is no mercy to them to stop at intellectually establishing the truth of Religion to them. Rather, true mercy towards them is to compel them so that Faith finds a way to their minds despite themselves. It is like a bitter medicine administered to a sick man. Moreover, there can be no compulsion without eliminating those who are a source of great harm or aggression, or liquidating their force, and capturing their riches, so as to render them incapable of posing any challenge to Religion. Thus their followers and progeny are able to enter the faith with free and conscious submission.[90]

Reading Islamic history, Shah Wali Allah saw the action of Allah, and he exhorted Muslims of his own day to enable the deity to act anew:

> Jihad made it possible for the early followers of Islam from the Muhajirun and the Ansar to be instrumental in the entry of the Quraysh and the people around them into the fold of Islam. Subsequently, God destined that Mesopotamia and Syria be conquered at their hands. Later on it was through

the Muslims of these areas that God made the empires of the Persians and Romans to be subdued. And again, it was through the Muslims of these newly conquered realms that God actualized the conquests of India, Turkey and Sudan. In this way, the benefits of jihad multiply incessantly, and it becomes, in that respect, similar to creating an endowment, building inns and other kinds of recurring charities....

Jihad is an exercise replete with tremendous benefits for the Muslim community, and it is the instrument of jihad alone that can bring about their victory.... The supremacy of his Religion over all other religions cannot be realized without jihad and the necessary preparation for it, including the procurement of its instruments. Therefore, if the Prophet's followers abandon jihad and pursue the tails of cows [that is, become farmers] they will soon be overcome by disgrace, and the people of other religions will overpower them.[91]

Shah Wali Allah accordingly wrote to Ahmad Shah Durrani: "We beseech you in the name of the Prophet to fight a jihad against the infidels of this region. This would entitle you to great rewards before God the Most High and your name would be included in the list of those who fought for jihad for His sake. As far as worldly gains are concerned, incalculable booty would fall into the hands of the Islamic *gazis* [warriors] and the Muslims would be liberated from their bonds."[92] The Afghan jihadis were able to pass into India without difficulty, and as the Maratha commander Sadashivrao Bhau put it, "The cup is now full to the brim and cannot hold another drop."[93]

The Marathas had to drink that cup in 1761 at Panipat, just north of Delhi, the site of two earlier pivotal battles that established and secured Mughal rule. Ahmad Shah Durrani (with Shah Wali Allah present) defeated them decisively and proved to the world that the Mughal Empire was only a shadow of what it had once been; the Afghan warriors routed the Hindus and destroyed the Maratha army. The Marathas were forced to withdraw from a good part of the territories they controlled. Ahmad

Shah Durrani wanted to press forward and conquer all of India, bringing it once again under Islamic rule, but was stopped by a mutiny among his soldiers, forcing him to return to Afghanistan.[94]

In his absence, the Marathas were able to regroup and hold on to power in much of central India, with two Muslim kingdoms in southern India. At this point, however, came a challenge to both Hindu and Muslim Indian rulers, which neither group proved able to withstand: the British colonialists. In 1765, the Mughal emperor Shah Alam II gave the East India Company the right to collect tax revenues in Bengal, which made the British the effective rulers of the area; from there they expanded their holdings until by 1820, most of India was under their control.

The presence and hegemony of the British presented the Muslim clerics of India with a question that had not previously been answered, as there had never before been occasion to consider it: was land that had previously been ruled by Muslims, but was now under the rule of infidels but with a substantial population of Muslims living there (as opposed to Spain, from which the Muslims had been expelled), *dar al-Islam* (the house of Islam) or *dar al-harb* (the house of war)? If India was still the house of Islam, jihad could not legitimately be waged against the British, but if it had become part of the house of war by dint of the British rule, it could.

A prominent Muslim cleric, Shah Abd al-Aziz, issued a fatwa in 1803 to answer this question. In doing so, he relied upon the idea that jihad is not necessarily always to be carried out by leaders of Muslim states or other polities, but when a Muslim land is attacked, jihad becomes the responsibility of every individual Muslim. In his fatwa, he lamented that in Delhi,

> ...the *Imam al-Muslimin* [leader of the Muslims] wields no authority at all whereas the authority of the leaders of the Christians is enforced without any trouble. By the enforcement of the rules of unbelief is meant that unbelievers can act on their own authority in governing and dealing with the subjects, in collecting land-tax, tolls, tithes, customs and excises, in punishing highway robbers and thieves, in settling disputes and punishing crimes. It is true that certain Islamic rules like those regarding the congregational

prayers of Friday and the festivals, the call for prayer and the slaughter of cows are not being interfered with. This, however, is because the essence of these things is of no value to them, for they demolish mosques without any scruples and Moslems or *dhimmis* can only enter this city or its surroundings by asking *aman* [protection] from them.[95]

This situation was intolerable for believers in a religion that mandated that unbelievers be subject to them. Resistance to British rule grew among Muslims until finally in 1821, Sayyid Ahmad Barelvi began a movement known as The Way of Muhammad (Tariqa-i Muhammadi). Barelvi exhorted the Muslims to take up the jihad once again: "One should know," he wrote, "that jihad is an advantageous and beneficial institution. Mankind derives benefits from its advantages in various ways, just like rain, the advantages of which are imparted upon both plants, animals and men."[96]

Barelvi promised that if Muslims waged jihad, they would receive "the blessings of heaven," including "timely downpour of rain, abundant vegetation, growth of profits and trade, absence of calamities and pestilences, growth of wealth and presence of men of learning and perfection."[97]

The idea that jihadis would be rewarded in this life was thoroughly Qur'anic. At one point in the Muslim holy book, Allah chastises a group of unbelievers and adds: "if they repent, it is better for them; but if they turn away, Allah will punish them with a painful punishment in this world and the Hereafter." (9:74) One can avoid the painful punishment in this world by repenting and doing Allah's will, which, of course, includes jihad. Allah tells the unbelievers, "already there has been for you a sign in the two armies which met" at Badr, "one fighting in the cause of Allah and another of disbelievers" (3:10). The sign is that Allah blesses those who do his will and punishes those who do not, in this world. At Badr, "Allah had certainly fulfilled His promise to you when you were killing the enemy by His permission until when you lost courage and fell to disputing about the order and disobeyed after he had shown you that which you love." (3:152)

Sayyid Ahmad wanted to drive the British from India but knew that his movement, although it was gaining a large following, had no chance of doing that. So instead, in 1826, he declared jihad against the

Sikhs who ruled in northwestern India, close to the Afghan border. In 1831, he was killed in a battle against the Sikhs at Balakot, just north of Islamabad. That same year, Titu Mir, another Tariqa-i Muhammadi leader, was killed as the jihadis battled the British army in West Bengal.

In 1857, the British captured Delhi and put an end to the Mughal Empire. Although there was hardly any Mughal Empire to conquer by that point, this was the official end of a thousand years of Islamic rule in India, and confirmation of the fact that India had now completely lost its independence. There was, accordingly, a large-scale uprising against British rule in India in which not only Muslims but Hindus also participated. Nonetheless, in the course of it, Tariqa-i Muhammadi clerics issued fatwas justifying armed jihad against the colonial rulers. Tariqa-i Muhammadi continued to wage jihad against the British until 1883, when the British army finally put a complete stop to its activities.[98]

There was never, however, a major jihadi uprising against the British in India, in large part because many Islamic authorities held that no such jihad was justified. The *ulama* (Islamic scholars) of northern India stated: "The Musalmens here are protected by the Christians, and there is no Jihad in a country where protection is afforded, as the absence of protection and liberty between Musalmens and Infidels is essential in a religious war and that condition does not exist here. Besides it is necessary that there should be a probability of victory to Musalman and glory to the Indian. If there be no such probability, the Jihad is unlawful."[99]

This was not just a prudential directive but an element of Islamic law. A manual of Islamic law dictates that "jihad is personally obligatory upon all those present in the battle lines," but that a Muslim may leave the field of battle "if the opposing non-Muslim army is more than twice the size of the Muslim force."[100] This did not efface the jihad imperative entirely, for the Muslims were to work to gain strength in order to fight more effectively later; but if the odds were prohibitive, Muslims were not obligated to walk into certain death. And so the Muslims in India, faced with the overwhelming might of the British imperial forces, for the most part did not wage jihad.

In the same vein, the Muhammadan Literary Society of Calcutta even went so far as to say that if some Muslims in India began to wage jihad, other Muslims would be obliged to fight with the British against them: "If anyone were to wage war against the Ruling Powers of this Country, British India, such war would be rightly pronounced rebellion; and rebellion is strictly forbidden by Muhammadan Law. Therefore such war will likewise be unlawful; and in case any one should wage war, the Muhammadan subjects would be bound to assist their Rulers, and, in conjunction with their Rulers, to fight with such rebels."[101]

Likewise, the nineteenth-century Indian Muslim reformer Sayyid Ahmad Khan determined that "an Infidel Government in which the Mahomedans enjoy every sort of peace and security, discharge their religious duties with perfect freedom, and which is connected with a Mahomedan Government by treaty, is not Dar-ul-Islam, because it is a Non-Mahomedan Government, but we may call it so as regards the peace and religious freedom which the Muslims enjoy under its protection; nor is it Dar-ul-Harb, because the treaty existing between it and the Moslem Government makes Jihad against it unlawful."[102]

The idea that Muslims must obey a non-Muslim ruler who was not interfering with their practice of Islam came from Muhammad himself, who is depicted in a *hadith* mandating obedience to rulers in all cases except when a ruler called upon a Muslim to sin:

> It is obligatory upon a Muslim that he should listen [to the ruler appointed over him] and obey him whether he likes it or not, except that he is ordered to do a sinful thing. If he is ordered to do a sinful act, a Muslim should neither listen to him nor should he obey his orders.[103]

Ultimately, in a non-Muslim state this put the Muslim population on a collision course with the rulers, for Islamic law mandates the submission and subjugation of the unbelievers, and so ultimately, nonenforcement of that subjugation is a sinful act that the Muslim population cannot tolerate. But this did not come to a head in British India.

Nonetheless, British colonialism increased Muslim anger, as Islam no longer dominated. Indian politician Muhammad Yusuf asked the British on May 3, 1883, for specifically Muslim representation in the raj's government: "But it would be an advantage and more fit recognition of the claims of the Muslim population if provision could be made in the bill for the election of Muslims by reserving a certain number of membership for that community."[104] Sayyid Ahmad Khan articulated why in 1888 when he declared that Muslims and Hindus in India were two nations that were at war with one another, and could never coexist in peace.

Indian Muslim politician Rahimtulla Mahomed Sayani explained why this was so in 1896: "Before the advent of the British in India, the Muslims were the rulers of the country. The rulers and their chiefs were Muslims, so were the great landlords and officials. The court language was their own [Persian was the official language of India till 1842]…. The Hindus were in awe of them. By a stroke of misfortune, the Muslims had to abdicate their position and descend to the level of their Hindu fellow-countrymen. The Muslims resented the treatment."[105]

That resentment would come to a head in the twentieth century.

IV. JIHAD AGAINST THE COLONIAL POWERS

While Muslims in India debated over whether jihad against the British was justified under Islamic law, Muslims under colonial rule elsewhere were not so hesitant. In 1830, the French invaded Algiers and defeated an Ottoman army. Almost immediately, a Muslim leader named Ahmed Bey declared jihad against the French and battled them for seven years until the French army forced him to flee into the desert.

An Islamic revival movement, the Qadiriyyah, also pursued the jihad against the French, and was so strong that in 1834 the French agreed to a treaty with its leader, Abd al-Qadir, recognizing his authority in western Algeria. But in accord with the dictates of Islamic law, that say treaties can be concluded with infidels only when the Muslims are weak and need time to gain strength, and can be broken when they are no longer useful, Abd al-Qadir soon resumed the jihad against the French, and concluded a new, more favorable agreement with them in 1837.[106]

Abd al-Qadir lamented "the serious and distressed situation in the land of Algiers, that has become a place where the crows of unbelief slaughter [the believers], since the enemy of the Religion attempts to subject and to enslave the Moslems, sometimes by means of the sword and sometimes by means of political intrigues."[107] Resolved to end this, he continued expanding the territory under his control, even writing to the French King Louis Philippe in 1839 to protest French encroachment upon what he said they had recognized as his territory. Because of this violation of the agreement, he said, he had no choice but to wage jihad against the French once again. Finally, the French had enough of it and pursued Abd al-Qadir vigorously, capturing him in 1847 and imprisoning him in France for five years. When he was released, he did not resume his jihad.[108] Others did, however. It wasn't until 1871 that French rule in Algiers was fully established.

The Mahdi Revolt

As if all this weren't enough, there was more coming for the Ottomans in the North African domains they nominally ruled. In 1881, the Sudanese Sufi sheikh Muhammad Ahmad proclaimed himself the Mahdi, the savior figure of Islamic apocalyptic literature. Muhammad himself, he announced, had chosen him for this role:

> The eminent lord [the Prophet Muhammad], on whom be blessing and peace, several times informed me that I am the *Mahdi*, the expected one, and [appointed] me [as] successor to himself, on whom he blessing and peace, to sit on the throne, and [as successors] to their excellencies the four ["Rightly-Guided Caliphs" (*khilafah*)] and Princes [of the Faith].... And he gave me the sword of victory of His Excellency [the Prophet Muhammad] on whom be blessing and peace; and it was made known to me that none of either race, human or *jinn*, can conquer him who has it.... He ordered me [to take my exile [*hijrah*]] to Jebel Kadeer close to Masat, and he commanded me to write thence to all entrusted with public offices. I wrote thus to the Emirs and Sheikhs of religion, and the wicked denied [my mission], but the righteous believed.... this is what the eminent lord [the Prophet Muhammad], on whom be blessing and peace, said to me: "He who doubts that thou art the *Mahdi* has blasphemed God and His Prophet."...If you have understood this, we order all the chosen ones to [make

their *hijrah*] unto us for the *jihad*…in the cause of God, to the nearest town, because God Most High has said, "slay the infidels who are nearest to you.".…Fear God and join the righteous, and help one another in righteousness, and in the fear of God and in the *jihad*…in the cause of God, and stand firm within the boundaries of God, for he who transgresses those boundaries will injure himself. Know that all things are in the hand of God. Leave all to Him and rely on Him. He who makes God his support has been guided into the straight way. Peace [be with you].[109]

The Mahdi also declared: "Cease to pay taxes to the infidel Turks and let everyone who finds a Turk kill him, for the Turks are infidels."[110] He declared jihad against the Ottomans and the Egyptians, and enacted a series of Messianic decrees reminiscent of the Qarmatians, who a thousand years before had forsworn mosque worship and the pilgrimage to Mecca in anticipation of the imminent arrival of the Mahdi.

Now Muhammad Ahmad, in the role of the Mahdi, likewise began to alter what orthodox Muslims considered the unchangeable aspects of Islam. He revised the profession of faith from "There is no god but Allah and Muhammad is his prophet" to "There is no god but Allah and Muhammad Ahmad is the Mahdi of Allah and the representative of his prophet."[111] He directed that *zakat*, Islamic almsgiving, be paid only to his movement, and replaced the *hajj*, the pilgrimage to Mecca, as a pillar of Islam with jihad.

The Mahdi called upon Muslims around the world to emigrate to his domains for the sake of Allah, after the manner of Muhammad's *hijrah* from Mecca to Medina. He wrote to Muslim leaders:

It is evident that times have changed and that the Sunnah has been abandoned. No one with faith and intelligence will approve of that. Therefore, it would be better that he leave his affairs and his country in order to establish the Religion and the Sunnah…Emigrating with the Religion is obligatory on the strength of the Book and the Sunnah. Allah has said: "Oh ye who have believed, respond to Allah and to the messenger when He calls you to what will give you life." [Qur'an 8:24] The prophet has said: "He who flees with his religion from one territory to another, even if it is [only the distance of] an inch, will be worthy of Paradise and be the companion of his father Ibrahim, Allah's bosom friend, and of His prophet Muhammad." And [there are] similar Koranic verses and Traditions.... If you understand this, [know then that] I have ordered all those [of you] who are legally capable, to emigrate to us for the sake of jihad in the way of Allah, or to the country that is nearest to you, on the strength of Allah's words: "Oh ye who have believed, fight the unbelievers who are near to you." [Qur'an 9:123]...If you understand this, then: onward to the jihad in His way.[112]

The Mahdi proceeded to wage that jihad against the Egyptians, until finally the Egyptian *khedive* Tewfik became determined to kill this imposter and put down this uprising. But the Mahdi was popular, and Tewfik and the Egyptian rulers, to say nothing of the Ottomans, were not. Thus, for help in finding and killing the Mahdi, Tewfik turned to the British. The Mahdi, enraged, wrote to Tewfik: "You were not right in taking the unbelievers as patrons in preference to Allah and asking their assistance while they were shedding the blood of the community of Mohammed."[113] He quoted the Qur'an: "O ye who have believed, do not choose Jews or Christians as patrons, they are patrons to each other; whoever makes patrons of them is one of them." (5:51) He exhorted the *khedive* to "declare yourself above being permanently the captive of Allah's enemies and do not lead to perdition those of the community of Mohammed that are with you."[114]

The *khedive* was unmoved. Ottoman Islamic scholars issued a number of fatwas refuting Muhammad Ahmad's claim to be the Mahdi, and charging that he was illegitimately killing fellow Muslims, in violation of the Qur'anic prohibition against doing so (4:92). These fatwas had little effect; the Ottomans and the Egyptians were hoping that the British would finish the Mahdi off for good.

Getting help from the British came at a price. Anti-English riots broke out in Egypt in June 1882. Ahmad Urabi, the *khedive's* minister of war, rebelled against the *khedive's* pro-English policy and led an army against the British, only to be condemned by the Ottoman sultan and the *khedive*. But in July 1882, however, Egyptian ulama published a call for jihad, calling for support of Urabi's army and reminding Muslims: "Those who sacrifice themselves in support of their Religion will attain success and acceptance [with Allah]."[115] But Urabi was defeated, and British rule in Egypt secured. The British army could now turn its attention to the Mahdi.

Calling in the British imperial army against the Mahdi was akin to calling in the police to swat a fly, and yet the fly won. To be sure, the British didn't commit nearly as much as they could have, and the Mahdi's forces far outnumbered those of the British, but the followers of the Mahdi still took the crushing defeat of the British at El-Obeid in the Sudan in 1883 as a sign that Muhammad Ahmad was indeed the Mahdi, and Allah was blessing their jihad, as he had blessed the pious Muslims at Badr. To ensure that they would not lose that divine favor, which came only as a reward for obedience, the Mahdi issued a sweeping decree after El-Obeid:

> Let all show penitence before Allah, and abandon all bad and forbidden habits, such as degrading acts of the flesh, the drinking of wine and smoking tobacco, lying, bearing false witness, disobedience to parents, brigandage, the non-restitution of goods to others, the clapping of hands, dancing, improper signs with the eyes, tears and lamentations at the bed of the dead, slanderous language, calumny, and the company of strange women. Clothe your women in a decent way and let them be careful not to speak to unknown persons. All those who do not pay attention to these principles disobey God and His Prophet, and they shall be punished in accordance with the law. Say your prayers at the prescribed hours. Give the tenth of your goods, handing it to our Prince, Sheikh Mansour [whom the Mahdi had

made governor of El Obeid] in order that he may forward
it to the treasury of Islam. Adore God, and hate not each
other, but assist each other to do good.[116]

Or else. The Mahdi endorsed the harshest Sharia punishments for
transgressors. This was because, he said, "well-being with Allah can only
be achieved by following the Religion, by reviving the Sunnah of His
prophet and His community, by suppressing these recent innovations
[*bida*] and errors and by turning repentantly to the Exalted One in all
situations."[117] Even reading a book other than the Qur'an or *hadith* collections could cost a man his life. And, for a time, it did appear as if
strict adherence to Sharia, as Allah had promised, would result in earthly
success. In 1884, the British sent to the Sudan the renowned general Sir
Charles "Chinese" Gordon. Gordon himself was less than enthusiastic
about fighting to secure control of this barren and desolate region, writing: "No one who has ever lived in the Sudan can escape the reflection
'What a useless possession is this land!'"[118]

Nonetheless, he did all he could, only to find himself betrayed by
his nominal allies. In March 1884, the Mahdi's army attacked Egyptian
troops at the oasis of Halfaya, near Khartoum. Gordon set out to retake
Halfaya from the Mahdi; as the British approached, the Egyptians inside
the oasis warned the Mahdi's troops to retreat or face annihilation. The
Mahdi's forces, cautious considering Gordon's reputation, complied, and
began a retreat, only to be suddenly and inexplicably called back by two
Egyptian officers. The rest of the Egyptian troops, seeing this betrayal, fled in panic. Gordon wrote in his diary: "Sixty horsemen defeated
two thousand men."[119] He questioned the Egyptian officers, who insisted that they were encouraging the Mahdists to surrender, not betraying
their own side. Gordon, however, was unconvinced. Were these followers
of the Mahdi within his own ranks? The possibility could not be dis-
counted. He had them executed.

The following year, flush with these unexpected victories, the Mahdi's army besieged Khartoum. Finding a way into the city, the Mahdists
found Gordon and cried out, "O cursed one, your time has come!"[120]
They beheaded Gordon and either killed or sold into slavery thirty thousand men, women, and children.

Again, the Mahdi and his followers had won a victory that shocked the world and reinforced the idea among them that Allah was blessing them and would lead them to final jihad victories over the Ottoman Empire, the British Empire, and infidels everywhere.

Yet this great jihad was never even to get past Khartoum. In June 1885, the Mahdi died suddenly and mysteriously. Although he continued to be a revered figure, after his death his movement was a spent force, unable to continue without his charismatic leadership. The principal lesson of the Mahdi revolt that like-minded Muslims carried into the twentieth century was that the Ottomans, Egyptians, and British could not defeat a determined group of pious, believing Muslims. The Ottoman Empire was truly, as it was often called, "the Sick Man of Europe," and its end was nigh, but the British Empire was at its zenith and had not been able to defeat the Mahdi.

So while there were currents within the decaying Ottoman Empire that were beginning to conclude that the empire's problems stemmed from its adherence to Islam, numerous Muslims elsewhere were concluding that the Ottomans' trouble was that they weren't Islamic enough, and that all that one needed for success against even the great powers of the world was a fanatical adherence to the will of Allah.

By the end of the nineteenth century, the idea that success came from obeying the will of Allah was decidedly in eclipse. The British had won control of India and Egypt, ending one long-lived Islamic empire (that of the Mughals) and contributing to the near-demise of another (the Ottomans), even while entering into alliances of convenience with it. As the twentieth century dawned, it looked as if, aside from a few fanatics such as the Mahdi, the era of jihad had been consigned to the dustbin of history.

CHAPTER NINE

RESURGENCE

Jihad in the Twentieth Century

I. THE END OF THE CALIPHATE

The Age of Defensive Jihad

The Ottoman Empire was in its death throes as the twentieth century began, and the days of Islamic states' declaring jihad against non-Muslim neighbors were drawing to a close. Sunni law authorized the caliph to declare only offensive jihad, and the caliph was weak and getting weaker. But that is not the only form of jihad warfare against infidels: Islamic law stipulates that when a Muslim land is attacked, defensive jihad becomes obligatory for every individual Muslim. The Islamic legal manual *Reliance of the Traveller* stipulates that "the caliph makes war upon Jews, Christians, and Zoroastrians…until they become Muslim or else pay the non-Muslim poll tax."[1] However, "when non-Muslims invade a Muslim country or near to one," jihad "becomes personally obligatory upon the inhabitants of that country, who must repel the non-Muslims with whatever they can."[2]

This applies not just to the Muslims in that country but to all Muslims. Ibn Taymiyya considered it an absolute: "If the enemy wants to attack the Muslims, then repelling him becomes a duty for all those under attack and for the others in order to help them. God, He is exalted, has said: 'Yet if they ask you for help, for religion's sake, it is your duty to help them.' (K[oran] 8:72) In the same vein the Prophet has ordered Muslims to help fellow Muslims. The assistance, which is obligatory both for the regular professional army and for others, must be given, according to everybody's possibilities, either in person, by fighting on foot or on horseback, or through financial contributions, be they small or large."³

The twentieth century was the age of defensive jihad. Because of the universal character of this responsibility and the absence, after 1924, of a caliph, the twentieth century saw, for the first time on a large scale, individuals and small groups mounting jihad attacks in service of the larger jihad agenda, not as part of an Islamic army.

Jihad Against Colonial Rule

In October 1911, an Italian army invaded Libya and confronted a vastly smaller Ottoman force there. The Italians encountered far greater resistance than they expected, however, because the Ottomans got help from a revivalist Muslim group known as the Sanusis, after its founder, Muhammad ibn Ali as-Sanusi. Its leader, al-Sayyid Ahmad al-Sharif, declared jihad against the Italians in January 1912, calling upon "all Moslems especially those in such countries as have been occupied by the enemies of Religion" to remember the requirements of defensive jihad and do "what is incumbent upon you, namely jihad against the enemies, giving them a rough time, establishing Islam, assisting the Religion and its adherents, raising Allah's Word and subjugating unbelief and the unbelievers."⁴

Al-Sharif's call was repeated by Islamic authorities worldwide, but nonetheless, the Italians did finally defeat the Ottomans and the Sanusis in October 1912. Al-Sharif did not give up. In 1914, he wrote to the Muslims in Libya: "How can you live with vipers and scorpions and with those who openly profess polytheism and the Trinity and who destroy the *mihrabs* [niches in the wall of a mosque showing the direction to Mecca for prayer]. How can the light of the sun of Islam shine over you when the Banner of the Cross and the Darkness flutters among you?"⁵

The Sanusis never gave up, even defeating the Italians in battle in April 1915. They continued their jihad against the Italians for decades thereafter, and after World War II began to work with the United Nations toward Libyan independence. In 1951, the Sanusi leader Prince Muhammad Idris bin Muhammad al-Mahdi as-Sanusi became King Idris I of Libya; he was deposed in a coup by Muammar Gaddafi in 1969.

The Ottoman Empire's Death Throes

The Ottoman Empire lost Bosnia to Austria-Hungary in 1908, parts of Greece to the independent Greek state and Rhodes to Italy in 1912, and Albania, Macedonia, and Thrace in 1913. By the time World War I began, the Ottoman domains in Europe that remained were the city of Edirne and the portion of East Thrace that surrounded it.

During the war, the Ottomans joined the Central Powers against their archenemy Russia, along with Russia's allies, Britain and France. The sultan Mehmet V declared that the war was a jihad, issuing a fatwa answering yes to this question:

> When it occurs that enemies attack the Islamic world, when it has been established that they seize and pillage Islamic countries and capture Moslem persons and when His Majesty the Padishah of Islam thereupon orders the jihad in the form of a general mobilization, has jihad then, according to the illustrious Koran verse: 'March out light and heavy [hearted], and strive with goods and persons [in the way of Allah; that will be better for you' (K[oran] 9:41)], become incumbent upon all Moslems in all parts of the world, be they young or old, on foot or mounted, to hasten to partake in the jihad with their goods and money?[6]

He likewise answered yes to this question:

> Now that it has been established that Russia, England, France and the governments that support them and are allied to them, are hostile to the Islamic Caliphate, since their warships and armies attack the Seat of the Islamic Caliphate and the Imperial Dominions and strive (Allah forbid) for extinguishing and annihilating the exalted light of Islam [cf. Qur'an 9:32], is it, in this case, also incumbent upon all Muslims that are being ruled by these governments, to proclaim jihad against them and to actually attack them?[7]

The Armenian Genocide Continues

The Sultan's call to jihad didn't arouse much enthusiasm. However, the Ottoman public hadn't lost its thirst for jihad altogether; it was just much more enthusiastic and willing to be roused to action by denunciations of the Armenians than by denunciations of the Russians, British, and French.

As the Ottoman Empire was crumbling and there were calls for Armenian independence, the Ottoman authorities cracked down hard. In October 1915, Ismail Enver, the Ottoman minister of war, declared that he planned to "solve the Greek problem during the war…in the same way he believe[d] he solved the Armenian problem."[8] Rafet Bey, an Ottoman official, said in November 1916 that "we must finish off the Greeks as we did with the Armenians…today I sent squads to the interior to kill every Greek on sight."[9] *The New York Times* reported in 1915 that "both Armenians and Greeks, the two native Christian races of Turkey, are being systematically uprooted from their homes en masse and driven forth summarily to distant provinces, where they are scattered in small groups among Turkish Villages and given the choice between immediate acceptance of Islam or death by the sword or starvation."[10]

The Ottoman interior minister, Mehmet Talat Pasha, explained to the ambassador from the United States, Henry Morgenthau, that one reason why the Armenian genocide was proceeding was because the Armenians had rebelled against the rule of the caliphate, thereby transgressing against the principle that Islam must dominate and not be dominated:

> We base our objections to the Armenians on three distinct grounds. In the first place, they have enriched themselves at the expense of the Turks. In the second place, they are determined to domineer over us and to establish a separate state. In the third place, they have openly encouraged our enemies. They have assisted the Russians in the Caucasus and our failure there is largely explained by their actions. We have therefore come to the irrevocable decision that we shall make them powerless before this war is ended.[11]

Mehmet Talat Pasha also boasted to Morgenthau that the deed was already largely done:

> It is no use for you to argue…we have already disposed of three-quarters of the Armenians; there are none at all left in Bitlis, Van, and Erzeroum. The hatred between the Turks and the Armenians is now so intense that we have got to finish with them. If we don't, they will plan their revenge…. We will not have Armenians anywhere in Anatolia. They can live in the desert but nowhere else.[12]

The Times of London noted somewhat later that Assyrian Christians in what is now Iraq suffered at the hands of the Turks as well: "Telegrams from Mesopotamia state that some 47,000 refugees largely Nestorians, have come into the British lines after having got through the Turkish lines. Many of these are being taken to camps near Baghdad. A further 10,000 have been absorbed in the towns of Kurdistan or are wandering among the hills. These refugees have come from the Urumia region, which was isolated during the Turkish advance in North-West Persia…. The day after this escape the Turks entered Urumia and massacred 200 unresisting people—mostly old men—while 500 Christian women are reported to have been distributed between the Turkish troops and the Moslem inhabitants."[13]

The New York Times predicted that unless the Ottomans lost the war, there would "soon be no more Christians in the Ottoman Empire."[14] The Ottoman Empire did lose the war, but the de-Christianization continued, as the secular Turkish government considered a depoliticized Islam to be essential to the Turkish national identity, and continued to persecute and drive out the nation's Christians, with the approval of Turkish Muslim clerics who still thought in terms of jihad.

All in all, about a million and a half Armenians were killed in the Armenian Genocide, seven hundred thousand Greeks, and 275,000 Assyrians were killed in Ottoman territories under similar circumstances.[15] Christian communities that had existed since the beginning of Christianity were wiped out. Constantinople, fifty percent Christian even in 1914, is today 99.99 percent Muslim.[16] Further effacing the historical identity of the city, the secular Turkish government on

March 28, 1930, officially changed the name of Constantinople to one of the names the Turks had used for centuries for the city but had never been official: Istanbul.[17]

Adolf Hitler was impressed with the brutal efficiency of how the Turks answered their "Armenian question," and used their example, and the world's forgetfulness regarding this atrocity, to justify his own extermination of the Poles. In August 1939, he told Wehermacht commanders:

> Our strength consists in our speed and in our brutality. Genghis Khan led millions of women and children to slaughter—with premeditation and a happy heart. History sees in him solely the founder of a state. It's a matter of indifference to me what a weak western European civilization will say about me.
>
> I have issued the command—and I'll have anybody who utters but one word of criticism executed by a firing squad—that our war aim does not consist in reaching certain lines, but in the physical destruction of the enemy. Accordingly, I have placed my death-head formations in readiness—for the present only in the East—with orders to send them to death mercilessly and without compassion, men, women, and children of Polish derivation and language. Only thus shall we gain the living space [*Lebensraum*] which we need. Who, after all, speaks today of the annihilation of the Armenians?[18]

The same could be said of the victims of jihad throughout history. Who, after all, speaks of the victims of Tariq ibn Ziyad, or Mahmoud of Ghazni, or Mehmet the Conqueror, or Aurangzeb?

The Demise of the Caliphate

With the war lost, there was widespread discontent in the diminished Ottoman domains against the Islamic leadership that had led the once great empire down the road to disaster. One Turkish woman reflected the sentiments of many when she asked, "Of what use was the Caliphate to us during the war? We proclaimed a holy war and what good did that do?"[19]

Kemal Ataturk, the founder of secular Turkey, agreed. The Turkish Grand National Assembly abolished the sultanate on November 1, 1922, but seventeen days later chose the Ottoman crown prince, Abdulmecid II, to be the caliph—the first and only Ottoman caliph who was not to be sultan of the empire. Ataturk declared: "The Caliph has no power or position except as a nominal figurehead."[20] When the caliph dared to ask Ataturk for an increase in his pay, Ataturk told Abdulmecid: "The caliphate, your office, is no more than an historical relic. It has no justification for existence. It is a piece of impertinence that you should dare write to any of my secretaries."[21]

Finally, on March 3, 1924, Ataturk abolished the caliphate altogether and sent Abdulmecid into exile. The last caliph boarded the Orient Express, bound for Switzerland. As his train sped past Szigetvar in Hungary, where his illustrious predecessor Suleiman the Magnificent's heart was buried after he died while on a jihad expedition, Abdulmecid said sadly: "My ancestor came with a horse and flags. Now I come as an exile."[22]

"Islam," said Ataturk, "this theology of an immoral Arab, is a dead thing."[23] Islam wasn't dead by any means, but the caliphate was, at least for the time being. Almost immediately, however, Muslims began working to bring it back. Initially, they were swimming against the stream. Ataturk's Republic of Turkey, consciously based on Western, secular models of governance, was an initial success. Many of the states that were created by the British and French out of former Ottoman holdings adopted Arab nationalist secular governments that did not implement Sharia, such that as the twentieth century approached its midpoint, most Muslims did not live under Islamic law.

For true believers, this was an intolerable affront to Allah, as well as the cause of the weakness of Muslims and of Islam itself. It could not be allowed to stand.

II. SAUDI ARABIA

One of the principal forces making sure that it would not stand, and that secular government would never gain a lasting foothold in Muslim countries, was the Kingdom of Saudi Arabia.

Exiled to Kuwait by the rival al-Rashid clan in 1891, Saudi leader Abdul-Aziz ibn Saud returned in 1902, defeated the Rashidis, and seized Riyadh.[24] Over the next few years, he gained control over more and more of Arabia, alarming the Ottomans, who were too weak to do much about it. In August 1906, Ibn Saud met with the Ottoman commander Sami Pasha, only to grow enraged when Sami Pasha would not relent on his insistence that the al-Qassim region of Arabia remain under Ottoman control. Ibn Saud shouted, "If you were not my guest, I should not spare your life," and stormed out of the meeting.[25] The Ottoman troops, meanwhile, were short on supplies and growing weary of the Arabian desert, which they called "Satan's daughter."[26] In November 1906, they withdrew from the area.

In 1914, the British and the Ottomans agreed to a partition of the Arabian Peninsula, with Ibn Saud nominally the viceroy of the Ottomans as the emir of Najd.[27] When the Hashemite Hussein ibn Ali, the sharif of Mecca, rose up against the Ottomans in 1916 with the intention of forming an independent Arab state, the British—including Colonel T. E. Lawrence, who came to be known as Lawrence of Arabia—supported him. The British did not, however, support Hussein's claim to be "King of the Arab Countries," and did not fulfill the promises they had made to him to support the independence of Arab lands.

Ibn Saud didn't like the "King of the Arab Countries" title either, and waged jihad against Hussein, eventually defeating him and driving him out of Arabia in 1924. After consolidating his control over the Arabian Peninsula, Ibn Saud proclaimed the Kingdom of Saudi Arabia on September 18, 1932.[28] He decreed that all laws "should correspond to Allah's Book, the Sunna of His Prophet (Allah's blessing be upon Him) and the rules to which the Prophet's Companions and the first pious generations adhered."[29]

The proclamation of the Kingdom of Saudi Arabia took on geopolitical significance on March 4, 1938, when massive oil deposits were discovered inside the kingdom.[30] Other discoveries followed, and within a few years the Saudis were exporting millions of barrels of oil every year. As the Saudi ruling class became more and more awash in luxury, it did not forget its Wahhabi roots. One of the chief exports of Saudi Arabia, particularly in the aftermath of the oil crisis of 1973, when unimaginable wealth flowed into Saudi coffers, was Wahhabi Islam.

Between 1979 and 2017, the Saudis spent more than seventy billion dollars to finance the construction of mosques and madrasas all over the world, and on Wahhabi literature with which to fill them.[31] One of the Wahhabis' notable successes was in Kosovo. In the late 1990s, U.S. president Bill Clinton backed Muslims in Kosovo in their fight for independence against Serbia. Grateful Kosovars named a street in Pristina Bill Clinton Boulevard.[32] But Kosovo's pro-Americanism did not last long, courtesy of Saudi Arabia.

Fatos Makolli, director of Kosovo's counterterrorism police, recounted in 2016 what happened when Saudi Wahhabis started pouring millions of euros into Kosovo in 1999: "They promoted political Islam. They spent a lot of money to promote it through different programs mainly with young, vulnerable people, and they brought in a lot of Wahhabi and Salafi literature. They brought these people closer to radical political Islam, which resulted in their radicalization.... There is no evidence that any organization gave money directly to people to go to Syria. The issue is they supported thinkers who promote violence and jihad in the name of protecting Islam."[33]

A Kosovar imam named Idriz Bilalli, who opposed the Saudi influence, later declared: "This is Wahhabism coming into our society. The first thing the Wahhabis do is to take members of our congregation, who understand Islam in the traditional Kosovo way that we had for generations, and try to draw them away from this understanding. Once they get them away from the traditional congregation, then they start bombarding them with radical thoughts and ideas. The main goal of their activity is to create conflict between people. This first creates division, and then hatred, and then it can come to what happened in Arab countries, where war starts because of these conflicting ideas."[34]

After Kosovo's declaration of independence in 2008, the Saudis sponsored the building of 240 mosques in that tiny country alone.[35] In those mosques, of course, they taught Wahhabism, but the Saudis were not able simply to buy the allegiance of Kosovars or anyone else. They spent enormous amounts of money to promote Wahhabism, but Wahhabism was still able to gain only footholds around the world because of its scrupulous adherence to the letter of the Qur'an and Sunnah. The Wahhabi message resonated among Muslims because of its basis in the teachings of the Qur'an and Muhammad.

The global result of this massive Saudi cash outlay was that in 2013, the European Parliament identified Wahhabism as a principal source of terrorism worldwide.[36] The Saudis were the chief financiers of the jihad movements that convulsed the world beginning in the last decades of the twentieth century.

Most of those movements were rooted in the Muslim Brotherhood.

III. THE RISE OF JIHAD MOVEMENTS

The Muslim Brotherhood:
The Qur'an and the Sword

Determined to fight Western influence and restore the caliphate, Hasan al-Banna founded the Muslim Brotherhood in Egypt in 1928. Al-Banna decried the abolition of the caliphate, which separated "the state from religion in a country which was until recently the site of the Commander of the Faithful." Al-Banna characterized it as just part of a larger "Western invasion which was armed and equipped with all [the] destructive influences of money, wealth, prestige, ostentation, power and means of propaganda."[37]

He saw this Western influence as all-pervasive. Al-Banna lamented that "a wave of dissolution which undermined all firm beliefs, was engulfing Egypt in the name of intellectual emancipation. This trend attacked the morals, deeds and virtues under the pretext of personal freedom. Nothing could stand against this powerful and tyrannical stream of disbelief and permissiveness that was sweeping our country."[38]

Like Islamic movements going back to Ibn Tumart's and those before him, Al-Banna's was a revivalist movement. In 1928, al-Banna decried the indifference of the Egyptian elite to Islam: "What catastrophe has befallen the souls of the reformers and the spirit of the leaders...? What calamity has made them prefer this life to the thereafter [sic]? What has made them...consider the way of struggle [*sabil al-*

jihad] too rough and difficult?"[39] When the Brotherhood was criticized for being a political group in the guise of a religious one, al-Banna met the challenge head-on:

> We summon you to Islam, the teachings of Islam, the laws of Islam and the guidance of Islam, and if this smacks of "politics" in your eyes, then it is our policy. And if the one summoning you to these principles is a "politician," then we are the most respectable of men, God be praised, in politics.... Islam does have a policy embracing the happiness of this world.... We believe that Islam is an all-embracing concept which regulates every aspect of life, adjudicating on every one of its concerns and prescribing for it a solid and rigorous order.[40]

The Brotherhood invoked the Qur'an—"Fight them until there is no fitnah [sedition] and worship is for Allah" (2:193)—in exhorting Muslims worldwide to recapture the glory days of Islam, to reestablish the caliphate and once again make it into a great power. Al-Banna also insisted that "every piece of land where the banner of Islam has been hoisted is the fatherland of the Muslims." In line with another Qur'anic directive, "drive them out from where they drove you out" (2:191), the Brotherhood urged Muslims to reconquer Spain, as well as Sicily and southern Italy and the former Ottoman domains in the Balkans.[41]

The Brotherhood grew in Egypt from 150 branches in 1936 to as many as fifteen hundred by 1944. In 1939 al-Banna referred to "100,000 pious youths from the Muslim Brothers from all parts of Egypt," and by 1944 membership was estimated as being between one hundred thousand and five hundred thousand.[42] By 1937 the group had expanded beyond Egypt, setting up "several branches in Sudan, Saudi Arabia, Palestine, Syria, Lebanon, and Morocco, and one each in Bahrain, Hadramawt, Hyderabad, Djibouti, and even in Paris."[43]

Thus many thousands of Muslims dispersed around the world heard al-Banna's call to "prepare for jihad and be lovers of death."[44] The Muslim Brotherhood's newspaper explained: "No justice will be dealt and no peace maintained on earth until the rule of the Koran and the bloc of Islam are established. Moslem unity must be established. Indonesia,

Pakistan, Afghanistan, Iran, Iraq, Turkey, Syria, Lebanon, Trans-Jordan, Palestine, Saudi-Arabia, Yemen, Egypt, Sudan, Tripoli, Tunis, Algeria and Morocco all form one bloc, the Moslem bloc, which God has promised to grant victory, saying: 'We shall grant victory unto the faithful.' But this is impossible to reach other than through the way of Islam."[45] Al-Banna told his followers: "Islam is faith and worship, a country and a citizenship, a religion and a state. It is spirituality and hard work. It is a Qur'an and a sword."[46]

Islam, the Answer to the World's Problems

The Armenian-American journalist Arthur Derounian met al-Banna in 1948. Writing later under the name John Roy Carlson, Derounian described al-Banna as "a short, squat ratty-faced man with puffed cheeks and fleshy nose.... We sat in the shade, under the shield showing the Koran above a pair of crossed swords.... I disliked him instantly and thoroughly. He was the most loathsome man I had yet met in Cairo."[47] Al-Banna told Derounian: "The Koran should be Egypt's constitution, for there is no law higher than Koranic law. We seek to fulfill the lofty, human message of Islam which has brought happiness and fulfillment to mankind in centuries past. Ours is the highest ideal, the holiest cause and the purest way. Those who criticize us have fed from the tables of Europe. They want to live as Europe has taught them—to dance, to drink, to revel, to mix the sexes openly and in public."[48]

Sayyid Qutb, the Muslim Brotherhood's great theorist, shared that puritanical revulsion. He sharpened his distaste for the West while living in the United States from November 1948 to August 1950.[49] Moving to Greeley, Colorado, he was impressed by the number of churches in the city but not with the piety they engendered: "Nobody goes to church as often as Americans do.... Yet no one is as distant as they are from the spiritual aspect of religion." He was thoroughly scandalized by a dance after an evening service at a local church: "The dancing intensified.... The hall swarmed with legs.... Arms circled arms, lips met lips, chests met chests, and the atmosphere was full of love."[50] The pastor further scandalized Qutb by dimming the lights, creating "a romantic, dreamy effect," and playing a popular record of the day:

"Baby, It's Cold Outside."[51] He regarded American popular music in general with a gimlet eye: "Jazz is the favorite music [of America]. It is a type of music invented by [American] Blacks to please their primitive tendencies and desire for noise."[52]

Ultimately he concluded: "I fear that when the wheel of life has turned and the file on history has closed, America will not have contributed anything." He didn't find American prosperity to be matched by a corresponding wealth of spirit. "I am afraid that there is no correlation between the greatness of the American material civilization and the men who created it.... In both feeling and conduct the American is primitive [*bida'a*]."[53]

Qutb's influential book *Milestones* positioned Islam as the true source of societal and personal order, as opposed to both capitalism and Communism. "Mankind today is on the brink of a precipice," he asserted in this Cold War–era manifesto, "not because of the danger of complete annihilation which is hanging over its head—this being just a symptom and not the real disease—but because humanity is devoid of those vital values which are necessary not only for its healthy development but also for its real progress." Perhaps with his time in America in mind, he went on: "Even the Western world realizes that Western civilization is unable to present any healthy values for the guidance of mankind. It knows that it does not possess anything which will satisfy its own conscience and justify its existence."

Qutb concluded: "It is essential for mankind to have new leadership!"[54] That new leadership would come from Islam. To Qutb, what the Muslim *umma* needed was a restoration of Islam in its fullness and purity, including all the rules of the Sharia for regulating society. "If we look at the sources and foundations of modern ways of living, it becomes clear that the whole world is steeped in *Jahiliyyah* [Ignorance of the Divine guidance], and all the marvelous material comforts and high-level inventions do not diminish this ignorance. This *Jahiliyyah* is based on rebellion against God's sovereignty on earth. It transfers to man one of the greatest attributes of God, namely sovereignty, and makes some men lords over others."[55]

He advanced Islam as "a challenge to all kinds and forms of systems which are based on the concept of the sovereignty of man; in other words, where man has usurped the Divine attribute. Any system in which the final decisions are referred to human beings, and in which the sources of all authority are human, deifies human beings by designating others than God as lords over men."[56]

Qutb taught that jihad was necessary in order to establish Sharia. "The establishing of the dominion of God on earth, the abolishing of the dominion of man, the taking away of sovereignty from the usurper to revert it to God, and the bringing about of the enforcement of the Divine Law [Sharia]…and the abolition of man-made laws cannot be achieved only through preaching. Those who have usurped the authority of God and are oppressing God's creatures are not going to give up their power merely through preaching; if it had been so, the task of establishing God's religion in the world would have been very easy for the Prophets of God! This is contrary to the evidence from the history of the Prophets and the story of the struggle of the true religion, spread over generations."[57]

Qutb emphasized Islam's universal character and call: "This religion is not merely a declaration of the freedom of the Arabs, nor is its message confined to the Arabs. It addresses itself to the whole of mankind, and its sphere of work is the whole earth.… This religion wants to bring back the whole world to its Sustainer and free it from servitude to anyone other than God."[58]

Al-Banna likewise explained: "We want an Arabian United States with a Caliphate at its head and every Arab state subscribing wholeheartedly to the laws of the Koran. We must return to the Koran, which preaches the good life, which forbids us to take bribes, to cheat, to kill one's brother. The laws of the Koran are suitable for all men at all times to the end of the world. This is the day and this is the time when the world needs Islam most."[59]

To impress upon Egypt its need for Islam, the Brotherhood attacked Jews who lived there and assassinated several leading officials, including several judges. Al-Banna ordered one young member of the Brotherhood, a twenty-three-year-old student named Abdel Magid Ahmed Hassan, to do his duty before Allah—which, a sheikh explained to the young man, involved killing "the enemies of Islam and of Arabism." Hassan agreed to murder anyone al-Banna told him to, and so on December 28, 1948, the young man gunned down Egypt's prime minister, Mahmoud El Nokrashy Pasha.[60] Al-Banna was himself assassinated on February 12, 1949, most likely in a revenge killing.[61] Qutb, hospitalized in Washington, D.C. for a respiratory ailment in February 1949, claimed implausibly that a radio broadcast of the news of al-Banna's assassination set the hospital staff to open rejoicing.[62]

Egypt's Arab Socialist ruler, Gamel Abdel Nasser, had no patience for the Brotherhood, and had Qutb imprisoned and tortured. Qutb wrote from his prison cell: "The whole of Egypt is imprisoned.... I was arrested despite my immunity as a judge, without an order of arrest... my sole crime being my critique of the non-application of the Sharia."[63] As his trial began, he declared: "The time has come for a Muslim to give his head in order to proclaim the birth of the Islamic movement."[64] When he was sentenced to death, he exclaimed: "Thank God! I performed jihad for fifteen years until I earned this martyrdom."[65] He was executed in 1966.

IV. THE JIHAD IN ISRAEL

Hajj Amin al-Husseini

One of the Muslim Brotherhood's foremost friends and supporters was Hajj Amin al-Husseini, the mufti of Jerusalem, who for years before the establishment of the state of Israel fought strenuously against Jewish settlement in the Holy Land, which had accelerated after Britain's 1917 Balfour Declaration calling for the establishment of a Jewish homeland in the Middle East.

Beginning in 1919, al-Husseini began organizing jihad attacks against Jews, as well as riots in Jerusalem in 1920 during which six Jews were killed and two hundred injured. The following year, British high commissioner Herbert Samuel responded to al-Husseini's instigation of jihad violence by appointing him mufti of Jerusalem, hoping that this gift would lead al-Husseini to be "devoted to tranquility."[66]

Instead, al-Husseini continued to incite violence, including riots in Petach Tikvah and Jaffa just weeks after he became mufti; forty-three Jews were killed. A British government report stated that "the Arab majority, who were generally the aggressors, inflicted most of the casualties."[67]

This continued to be true as Muslim Arabs attacked Jews over the next two decades, largely at al-Husseini's instigation. Instead of confronting its mufti, in May 1939 the British government limited Jewish settlement in Palestine to seventy-five thousand over the next five years, thereby rewarding jihad violence by giving the mufti part of what he wanted (if it had been up to him, Jewish entry into the Holy Land would have been halted entirely, and the Jews there expelled) and condemning to death in the Holocaust untold numbers of Jews who might have escaped.

Al-Husseini stirred up the mobs by claiming that Jews had designs on large portions of the Islamic world: "Palestine does not satisfy the Jews, because their goal is to rule over the rest of the Arab nations, over Lebanon, Syria, and Iraq, and even over the lands of Khyber in Saudi Arabia, under the pretext that this city was the homeland of the Jewish tribes in the seventh century."[68]

Had that been true, Islamic law would have obligated Muslims to wage a defensive jihad against the Jews, for, as noted previously, defensive jihad becomes obligatory upon every Muslim whenever a Muslim land is attacked. As far as al-Husseini was concerned, his effort against the Jews was indeed a jihad. At a conference in Syria in 1937, he contributed an address entitled "Islam and the Jews," in which he explained:

> The battle between Jews and Islam began when Mohammed fled from Mecca to Medina.... In those days the Jewish methods were exactly the same as they are today. Then as now, slander was their weapon. They said Mohammed was a swindler.... They tried to undermine his honor.... They began to pose senseless and unanswerable questions to Mohammed...and then they tried to annihilate the Muslims. Just as the Jews were able to betray Mohammed, so they will betray the Muslims today...the verses of the Koran and the Hadith assert that the Jews were Islam's most bitter enemy and moreover try to destroy it.[69]

From 1941 to 1945, al-Husseini lived in Berlin, where he became close friends with Adolf Eichmann and Heinrich Himmler, and met with

Adolf Hitler. Eichmann's assistant, Dieter Wisliczeny, testified at the Nuremberg Trials that the mufti had been a central figure in the planning of the genocide of the Jews:

> The Grand Mufti has repeatedly suggested to the Nazi authorities—including Hitler, von Ribbentrop and Himmler—the extermination of European Jewry. He considered this a comfortable solution to the Palestine problem....The Mufti was one of the initiators of the systematic extermination of European Jewry and had been a collaborator and adviser of Eichmann and Himmler in the execution of this plan. He was one of Eichmann's best friends and had constantly incited him to accelerate the extermination measures. I heard him say, accompanied by Eichmann, he had visited incognito the gas chambers of Auschwitz.[70]

Eichmann denied this, but in any case, there is no doubt of the fact that the mufti was openly calling for the mass murder of Jews. In a broadcast on July 7, 1942, the mufti exhorted Muslims in Egypt, Syria, Iraq, and Palestine to kill Jews, basing his exhortation on a flagrant lie:

> A large number of Jews residing in Egypt and a number of Poles, Greeks, Armenians and Free French, have been issued with revolvers and ammunition in order to help them against the Egyptians at the last moment, when Britain is forced to evacuate Egypt.
>
> In the face of this barbaric procedure by the British we think it best, if the life of the Egyptian nation is to be saved, that the Egyptians rise as one man to kill the Jews before they have a chance of betraying the Egyptian people. It is the duty of the Egyptians to annihilate the Jews and to destroy their property....
>
> You must kill the Jews, before they open fire on you. Kill the Jews, who have appropriated your wealth and who are plotting against your security. Arabs of Syria, Iraq and Palestine, what are you waiting for? The Jews are planning to violate your women, to kill your children and to destroy

you. According to the Muslim religion, the defense of your life is a duty which can only be fulfilled by annihilating the Jews. This is your best opportunity to get rid of this dirty race, which has usurped your rights and brought misfortune and destruction on your countries. Kill the Jews, burn their property, destroy their stores, annihilate these base support-ers of British imperialism. Your sole hope of salvation lies in annihilating the Jews before they annihilate you.[71]

Al-Husseini also actively intervened on numerous occasions to ensure that Jews were not deported from Europe—thereby ensuring that exter-mination was the only option left for the fanatical Nazi Jew-haters. As late as July 25, 1944, al-Husseini wrote to Joachim von Ribbentrop, the German minister for foreign affairs:

I have previously called the attention of your Excellen-cy to the constant attempts of the Jews to emigrate from Europe in order to reach Palestine and asked your Ex-cellency to undertake the necessary steps so as to prevent the Jews from emigrating. I had also sent you a letter, un-der date of June 5, 1944, in regard to the plan for an ex-change of Egyptians living in Germany with Palestinian Germans, in which I asked you to exclude the Jews from this plan of exchange. I have, however, learned that the Jews did depart on July 2, 1944, and I am afraid that fur-ther groups of Jews will leave for Palestine from Germa-ny and France to be exchanged for Palestinian Germans.

This exchange on the part of the Germans would en-courage the Balkan countries likewise to send their Jews to Palestine. This stop would be incomprehensible to the Arabs and Moslems after your Excellency's declaration of November 2, 1943 that "the destruction of the so-called Jewish national home in Palestine is an immutable part of the policy of the greater German Reich" and it would create in them a feeling of keen disappointment.

It is for this reason that I ask your Excellency to do

all that is necessary to prohibit the emigration of Jews to Palestine, and in this way your Excellency would give a new practical example of the policy of the naturally allied and friendly Germany towards the Arab Nation.[72]

According to the Arab Higher Committee, "In virtually identical letters, the Mufti, in the summer of 1944, approached Germany, Romania, Bulgaria, and Hungary to speed up the extermination of the Jews by sending them to Poland where the Nazi death chambers were located."[73]

Whatever the mufti's actual role in the establishment of the Nazi death camps, he certainly approved of their work, saying confidently: "The Arab nation awaits the solution of the world Jewish problem by its friends, the Axis powers."[74]

Al-Husseini was a committed collaborator with the Nazis, traveling from Berlin to Bosnia in 1943 to raise up a Muslim SS division, which was responsible for killing ninety percent of the Jews in Bosnia, as well as for the burning of numerous Serbian churches.[75] He noted the convergence of the goals of Islamic jihad and those of the Nazis. "It is the duty of Muhammadans in general and Arabs in particular to…drive all Jews from Arab and Muhammadan countries…. Germany is also struggling against the common foe who oppressed Arabs and Muhammadans in their different countries. It has very clearly recognized the Jews for what they are and resolved to find a definitive solution [*endgültige Lösung*] for the Jewish danger that will eliminate the scourge that Jews represent in the world."[76]

The mufti also made radio broadcasts in Arabic from Berlin that were beamed into the Arabic-speaking world, using Islam to bring Arabs over to Hitler's side. On May 9, 1941, he broadcast a fatwa calling upon Muslims in Iraq to wage jihad against the British. In response, Muslims in Iraq began murdering Jews, ultimately killing 128 while destroying well over a thousand Jewish businesses and homes.[77]

That was just what the mufti wanted, and he wanted much more. On November 2, 1943, he decried "the overwhelming egoism which lies in the character of Jews, their unworthy belief that they are God's chosen nation and their assertion that all was created for them and that other people are animals."[78] All that, he said, made Jews "incapable of being trusted. They cannot mix with any other nation but live as parasites among the nations, suck out their blood, embezzle their property, corrupt their morals." In a 1944 broadcast, he was more succinct: "Kill the Jews wherever you find them. This pleases God, history, and religion."[79] His call was an echo of the Qur'an's call to "kill them wherever you find them" (2:191, 4:89) and to "kill the idolaters wherever you find them." (9:5)

Al-Husseini was arrested by French troops in May 1945, but the French refused requests from the British to turn him over to their custody. The British may have wanted to put him on trial, as he was a British citizen (of their Palestinian mandate) and a collaborator with the Nazis. Instead, the French put him on a plane to Cairo, where he resumed his jihad against the Jews. The Muslim Brotherhood successfully prevailed upon the Egyptian government to grant him asylum.[80]

Strangling Israel in its Cradle

In October 1947, al-Banna told the Brotherhood to begin preparing for jihad.[81] The Brothers were ready for this call, as the Brotherhood was dedicated to an Islamic revival, and since the Qur'an and Sunnah teach warfare, jihad war was part of that revival. The Brotherhood had weapons and a military wing, preaching revival openly while secretly amassing weapons and preparing for jihad.

U.S. president Franklin D. Roosevelt ,who died in 1945, had declined to give any significant support to the Zionist project. When Rabbis Stephen S. Wise and Abba Hillel Silver tried to convince him that Jewish refugees from Europe should be moved to the Holy Land, he responded: "Do you want to be responsible by your actions for the loss of hundreds of thousands of lives? Do you want to start a holy jihad?"[82] (In saying this, he demonstrated far greater awareness of history and Islam than many of his successors, but about their same level of resolve to confront it.) After a conversation with his friend, the Saudi king, Roosevelt recounted happily to Congress: "I learned more about the whole problem by talking with Ibn Saud for five minutes than I could have learned in an exchange of two or three dozen letters."[83] That the king's perspective was formed by jihadi assumptions about who rightfully owned the land did not appear to trouble Roosevelt in the least.

After the horrors of the Holocaust were revealed, however, the Zionist movement was able to gain a great deal of international support, most notably from Roosevelt's successor as president, Harry S. Truman. The state of Israel declared its independence on May 14, 1948.

The Muslim Brotherhood was in the front line of the jihad effort to smother the Jewish state in its cradle. Al-Banna predicted: "All Arabs shall arise and annihilate the Jews. We shall fill the sea with their corpses."[84] Abdul Rahman Azzam, the secretary-general of the Arab League, said: "I personally wish that the Jews do not drive us to this war, as this will be a war of extermination and momentous massacre which will be spoken of like the Tartar massacre or the Crusader wars."[85]

Hajj Amin al-Husseini emphasized that this was not just a war but a jihad, saying: "I declare a holy war, my Muslim brothers! Murder the Jews! Murder them all!"[86] The idea that the Arab war against the new Jewish state was not just a conflict over territory but an Islamic jihad was based on the Qur'anic command to "drive them out from where they drove you out" (2:191), the same command that the Muslim Brotherhood invoked to call for Islamic reconquest of Spain and the Balkans. The Islamic principle that no land that had ever been ruled by the laws of Islam could ever legitimately revert to rule by the infidels, and that all land once won by Islam belonged to Islam forever, meant that a state of Israel ruled by Jews would never be acceptable in any form. Israel was even more of an insult because of the Qur'an's many anti-Semitic passages, portraying Jews as dishonest schemers, enemies of Allah, and enemies of the Muslims: "You will surely find the most intense of the people in animosity toward the believers to be the Jews" (5:82). Arab leaders consequently rejected the United Nations' partition of the area and creation of an Arab state alongside the Jewish state and called instead for war.

Many Muslims heeded this call, massacring forty-one Jews at the Haifa oil depot in December 1947; burning Jews alive at the Ein Zeitun settlement in January 1948; ambushing and murdering thirty-five Jews on a Jerusalem road that same month and sexually mutilating the corpses; killing one and injuring twenty with a bomb in the Jerusalem Post offices in February 1948; murdering forty-six and injuring 130 with a bomb at the Ben Yehuda market later that month; murdering fourteen and injuring forty with still another bomb at the Jewish Agency building in March 1948; ambushing and murdering 105 Jews on another road in April 1948; destroying thirty-five synagogues and other Jewish institutions in May 1948; disemboweling several women at Nitzanim in June 1948; and on and on. The mufti's Arab Liberation Army killed three hundred Jews at Kfar Etzion, south of Jerusalem, in jihad attacks in the opening months of 1948; the Muslims blew up one house with twenty Jewish girls inside it.[87]

On April 4, 1948, Easter Sunday, Arabic-language notices were posted in Jerusalem saying, "The Government is with us, Allenby is with us, kill the Jews; there is no punishment for killing Jews."[88] Allenby was the English field marshal viscount Edmund Allenby, who had won the admiration of Muslims in Jerusalem when he took the city from the Ottomans in 1917 while emphasizing that he was only fighting the sultanate, not crusading against Islam. Allenby brushed aside celebrations of him as being the Christian commander who had liberated Jerusalem from 730 years of Turkish rule; he was not religious, and his war was no Crusade.[89] Allenby died in 1936, so the authors of these posters were invoking his spirit and claiming his blessing on their pogrom. A Muslim mob chanting, "Palestine is our land, kill the Jews" and, "We will drink the blood of the Jews" began rampaging through the city; at the end of the day, five Jews were dead and 216 injured.[90] There would be much, much more of this to come in the years and decades ahead: Muslim Arabs never stopped waging jihad against Israel.

Arthur Derounian met Hasan al-Banna while in Cairo to cover the jihad that the Muslim Brotherhood and other Muslims were preparing against Israel. He found a great deal of excitement and enthusiasm for the jihad against the Jews. He also met with Saleh Harb Pasha, Egypt's former minister of defense and a close friend of al-Banna's; Harb Pasha expressed regret at the outcome of World War II: "If Rommel had won we would be independent now. If the Nazis and Fascists had won, they would have been friends to the whole Arab world. And there would have been no Zionist problem because there would have been no Zionist Jews…or any Jews at all left."[91]

An imam told Derounian: "I pray to Allah to destroy the Jews. I pray to Allah to punish President Truman because he has been on the Zionist side. I used to pray against President Roosevelt, a very bad man.... May Balfour and Roosevelt take the first place in hell. Allah, Allah, may this be done."[92] One jihadi assured the American journalist: "Our God is the strongest. We are not afraid to die. The Jews are cowards because they want to live. The Arabs would rather lose ten men than one gun. The Jews are the opposite. They want to save their lives and lose their guns. That is one difference between us."[93]

The jihadi was wrong. The nascent state of Israel defeated forces from Egypt, Iraq, Syria, Transjordan, Lebanon, Saudi Arabia, and Yemen that had been determined to destroy it utterly. The jihad against it continued, but it held firm, defeating Egypt, Iraq, Syria, Jordan, and Lebanon again in the Six-Day War in 1967, and Egypt and Syria yet again in the 1973 Yom Kippur War. In winning these victories against enormous odds, Israel won the admiration of the free world, leading to the largest-scale and most audacious application in Islamic history of Muhammad's dictum "War is deceit."[94]

In order to destroy the impression of the tiny Jewish state's facing enormous Muslim Arab foes and prevailing, the Soviet KGB (the Soviet Committee for State Security) developed the fiction of an even smaller people, the "Palestinians," menaced by a well-oiled and ruthless Israeli war machine. In A.D. 134, the Romans had expelled the Jews from Judea after the Bar Kokhba revolt and renamed the region Palestine, a name they plucked from the Bible, the name of the Israelites' ancient enemies, the Philistines. But never had the name Palestinian referred to anything but a region, not to a people or an ethnicity. In the 1960s, however, the KGB and Hajj Amin al-Husseini's nephew Yasir Arafat created both these allegedly oppressed people and the instrument of their freedom, the Palestine Liberation Organization (PLO).

Ion Mihai Pacepa, who had served as acting chief of Cold War–era Communist Romania's spy service, later revealed that "the PLO was dreamt up by the KGB, which had a penchant for 'liberation' organizations. There was the National Liberation Army of Bolivia, created by the KGB in 1964 with help from Ernesto 'Che' Guevara...the KGB also created the Democratic Front for the Liberation of Palestine, which carried out numerous bombing attacks…. In 1964 the first PLO Council, consisting of 422 Palestinian representatives handpicked by the KGB, approved the Palestinian National Charter—a document that had been drafted in Moscow. The Palestinian National Covenant and the Palestinian Constitution were also born in Moscow, with the help of Ahmed Shuqairy, a KGB influence agent who became the first PLO chairman."[95]

For Arafat to head up the PLO, he had to be a Palestinian. Pacepa explained that "he was an Egyptian bourgeois turned into a devoted Marxist by KGB foreign intelligence. The KGB had trained him at its Balashikha special-operations school east of Moscow and in the mid-1960s decided to groom him as the future PLO leader. First, the KGB destroyed the official records of Arafat's birth in Cairo, and replaced them with fictitious documents saying that he had been born in Jerusalem and was therefore a Palestinian by birth."[96]

Arafat may have been a Marxist, at least at first, but he and his Soviet handlers made copious use of Islamic anti-Semitism. KGB chief Yuri Andropov noted that "the Islamic world was a waiting petri dish in which we could nurture a virulent strain of America-hatred, grown from the bacterium of Marxist-Leninist thought. Islamic anti-Semitism ran deep…. We had only to keep repeating our themes—that the United States and Israel were 'fascist, imperial-Zionist countries' bankrolled by rich Jews. Islam was obsessed with preventing the infidels' occupation of its territory, and it would be highly receptive to our characterization of the U.S. Congress as a rapacious Zionist body aiming to turn the world into a Jewish fiefdom."[97]

PLO executive committee member Zahir Muhsein explained the strategy more fully in a 1977 interview with the Dutch newspaper *Trouw*:

> The Palestinian people does not exist. The creation of a Palestinian state is only a means for continuing our struggle against the state of Israel for our Arab unity. In reality today there is no difference between Jordanians, Palestinians, Syrians and Lebanese. Only for political and tactical reasons do we speak today about the existence of a Palestinian people, since Arab national interests demand that we posit the existence of a distinct "Palestinian people" to oppose Zionism.

> For tactical reasons, Jordan, which is a sovereign state
> with defined borders, cannot raise claims to Haifa and Jaffa,
> while as a Palestinian, I can undoubtedly demand Haifa,
> Jaffa, Beer-Sheva and Jerusalem. However, the moment we
> reclaim our right to all of Palestine, we will not wait even a
> minute to unite Palestine and Jordan.[98]

Once the people had been created, their desire for peace could be easily fabricated as well. Romanian dictator Nicolae Ceausescu tutored Arafat in how to play the West like a fiddle. Pacepa recounted: "In March 1978, I secretly brought Arafat to Bucharest for final instructions on how to behave in Washington. 'You simply have to keep on pretending that you'll break with terrorism and that you'll recognize Israel—over, and over, and over,' Ceausescu told him [Arafat].... Ceausescu was euphoric over the prospect that both Arafat and he might be able to snag a Nobel Peace Prize with their fake displays of the olive branch.... Ceausescu failed to get his Nobel Peace Prize. But in 1994 Arafat got his—all because he continued to play the role we had given him to perfection. He had transformed his terrorist PLO into a government-in-exile (the Palestinian Authority), always pretending to call a halt to Palestinian terrorism while letting it continue unabated. Two years after signing the Oslo Accords, the number of Israelis killed by Palestinian terrorists had risen by 73 percent."[99]

This strategy continued to work beautifully, through U.S.-brokered "peace process" after "peace process," from the 1978 Camp David Accords into the presidency of Barack Obama and beyond, with no end in sight. Western authorities never seem to ponder why so many attempts to achieve a negotiated peace between Israel and the "Palestinians," whose historical existence everyone by now takes for granted, have all failed. The answer, of course, lies in the Islamic doctrine of jihad. "Drive them out from where they drove you out" is a command that contains no mitigation and accepts none.

While all of the Palestinian factions made the fact clear (at least to those who were paying attention) that they would never accept the existence of Israel in any form, and that their war against it was a jihad, none have made this clearer than Hamas (Harakat Muqawama Islamiyya—the Islamic Resistance Movement), founded in 1988. The

Hamas charter calls for Islamic rule in Palestine, describing the PLO's idea of a secular state as a Western colonial imposition upon the Muslim world: "Secular thought is diametrically opposed to religious thought. Thought is the basis for positions, for modes of conduct and for resolutions. Therefore, in spite of our appreciation for the PLO and its possible transformation in the future, and despite the fact that we do not denigrate its role in the Arab-Israeli conflict, we cannot substitute it for the Islamic nature of Palestine by adopting secular thought. For the Islamic nature of Palestine is part of our religion, and anyone who neglects his religion is bound to lose."[100] The charter follows this with a quotation from the Qur'an: "And who forsakes the religion of Abraham, save him who befools himself?" (2:130)

Islam is the only unifying factor of the Palestinian factions: "When the PLO adopts Islam as the guideline for life, then we shall become its soldiers, the fuel of its fire which will burn the enemies."[101]

Significantly, Hamas identifies itself in its charter as "one of the wings of the Muslim Brothers in Palestine. The Muslim Brotherhood Movement is a world organization, the largest Islamic Movement in the modern era. It is characterized by a profound understanding, by precise notions and by a complete comprehensiveness of all concepts of Islam in all domains of life: views and beliefs, politics and economics, education and society, jurisprudence and rule, indoctrination and teaching, the arts and publications, the hidden and the evident, and all the other domains of life."[102]

The charter quotes al-Banna: "Israel will rise and will remain erect until Islam eliminates it as it had eliminated its predecessors."[103] In keeping with this guiding idea that Islam must be and will be the force that ultimately eliminates Israel, and that Islamic principles must rule all aspects of life, Hamas states that "the Islamic Resistance Movement consists of Muslims who are devoted to Allah and worship Him verily.... As the Movement adopts Islam as its way of life, its time dimension extends back as far as the birth of the Islamic Message and of the Righteous Ancestor. Its ultimate goal is Islam, the Prophet its model, the Quran its Constitution."[104]

Hamas sees its Islamic mission as part of the universal Islamic mission of jihad: "Its spatial dimension extends wherever on earth there are Muslims, who adopt Islam as their way of life; thus, it penetrates to the deepest reaches of the land and to the highest spheres of Heavens.... By virtue of the distribution of Muslims, who pursue the cause of the Hamas, all over the globe, and strive for its victory, for the reinforcement of its positions and for the encouragement of its Jihad, the Movement is a universal one."[105]

Also, in contrast to the PLO's taste for negotiations as a means to wring concessions from Israel and its allies, Hamas disdains peace talks: "[Peace] initiatives, the so-called peaceful solutions, and the international conferences to resolve the Palestinian problem, are all contrary to the beliefs of the Islamic Resistance Movement. For renouncing any part of Palestine means renouncing part of the religion; the nationalism of the Islamic Resistance Movement is part of its faith, the movement educates its members to adhere to its principles and to raise the banner of Allah over their homeland as they fight their Jihad: 'Allah is the all-powerful, but most people are not aware.'"[106]

Hamas and other Palestinian jihad groups have continued the practice of murdering Israeli civilians, justifying this action as defensive jihad, hoping thereby to weaken and demoralize the Jewish state, while characterizing all of Israel's defensive efforts as disproportionate, unwarranted, and unjust. It is a jihad of the pen and the tongue combined with that of the sword, wielded as much in the court of public opinion as in Jerusalem, Tel Aviv, and other areas of Israel.

In keeping with Muhammad's dictum "War is deceit," Palestinian propagandists worked assiduously to create a picture for the international media of a beleaguered Palestinian people menaced by a remorseless and ruthless Israeli war machine. Numerous Israeli atrocities were manufactured for eager consumption and propagation by the international media, the most notorious of these being a video purportedly showing a twelve-year-old boy, Muhammad al-Dura, wantonly murdered by the Israeli Defense Force in 2000. In reality, there was no murder—and may not even have been a Muhammad al-Dura. Before that was definitively established, a Palestinian *intifada*, or uprising, against Israel killed around a thousand Israelis.[107]

The Palestinian propaganda barrage was a magnificent success. Global opinion, once strongly on the side of Israel, turned so sharply against the Jewish state that by the end of the twentieth century and the beginning of the twenty-first, Israel had become the chief target of United Nations human rights condemnations, and the primary target of demonstrations on campuses in the United States and elsewhere in the West. It was a new and highly successful jihad tactic, recognized by few as such but nonetheless unmistakably just that: all part of an effort to isolate, destabilize, and ultimately destroy Israel so that it could be replaced by an Islamic government.

V. JIHAD AND THE PARTITION OF INDIA

After World War II, as the sun was setting on the British Empire, India was partitioned into a majority-Hindu area, known as India, and two majority-Muslim areas, known as East Pakistan (later Bangladesh) and West Pakistan. The name Pakistan was an amalgamation of the names of the regions that made it up: Punjab, Afghania, Kashmir, Sindh, and Baluchistan. "*Pak*," however, also means "pure" in Urdu and Persian, and for many Muslims, Pakistan, a land created specifically for Muslims, was to be the land of the pure expression of the faith.

The seeds of the partition were planted with the first jihad invasion of India in the eighth century, which was a manifestation of Islam's hatred of and contempt for the infidels. Centuries of bloody oppression led to significant levels of resentment of Muslims among the Hindu population of India. In the aftermath of World War I, the Khilafat movement among Muslims in India protested against the secular Turkish marginalization, and subsequent abolition, of the caliphate. In doing so, it promoted the idea that the Muslims of the world should be united in a single state, although this had not actually been the case at any point in history except, arguably, in the age of the "Rightly-Guided Caliphs" before the Sunni/Shi'a split became formalized, but the new propagation of this idea undermined prospects for Indian unity.[108]

Although Pakistani leader Muhammad Ali Jinnah was not a doctrinaire Muslim and did not found Pakistan as a state ruled by Islamic law, the proponents of jihad and Sharia backed the partition because it was unacceptable to them for Muslims to live under infidel rule. The partition itself was acrimonious, with over a million people killed and fifteen million made refugees.[109] Almost immediately, the new state of Pakistan began waging jihad against India, in September 1947 arming militias fighting against Indian rule in the disputed state of Jammu and Kashmir.[110] Arif Jamal, a historian of the jihad in Kashmir, notes that "Jinnah had signed a stand-still agreement with the Maharaja [ruler] of Jammu and Kashmir, and jihad by tribesmen violated that agreement. The Maharaja then invited Indian troops to defend the state, which led to the first war between India and Pakistan and the division of Kashmir by the end of 1948."[111]

A historian of Kashmir, Talat Bhat, notes that the drive for Kashmiri independence from India grew progressively more jihadist in character toward the end of the twentieth century, thanks to Pakistani government interference: "Kashmir's independent movement began in 1948 and kept gaining strength in Indian-occupied areas until 1985, a year after the hanging of the separatist leader Maqbool Bhat in 1984. His Jammu and Kashmir Liberation Front (JKLF) party declared war on India in 1988, which also led to a popular independence movement. But in 1991, Pakistan's ISI created Hizbul Mujadeen (HM), an Islamist militant organization, to counter secular JKLF. Between 1991 and 1993, most JKLF commanders were either killed or jailed by HM or Indian troops. In 1994, JKLF declared unilateral ceasefire but Islamabad sent more Islamists, who had fought the war in Afghanistan, to Kashmir."[112]

Pakistan and India have remained in an ongoing state of war since the partition, due to Pakistan's jihadi intransigence and fanaticism, with 9,471 outbreaks of actual violence in 1947, 1965, 1971, and 1999. In a telling incident in 1964, the government of Indian prime minister Jawaharlal Nehru sent the Kashmiri Muslim leader Sheikh Mohammad Abdullah and his lieutenant, Mirza Mohammad Afzal Beg, to Pakistan for talks with its military ruler, Field Marshal Ayub Khan. Nehru's offer was audacious: the reunion of the subcontinent.

Ayub Khan would have none of it. He later complained that all Abdullah and Mirza Afzal Beg had brought him was an "absurd proposal of confederation between India, Pakistan and Kashmir." Ayub recounted: "I told him plainly that we would have nothing to do with it. It was curious that whereas we were seeking the salvation of Kashmiris, they had been forced to mention an idea which, if pursued, would lead to our enslavement." What most annoyed Ayub was that "a confederal arrangement would undo the Partition and place the Hindu majority in a dominant and decisive position."[113] This was intolerable, as it contradicted the Islamic imperative to dominate and hold political power over infidels.

The Hizbul Mujadeen commander Burhan Wani has emphasized that his organization's "jihad is for a Caliphate."[114] As always.

VI. IRAN'S ISLAMIC REVOLUTION

The Fall of the Shah

On October 8, 1962, Mohammed Reza Pahlavi, the Western-oriented shah of Iran, whose father, Reza Shah, had admired Kemal Ataturk and set Iran on a secular path, granted women the right to vote in elections for local councils and gave permission for those elected to take their oaths of office on any sacred book, not just the Qur'an—which meant that they didn't have to be Muslim.[115]

In response, a little-known ayatollah named Ruhollah Khomeini and his colleagues instructed Shi'ite clergy all over the country to denounce the government. Several weeks later, the shah relented: his prime minister, Assadollah Alam, announced that candidates for local councils would have to be Muslim, that oaths must be sworn on the Qur'an only, and that the Majlis would decide the question of women's suffrage.[116]

Then, in January 1963, the shah announced a series of reforms he called the White Revolution, including distributing land to the poor and allowing women not only to vote but also to run for office. Khomeini declared, "What is happening is a calculated plot against Iranian independence and the Islamic nation, and it is threatening the foundation of Islam."[117] He and other Shi'ite clergy called for demonstrations, which so unnerved the shah that on January 24, 1963, during a presentation on the glories of land reform, he gave an impromptu speech attacking the ayatollahs and their allies as "a stupid and reactionary bunch whose brains have not moved...stupid men who don't understand and are ill-intentioned...they don't want to see this country develop."[118]

The "stupid and reactionary bunch" didn't give up, and over the years, tensions increased. The shah exiled Khomeini, but that didn't calm the situation. In exile in Iraq in 1970, Khomeini articulated a view called *velayat-e faqih* (guardianship of the jurist). Islam, Khomeini argued, had not just given mankind a set of laws. "A body of laws alone," said Khomeini, "is not sufficient for a society to be reformed. In order for law to ensure the reform and happiness of man, there must be an executive power and an executor. For this reason, God Almighty, in addition to revealing a body of law [that is, the ordinances of the Sharia]...has laid down a particular form of government together with executive and administrative institutions."[119]

Where were these divinely ordained executive and administrative institutions to be found? Khomeini argued that clerical rule, which many dismissed as an unacceptable innovation in Islam, was mandated by the example of Muhammad himself, whom the Qur'an declared to be the supreme model for Muslims (33:21): "The Most Noble Messenger (peace and blessings be upon him) headed the executive and administrative institutions of Muslim society. In addition to conveying the revelation and expounding and interpreting the articles of faith and the ordinances and institutions of Islam, he undertook the implementation of law and the establishment of the ordinances of Islam, thereby bringing into being the Islamic state."[120]

So, Khomeni argued, following the example of Muhammad, modern-day Shi'ite clerics should rule Iran and make it an Islamic state. He explained: "The fundamental difference between Islamic government, on the one hand, and constitutional monarchies and republics, on the other, is this: whereas the representatives of the people or the monarch in such regimes engage in legislation, in Islam the legislative power and competence to establish laws belongs exclusively to God Almighty."[121]

The unrest in Iran grew, and repressive measures from the shah only made matters worse. Finally, on January 16, 1979, after riots and numerous calls for him to go, a tearful shah and his family left Iran.[122] Two weeks later, on February 1, Khomeini returned to Iran after fourteen years of exile. He announced the formation of a new government, declaring: "This is not an ordinary government. It is a government based on the *shari'a*. Opposing this government means opposing the *shari'a* of Islam and revolting against the *shari'a*, and revolt against the government of the *shari'a* has its punishment in our law…it is a heavy punishment in Islamic jurisprudence. Revolt against God's government is a revolt against God. Revolt against God is blasphemy."[123]

On November 4, 1979, a group calling itself Muslim Students Following the Imam's Line (that is, Khomeini's line) entered the U.S. embassy compound in Tehran and took hostage the skeleton staff of sixty-six that was still serving there after the fall of the shah.[124]

Khomeini was delighted, dubbing the hostage-taking "the Second Revolution."[125] He told a reporter, "I regard the occupation of the American Embassy as a spontaneous and justified retaliation of our people."[126] He explained that the hostage crisis would assist the Islamic Republic in consolidating power: "This action has many benefits. The Americans do not want to see the Islamic Republic taking root. We keep the hostages, finish our internal work, then release them."[127] Fifty-two of the American hostages remained in captivity for 444 days, until January 20, 1981.[128]

Khomeini continued to ensure that the Islamic Republic would be Islamic, and nothing but. He declared, "What the nation wants is an Islamic Republic. Not just a Republic, not a democratic Republic, not a democratic Islamic Republic. Do not use the word 'democratic' to describe it. That is the Western style."[129] Indeed, there was nothing democratic about his regime. Khomeini embarked on a reign of terror, executing his political foes in large numbers and shutting down opposition newspapers and magazines.[130] He told secularists, "The 'clog-wearer and the turbaned' have given you a chance. After each revolution several thousand of these corrupt elements are executed in public and burnt and the story is over. They are not allowed to publish newspapers.…We will close all parties except the one, or a few which act in a proper manner.… We all made mistakes. We thought we were dealing with human beings. It is evident we are not. We are dealing with wild animals. We will not tolerate them any more."[131]

The Sharia state that Khomeini constructed gave Iranians neither democracy nor equality of rights under the law. In 1985, Sa'id
Raja'i-Khorassani, the permanent delegate to the United Nations from
the Islamic Republic of Iran, declared that "the very concept of human
rights was 'a Judeo-Christian invention' and inadmissible in Islam....
According to Ayatollah Khomeini, one of the shah's 'most despicable
sins' was the fact that Iran was among the original group of nations that
drafted and approved the Universal Declaration of Human Rights."[132]

Khomeini thundered that fighting was an Islamic duty: "Jihad or
Holy War, which is for the conquest of [other] countries and kingdoms,
becomes incumbent after the formation of the Islamic State in the
presence of the Imam or in accordance with his command. Then Islam
makes it incumbent on all adult males, provided they are not disabled or
incapacitated, to prepare themselves for the conquest of countries so that
the writ of Islam is obeyed in every country in the world.... Islam's Holy
War is a struggle against idolatry, sexual deviation, plunder, repression
and cruelty.... But those who study Islamic Holy War will understand
why Islam wants to conquer the whole world."[133] The goal of this conquest would be to establish the hegemony of Islamic law.

Khomeini had no patience for those who insisted that Islam was a
religion of peace:

> Those who know nothing of Islam pretend that Islam
> counsels against war. Those [who say this] are witless. Islam
> says: Kill all the unbelievers just as they would kill you all!
> Does this mean that Muslims should sit back until they are
> devoured by [the unbelievers]? Islam says: Kill them [the
> non-Muslims], put them to the sword and scatter [their
> armies]. Does this mean sitting back until [non-Muslims]
> overcome us? Islam says: Kill in the service of Allah those
> who may want to kill you! Does this mean that we should
> surrender [to the enemy]? Islam says: Whatever good there
> is exists thanks to the sword and in the shadow of the sword!
> People cannot be made obedient except with the sword! The
> sword is the key to Paradise, which can be opened only for
> the Holy Warriors! There are hundreds of other [Qur'anic]

psalms and Hadiths [sayings of the Prophet] urging Muslims to value war and to fight. Does all this mean that Islam is a religion that prevents men from waging war? I spit upon those foolish souls who make such a claim.[134]

Under the Islamic Republic, Iran became a totalitarian Sharia backwater and a chief financier of global jihad terrorism. Iran was the embodiment of a notorious statement of Khomeini's: "Allah did not create man so that he could have fun. The aim of creation was for mankind to be put to the test through hardship and prayer. An Islamic regime must be serious in every field. There are no jokes in Islam. There is no humor in Islam. There is no fun in Islam. There can be no fun and joy in whatever is serious. Islam does not allow swimming in the sea and is opposed to radio and television serials. Islam, however, allows marksmanship, horseback riding and competition."[135]

The Party of Allah

There was no fun in Islam—or in Iran, either. Through its proxy, the Lebanese jihad terror group Hizballah (Party of Allah), the Islamic Republic pursued jihad against the United States. On October 23, 1983, Hizballah bombed military barracks in Beirut, murdering 241 American servicemen (including 220 Marines) and fifty-eight French military personnel. Hizballah and Iran denied involvement in that bombing, but there was considerable evidence to the contrary—not least the fact that the truck carrying the over twenty-one thousand pounds of TNT that exploded at the barracks was driven by Ismail Ascari, an Iranian national. On May 30, 2003, U.S. District Court judge Royce Lamberth found Iran and Hizballah responsible for the bombing, which he called "the most deadly state-sponsored terrorist attack made against United States citizens before September 11, 2001."[136]

The Lebanese terror group also won notoriety for its jihad suicide bombing at the U.S. Embassy in Beirut on April 18, 1983, which killed sixty-three people, including seventeen Americans. As he did in the barracks case, Lamberth found that the embassy bombing had been carried out by Hizballah and financed by Iranian officials.

Hizballah continued its actions against the United States by kidnapping the CIA station chief in Lebanon, William Buckley, on March 16, 1984. Buckley's captors subsequently delivered several videos to American embassies showcasing how they were torturing him. After viewing the first, CIA director William Casey said: "I was close to tears. It was the most obscene thing I had ever witnessed. Bill was barely recognizable as the man I had known for years. They had done more than ruin his body. His eyes made it clear his mind had been played with. It was horrific, medieval and barbarous."[137] No one knows for certain when William Buckley died. The likeliest time is sometime during the night of June 3, 1985, the 444th day of his captivity."[138]

Hizballah's primary mission, of course, was to wage jihad against Israel. Hizballah founder Hassan Nasrallah has said, "If they [Jews] all gather in Israel, it will save us the trouble of going after them worldwide."[139] Hizballah menaced the Jewish state from Lebanon in the North, while Hamas (Sunni, but also funded by Iran) harassed it from Gaza in the South.

The Islamic Republic's Example

In the last two decades of the twentieth century, the Islamic Republic of Iran became for those who believed that Islamic law was the sole legitimate source of law for every society what the Republic of Turkey had been for secular Muslims in the middle of the century: an example and an inspiration, an indication that a group with their perspective could succeed in overthrowing an established national government and take and hold power in a state.

Bringing down the biggest infidel state of all in the second half of the twentieth century was the goal of other jihad groups.

VII. JIHAD TERRORISM GOES GLOBAL

In 1969 and 1970, Egypt, Sudan, and Algeria helped Nigeria fight the rebellious Republic of Biafra, formed from several southeastern Nigerian provinces. Biafran leader Emeka Ojukwu charged that this was because those states were Muslim, and Biafra Christian: "It is now evident why the fanatic Arab-Muslim states like Algeria, Egypt and the Sudan have come out openly and massively to support and aid Nigeria in her present war of genocide against us.... Biafra is one of the few African states untainted by Islam." The rebellion was crushed. But the most arresting manifestation of the globalization of the jihad in the twentieth century was the formation of global jihad terror groups.

Al-Qaeda

Sheikh Abdullah Azzam was, according to *Jane's Intelligence Review*, "an influential figure in the Muslim Brotherhood" and "the historical leader of Hamas," as well as the man who shaped Osama bin Laden's view of the world.[140] Born in a Palestinian village in 1941, Azzam was raised in a pious Muslim household and earned a degree in Sharia from the Sharia College of Damascus University in 1966. In 1973, he received a Ph.D. in Islamic jurisprudence from al-Azhar University in Cairo, the oldest, most respected, and most influential institute of higher learning in the Muslim world. While in Egypt, he met members of key Muslim Brotherhood theorist Sayyid Qutb's family, who revered the author of *Milestones* as a martyr.

Azzam then joined the jihad against Israel, but soon grew frustrated, furious that his fellow jihadis spent their off-hours gambling and playing music, both forbidden activities according to Islamic law—particularly in the interpretation of the Shafi'i school, which holds sway at al-Azhar.[141] Ultimately, Azzam decided that "this revolution has no religion behind it" and traveled to Saudi Arabia to teach.[142] There he taught that the Muslims' philosophy, in conflicts with non-Muslims, ought to be "jihad and the rifle alone. NO negotiations, NO conferences and NO dialogue."[143]

In 1980, attracted by the jihad against the Soviets in Afghanistan, he went to Pakistan to get to know the movement's leaders. He taught for a while at the International Islamic University in Islamabad, but soon resigned to devote himself full-time to jihad. In 1988, Azzam and his "dear friend," a wealthy Saudi named Osama bin Laden, founded al-Qaeda (The Base). In a 2001 interview, however, bin Laden emphasized that al-Qaeda was simply a group of Muslims waging jihad for the sake of Allah:

> This matter isn't about any specific person, and that it is not about the al-Qai'dah Organization. We are the children of

an Islamic Nation, with Prophet Muhammad as its leader, our Lord is one, our Prophet is one, our Qibla [the direction Muslims face during prayer] is one, we are one nation [*ummah*], and our Book [the Qur'an] is one. And this blessed Book, with the tradition [*sunnah*] of our generous Prophet, has religiously commanded us [*alzamatna*] with the brotherhood of faith [*ukhuwat al-imaan*], and all the true believers [*mu'mineen*] are brothers. So the situation isn't like the West portrays it, that there is an "organization" with a specific name (such as "al-Qai'dah") and so on.[144]

Azzam's written exhortation to Muslims to join the jihad in Afghanistan, *Join the Caravan*, is likewise studded with Qur'anic quotations and references to the life of Muhammad. Azzam denied that Muhammad ever understood jihad solely as a spiritual struggle. "The saying, 'We have returned from the lesser Jihad [battle] to the greater Jihad,' which people quote on the basis that it is a hadith, is in fact a false, fabricated hadith which has no basis. It is only a saying of Ibrahim bin Abi Ablah, one of the Successors, and it contradicts textual evidence and reality." He quotes several authorities charging that *ahadith* narrated by Ibrahim bin Abi Ablah are false, including one who reports: "He was accused of forging hadith." Azzam also invokes the medieval Islamic scholar Ibn Taymiyya, who wrote: "This hadith has no source and nobody whomsoever in the field of Islamic knowledge has narrated it. Jihad against the disbelievers is the most noble of actions and moreover it is the most important action for the sake of mankind."[145]

For this important action, jihadis receive especial rewards. Azzam held out as enticements to would-be jihadis statements like this from Muhammad: "Paradise has one-hundred grades [or levels] which Allah has reserved for the *Mujahidun* [warriors of jihad] who fight in His Cause, and the distance between each of two grades is like the distance between the heaven and the earth."[146]

"Jihad and hijrah [emigration] to Jihad," writes Azzam, "have a deep-rooted role which cannot be separated from the constitution of this religion."[147]

Azzam points out in *Join the Caravan* that Muhammad himself went on twenty-seven "military excursions" and that "he himself fought in nine of these." After summarizing Muhammad's military career, Azzam notes that "this means that the Messenger of Allah (SAWS) used to go out on military expeditions or send out an army at least every two months."[148] He quotes a *hadith* in which Muhammad says that Islam's "highest peak" is jihad.[149]

Azzam quotes the medieval Qur'an commentator Abu Abdullah Muhammad Al-Qurtubi, who declared that "going out for Jihad is compulsory in times of need, of advent of the disbelievers, and of severe furore [sic] of fighting."[150]

Osama bin Laden carried on with al-Qaeda after Azzam's death in 1989, waging jihad first against the Soviets in Afghanistan and then turning to other infidels. The group grew quickly into a worldwide movement, with help from (according to U.S. State Department estimates) as much as two billion dollars from the Saudi government.[151] It demonstrated its reach on February 26, 1993, when al-Qaeda operatives exploded an eleven-hundred-pound bomb at the World Trade Center in New York City, killing six people and injuring a thousand.[152] As it happened, the jihadis had placed the bomb poorly, minimizing the damage; they had hoped to bring down the Twin Towers and murder tens of thousands.

Al-Qaeda operatives also took their jihad to the Balkans, streaming into the former Ottoman holdings in Eastern Europe in the early 1990s, when the dissolution of Yugoslavia provided them a new opportunity to conquer and Islamize the land once and for all.

The jihad commander Abu Abdel Aziz Barbaros, his two-foot-long beard dyed with henna after the example of the Prophet Muhammad, declared that the Bosnian war "confirmed the saying of the Prophet, peace and blessings be upon him, 'Verily, the jihad will endure until the Day of Judgment.' A new jihad was beginning in Bosnia; we went there, and we joined the battle, according to God's will."[153] In a 1994 interview for a Muslim newspaper in the United States, Aziz firmly rejected the prevailing view that jihad rhetoric was a cover for political motivations: "As to your question about the characteristics needed for someone to be a Mujahid [warrior of jihad], I say: Belief in Allah, praised be He [comes first]. He should be in our sight, heart and mind. We have to make Jihad to make His word supreme, not for a nationalistic cause, a tribal cause, a group feeling or any other cause. This matter is of great importance in this era, especially since many groups fight and want to see to it that their fighting is Jihad and their dead ones are martyrs. We have to investigate this matter and see under what banner one fights."[154]

Al-Qaeda moved into Chechnya as well. Muslim Chechens have been waging jihad against the Russians for over two centuries.[155] As long ago as the 1780s, a convert to Islam from Catholicism who called himself Sheikh Mansour led a jihad against the Russians in Chechnya on behalf of the Ottoman Sultan. Later, Ghazi Mullah, a disciple of the Naqshbandi Sufi mullah Muhammad Yaraghi, proclaimed a jihad against the Russians and attempted to institute the Sharia in Chechnya. Ghazi's Sufi ties—and the Sufi army he raised—are interesting in that present-day Westerners generally regard Muslim Sufis as peaceful; this may be true, but it would be hasty to assume that they have all rejected the Islamic doctrines of jihad. His disciple, the imam Shamyl, actually presided over what Chechens still remember as the "Time of Sharia in the Caucasus." In the 1990s, Chechen struggles for independence took on a decidedly Islamic cast. With material and religious aid from Wahhabi Saudi Arabia, a disciple of Osama bin Laden named Omar Ibn al Khattab positioned the Chechen independence fight as part of the global jihad.[156]

In August 1996, bin Laden published a fatwa entitled "Declaration of War against the Americans Occupying the Land of the Two Holy Places," declaring jihad against the United States for daring to base its troops in Saudi Arabia, first to defeat Saddam Hussein's Iraq in late 1990 and early 1991, and force it to relinquish its claim to Kuwait as an Iraqi province, and then to keep the peace in the region. Bin Laden retailed grievances, thereby basing his call for jihad firmly within the Islamic theology of defensive jihad: "It should not be hidden from you that the people of Islam had suffered from aggression, iniquity and injustice imposed on them by the Zionist-Crusaders alliance and their collaborators; to the extent that the Muslims' blood became the cheapest and their wealth as loot in the hands of the enemies."[157]

Bin Laden listed areas around the world where Muslim blood was supposedly being spilled, and then declared: "The people of Islam awakened and realised that they are the main target for the aggression of the Zionist-Crusaders alliance."[158] And "the latest and the greatest of these aggressions, incurred by the Muslims since the death of the Prophet, is the occupation of the land of the two Holy Places—the foundation of the house of Islam, the place of the revelation, the source of the message and the place of the noble Ka'ba, the Qiblah of all Muslims—by the armies of the American Crusaders and their allies."[159]

Addressing Americans, bin Laden wrote: "Terrorising you, while you are carrying arms on our land, is a legitimate and morally demanded duty. It is a legitimate right well known to all humans and other creatures. Your example and our example is like a snake which entered into a house of a man and got killed by him. The coward is the one who lets you walk, while carrying arms, freely on his land and provides you with peace and security."[160]

Also, in 1996, bin Laden moved to Afghanistan, joining forces with the Taliban ("Students"), a jihad group that proclaimed the Islamic Emirate of Afghanistan that year. His vision, however, continued to be global. On February 23, 1998, he joined jihad leaders from Egypt, Pakistan, and Bangladesh in what they called the World Islamic Front and issued a statement entitled "Jihad Against Jews and Crusaders." It begins by invoking martial statements of the Qur'an and Muhammad:

> Praise be to Allah, who revealed the Book, controls the clouds, defeats factionalism, and says in His Book: "But when the forbidden months are past, then fight and slay the pagans wherever ye find them, seize them, beleaguer them, and lie in wait for them in every stratagem [of war]"; and peace be upon our Prophet, Muhammad Bin-'Abdallah, who said: "I have been sent with the sword between my hands to ensure that no one but Allah is worshipped, Allah who put my livelihood under the shadow of my spear and who inflicts humiliation and scorn on those who disobey my orders."[161]

Then, after reiterating many of the charges of American aggression against Muslims from the 1996 statement, it adds: "All these crimes and sins committed by the Americans are a clear declaration of war on Allah, his messenger, and Muslims. And *ulema* [Muslim scholars] have throughout Islamic history unanimously agreed that the jihad is an individual duty if the enemy destroys the Muslim countries."[162] Therefore,

...the ruling to kill the Americans and their allies—civilians and military—is an individual duty for every Muslim who can do it in any country in which it is possible to do it, in order to liberate the al-Aqsa Mosque and the holy mosque [Mecca] from their grip, and in order for their armies to move out of all the lands of Islam, defeated and unable to threaten any Muslim. This is in accordance with the words of Almighty Allah, "and fight the pagans all together as they fight you all together,'" and "fight them until there is no more tumult or oppression, and there prevail justice and faith in Allah."...

We—with Allah's help—call on every Muslim who believes in Allah and wishes to be rewarded to comply with Allah's order to kill the Americans and plunder their money wherever and whenever they find it. We also call on Muslim ulema, leaders, youths, and soldiers to launch the raid on Satan's U.S. troops and the devil's supporters allying with them, and to displace those who are behind them so that they may learn a lesson.[163]

On August 7, 1998, Al-Qaeda killed 223 people in jihad attacks on the American embassies in Kenya and Tanzania, but Osama bin Laden and his followers would teach their most memorable and resounding lesson on September 11, 2001.[164]

Yet, as the warriors of jihad were preparing for a new onslaught against the West, their targets began to display a most peculiar reaction: a denial that any of it was happening because of the jihadis' stated motivations, despite fourteen hundred years of history showing that warfare against the unbelievers was indeed a genuine priority of believers in Islam. In 1998, U.S. President Bill Clinton said this at the United Nations:

Many believe there is an inevitable clash between Western civilization and Western values, and Islamic civilizations and values. I believe this view is terribly wrong. False prophets may use and abuse any religion to justify whatever political objectives they have—even cold-blooded murder. Some may have the world believe that almighty God himself, the merciful, grants a license to kill. But that is not our understanding of Islam.... Americans respect and honor Islam.[165]

In time, even as the new jihad against the West escalated, Clinton's words would become cliché, repeated by Western politicians ad infinitum after every new jihad attack.

CHAPTER TEN

THE WEST LOSES THE WILL TO LIVE

Jihad in the Twenty-First Century

SEPTEMBER 11

On September 11, 2001, al-Qaeda initiated a new phase of the jihad against the United States, and the free world in general, only to find that the traditional foes of the warriors of jihad were no longer interested in fighting, or at least in conceiving of the conflict as it had historically.

On that day, al-Qaeda operatives hijacked jetliners and flew them into the Twin Towers of the World Trade Center in New York City and the Pentagon in Washington, D.C. Passengers resisted on a fourth jet and managed to bring it down in rural Pennsylvania, far from its intended Washington target, which may have been the White House or the Capitol building. Nearly three thousand people were killed.

This was jihad, but it was markedly different from jihad attacks that the West had faced before. The free world was not facing a state that had declared jihad against it, but an international organization operating in the name of Islam, not dependent upon a charismatic leader (although it had one) or centered in any particular geographical location. Yet this was not a "hijacking" of Islam either, as was widely claimed at the time; the underlying principles of jihad remained the same.

Why did al-Qaeda strike New York and Washington? Osama bin Laden explained in a 2004 interview that al-Qaeda's overall objective was to drain the United States economically, a shrewd jihad objective to bring down an enemy many times stronger than the jihad force: "We are continuing this policy in bleeding America to the point of bankruptcy. Allah willing, and nothing is too great for Allah.... We, alongside the mujahedeen, bled Russia for 10 years until it went bankrupt and was forced to withdraw in defeat."[1] He boasted that it was "easy for us to provoke and bait this administration. All that we have to do is to send two mujahedeen to the furthest point east to raise a piece of cloth on which is written al Qaeda, in order to make generals race there to cause America to suffer human, economic and political losses without their achieving anything of note other than some benefits for their private corporations."[2]

Noting a British estimate that 9/11 cost al-Qaeda five hundred thousand dollars, bin Laden said: "Every dollar of al Qaeda defeated a million dollars, by the permission of Allah, besides the loss of a huge number of jobs. As for the economic deficit, it has reached record astronomical numbers estimated to total more than a trillion dollars.... And it all shows that the real loser is you. It is the American people and their economy.... So the war went ahead, the death toll rose, the American economy bled, and Bush became embroiled in the swamps of Iraq that threaten his future."[3]

But why did al-Qaeda want to bring America down? In the November 24, 2002, "Letter to the American People" that bore his name, bin Laden explained: "Why are we fighting and opposing you? The answer is very simple: Because you attacked us and continue to attack us."[4] That stated neatly the requirements of defensive jihad, but the overarching goal of jihad warfare remained: the war against the United States would not end with the U.S.' ceasing to attack the Muslims; it would end only with the submission of the United States to the warriors of jihad, as bin Laden stated succinctly: "The first thing that we are calling you to is Islam."[5]

Other al-Qaeda plotters involved in planning the September 11 attacks, including Khalid Sheikh Mohammed, issued a statement in 2009 that explicitly grounded their actions in Islamic religious terms: the very motive that neither the media nor the government showed any inclination of wanting to acknowledge or examine. The statement was even entitled "The Islamic Response to the Government's Nine Accusations."

"Many thanks to God," they wrote about the attacks, "for his kind gesture, and choosing us to perform the act of Jihad for his cause and to defend Islam and Muslims. Therefore, killing you and fighting you, destroying you and terrorizing you, responding back to your attacks, are all considered to be great legitimate duty in our religion. These actions are our offerings to God. In addition, it is the imposed reality on Muslims in Palestine, Lebanon, Afghanistan, Iraq, in the land of the two holy sites [Mecca and Medina, Saudi Arabia], and in the rest of the world, where Muslims are suffering from your brutality, terrorism, killing of the innocent, and occupying their lands and their holy sites."

They emphasized, however, that this was not solely a response to American attacks. It stemmed ultimately from the fact that the United States was not an Islamic polity: "Nevertheless, it would have been the greatest religious duty to fight you over your infidelity. However, today, we fight you over defending Muslims, their land, their holy sites, and their religion as a whole."[6]

Denial

Despite the open avowals of the perpetrators, one of the most controverted aspects of the September 11 attacks became the question of whether or not they had anything to do with Islam and jihad. The foremost personage to deny the connection was the putative leader of the free world. On September 17, 2001, U.S. President George W. Bush appeared at the Islamic Center of Washington, D.C., in the company of several prominent Muslim leaders, and said:

> These acts of violence against innocents violate the fundamental tenets of the Islamic faith. And it's important for my fellow Americans to understand that.
>
> The English translation is not as eloquent as the original Arabic, but let me quote from the Koran, itself: In the long run, evil in the extreme will be the end of those who do evil. For that they rejected the signs of Allah and held them up to ridicule.

The face of terror is not the true faith of Islam. That's not what Islam is all about. Islam is peace. These terrorists don't represent peace. They represent evil and war.

When we think of Islam we think of a faith that brings comfort to a billion people around the world. Billions of people find comfort and solace and peace. And that's made brothers and sisters out of every race—out of every race.[7]

As Americans still searched the smoking ruins of the World Trade Center for the remains of their loved ones, President Bush cautioned Americans against thinking ill of Muslims, as if the 9/11 attacks had been perpetrated by Americans targeting Muslims:

America counts millions of Muslims amongst our citizens, and Muslims make an incredibly valuable contribution to our country. Muslims are doctors, lawyers, law professors, members of the military, entrepreneurs, shopkeepers, moms and dads. And they need to be treated with respect. In our anger and emotion, our fellow Americans must treat each other with respect.

Women who cover their heads in this country must feel comfortable going outside their homes. Moms who wear cover must be not intimidated in America. That's not the America I know. That's not the America I value.

I've been told that some fear to leave; some don't want to go shopping for their families; some don't want to go about their ordinary daily routines because, by wearing cover, they're afraid they'll be intimidated. That should not and that will not stand in America.

Those who feel like they can intimidate our fellow citizens to take out their anger don't represent the best of America, they represent the worst of humankind, and they should be ashamed of that kind of behavior.

This is a great country. It's a great country because we share the same values of respect and dignity and human worth. And it is my honor to be meeting with leaders

who feel just the same way I do. They're outraged, they're
sad. They love America just as much as I do.[8]

Muslims were not being subjected to wholesale vigilante attacks in the
United States, at that time or at any point subsequently. This speech was
an exercise in vassalage that would have made the late-fourteenth- and
early-fifteenth-century Byzantine emperors ashamed, yet Bush was by
no means alone. Political leaders all over the West echoed his words
about Islam's being a religion of peace, having nothing to do with terrorism. After September 11, this became a commonplace of the Western
political discourse, rejected only by a small minority, who were quickly
stigmatized as cranks.

The Saudi Involvement in September 11

Why Bush turned so quickly after the September 11 attacks to dissembling about their motivating ideology remains a mystery, but the best
explanation for it remains Saudi influence in Washington, including
within his administration itself.

For many years this involvement was concealed. The twenty-
eight-page section of the 9/11 report detailing Saudi involvement in
the September 11, 2001, jihad attacks was finally released in July 2016
(albeit with substantial portions redacted), and made it clear why one
president who held hands with the Saudi king (George W. Bush) and
another who bowed to him (Barack Obama) worked so hard for so
many years to keep these pages secret: they confirmed that the 9/11
jihad murderers received significant help from people at the highest
levels of the Saudi government.[9]

The report states that Omar al-Bayoumi, who "may be a Sau-
di intelligence officer," gave "substantial assistance to hijackers Khalid
al-Mindhar and Nawaf al-Hamzi after they arrived in San Diego in
February 2000.[10] Al-Bayoumi met the hijackers at a public place shortly
after his meeting with an individual at the Saudi consulate."[11] Around
the same time, al-Bayoumi "had extensive contact with Saudi Government establishments in the United States and received financial support
from a Saudi company affiliated with the Saudi Ministry of Defense."[12]
That company "reportedly had ties to [O]sama bin Ladin and al-

Qa'ida."[13] The Saudis also gave al-Bayoumi 400,000 dollars to finance the construction of a mosque in San Diego.[14]

Another possible Saudi agent, Osama Bassnan, who "has many ties to the Saudi government" and was also a supporter of Osama bin Laden, boasted that he did more for al-Mindhar and al-Hamzi than al-Bayoumi did.[15] He also "reportedly received funding and possibly a fake passport from Saudi government officials."[16] The report says that at one point, "a member of the Saudi Royal Family provided Bassnan with a significant amount of cash," and that "he and his wife have received financial support from the Saudi ambassador to the United States and his wife."[17] That ambassador was Prince Bandar, about whom *The New York Times* later noted: "No foreign diplomat has been closer or had more access to President Bush, his family and his administration than the magnetic and fabulously wealthy Prince Bandar bin Sultan of Saudi Arabia."[18]

Bassnan "spoke of bin Laden 'as if he were a god.' Bassnan also stated to an FBI asset that he heard that the U.S. government had stopped approving visas for foreign students. He considered such measures to be insufficient as there are already enough Muslims in the United States to destroy the United States and make it an Islamic state within ten to fifteen years."[19]

Then there was Shaykh al-Thumairy, "an accredited diplomat at the Saudi consulate in Los Angeles and one of the 'imams' at the King Fahad mosque in Culver City, California," who also "may have been in contact" with al-Mindhar and al-Hamzi.[20]

Saleh al-Hussayen, "reportedly a Saudi Interior Ministry official, stayed at the same hotel in Herndon, Virginia where al-Hazmi was staying. While al-Hussayen claimed after September 11 not to know the hijackers, FBI agents believed he was being deceptive. He was able to depart the United States despite FBI efforts to locate and re-interview him."[21]

The name of "another Saudi national with close ties to the Saudi Royal Family" was redacted, but the report notes that he was "the subject of FBI counterterrorism investigations and reportedly was checking security at the United States' southwest border in 1999 and discussing the possibility of infiltrating individuals into the United States."[22] There is no telling who this could have been, but Prince Bandar's unlisted phone number turned up in a phone book of Abu Zubaida, "a senior al-Qa'ida operative captured in Pakistan in March 2002."[23] Abu Zubaida also had the number of "a bodyguard at the Saudi Embassy in Washington, DC."[24]

The report also mentions a CIA memorandum that "discusses alleged financial connections between the September 11 hijackers, Saudi Government officials, and members of the Saudi Royal Family."[25] This memorandum was passed on to an FBI investigator; yet "despite the clear national implications of the CIA memorandum, the FBI agent included the memorandum in an individual case file and did not forward it to FBI Headquarters."[26] Why?

The declassified twenty-eight pages also revealed a great deal about Saudi mosque financing inside the United States. The King Fahad mosque in Culver City, California, "was built in 1998 from funding provided by Saudi Arabia's Crown Prince Abdelaziz. The mosque is reportedly attended by members of the Saudi consultant in Los Angeles and is widely recognized for its anti-Western views," and is a "site of extremist-related activity."[27] In fact, "several subjects of FBI investigations prior to September 11 had close connections to the mosque and are believed to have laundered money through this mosque to non-profit organizations overseas affiliated with [O]sama bin Ladin. In an interview, an FBI agent said he believed that Saudi government money was being laundered through the mosque."[28]

David D. Aufhauser, a former Treasury Department general counsel, told a Senate committee in June 2004 that estimates of how much money the Saudis had spent worldwide since the 1970s to promote Wahhabism went "north of seventy-five billion dollars." The money went to mosques, Islamic centers, Islamic schools, Islamic preachers, and the printing of hundreds of millions of copies of the Qur'an and other Islamic religious books.[29]

Terrorism expert Yehudit Barsky noted in 2005: "The people now in control of teaching religion [to American Muslims] are extremists. Who teaches the mainstream moderate non-Saudi Islam that people used to have? It's in the homes, but there's no infrastructure. Eighty percent of the infrastructure is controlled by these extremists."[30] Nor was this happening in the United States alone. In December 2015,

German vice chancellor Sigmar Gabriel declared: "We have to make clear to the Saudis that the time of looking away is over. Wahhabi mosques all over the world are financed by Saudi Arabia. Many Islamists who are a threat to public safety come from these communities in Germany."[31]

Seven years after the September 11 attacks, a U.S. government cable noted: "Government and non-governmental sources claimed that financial support estimated at nearly 100 million USD annually was making its way to Deobandi and Ahl-e-Hadith clerics in the region from 'missionary' and 'Islamic charitable' organizations in Saudi Arabia and the United Arab Emirates ostensibly with the direct support of those governments."[32] The Deobandi was a Sunni revivalist movement found primarily in India, Pakistan, Afghanistan, and Bangladesh; the Ahl-e-Hadith was another revivalist movement based in India. As we have seen throughout Islamic history, revivalist movements quite frequently resort to jihad.

The following year, Secretary of State Hillary Clinton's office noted:

> While the Kingdom of Saudi Arabia (KSA) takes seriously the threat of terrorism within Saudi Arabia, it has been an ongoing challenge to persuade Saudi officials to treat terrorist financing emanating from Saudi Arabia as a strategic priority. Due in part to intense focus by the USG over the last several years, Saudi Arabia has begun to make important progress on this front and has responded to terrorist financing concerns raised by the United States through proactively investigating and detaining financial facilitators of concern. Still, donors in Saudi Arabia constitute the most significant source of funding to Sunni terrorist groups worldwide.... [M]ore needs to be done since Saudi Arabia remains a critical financial support base for al-Qa'ida, the Taliban, LeT, and other terrorist groups, including Hamas, which probably raise millions of dollars annually from Saudi sources, often during Hajj and Ramadan. In contrast to its increasingly aggressive efforts to disrupt al-Qa'ida's access to funding from Saudi sources, Riyadh has taken only

limited action to disrupt fundraising for the UN 1267-list-
ed Taliban and LeT-groups that are also aligned with al-
Qa'ida and focused on undermining stability in Afghanistan and Pakistan.[33]

In an October 2013 speech, Clinton declared: "Some of us thought,
perhaps, we could, with a more robust, covert action trying [sic] to
vet, identify, train and arm cadres of rebels that would at least have the
firepower to be able to protect themselves against both Assad and the
Al-Qaeda-related jihadist groups that have, unfortunately, been attracted to Syria. That's been complicated by the fact that the Saudis and
others are shipping large amounts of weapons—and pretty indiscriminately—not at all targeted toward the people that we think would be
the more moderate, least likely, to cause problems in the future, but this
is another one of those very tough analytical problems."[34]

But there was still no hint of a rift in the U.S.–Saudi alliance. It was
a tough analytical problem because the United States, even as it faced a
comprehensive jihad challenge, was politically and economically entan-
gled with one of the chief financiers of the jihad. But no Washington
analysts appeared willing to ponder the implications of that, or to try to
devise ways to extricate the nation from this conundrum.

And when there was a regime change in Washington and Donald
Trump became president of the United States, he did the sword dance in
Riyadh with Saudi royals.

The Iranian Involvement in 9/11

Less noted but no less significant is the Islamic Republic of Iran's
role in the September 11 attacks—also a subject of U.S. government
cover-up attempts.[35]

On December 22, 2011, U.S. District judge George B. Daniels ruled
in *Havlish, et al. v. bin Laden, et al.*, that Iran and Hizballah were liable
for damages to be paid to relatives of the victims of the September 11,
2001, jihad attacks in New York and Washington, as both the Islamic
Republic and its Lebanese proxy had actively aided al-Qaeda in planning
and executing those attacks.[36]

Daniels found that Iran and Hizballah had cooperated and collaborated with al-Qaeda before 9/11 and continued to do so after the attacks.

Before 9/11, Iran and Hizballah were implicated in efforts to train al-Qaeda members to blow up large buildings—resulting in the bombings of the Khobar Towers in Saudi Arabia in 1996, the bombings of the U.S. embassies in Kenya and Tanzania in 1998, and the attack on the USS *Cole* in 2000.[37]

Shortly after the *Cole* attack, the 9/11 jihad plot began to come together—and Iran was involved. Former MOIS operative Abolghasem Mesbahi, a defector from Iran, testified that during the summer of 2001, he received messages from Iranian government officials regarding a plan for unconventional warfare against the U.S., entitled "*Shaitan dar Atash*" ("Satan in Flames").[38]

"Satan in Flames" was the elaborate plot to hijack three passenger jets, each packed full of people, and crash them into American landmarks: the World Trade Center, which jihadis took to be the center of American commerce; the Pentagon, the center of America's military apparatus; and the White House.[39]

A classified National Security Agency analysis referred to in the 9/11 Commission report reveals that eight to ten of the 9/11 hijackers traveled to Iran repeatedly in late 2000 and early 2001. The 9/11 Commission called for a U.S. government investigation into Iran's role in 9/11, but none was ever undertaken. Kenneth R. Timmerman of the Foundation for Democracy in Iran was, in his words, "engaged by the *Havlish* attorneys in 2004 to carry out the investigation the 9/11 Commission report called on the U.S. government to handle."[40]

Timmerman noted that during the 9/11 hijackers' trips to Iran, they were "accompanied by 'senior Hezbollah operatives' who were in fact agents of the Iranian regime."[41] Iranian border agents did not stamp their passports, so that their having been inside the Islamic Republic would not arouse suspicion against them when they entered the United States.[42]

The CIA, embarrassed by its failure to recognize the import of these trips, tried to suppress this revelation.[43] But Timmerman contends that even the available evidence is explosive enough, revealing that the Islamic Republic of Iran, in his words:

- helped design the 9/11 plot;

- provided intelligence support to identify and train the operatives who carried it out;

- allowed the future hijackers to evade U.S. and Pakistani surveillance on key trips to Afghanistan where they received the final order of mission from Osama bin Laden, by escorting them through Iranian borders without passport stamps;

- evacuated hundreds of top al-Qaeda operatives from Afghanistan to Iran after 9/11 just as U.S. forces launched their offensive;

- provided safe haven and continued financial support to al-Qaeda cadres for years after 9/11;

- allowed al-Qaeda to use Iran as an operational base for additional terror attacks, in particular the May 2003 bombings in Riyadh, Saudi Arabia.[44]

The Ayatollah Khamenei knew about the plot. During the summer of 2001, he instructed Iranian agents to be careful to conceal their tracks and told them to communicate only with al-Qaeda's second in command, Ayman al-Zawahiri, and Imad Mughniyah of Hizballah.[45]

Mughniyah was Iran's key player in the 9/11 "Satan in Flames" plot. During the *Havlish* trial, former CIA agents Clare M. Lopez and Bruce D. Tefft submitted an affidavit stating that "Imad Mughniyah, the most notable and notorious world terrorist of his time, an agent of Iran and a senior operative of Hizballah, facilitated the international travel of certain 9/11 hijackers to and from Iran, Lebanon, Saudi Arabia, and Afghanistan, and perhaps various other locations for the purpose of executing the events of September 11, 2001. This support enabled two vital aspects of the September 11, 2001 plot to succeed: (1) the continued training of the hijackers in Afghanistan and Iran after securing their United States visas in Saudi Arabia, and (2) entry into the United States."[46]

The Obama-era CIA went to great pains to try to ensure that information about Iran's role in 9/11 did not come out in the *Havlish* case. In August 2010, a CIA official pressured a *Havlish* witness to withdraw his testimony in exchange for a new identity, new passport, and new job. In December of that year, another CIA operative approached a different *Havlish* witness, showed him documents stolen from the case, and took him to a U.S. embassy, where he was subjected to five hours of interrogation and finally offered cash if he recanted his testimony. Says Timmerman, "After I reported those attempts at witness tampering to a Congressional oversight committee, they ceased."[47]

Judge Daniels determined that Iran, Hizballah, the Islamic Revolutionary Guard Corps, the Iranian Ministry of Intelligence and Security, and other Iranian government departments, as well as the Ayatollah Khamenei himself and former Iranian president Ali Akbar Hashemi Rafsanjani were all directly implicated in Iranian efforts to aid al-Qaeda in its 9/11 plot.[48] He awarded the plaintiffs in the *Havlish* case 394,277,884 dollars for economic damages, as well as ninety-four million dollars for pain and suffering, eighty hundred and seventy-four million for mental anguish and grief, and 4,686,235,921 dollars in punitive damages, along with nine hundred and sixty-eight million in prejudgment interest, for a total of 7,016,513,805 dollars.[49]

The *Havlish* plaintiffs were unlikely to receive a check for that amount from the Islamic Republic of Iran neatly signed by the Ayatollah Khamenei. However, in March 2014, as part of the *Havlish* judgment, the plaintiffs were awarded ownership of a five-hundred-million-dollar office tower in midtown Manhattan—one that had been owned by Iranian companies.[50]

This award provided a small bit of compensation for the loss of life and the years of trauma that these families had suffered as a result of the Islamic Republic's war against the United States. More important, it stood as a tangible acknowledgment of Iran's role in the 9/11 attacks.

Confirming all of this was the revelation in November 2017 of a document captured in the May 2, 2011, American raid on Osama bin Laden's hideout in Pakistan. It details a mutual agreement between al-Qaeda and the Islamic Republic of Iran to strike American interests in "Saudi Arabia and the Gulf"; the Iranians agreed to supply al-Qaeda "money, arms," and "training in Hizbollah camps in Lebanon."[51]

Infiltration

Standing with President Bush in the mosque in September 2001 was Abdurrahman Alamoudi, who was then one of the most prominent Muslim leaders in the United States. During the presidency of Bill Clinton, Alamoudi served as a State Department "goodwill ambassador" to Muslim lands.[52] In June 2001, he attended a White House briefing on George W. Bush's faith-based initiative program.[53]

Even though it was universally taken for granted that Alamoudi was a "moderate," he never bothered to conceal his true allegiances. In 1994 he declared his support for the jihad terror group Hamas. He claimed that "Hamas is not a terrorist group" and that it did "good work."[54] In 1996, Alamoudi defended Hamas leader Mousa Abu Marzouk, who was ultimately deported because of his work with Hamas and currently leads a branch of the terror group in Syria. "I really consider him to be from among the best people in the Islamic movement," said Alamoudi of Marzouk. "Hamas…and I work together with him."[55]

At a rally in October 2000, he encouraged those in the crowd to show their support for Hamas and Hizballah. As the crowd cheered, Alamoudi shouted: "I have been labeled by the media in New York to be a supporter of Hamas. Anybody supports Hamas here?" As the crowd cheered, "Yes," Alamoudi asked the same question again, and then added: "Hear that, Bill Clinton, we are all supporters of Hamas, *Allahu akbar*. I wish they added that I am also a supporter of Hizballah. Anybody supports Hizballah here?" The crowd again roared its approval.[56] But even that did not raise any concern among those in Washington who were confident that he was a sterling and reliable "moderate Muslim." And so, in January 2001, the year he was invited to the Bush White House, Alamoudi traveled to Beirut to attend a conference with leaders of al-Qaeda, Hamas, Hizballah, and Islamic Jihad.[57]

Then, in September 2003, Alamoudi was arrested in London's Heathrow Airport while carrying three hundred and forty thousand dollars in cash—money that, as it turned out, he had received from Libyan president Muammar Gaddafi in order to finance an al-Qaeda plot to murder the Saudi crown prince, the future King Abdullah.[58] Indicted on numerous charges, Alamoudi was found to have funneled over one million dollars to al-Qaeda; he pled guilty to being a senior al-Qaeda financier and was sentenced in October 2004 to twenty-three years in prison.[59] In 2011, the Obama administration reduced Alamoudi's sentence by six years, without making public its reasons for doing so.[60]

So, as he proclaimed that Islam was a religion of peace that had no connection to the September 11 attacks, George W. Bush was standing in the company of a financier of the organization that was responsible for those attacks. Nor was that by any means the extent of the influence in Washington of groups with ties to others that applauded or even had involvement in the attacks. It was due to the influence of these groups that the world's chief superpower, while expending massive resources in tracking down and neutralizing various jihadi individuals *and* groups, committed itself to a policy of complete denial regarding why the jihad was being fought in the first place.

That denial made the American response to 9/11 curious and wrongheaded in numerous ways. The war went ahead in both Iraq and Afghanistan, both rather off the point if the United States really wanted to confront the sources of jihad activity worldwide. The invasion of Afghanistan made some sense, since the Taliban government was cooperating with al-Qaeda and allowing it to operate training camps on its soil. The invasion of Iraq, however, was based on allegations of cooperation between bin Laden and Iraqi dictator Saddam Hussein that were much more tenuous. In both cases, the invasions were predicated on the assumption that the people of each country would welcome the Americans. Vice President Dick Cheney said on March 16, 2003: "I think things have gotten so bad inside Iraq from the standpoint of the Iraqi people, my belief is we will, in fact, be greeted as liberators."[61] Of course, he was proven wrong: operations in both Afghanistan and Iraq became quagmires, immense drains on American personnel, money, and materiel, with little to no upside.

Cheney's odd idea that the Americans would be greeted as liberators seems to have been based upon the Bush administration's ahistorical belief that Islam was a religion of peace and compatible with Western notions of secular and democratic rule, such that the Iraqis would welcome the fall of the oppressor and the chance to express themselves at the ballot box. This view completely ignored Islam's political character, and the idea of Sharia as the immutable and perfect law of Allah that was superior to any man-made law.

This may have been attributable to Muslim Brotherhood influence in the United States government. The Muslim Brotherhood spelled out its goals for the United States in an internal document seized by the FBI in 2005 in the Northern Virginia headquarters of an Islamic charity, the Holy Land Foundation. The Holy Land Foundation, once the largest Islamic charity in the United States, was shut down for sending charitable contributions to Hamas. The captured document was entitled, "An Explanatory Memorandum on the General Strategic Goal for the Group in North America."[62]

In it, Muslim Brotherhood members were told that the Brotherhood was working on presenting Islam as a "civilizational alternative" to non-Islamic forms of society and governance, and supporting "the global Islamic state wherever it is."[63] In working to establish that Islamic state, Muslim Brotherhood members in the United States: "must understand that their work in America is a kind of grand jihad in eliminating and destroying the Western civilization from within and 'sabotaging' its miserable house by their hands and the hands of the believers so that it is eliminated and Allah's religion is made victorious over all other religions."[64]

The Muslim Brotherhood has been active in the United States for decades, and is the moving force behind virtually all of the mainstream Muslim organizations in America: the Islamic Society of North America (ISNA), the Islamic Circle of North America (ICNA), the Muslim American Society (MAS), the Muslim Students Association (MSA), the Council on American Islamic Relations (CAIR), the International Institute for Islamic Thought (IIIT), and many others.

Obama in Cairo

Against this backdrop, it is no surprise that when President Barack Obama made his outreach speech to the Muslim world from Cairo on June 4, 2009, he included fulsome praise of Islam that played fast and loose with the historical record:

> As a student of history, I also know civilization's debt to
> Islam. It was Islam—at places like Al-Azhar—that carried

the light of learning through so many centuries, paving the way for Europe's Renaissance and Enlightenment. It was innovation in Muslim communities—it was innovation in Muslim communities that developed the order of algebra; our magnetic compass and tools of navigation; our mastery of pens and printing; our understanding of how disease spreads and how it can be healed. Islamic culture has given us majestic arches and soaring spires; timeless poetry and cherished music; elegant calligraphy and places of peaceful contemplation. And throughout history, Islam has demonstrated through words and deeds the possibilities of religious tolerance and racial equality.

I also know that Islam has always been a part of America's story. The first nation to recognize my country was Morocco. In signing the Treaty of Tripoli in 1796, our second President, John Adams, wrote, "The United States has in itself no character of enmity against the laws, religion or tranquility of Muslims." And since our founding, American Muslims have enriched the United States. They have fought in our wars, they have served in our government, they have stood for civil rights, they have started businesses, they have taught at our universities, they've excelled in our sports arenas, they've won Nobel Prizes, built our tallest building, and lit the Olympic Torch. And when the first Muslim American was recently elected to Congress, he took the oath to defend our Constitution using the same Holy Koran that one of our Founding Fathers—Thomas Jefferson—kept in his personal library.

The Jefferson and Adams who were told by the Tripolitanian ambassador Sidi Haji Abdrahaman that Tripoli "was founded on the Laws of the Prophet, that it was written in their Koran, that all nations who should not have answered their authority were sinners, that it was their right and duty to make war upon them wherever they could be found" might have found Obama's insinuation that they admired and respected Islam startling.[65] Undaunted by facts, Obama continued:

So I have known Islam on three continents before coming to the region where it was first revealed. That experience guides my conviction that partnership between America and Islam must be based on what Islam is, not what it isn't. And I consider it part of my responsibility as President of the United States to fight against negative stereotypes of Islam wherever they appear.[66]

Where this executive duty to defend Islam appeared in the Constitution, he did not explain.

In September 2012 at the United Nations, in the wake of the jihad massacre of four Americans by al-Qaeda operatives in Benghazi in Libya, which key members of his administration falsely and repeatedly attributed to a spontaneous demonstration arising over a video criticizing Muhammad on YouTube, Obama went even farther, saying: "The future must not belong to those who slander the prophet of Islam."[67] The specter of the leader of the free world vowing to enforce Islamic blasphemy laws was not just rhetoric. The idea that Islam in America was beset by negative stereotypes that same year helped to defeat an attempt to investigate Muslim Brotherhood influence within the United States government.

Efforts to Investigate Infiltration Stymied

In 2012, Rep. Michele Bachmann (R-MN) tried to call attention to this influence, asking for an investigation into Muslim Brotherhood infiltration into the U.S. government. She accused the first Muslim member of Congress, Rep. Keith Ellison (D-MN) of having a "long record of being associated" with CAIR and the Muslim Brotherhood.[68]

In response, Ellison accused Bachmann of religious bigotry.[69] Yet he really did have a "long record of being associated" with Hamas-linked CAIR and the Muslim Brotherhood. As long ago as 2006, Ellison's closeness to CAIR's cofounder and National Executive Director Nihad Awad was a matter of public record.[70] Awad, who notoriously said in 1994 that he was "in support of the Hamas movement," spoke at fundraisers for Ellison, raising considerable sums for his first congressional race. Ellison has appeared frequently at CAIR events since then.[71]

Investigative journalist Patrick Poole explained that "according to Justice Department, Awad is a longtime Hamas operative. Multiple statements made by federal prosecutors identify Awad as one of the attendees at a 1993 meeting of US Muslim Brotherhood Palestine Committee leaders in Philadelphia that was wiretapped by the FBI under a Foreign Intelligence Surveillance Act (FISA) warrant. The topic of discussion during that 1993 meeting was how to help Hamas by working in the U.S. to help sabotage the Oslo Peace Accords."[72] But none of that fazed Ellison. Nor has he ever expressed any concern over the fact that CAIR is also linked to the Muslim Brotherhood through its parent group, the Islamic Association for Palestine (IAP).

Ellison's ties to the Muslim Brotherhood were also more direct. In 2008, Ellison accepted 13,350 dollars from the Muslim American Society (MAS) to go on a pilgrimage to Mecca.[73] As we have seen, the Muslim American Society is the principal arm of the Muslim Brotherhood in the United States.

In December 2012, possible corroboration of some of Bachmann's allegations came from an unlikely quarter: Egypt's *Rose El-Youssef* magazine, which asserted in a December 2012 article that six highly placed Muslim Brotherhood infiltrators within the Obama Administration had transformed the United States "from a position hostile to Islamic groups and organizations in the world to the largest and most important supporter of the Muslim Brotherhood."[74]

The article said that "the six named people include: Arif Alikhan, assistant secretary of Homeland Security for policy development; Mohammed Elibiary, a member of the Homeland Security Advisory Council; Rashad Hussain, the U.S. special envoy to the Organization of the Islamic Conference [OIC]; Salam al-Marayati, co-founder of the Muslim Public Affairs Council (MPAC); Imam Mohamed Magid, president of the Islamic Society of North America (ISNA); and Eboo Patel, a member of President Obama's Advisory Council on Faith-Based Neighborhood Partnerships."[75]

Besides Elibiary and Magid, Bachmann also raised concerns about the OIC, to which Hussain was Barack Obama's ambassador. And so the Egyptian article stood as vindication of her concerns, and showed that her request an investigation be opened of the Muslim Brotherhood's infiltration was entirely reasonable and not a manifestation of "bigotry," "racism," or "McCarthyism"—contrary to the hysterical (and formulaic) claims of her leftist detractors.

Of course, the Egyptian article had to be taken with a grain of salt. It could have been the product of a Muslim Brotherhood advocate in Egypt, anxious to bolster perceptions of his movement's clout and credibility. While that was possible, however, it could not responsibly be assumed to be the case without closer examination; it was equally possible that the article represented a genuine indication that Bachmann's concerns were justified, and that the Muslim Brotherhood had indeed penetrated the highest levels of the U.S. government.

Infiltration in American institutions was undeniable. Louay Safi, a Muslim activist, had ties to two Muslim Brotherhood entities—the Islamic Society of North America and the International Institute of Islamic Thought—as well as to convicted jihad leader Sami al-Arian. Yet Safi was training troops and even meeting with the families of victims at Fort Hood in December 2009, the month after a Muslim Army major, Nidal Hasan, massacred thirteen people there while shouting, "*Allahu akbar*."[76] Safi later became a leader of the Syrian opposition to Bashar Assad that was dominated by al-Qaeda and other pro-Sharia Islamic supremacist groups.[77]

And Gehad El-Haddad, a top Muslim Brotherhood official in Egypt, was for five years employed with the Clinton Foundation.[78] The Clinton Foundation, of course, is not a government agency, but his involvement with it afforded El-Haddad access to a former president of the United States and his associates, including present and former government officials. In September 2013, Egypt's military government arrested El-Haddad for his Muslim Brotherhood activities.[79]

For all of the furor over Bachmann's call for an investigation of Muslim Brotherhood influence in Washington, nothing caused as much controversy as her naming Huma Abedin, then Secretary of State Hillary Clinton's closest personal assistant and adviser. Abedin is an observant Muslim who lived in Saudi Arabia as a child; her brother Hassan works "as a fellow and partner with a number of Muslim Brotherhood members." Her mother, Saleha Mahmoud Abedin, is a professor in Saudi Arabia and a member of the Brotherhood's woman's division, the Muslim Sisterhood.[80] Her father, Syed Z. Abedin, was a professor in Saudi Arabia who founded the Institute for Muslim Minority Affairs, an organization supported by the Muslim World League, a Brotherhood organization.[81]

Despite this evidence, there was no investigation. Yet, in an article about Abedin and her influence, former U.S. prosecutor Andrew C. McCarthy listed a great many strange collaborations between the State Department of Barack Obama and Hillary Clinton and Muslim Brotherhood organizations, including:

- The State Department announced that the Obama administration would be "satisfied" with the election of a Muslim Brotherhood–dominated government in Egypt.

- Secretary Clinton personally intervened to reverse a Bush-administration ruling that barred Tariq Ramadan, grandson of the Brotherhood's founder and son of one of its most influential early leaders, from entering the United States.

- The State Department collaborated with the Organization of Islamic Cooperation, a bloc of governments heavily influenced by the Brotherhood, in seeking to restrict American free-speech rights in deference to Sharia proscriptions against negative criticism of Islam.

- The State Department excluded Israel, the world's leading target of terrorism, from its "Global Counterterrorism Forum," a group that brings the United States together with several Islamist governments, prominently including its cochair, Turkey—which now finances Hamas and avidly supports the flotillas that seek to break Israel's blockade of Hamas. At the forum's kickoff, Secretary Clinton decried various terrorist attacks and groups, but she did not mention Hamas or attacks against Israel—in transparent deference to the Islamist governments, which echo the Brotherhood's position that Hamas is not a terrorist organization and that attacks against Israel are not terrorism.

- The State Department and the Obama administration waived congressional restrictions in order to transfer 1.5 billion dollars in aid to Egypt after the Muslim Brotherhood's victory in the parliamentary elections.

- The State Department and the Obama administration waived congressional restrictions in order to transfer millions of dollars in aid to the Palestinian territories, notwithstanding that Gaza is ruled by the terrorist organization Hamas, the Muslim Brotherhood's Palestinian branch.

- The State Department and the administration hosted a contingent from Egypt's newly elected parliament that included not only Muslim Brotherhood members but a member of the Islamic Group (Gamaa al-Islamiyya), which is formally designated as a foreign terrorist organization. The State Department refused to provide Americans with information about the process by which it issued a visa to a member of a designated terrorist organization, about how the members of the Egyptian delegation were selected, or about what security procedures were followed before the delegation was allowed to enter our country.[82]

During the Bush and Obama administrations, it became socially and politically unacceptable even to raise questions about Muslim Brotherhood influence, or to express any skepticism about the politically correct dogmas regarding Islam and jihad. For in Abedin's case, it certainly was not that the evidence was lacking. It was that the political elites had forbidden any examination or discussion of it.

Stigmatizing Resistance to Jihad

The crowning victory in the effort to stigmatize resistance to jihad terror and Islamic supremacism came in February 2012, when the Obama administration purged more than a thousand documents and presentations from counterterror training materials for the FBI and other agencies. This material was discarded at the demand of Muslim groups, which had deemed it inaccurate (by their own account) or offensive to Muslims.[83]

This triumph was several years in the making. The movement toward it began in earnest in August 2010, when I gave a presentation on Islam and jihad to the FBI's Joint Terrorism Task Force—one of many such talks I gave to government agencies and military groups in those years. CAIR sent a series of letters to FBI director Robert Mueller and others, demanding that I be dropped as a counterterror trainer; the organization even started a "coalition" echoing this demand, which black activist leader Jesse Jackson and others joined.[84]

And indeed, Mueller made no public comment on CAIR's demand, and so it initially appeared that the effort had failed—although I was never again invited to provide counterterror training for any government agency, after having done so fairly regularly for the previous five years. Although Mueller was publicly silent, the Islamic supremacists and their leftist allies didn't give up. In the summer and fall of 2011, the online tech journal *Wired* published several "exposés" by far-left journalist Spencer Ackerman, who took the FBI to task for training material that spoke forthrightly and truthfully about the nature and magnitude of the jihad threat.

In a typical sally from these exposés, Ackerman reported that "the FBI is teaching its counterterrorism agents that 'main stream' [sic] American Muslims are likely to be terrorist sympathizers; that the Prophet Mohammed was a 'cult leader'; and that the Islamic practice of giving charity is no more than a 'funding mechanism for combat.' At the Bureau's training ground in Quantico, Virginia, agents are shown a chart contending that the more 'devout' a Muslim, the more likely he is to be 'violent.' Those destructive tendencies cannot be reversed, an FBI instructional presentation adds: 'Any war against non-believers is justified' under Muslim law; a 'moderating process cannot happen if the Koran continues to be regarded as the unalterable word of Allah.'"[85]

Like virtually all leftist and Islamic supremacist critiques of antijihad and antiterror material from this period, Ackerman's piece took for granted that such assertions are false, without bothering to explain how or why. Apparently, Ackerman believed that their falsity was so self-evident as to require no demonstration; unfortunately for him, however, there was considerable evidence that what this FBI training material asserted was true. Nonetheless, in the face of Ackerman's reports, the FBI went into full retreat: in September 2011, it announced that it was dropping one of the programs that Ackerman had zeroed in on.[86]

The Islamic supremacists didn't rest on their laurels. On October 19, 2011, Salam al-Marayati of the Muslim Public Affairs Council

(MPAC) took this campaign to the mainstream media, writing in the *Los Angeles Times* that "a disturbing string of training material used by the FBI and a U.S. attorney's office came to light beginning in late July that reveals a deep anti-Muslim sentiment within the U.S. government." Al-Marayati warned that "if this matter is not immediately addressed, it will undermine the relationship between law enforcement and the Muslim American community—another example of the ineptitude and/or apathy undermining bridges built with care over decades." He also noted that the FBI was beginning to move on these demands, although as far as al-Marayati was concerned, much more was needed: "It is not enough to just call it a 'very valid concern,' as FBI Director Robert Mueller told a congressional committee this month."[87]

The same day that al-Marayati's op-ed was published, Farhana Khera of Muslim Advocates, who had complained for years about supposed Muslim profiling and entrapment, wrote a letter to John Brennan, who was then the assistant to the president on national security for homeland security and counterterrorism. The letter was signed not just by Khera but by the leaders of virtually all the significant Islamic groups in the United States: fifty-seven Muslim, Arab, and South Asian organizations, including many with ties to Hamas and the Muslim Brotherhood, including CAIR, ISNA, MAS, the Islamic Circle of North America (ICNA), Islamic Relief USA, and the Muslim Public Affairs Council (MPAC).[88]

The letter denounced what it characterized as U.S. government agencies' "use of biased, false and highly offensive training materials about Muslims and Islam," and emphasized that they regarded this as an issue of the utmost importance: "The seriousness of this issue cannot be overstated, and we request that the White House immediately create an interagency task force to address this problem, with a fair and transparent mechanism for input from the Muslim, Arab, and South Asian communities, including civil rights lawyers, religious leaders, and law enforcement experts."[89]

This was needed because "while recent news reports have highlighted the FBI's use of biased experts and training materials, we have learned that this problem extends far beyond the FBI and has infected other government agencies, including the U.S. Attorney's Anti-Terrorism Advisory Councils, the U.S. Department of Homeland Security, and the U.S. Army. Furthermore, by the FBI's own admission, the use of bigoted and distorted materials in its trainings has not been an isolated occurrence. Since last year, reports have surfaced that the FBI, and other federal agencies, are using or supporting the use of biased trainers and materials in presentations to law enforcement officials."[90]

In a November 3, 2011, response to Khera, that—significantly—was written on White House stationery, Brennan accepted Khera's criticisms without a murmur of protest and assured her of his readiness to comply. "Please allow me to share with you the specific steps we are taking," Brennan wrote to Khera, "to ensure that federal officials and state, local and tribal partners receive accurate, evidence-based information in these crucial areas."[91]

"I am aware," Brennan went on, "of recent unfortunate incidents that have highlighted substandard and offensive training that some United States Government elements have either sponsored or delivered. Any and all such training runs completely counter to our values, our commitment to strong partnerships with communities across the country, our specific approach to countering violent extremist recruitment and radicalization, and our broader counterterrorism (CT) efforts. Our National Strategy for Empowering Local Partners to Prevent Violent Extremism in the United States highlights competent training as an area of primary focus and states that 'misinformation about the threat and dynamics of radicalization to violence can harm our security by sending local stakeholders in the wrong direction and unnecessarily creating tensions with potential community partners.' It also emphasizes that our security is 'inextricably linked to our values,' including 'the promotion of an inclusive society.'"[92]

Brennan then assured Khera that all her demands would be met: "Your letter requests that 'the White House immediately create an interagency task force to address this problem,' and we agree that this is necessary." He then detailed the specific actions being undertaken to ensure this, including "collecting all training materials that contain cultural or religious content, including information related to Islam or Muslims."[93]

This material wouldn't just be "collected"; it would be purged of anything that Farhana Khera and others like her found offensive—that is, any honest discussion of how Islamic jihadists used Islamic teachings to justify violence.

The alacrity with which Brennan complied was unfortunate on many levels. Not only were numerous books and presentations that presented a perfectly accurate view of Islam and jihad purged, but Brennan was complying with demands from quarters that could hardly be considered authentically moderate.

America was going to war against jihadists while forbidding itself to understand jihad.

Brennan also attempted to distance Islam and the concept of jihad from contemporary Islamic terrorism long before he told Farhana Khera that he would give her everything she wanted. In August 2009, Brennan noted that Barack Obama did not see the struggle against al-Qaeda "as a fight against jihadists. Describing terrorists in this way, using the legitimate term 'jihad,' which means to purify oneself or to wage a holy struggle for a moral goal, risks giving these murderers the religious legitimacy they desperately seek but in no way deserve."[94]

Brennan declared at New York University Law School in February 2010:

As Muslims you have seen a small fringe of fanatics who cloak themselves in religion, try to distort your faith, though they are clearly ignorant of the most fundamental teachings of Islam. Instead of finding the inherent dignity and decency in other human beings, they practice a medieval brand of intolerance. Instead of saving human lives, as the Quran instructs, they take innocent life. Instead of creating, they destroy—bombing mosques, schools and hospitals. They are not jihadists, for jihad is a holy struggle, an effort to purify for a legitimate purpose, and there is nothing, absolutely nothing holy or pure or legitimate or Islamic about murdering innocent men, women and children."[95]

Going even farther, he said on May 26, 2010, in an address at the Center for Strategic and International Studies: "Nor do we describe our enemies as jihadists or Islamists because jihad is a holy struggle, a legitimate tenet of Islam meaning to purify oneself or one's community."[96] In a press release the next day, CAIR "expressed appreciation" for Brennan's remarks.[97]

In the same speech, Brennan added: "And there is nothing holy or legitimate or Islamic about murdering innocent men, women and children. Indeed, characterizing our adversaries this way would actually be counterproductive. It would play into the false perception that they are religious leaders defending a holy cause when in fact, they are nothing more than murderers, including the murder of thousands upon thousands of Muslims."[98]

So many warriors of jihad throughout history would have disagreed with Brennan, and one reporter in 2010 had the temerity to challenge him on this point. A *Washington Times* interviewer asked Brennan: "Can you give me an example of a jihad in history? Like, has there ever been a jihad…an armed jihad anywhere in history? Has it ever existed for real, or is it just a concept?"[99]

When Brennan responded, "I'm not going to go into this sort of history discussion here," the interviewer explained: "But it's important to frame the concept, because we want to say that what al-Qaeda is doing is not jihad. They say it is." The interviewer then paraphrased for Brennan the jihadist claim, as repeated by al-Qaeda cofounder Abdullah Azzam, that the idea that the spiritual jihad was the "greater jihad" had no basis in Islamic theology: "Abdul Azzam has said, in fact, 'there's not even a greater jihad.' [Azzam has said] that that's just a myth—that hadith didn't even really happen."[100]

Azzam claimed, the interviewer continued, "that there's only armed jihad. Ayatollah Khomeini said 'there is only armed jihad,' and it would be useful to be able to characterize or to contrast what they're doing and what they claim against a legitimate armed jihad in the past."[101]

Rather than explain on what grounds he found these usages of the word "jihad" as armed struggle to be illegitimate from an Islamic standpoint, Brennan said abruptly: "I think we've finished. I have to get going," and left.[102]

Brennan was instrumental in the Obama administration's recasting of the defense against terror as a localized struggle against al-Qaeda.

The Migrant Influx

Meanwhile, after September 11, European nations began admitting tens of thousands of Muslim immigrants, such that by 2017, many European cities had majority-Muslim enclaves, and the Muslim population of Europe was in the millions and growing much more quickly than the non-Muslim population.

The influx picked up sharply in 2015. German chancellor Angela Merkel, keen to alleviate the humanitarian crisis in Syria and the surrounding regions, opened Germany's doors to hundreds of thousands of Muslim migrants. Other Western European countries did as well. Yet while there was no doubt that some of the refugees were grateful for the hospitality they were being shown, others clearly weren't. All of the Islamic jihadis who murdered 130 people in Paris in a series of jihad attacks in November 2015 were putative refugees who had recently been welcomed into Europe.[103] Germany's domestic intelligence agency admitted in July 2017 that hundreds of jihadis had entered the country among the refugees, and that twenty-four thousand jihadis were active in Germany.[104]

Muslim migrants in Europe were also responsible for an appalling epidemic of rape, sexual assault, theft, petty crime, and looting. In the first half of 2016, migrants in Germany, who were overwhelmingly Muslim, committed 142,500 crimes, an average of 780 every day. This was a significant increase from 2015, during which migrants committed two hundred thousand crimes during the entire year.[105]

On New Year's Eve, December 31, 2015, Muslim migrants committed as many as two thousand mass rapes and sexual assaults in Cologne, Stockholm, and other major European cities.[106] Such assaults weren't limited to that day alone; Sweden was called the "rape capital of the world" because of the notorious activities of Muslim migrants.[107] Muslim migrants made Malmö, once a peaceful city, crime-ridden and hazardous.[108]

In Sweden, Muslim migrants from Afghanistan were found in 2017 to be seventy-nine times more likely to commit rape and other sexual crimes than native Swedes. Migrants and refugees committed ninety-two percent of rapes in Sweden. Rapists in Sweden have come from Iraq, Afghanistan, Somalia, Eritrea, Syria, Gambia, Iran, Palestine, Chile, and Kosovo, in that order; rapists of Swedish background do not exist in sufficient numbers to make the top ten, and all the nations on that list except Chile and Eritrea are majority Muslim.[109]

In the British town of Rotherham, Muslim gangs brutalized, sexually assaulted, and raped over fourteen hundred young British girls, while authorities remained extremely reluctant to say or do anything in response, for fear of being labeled racist.[110]

Yet hardly anything was being said about this. In the summer of 2016, Krystyna Pawłowicz, a member of the Polish parliament, charged German authorities with attempting to "cover up the crimes of their Arab guests, or even shift the blame upon themselves."[111] There was also evidence that migrant crimes were being covered up in the Netherlands and Sweden as well.[112]

These cover-ups apparently proceeded from a fear that non-Muslims would begin to have negative views of Islam; yet the sexual assaults *did* have to do with Islam. The Qur'an dictates that a Muslim man may have sexual relations with the "captives of the right hand," that is, captured non-Muslim women (4:3; 4:24; 23:1–6; 33:50; 70:30). The Qur'an also says that women should veil themselves so that they may not be molested (33:59), with the implication being that if they are not veiled, they may indeed be molested.

The Catholic Church

The Catholic Church, on the forefront of resistance to the jihad for centuries, likewise abdicated early in the twenty-first century. Of course, the Church had not called a Crusade for centuries, and by September 11 no one would have expected it to do so. Not only were the Crusades by then a dim historical memory, ill-remembered and even less understood, among most Catholics, but schools all over the West that had adopted the name Crusaders during the twentieth century began shedding the label. Historical pride quickly gave way to historical shame.

Early in the twenty-first century, the Catholic Church went even farther, not only not sounding the alarm about the advancing jihad, but demonstrating that it had no historical memory of why the Crusades had been fought, as well as no awareness that this jihad, which had historically targeted the Church, was continuing and had found renewed energy. There were to be no reminders from the Catholic Church about how Islam had been set against Europe for fourteen hundred years and that mass Muslim migration into Europe might not be such a good idea.

However, Pope Benedict XVI did touch off a worldwide controversy in 2006 by quoting the fourteenth-century Byzantine emperor Manuel II Paleologus' words about Muhammad's bringing nothing new but what was evil and inhumane. Benedict at least demonstrated that he was aware that Islam somehow posed a problem for Europe and the free world in general; after the Muslim riots and murders that followed his remarks, and fulmination from Egypt's al-Azhar over his statements after a jihad mass murder attack in an Egyptian cathedral, Benedict fell silent.

His successor, Pope Francis, was anything but silent. In a November 2013 Apostolic Exhortation, he declared: "Faced with disconcerting episodes of violent fundamentalism, our respect for true followers of Islam should lead us to avoid hateful generalisations, for authentic Islam and the proper reading of the Koran are opposed to every form of violence."[113]

This statement, remarkable for the dogmatic confidence with which its false claim was made, was not singular. Pope Francis was not just a defender of Islam and the Qur'an but of the Sharia death penalty for blasphemy: after Islamic jihadists in January 2015 murdered cartoonists from the French satirical magazine *Charlie Hebdo*, Francis obliquely justified the murders by saying that "it is true that you must not react violently, but although we are good friends if [an aide] says a curse word against my mother, he can expect a punch, it's normal. You can't make a toy out of the religions of others. These people provoke and then [something can happen]. In freedom of expression there are limits."[114]

For the pope, it can thus be assumed, murdering people for violating Sharia blasphemy laws was "normal," and it wasn't terrorism anyway, for "Christian terrorism does not exist, Jewish terrorism does not exist, and Muslim terrorism does not exist. They do not exist," as he said in a speech in February 2017.[115] "There are fundamentalist and violent individuals in all peoples and religions—and with intolerant generalizations they become stronger because they feed on hate and xenophobia."[116]

There was no Islamic terrorism, as far as the pope was concerned, but if one engaged in "intolerant generalizations," one could "expect a punch." The pope apparently believed that the problem was not jihad terror but non-Muslims talking about jihad terror; Muslims would be peaceful if non-Muslims would simply censor themselves and self-impose Sharia blasphemy restrictions regarding criticism of Islam.

In July 2017, Ahmed al-Tayeb, the grand imam of Cairo's al-Azhar, thanked Pope Francis for his "defense of Islam against the accusation of violence and terrorism."[117] Then, in September 2017, the pope met in the Vatican with Dr. Muhammad bin Abdul Karim Al-Issa, the secretary general of the Muslim World League (MWL), a group that has been linked to the financing of jihad terror.[118]

During the meeting, Al-Issa thanked the pope for his "fair positions" on what he called the "false claims that link extremism and violence to Islam."[119] In other words, he thanked the Pope for dissembling about the motivating ideology of jihad terror, which his group had been accused of financing, and for defaming other religions in an effort to whitewash Islam.

Francis' predecessors Urban II and Calixtus IV would have been astonished. As the jihad advanced in Europe, historically the heart of Christendom, the Catholic Church that had stood against the jihad for centuries now told its people that it was xenophobic and racist to resist mass Muslim immigration, and that even security concerns about the Muslim migrants did not override this.

In his message for the World Day of Peace on January 1, 2018, Pope Francis declared: "In a spirit of compassion, let us embrace all those fleeing from war and hunger, or forced by discrimination, persecution, poverty and environmental degradation to leave their homelands." He warned: "Many destination countries have seen the spread of rhetoric decrying the risks posed to national security or the high cost of welcoming new arrivals, and thus demeaning the human dignity due to all as sons and daughters of God. Those who, for what may be political reasons, foment fear of migrants instead of building peace are sowing violence, racial discrimination and xenophobia, which are matters of great concern for all those concerned for the safety of every human being."[120]

Yet those security concerns were real. All of the jihadis who murdered 130 people in Paris in November 2015 had just entered Europe as refugees.[121] This followed the Islamic State's February 2015 boast that it would soon flood Europe with as many as five hundred thousand refugees.[122] In September 2015, Elias Bou Saab, the Lebanese education minister, disclosed that there were twenty thousand jihadis among the refugees in camps in his country, waiting for the opportunity to go to Europe and North America.[123] That same month, it was revealed that eighty percent of migrants who had come to Europe claiming to be fleeing the war in Syria were not really from Syria at all.[124]

Why were they claiming to be Syrian and streaming into Europe, and the U.S. as well? An Islamic State operative gave the answer when he boasted in September 2015, shortly after the migrant influx began, that among the flood of refugees, four thousand Islamic State jihadis had already entered Europe. He explained their purpose: "It's our dream that there should be a caliphate not only in Syria but in all the world, and we will have it soon, *inshallah*."[125] These Muslims were going to Europe in the service of that caliphate: "They are going like refugees," he said, but they were going with the plan of sowing blood and mayhem on European streets. As he told this to journalists, he smiled and said, "Just wait."[126]

On May 10, 2016, Patrick Calvar, the head of France's DGSI internal intelligence agency, said that the Islamic State was using migrant routes through the Balkans to get jihadis into Europe.[127]

But for Pope Francis, concern for all of this was simply "xenophobia." "It is hypocritical," he thundered in October 2016, "to call yourself a Christian and to chase away a refugee, or anyone who needs your help. Jesus taught us what it means to be a good Christian in the parable of the Good Samaritan."[128] He cited Scripture: "You shall not wrong a stranger or oppress him, for you were strangers in the land of Egypt."[129]

The Islamic State, meanwhile, had its own scripture in mind. With marked ingratitude, in November 2017 it threatened "Christmas blood" at the Vatican and released an image of Pope Francis beheaded.[130]

A year before that, the same group had explained that, contrary to Pope Francis' fond imaginings, their struggle was all about Islam. Addressing the free world, the Islamic State declared in an article in its glossy online magazine *Dabiq*:

> We hate you, first and foremost, because you are disbelievers; you reject the oneness of Allah—whether you realize it or not—by making partners for Him in worship, you blaspheme against Him, claiming that He has a son, you

fabricate lies against His prophets and messengers, and you indulge in all manner of devilish practices....

We hate you because your secular, liberal societies permit the very things that Allah has prohibited while banning many of the things He has permitted, a matter that doesn't concern you because you [sic] Christian disbelief and paganism separate between religion and state, thereby granting supreme authority to your whims and desires via the legislators you vote into power....

In the case of the atheist fringe, we hate you and wage war against you because you disbelieve in the existence of your Lord and Creator.

We hate you for your crimes against Islam and wage war against you to punish you for your transgressions against our religion.

We hate you for your crimes against the Muslims; your drones and fighter jets bomb, kill, and maim our people around the world, and your puppets in the usurped lands of the Muslims oppress, torture, and wage war against anyone who calls to the truth.

We hate you for invading our lands and fight you to repel you and drive you out. As long as there is an inch of territory left for us to reclaim, jihad will continue to be a personal obligation on every single Muslim....

What's important to understand here is that although some might argue that your foreign policies are the extent of what drives our hatred, this particular reason for hating you is secondary, hence the reason we addressed it at the end of the above list.

The fact is, even if you were to stop bombing us, imprisoning us, torturing us, vilifying us, and usurping our lands, we would continue to hate you because our primary reason for hating you will not cease to exist until you embrace Islam.[131]

Neither Tariq ibn Ziyad nor Mahmud Ghazni could have said it more clearly. Nonetheless, neither Pope Francis nor other Catholic leaders took any notice.

The Islamic State

The Islamic State (commonly but erroneously known as ISIS, an acronym for its former and rejected name, the Islamic State of Iraq and al-Sham [the Levant]) that threatened Pope Francis and the West is best known for its audacious attempt from 2014 to 2017 to restore the caliphate. It declared its caliphate in the territory it controlled in Iraq and Syria on June 29, 2014, the same day it issued an explanatory document entitled "This is the Promise of Allah."

The declaration, similar to so many other Islamic declarations throughout Islamic history, asserted that the caliphate frees human beings from oppression and subjugation: it is meant "for the purpose of compelling the people to do what the Sharia (Allah's law) requires of them concerning their interests in the hereafter and worldly life, which can only be achieved by carrying out the command of Allah, establishing His religion, and referring to His law for judgment."[132]

Before Islam, according to "This is the Promise of Allah," the Arabs were weak and disunited; once they accepted Islam, Allah granted them unity and power. Then followed success unprecedented in world history. Referring to the jihad victories of the seventh century, it declared: "Our dear ummah—the best of peoples—Allah (the Exalted) decrees numerous victories for this ummah to occur in a single year, which He does not grant others in many years or even centuries. This ummah succeeded in ending two of the largest empires known to history in just 25 years, and then spent the treasures of those empires on jihad in the path of Allah. They put out the fire of the Magians (fire-worshippers) forever, and they forced the noses of the cross-worshippers onto the ground with the most miserable of weapons and weakest of numbers.... Yes, my ummah, those barefoot, naked, shepherds who did not know good from evil, nor truth from falsehood, filled the earth with justice after it had been filled with oppression and tyranny, and ruled the world for centuries."[133]

As far as the Islamic State was concerned, nothing had changed—or should have changed: "The God of this ummah yesterday is the same God of the ummah today, and the One who gave it victory yesterday is the One who will give it victory today."[134] Accordingly, "The time has come for those generations that were drowning in oceans of disgrace, being nursed on the milk of humiliation, and being ruled by the vilest of all people, after their long slumber in the darkness of neglect—the time has come for them to rise."[135] The "vilest of all people" is a Qur'anic epithet for the "unbelievers among the People of the Book"—that is, Jews, Christians, and Zoroastrians who do not become Muslims (98:6).

The Islamic State also announced: "The sun of jihad has risen. The glad tidings of good are shining. Triumph looms on the horizon. The signs of victory have appeared." It made its case for embodying the caliphate based on the fact that in its domains, the Muslims were exalted, and the infidels were humiliated, paying the Qur'anic tax (*jizya*) and submitting in humiliation to the Muslims, as specified in the Qur'an (9:29)—in the process, sketching out a chilling picture of non-Muslims subjugated under the supremacy of Islam:

> Here the flag of the Islamic State, the flag of tawhid [mono-theism], rises and flutters. Its shade covers land from Aleppo to Diyala. Beneath it, the walls of the tawaghit [rulers claiming the rights of Allah] have been demolished, their flags have fallen, and their borders have been destroyed. Their soldiers are either killed, imprisoned, or defeated. The Muslims are honored. The kuffar [infidels] are disgraced. Ahlus-Sunnah [the Sunnis] are masters and are esteemed. The people of bid'ah [heresy] are humiliated. The hudud [Sharia penalties] are implemented—the hudud of Allah—all of them. The frontlines are defended. Crosses and graves are demolished. Prisoners are released by the edge of the sword. The people in the lands of the State move about for their livelihood and journeys, feeling safe regarding their lives and wealth. Wulat [plural of *wali*, or governors] and judges have been appointed. Jizyah [a tax imposed on kuffar] has been enforced. Fay' [money taken from the kuffar without battle] and zakat [obligatory alms] have been collected. Courts

have been established to resolve disputes and complaints. Evil has been removed. Lessons and classes have been held in the masajid [plural of *masjid*] and, by the grace of Allah, the religion has become completely for Allah. There only remained one matter, a wajib kifa'i [collective obligation] that the ummah sins by abandoning. It is a forgotten obligation. The ummah has not tasted honor since they lost it. It is a dream that lives in the depths of every Muslim believer. It is a hope that flutters in the heart of every mujahid muwahhid [monotheist]. It is the khilafah [caliphate]. It is the khilafah—the abandoned obligation of the era.[136]

Consequently, all Muslims now owed allegiance to this caliphate: "We clarify to the Muslims that with this declaration of khilafah, it is incumbent upon all Muslims to pledge allegiance to the khalifah Ibrahim and support him (may Allah preserve him). The legality of all emirates, groups, states, and organizations, becomes null by the expansion of the khilafah's authority and arrival of its troops to their areas." And "the khalifah [caliph] Ibrahim (may Allah preserve him) has fulfilled all the conditions for khilafah [caliphate] mentioned by the scholars."[137]

Thus, the Islamic State exhorted all Muslims to join it and give it allegiance, as the Mahdi in Sudan and so many other Muslim revivalists had throughout Islamic history:

So rush O Muslims and gather around your khalifah, so that you may return as you once were for ages, kings of the earth and knights of war.... By Allah, if you disbelieve in democracy, secularism, nationalism, as well as all the other garbage and ideas from the west, and rush to your religion and creed, then by Allah, you will own the earth, and the east and west will submit to you. This is the promise of Allah to you. This is the promise of Allah to you.[138]

Less than a week after declaring itself the caliphate, the Islamic State gave the world a look at the new caliphate, releasing a video on July 5, 2014, of Abu Bakr al-Baghdadi speaking in the twelfth-century Great Mosque of al-Nuri in Mosul.[139]

He said that after the fall of the last caliphate, "the disbelievers were able to weaken and humiliate the Muslims, dominate them in every region, plunder their wealth and resources, and rob them of their rights." They did this by "attacking and occupying their lands, placing their treacherous agents in power to rule the Muslims with an iron fist, and spreading dazzling and deceptive slogans such as: civilization, peace, co-existence, freedom, democracy, secularism, baathism, nationalism, and patriotism, among other false slogans. Those rulers continue striving to enslave the Muslims, pulling them away from their religion with those slogans."[140]

The warriors of jihad should not worry about the formidable military might of the infidels, because just as at the Battle of Badr, success would come through obedience to Allah, not by means of weapons:

> O soldiers of the Islamic State, do not be awestruck by the great numbers of your enemy, for Allah is with you. I do not fear for you the numbers of your opponents, nor do I fear your neediness and poverty, for Allah (the Exalted) has promised your Prophet (peace be upon him) that you will not be wiped out by famine, and your enemy will not himself conquer you and violate your land. Allah placed your provision under the shades of your spears.[141]

He called upon them also to "persevere in reciting the Quran with comprehension of its meanings and practice of its teachings. This is my advice to you. If you hold to it, you will conquer Rome and own the world, if Allah wills."[142]

In June 2014, a video circulated of a masked Islamic State commander telling a cheering crowd: "By Allah, we embarked on our Jihad only to support the religion of Allah.... Allah willing, we will establish a state ruled by the Quran and the Sunna.... All of you honorable Muslims are the soldiers of the Muslim State." He promised that the Islamic State would establish "the Sharia of Allah, the Quran, and the Sunna" as the crowed repeatedly responded with cries of "*Allahu akbar*."[143]

The Islamic State is Not Islamic

U.S. and Western European leaders immediately denied that the Islamic State had anything to do with Islam. "ISIL does not operate in the name of any religion," said Deputy State Department spokesperson Marie Harf in August 2014. "The president has been very clear about that, and the more we can underscore that, the better."[144] CIA director John Brennan said in March 2015: "They are terrorists, they're criminals. Most—many—of them are psychopathic thugs, murderers who use a religious concept and masquerade and mask themselves in that religious construct. Let's make it very clear that the people who carry out acts of terrorism—whether it be al-Qaeda or the Islamic State of Iraq and the Levant—are doing it because they believe it is consistent with what their view of Islam is. It is totally inconsistent with what the overwhelming majority of Muslims throughout the world [believe]."[145] In September 2014, French foreign minister Laurent Fabius announced: "This is a terrorist group and not a state. I do not recommend using the term Islamic State because it blurs the lines between Islam, Muslims and Islamists."[146]

The Islamic State professed contempt and amusement over all this confusion and denial. In his September 21, 2014, address calling for jihad strikes in the U.S. and Europe, Islamic State spokesman Abu Muhammad Adnani ridiculed John Kerry ("that uncircumcised old geezer") and Barack Obama for declaring that the Islamic State was not Islamic, as if they were Islamic authorities.[147]

And indeed, everything the Islamic State did was clearly based on Islamic texts and teachings. Its public beheadings applied the Qur'an's directive: "When you meet the unbelievers, strike the necks." (47:4)

Similar calculations hold true regarding the Islamic State's practice of kidnapping Yazidi and Christian women and pressing them into sex slavery. The Qur'an says straightforwardly that in addition to wives ("two or three or four"), Muslim men may enjoy the "captives of the right hand" (4:3, 4:24). These are specified as being women who have been seized as the spoils of war (33:50) and are to be used specifically for sexual purposes, as men are to "guard their private parts except from their wives or those their right hands possess." (23:5–6).

If these women are already married, no problem. Islamic law directs that "when a child or a woman is taken captive, they become slaves by the fact of capture, and the woman's previous marriage is immediately annulled."[148]

In May 2011, a female Kuwaiti activist and politician, Salwa al-Mutairi, noted that Harun al-Rashid, the renowned Abbasid caliph from 786 to 809, "had 2,000 sex slaves."[149]

On December 15, 2014, the Islamic State released a document entitled "Clarification [regarding] the Hudud"—that is, punishments Allah specifies in the Qur'an. This was essentially the Islamic State's penal code, and every aspect of it was drawn from Islamic teaching.[150] Blasphemy against Islam was punishable by death, also as per the Qur'an: "If they violate their oaths after pledging to keep their covenants, and attack your religion, you may fight the leaders of paganism—you are no longer bound by your covenant with them—that they may refrain." (Qur'an 9:12) Adulterers were to be stoned to death; fornicators would be give one hundred lashes and exile. Stoning was in the *hadith*—a *hadith* in which the caliph Umar said it had once been in the Qur'an:

> Umar said, "I am afraid that after a long time has passed, people may say, 'We do not find the Verses of the Rajam [stoning to death] in the Holy Book,' and consequently they may go astray by leaving an obligation that Allah has revealed. Lo! I confirm that the penalty of Rajam be inflicted on him who commits illegal sexual intercourse, if he is already married and the crime is proved by witnesses or pregnancy or confession." Sufyan added, "I have memorized this narration in this way." Umar added, "Surely Allah's Apostle carried out the penalty of Rajam, and so did we after him."[151]

Sodomy (homosexuality) was also to be punished by death, as per Muhammad's reported words: "If you find anyone doing as Lot's people did, kill the one who does it, and the one to whom it is done."[152]

The Islamic State's rapid success was partly attributable to its fidelity to Islam and partly also to its financial backing, which came, predictably enough, in great part from Saudi Arabia. In August 2014, Hillary

Clinton wrote to John Podesta, an adviser to President Barack Obama: "We need to use our diplomatic and more traditional intelligence assets to bring pressure on the governments of Qatar and Saudi Arabia, which are providing clandestine financial and logistic support to ISIL [Isis] and other radical Sunni groups in the region. This effort will be enhanced by the stepped-up commitment in the [Kurdish Regional Government]. The Qataris and Saudis will be put in a position of balancing policy between their ongoing competition to dominate the Sunni world and the consequences of serious US pressure."[153]

But nothing was done.

At its height, the Islamic State controlled a territory larger than Great Britain and attracted thirty thousand foreign fighters from a hundred countries to travel to Iraq and Syria to join the caliphate. It gained the allegiance of other jihad groups in Libya, Nigeria, the Philippines, and elsewhere. Muslims took its apparent success as a sign of Allah's favor: the caliphate had indeed returned.

It didn't last long, however. When Donald Trump replaced Barack Obama as president of the United States, Iraqi forces and others began rolling up Islamic State strongholds, such that within a year of the beginning of the Trump presidency, the Islamic State had lost ninety-eight percent of its territory. The jihad threat posed by the Islamic State did not lessen, however, as those foreign fighters who survived returned to their home countries, often welcomed back by Western leaders who were convinced that kind treatment would compel them to turn away from jihad.

The Jihad Continues

In any case, the Islamic State was gone from Iraq and Syria, but the dream of the caliphate and the obligation to jihad remained, and other Muslims were quite willing, even eager, to take up arms in service of both.

The early twenty-first century saw a sharp rise in jihad massacres perpetrated all over the West by individuals or small groups of Muslims: in London, Manchester, Paris, Toulouse, Nice, Amsterdam, Madrid, Brussels, Berlin, Munich, Copenhagen, Malmö, Stockholm, Turku (in Finland), Moscow, St. Petersburg, and Beslan, among other places. Filmmaker Theo van Gogh was massacred on an Amsterdam street in 2004 for offending Islam; as mentioned previously, the cartoonists of the satirical magazine *Charlie Hebdo* were murdered in Paris in January 2015 for the same offense. In July 2016, Islamic jihadists murdered a French priest, Father Jacques Hamel, at the altar of his church for the crime of being Christian.

After each one of these atrocities, the local and national authorities called for prayer vigils and vowed their resolve against the "terrorists" of unspecified ideology, but they did nothing to address the immigration and appeasement policies that had led to these attacks in the first place.

As crime rates skyrocketed and jihad terror attacks became an increasingly common feature of the landscape in Europe, authorities all over the West seemed more concerned with making sure their people did not think negatively about Islam than defending them against the jihad onslaught.

The Jihad Against Myanmar

One notable example of this came in 2017 when the international media focused in horror upon the South Asian country of Myanmar (formerly Burma), which was, according to press reports, destroying the homes, exiling, and often massacring the nation's Muslim community, known as the Rohingyas.

According to news reports, this was entirely the fault of Buddhist leaders in Myanmar who were stirring up hatred against the Muslims. This was the media's consistent line. In 2013, *TIME* magazine's cover featured a Buddhist monk glowering over the caption: "The Face of Buddhist Terror: How Militant Monks Are Fueling Anti-Muslim Violence in Asia."[154] When the violence intensified in 2017, the UK's *Guardian* newspaper claimed that the Buddhists of Myanmar had been stirred up against the Rohingyas by a fanatical monk named Ashin Parathu who was, it charged, "stoking religious hatred across Burma. His paranoia and fear, muddled with racist stereotypes and unfounded rumors, have helped to incite violence and spread disinformation."[155]

The government of Myanmar denied committing any atrocities against the Rohingyas, asserting that many widely reported incidents had been fabricated, but the media generally brushed aside these denials.[156] Few news outlets reported that the conflict had intensified in the summer and fall of 2017 because of an August 2017 jihad attack on Myanmar police and border posts.[157] And hardly any news reports informed the public about the roots of the conflict: the Rohingya Muslims had actually been waging jihad against the Buddhists of Myanmar for nearly two centuries.

As is so often the case, the British were behind this. After they annexed Arakan, the area of western Burma now known as Rakhine state, in 1826, they began encouraging Muslims to move to the area to serve as a source of cheap farm labor.[158] The Muslim population grew rapidly, as did tensions with the Buddhists. In 1942, the British armed the Rohingyas to fight the Japanese, but the Rohingyas instead turned their weapons on the Buddhists, destroying whole villages, as well as Buddhist monasteries.[159] When the British withdrew that same year in the face of the Japanese advance, the Rohingyas set upon the Buddhists of Arakan in force, killing at least 20,000.[160] In 1946, as the partition of India was beginning, Rohingya leaders asked Muslim leader Mohammed Ali Jinnah to make Rakhine state part of East Pakistan (now Bangladesh).[161] Jinnah refused, whereupon Rohingya jihadis began a series of attacks against the Burmese government with the aim of joining East Pakistan or forming an independent Islamic state of their own.[162]

Those attacks have continued up to the present. But for the media, the crisis in Myanmar was simply a matter of "anti-Muslim bigotry," as was resistance to the Muslim migrant influx in Europe.

The End?

The failure of today's leadership and the international media to inform the public about what was really going on was an abdication of responsibility unparalleled in history, and one that rebuked the leaders throughout history who died to defend their people from the advancing jihad. On May 28, 1453, the day before the warriors of jihad finally broke through the defenses of Constantinople and realized their seven-hundred-year-old dream of conquering the great city, the last Byzantine emperor, Constantine XI Paleologus, said to his officers:

> You know well that the hour has come: the enemy of our faith wishes to oppress us even more closely by sea and land with all his engines and skill to attack us with the entire strength of this siege force, as a snake about to spew its venom; he is in a hurry to devour us, like a savage lion. For this reason I am imploring you to fight like men with brave souls, as you have done from the beginning up to this day, against the enemy of our faith. I hand over to you my glorious, famous, respected, noble city, the shining Queen of cities, our homeland. You know well, my brothers, that we have four obligations in common, which force us to prefer death over survival: first our faith and piety; second our homeland; third, the emperor anointed by the Lord and fourth; our relatives and friends.
>
> Well, my brothers, if we must fight for one of these obligations, we will be even more liable under the command strength of all four; as you can clearly understand. If God grants victory to the impious because of my own sins, we will endanger our lives for our holy faith, which Christ gave us with his own blood. This is most important of all. Even if one gains the entire world but loses his soul in the process, what will it benefit! Second, we will be deprived of such famous homeland and of our liberty. Third, our empire, renowned in the past but presently humbled, low and exhausted, will be ruled by a tyrant and an impious man. Fourth, we will be separated from our dearest children, wives and relatives....
>
> Now he wants to enslave her and throw the yoke upon the Mistress of Cities, our holy churches, where the Holy Trinity was worshipped, where the Holy Ghost was glorified in hymns, where angels were heard praising in chant the deity of and the incarnation of God's word, he wants to

turn into shrines of his blasphemy, shrines of the mad and false Prophet, Mohammed, as well as into stables for his horses and camels.

Consider then, my brother and comrades in arms, how the commemoration of our death, our memory, fame and freedom can be rendered eternal.[163]

In the twenty-first century, the leaders of Europe, as well as many in North America, have brought almost certain doom on their countries no less unmistakable than that which befell Constantinople on May 29, 1453. Instead of taking responsibility for what they have done, they have doggedly stayed their course. They would have denounced the doomed Emperor Constantine XI, like his tragic predecessor Manuel II, as "Islamophobic," and his exhortation to defend Constantinople to the death as "militaristic" and "xenophobic."

Muhammad is supposed to have said it so long ago: "I have been made victorious through terror."[164] In the early twenty-first century, he is being proven correct. As the fourteen-hundred-year Islamic jihad against the free world continues to advance, the best allies the warriors of jihad have are the very people they have in their sights.

ENDNOTES

Introduction

1 Imam Muslim, *Sahih Muslim*, rev. ed., translated by Abdul Hamid Siddiqi, bk. 19, no. 4294 (Kitab Bhavan, 2000).

2 Ahmed ibn Naqib al-Misri, *Reliance of the Traveller ('Umdat al-Salik): A Classic Manual of Islamic Sacred Law*, translated by Nuh Ha Mim Keller (Amana Publications, 1999), section o9.0.

3 *Reliance of the Traveller*, o9.8.

4 *Al-Hidayah*, vol. Ii. P. 140, in Thomas P. Hughes, "Jihad," in *A Dictionary of Islam*, (W.H. Allen, 1895), pp. 243–248.

5 *Al-Hidayah*, vol. Ii. P. 140, in Thomas P. Hughes, "Jihad," in *A Dictionary of Islam*, (W.H. Allen, 1895), pp. 243–248.

6 Ibn Khaldun, *The Muqaddimah: An Introduction to History*, translated by Franz Rosenthal; edited and abridged by N. J. Dawood, (Princeton University Press, 1967), 183.

7 Ibn Taymiyya, "Jihad," in Rudolph Peters, *Jihad in Classical and Modern Islam*, (Markus Wiener Publishers, 1996), 49.

Chapter One

1 Muhammed Ibn Ismaiel Al-Bukhari, *Sahih al-Bukhari: The Translation of the Meanings*, translated by Muhammad M. Khan, vol. 4, bk. 56, no. 2977 (Darussalam, 1997).

2 Ibid., bk. 64, no. 4428.

3 Ibid., bk. 56, no. 2977.

4 For much more on this, see my book *Did Muhammad Exist? An Inquiry Into Islam's Obscure Origins* (ISI Books, 2010).

5 Ibn Ishaq, *The Life of Muhammad: A Translation of Ibn Ishaq's Sirat Rasul Allah*, translated by Alfred Guillaume (Oxford University Press, 1955), 131.

6 Ibid., 287–88.

7 Ibid., 288.

8 Ibn Sa'd, *Kitab Al-Tabaqat Al-Kabir*, translated by S. Moinul Haq and H. K. Ghazanfar, vol. 2 (Kitab Bhavan, n.d.), 9.

9 Ishaq, *The Life of Muhammad*, 294.

10   Ibid., 297.

11   Ibid., 298.

12   For various estimates on the number of Muslim warriors, see Ibn Sa'd, *Kitab Al-Tabaqat Al-Kabir*, 20–21.

13   Ishaq, *The Life of Muhammad*, 300.

14   Ibid.

15   Ibid.

16   Ibid., 301.

17   Al-Bukhari, *Sahih al-Bukhari*, vol. 4, bk. 58, no. 3185.

18   Ibid., vol. 1, bk. 8, no. 520.

19   Ishaq, *The Life of Muhammad*, 308.

20   Ibid., 304.

21   Al-Bukhari, *Sahih al-Bukhari*, vol. 4, bk. 57, no. 3141.

22   Ibid., vol. 4, bk. 58, no. 3185.

23   Ishaq, *The Life of Muhammad*, 306.

24   Sa'd, *Kitab Al-Tabaqat Al-Kabir*, 40.

25   "*Banu*" means "tribe."

26   Abu Ja'far Muhammad bin Jarir al-Tabari, *The History of al-Tabari*, vol. 7, *The Foundation of the Community*, translated by M. V. McDonald (State University of New York Press, 1987), 86.

27   Ishaq, *The Life of Muhammad*, 363.

28   Ibid.

29   Ibid., 367.

30   Al-Bukhari, *Sahih al-Bukhari*, vol. 5, bk. 64, no. 4037.

31   Ibid.

32   Ibid.; Sa'd, *Kitab Al-Tabaqat Al-Kabir*, 37.

33   Sa'd, *Kitab Al-Tabaqat Al-Kabir*, 37.

34   Ishaq, *The Life of Muhammad*, 369; Sa'd, *Kitab Al-Tabaqat Al-Kabir*, 36.

35   Ishaq, *The Life of Muhammad*, 369.

36   Al-Bukhari, *Sahih al-Bukhari*, vol. 5, bk. 64, no. 4065.

37   Ishaq, *The Life of Muhammad*, 382.

38   Ibid., 386.

39   Al-Tabari, *The History of al-Tabari*, vol. 7, 158.

40   Ibid., 159.

41   Imam Muslim, *Sahih Muslim*, rev. ed., translated by Abdul Hamid Siddiqi, bk. 19, no. 4326 (Kitab Bhavan, 2000).

42   Ishaq, *The Life of Muhammad*, 437.

43   Sa'd, *Kitab Al-Tabaqat Al-Kabir*, 70.

44   Ishaq, *The Life of Muhammad*, 438.

45   Ibid., 450.

46 Ibid., 452.

47 Al-Tabari, *The History of al-Tabari*, vol. 8, *The Victory of Islam*, translated by Michael Fishbein (State University of New York Press, 1997), 11.

48 Ishaq, *The Life of Muhammad*, 452.

49 Al-Tabari, *The History of al-Tabari*, vol. 8, 12.

50 Ishaq, *The Life of Muhammad*, 452.

51 Ibid., 454.

52 Ibid., 460.

53 Muhammed Ibn Ismaiel Al-Bukhari, *Sahih al-Bukhari: The Translation of the Meanings*, translated by Muhammad M. Khan, vol. 4, bk. 56, no. 2813 (Darussalam, 1997).

54 Ishaq, *The Life of Muhammad*, 461.

55 Al-Bukhari, *Sahih al-Bukhari*, vol. 4, bk. 56, no. 3043.

56 Sa'd, *Kitab Al-Tabaqat Al-Kabir*, vol. 2, 93; *cf.* Ishaq, *The Life of Muhammad*, 464.

57 Abu-Dawud Sulaiman bin Al-Aash'ath Al-Azdi as-Sijistani, *Sunan abu-Dawud*, translated by Ahmad Hasan, bk. 38, no. 4390 (Kitab Bhavan, 1990).

58 Ishaq, *The Life of Muhammad*, 464.

59 Sa'd, *Kitab Al-Tabaqat Al-Kabir*, vol. 2, 93.

60 Ishaq, *The Life of Muhammad*, 464.

61 Al-Bukhari, *Sahih al-Bukhari*, vol. 4, bk. 57, no. 3128.

62 Ishaq, *The Life of Muhammad*, 490.

63 Al-Bukhari, *Sahih al-Bukhari*, vol. 9, bk. 97, no. 7409.

64 Ishaq, *The Life of Muhammad*, 504.

65 Ibid., 509.

66 Yahiya Emerick, *The Life and Work of Muhammad* (Alpha Books, 2002), 239.

67 Ibid., 240.

68 Ishaq, *The Life of Muhammad*, 511.

69 Ibid.

70 Sa'd, *Kitab Al-Tabaqat Al-Kabir*, vol. 2, 132–33.

71 Ishaq, *The Life of Muhammad*, 515.

72 Sa'd, *Kitab Al-Tabaqat Al-Kabir*, vol. 2, 136.

73 Ibid., 137.

74 Al-Bukhari, *Sahih al-Bukhari*, vol. 4, bk. 57, no. 3152.

75 Imam Muslim, *Sahih Muslim*, bk. 10, no. 3761.

76 Ishaq, *The Life of Muhammad*, 515.

77 Sa'd, *Kitab Al-Tabaqat Al-Kabir*, vol. 2, 137.

78 Al-Bukhari, *Sahih al-Bukhari*, vol. 5, bk. 64, no. 4200.

79 Sa'd, *Kitab Al-Tabaqat Al-Kabir*, vol. 2, 142.

80 Al-Bukhari, *Sahih al-Bukhari*, vol. 1, bk. 8, no. 371.

81 Imam Muslim, *Sahih Muslim*, bk. 8, no. 3329.

82 Al-Bukhari, *Sahih al-Bukhari*, vol. 1, bk. 8, no. 371.

83 Ibid.

84 Ishaq, *The Life of Muhammad*, 545.

85 Ibid., 546.

86 Ibid., 547.

87 Ibid.

88 Sa'd, *Kitab Al-Tabaqat Al-Kabir*, vol. 2, 168.

89 As-Sijistani, *Sunan abu-Dawud*, bk. 38, no. 4346.

90 Ishaq, *The Life of Muhammad*, 567.

91 Ibid., 569.

92 Guillaume explains: "*Ha'it* means wall and also the garden which it surrounds."

93 Ishaq, *The Life of Muhammad*, 589.

94 Ibid., 595–96.

95 Al-Bukhari, *Sahih al-Bukhari*, vol. 4, bk. 56, no. 2941.

96 Ibid., vol. 5, bk. 64, no. 4424.

97 Ibid., vol. 4, bk. 61, no. 3618.

98 Muslim, *Sahih Muslim*, bk. 19, no. 4294.

99 Al-Bukhari, *Sahih al-Bukhari*, vol. 4, bk. 56, no. 2785.

100 Muslim, *Sahih Muslim*, bk. 10, no. 31; *cf.* Al-Bukhari, *Sahih al-Bukhari*, vol. 1, bk. 2, no. 25.

101 Ishaq, *The Life of Muhammad*, 645–46.

102 Ibid., 643.

103 Muslim, *Sahih Muslim*, bk. 19, no. 4366.

104 Sa'd, *Kitab Al-Tabaqat Al-Kabir*, vol. 1, 328.

105 Ibid., vol. 1, 328–29.

106 Ishaq, *The Life of Muhammad*, 659–60. "T." refers to al-Tabari, a ninth-century Muslim historian whose recension of this material provides additional information.

Chapter Two

1   Muslim, *Sahih Muslim*, bk. 31, no. 5916.

2   Al-Bukhari, *Sahih al-Bukhari*, vol. 4, bk. 55, no. 2741.

3   At-Tirmidhi, vol. 1, bk. 46, no. 3673. Sunnah.com. http://sunnah.com/urn/635490

4   Al-Tabari, *The History of al-Tabari*, vol. 10, *The Conquest of Arabia*, translated by Fred M. Donner (State University of New York Press, 1993), 7.

5   Ibid., 8.

6   Ibid., 8–9.

7   Ishaq, *The Life of Muhammad*, 183.

8   Al-Bukhari, *Sahih al-Bukhari*, vol. 5, bk. 62, no. 3667.

9   Al-Tabari, *The History of al-Tabari*, vol. 10, 11–12.

10 Akbar Shah Najeebabadi, *The History of Islam*, vol. 1 (Darussalam, 2000), 276.

11 Fred Donner, *Muhammad and the Believers at the Origins of Islam* (The Belknap Press of Harvard University Press, 2010), 100–01.

12 Al-Tabari, *The History of al-Tabari*, vol. 10, 41.

13 Al-Bukhari, *Sahih al-Bukhari*, vol. 9, bk. 88, no. 6922; *cf.* vol. 4, bk. 56, no. 3017.

14 Al-Tabari, *The History of al-Tabari*, vol. 10, 103.

15 Ibid., 100–01.

16 Ibid., 100.

17 Ibid., 104.

18 Ibid.

19 Ibid., 102.

20 Ibid., 121.

21 Ibid., 133.

22 Ibid.

23 Ibid.

24 Abubakr Asadulla, *Islam vs. West: Fact or Fiction? A brief historical, political, theological, philosophical, and psychological perspective* (iUniverse, 2009), 42.

25 Modern-day Basra in Iraq.

26 Al-Tabari, *The History of al-Tabari*, vol. 11, *The Challenge to the Empires*, translated by Khalid Yahya Blankinship (State University of New York Press, 1993), 1–2.

27 Ibid., 4.

28 Ibid., 6.

29 Ibid., 4.

30 Ibid., 7.

31 Ibid.

32 Ibid., 59–60.

33 Ibid., 67.

34 Ibid., 68.

35 Ibid.

36 Agha Ibrahim Akram, *Islamic Historical General Khalid Bin Waleed* (Lulu Press, 2016).

37 Al-Tabari, *The History of al-Tabari*, vol. 11, 129.

38 Ibid., 158.

39 Al-Tabari places the battle at the end of Abu Bakr's reign as caliph, during Khalid's stint as commander of the Muslim armies; most historians, however, place it several years later.

40 Al-Tabari, *The History of al-Tabari*, vol. 11, 94.

41 Ibid., 94.

42 Ibid., 103.

43 H. U. Rahman, *Chronology of Islamic History, 570-1000 CE* (Ta-Ha Publishers, 1999), 59–60, 63–64.

44 At-Tirmidhi, vol. 3, bk. 19, no. 1606. Sunnah.com, https://sunnah.com/tirmidhi/21/69.

45 Najeebabadi, *The History of Islam*, vol. 1, 327.

46 Al-Bukhari, *Sahih al-Bukhari*, vol. 4, bk. 58, no. 3162.

47 Al-Tabari, *The History of al-Tabari*, vol. 11, 173.

48   Ibid., 174.

49   Najeebabadi, *The History of Islam*, vol. 1, 334.

50   Al-Tabari, *The History of al-Tabari*, vol. 12, *The Battle of al-Qadisiyyah and the Conquest of Syria and Palestine*, translated by Yohanan Friedman (State University of New York Press, 1992), 31.

51   Ibid., 31.

52   Ibid., 32.

53   Ibid., 34.

54   Ibid., 36.

55   Ibid., 39.

56   Ibid.

57   Ibid., 167.

58   Najeebabadi, *The History of Islam*, vol. 1, 367.

59   Ibid.

60   Ibid., 376.

61   Al-Tabari, *The History of al-Tabari*, vol. 12, 191.

62   Robert G. Hoyland, *Seeing Islam As Others Saw It: A Survey and Evaluation of Christian, Jewish and Zoroastrian Writings On Early Islam* (Darwin Press, 1997), 69.

63   Ibid., 72–73.

64   Steven Runciman, *A History of the Crusades*, vol. 1 (Cambridge University Press, 1951), 3.

65   Ibid., 4.

66   Al-Tabari, *The History of al-Tabari*, vol. 13, *The Conquest of Iraq, Southwestern Persia, and Egypt*, translated by Gautier H. A. Juynboll (State University of New York Press, 1989), 108.

67   Ibid.

68   Ibid.

69   Abu Ja'far Muhammad bin Jarir al-Tabari, *The History of al-Tabari*, vol. 3, 9, in *Kalid Ibn Al-Walid* (Brother Noah Publishing, 2015), 224.

70   Bat Ye'or, *The Decline of Eastern Christianity Under Islam: From Jihad to Dhimmitude* (Fairleigh Dickinson University Press, 1996), 271–72.

71   Ibid.

72   Ibid.

73   Al-Tabari, *The History of al-Tabari*, vol. 13, 165.

74   Hoyland, *Seeing Islam As Others Saw It*, 121.

75   Ye'or, *The Decline of Eastern Christianity Under Islam*, 274.

76   Ibid., 275.

77   "Khalifa Umar bin al-Khattab—Death of Umar," Alim, http://www.alim.org/library/biography/khalifa/content/KUM/19/2

78   Ignaz Goldziher, *Muslim Studies*, translated by C. R. Barber and S. M. Stern (George Allen & Unwin Ltd., 1971), 118.

79   Al-Bukhari, *Sahih al-Bukhari*, vol. 5, bk. 62, no. 3699.

80   Theophanes the Confessor, *The Chronicle of Theophanes: Anni Mundi 6095-6305 (A.D. 602-813)*, translated by Harry Turtledove (University of Pennsylvania Press, 1982), 44.

81   Yehuda D. Nevo and Judith Koren, *Crossroads to Islam* (Prometheus Books, 2003), 229.

82   Al-Bukhari, *Sahih al-Bukhari*, vol. 6, bk. 65, no. 4784.

83   Rahman, *Chronology of Islamic History, 570-1000 CE*, 77–79.

84   Al-Tabari, *The History of al-Tabari*, vol. 15, *The Crisis of the Early Caliphate*, translated by R. Stephen Humphreys (State University of New York Press, 1990), 185.

85   Al-Tabari, *The History of al-Tabari*, vol. 16, *The Community Divided*, translated by Adrian Brockett (State University of New York Press, 1997), 39.

86   Ibid., 52–166 *passim*.

87   Al-Tabari, *The History of al-Tabari*, vol. 17, *The First Civil War*, translated by G. R. Hawting (State University of New York Press, 1996), 29.

88   Ibid., 34.

89   Ibid., 79.

90   Ibid.

91   Ibid., 101.

92   Ibid.

93   Al-Tabari, *The History of al-Tabari*, vol. 18, *Between Civil Wars: The Caliphate of Mu'awiyah*, translated by Michael G. Morony (State University of New York Press, 1987), 3–4.

94   Al-Tabari, *The History of al-Tabari*, vol. 2, 112, in *Muslim Studies* by Goldziher, 44.

95   Goldziher, *Muslim Studies*, 105.

96   Allamah Sayyid Muhammad Husayn Tabatabai, *Shi'ite Islam*, 2nd ed., translated by Seyyed Hossein Nasr (State University of New York Press, 1977), 195.

97   Maxime Rodinson, *Muhammad*, translated by Anne Carter (Pantheon Books, 1971), 190.

98   Al-Bukhari, *Sahih al-Bukhari*, vol. 4, bk. 56, no. 2924.

99   Wilferd Madelung, "Hasan B., Ali B. Abi Taleb," Encyclopedia Iranica, December 15, 2003, http://www.iranicaonline.org/articles/hasan-b-ali.

100   Rahman, *Chronology of Islamic History, 570-1000 CE*, 99–101.

101   Al-Tabari, *The History of al-Tabari*, vol. 19, *The Caliphate of Yazid b. Mu'awiyah*, translated by I. K. A. Howard (State University of New York Press, 1990), 129.

102   Ibid., 131–32.

103   Ibid., 136–37.

104   Ibid.

105   Ibid.

106   Edward Gibbon, *The History of the Decline and Fall of the Roman Empire* (1782), vol. 5, ch. 51, part 8, 256.

107   Ibid.

108   H. Z. (J. W.) Hirschberg, "The Problem of the Judaized Berbers," *Journal of African History* 4, no. 3 (1963): 317–18.

109   L. W. Barnard, *The Graeco-Roman and Oriental Background of the Iconoclastic Controversy* (E. J. Brill, 1974), 18.

Chapter Three

1 Ibn Abd al-Hakam, *Dhikr Fath Al-Andalus* (*History of the Conquest of Spain*), translated by John Harris Jones (Williams & Norgate, 1858), 18.

2 Ibid.

3 Ibid.

4 Ibid., 19.

5 Ibid.

6 Ibid., 19–20.

7 "Al Maggari: Tarik's Address to His Soldiers, 711 CE, from The Breath of Perfumes," Internet Medieval Source Books, https://sourcebooks.fordham.edu/source/711Tarik1.asp.

8 Ibid.

9 Ibid.

10 Al-Hakam, *Dhikr Fath Al-Andalus*, 22.

11 Gibbon, *The History of the Decline and Fall of the Roman Empire*, vol. 5, ch. 51, part 8, 267.

12 Ibid.

13 Warren H. Carroll, *The Building of Christendom* (Christendom College Press, 1987), 269.

14 *Chronicle of Alfonso III*, 9, in *The Building of Christendom* by Carroll, 263.

15 Ibid.

16 Bat Ye'or, *The Dhimmi: Jews and Christians Under Islam*, translated by David Maisel, Paul Fenton, and David Littman (Fairleigh Dickinson University Press, 1985), 182.

17 Ibid., 182–83.

18 Jan Hogendorn, "The Hideous Trade: Economic Aspects of the 'Manufacture' and Sale of Eunuchs," *Paideuma* 45 (1999): 139.

19 Derryl N. MacLean, *Religion and Society in Arab Sind* (Brill, 1989), 37.

20 Ibid., 37.

21 K. S. Lal, *The Legacy of Muslim Rule in India* (Aditya Prakashan, 1992), 118.

22 Arun Shourie, Harsh Narain, Jay Dubashi, Ram Swarup, and Sita Ram Goel, *Hindu Temples: What Happened to Them*, vol. 1, *A Preliminary Survey* (Voice of India, 1990), 264.

23 MacLean, *Religion and Society in Arab Sind*, 38.

24 Shourie et al., *Hindu Temples*, 264.

25 MacLean, *Religion and Society in Arab Sind*, 39.

26 B. R. Ambedkar, *Thoughts on Pakistan* (Thacker and Company Ltd., 1941), 50.

27 Shourie et al., *Hindu Temples*, 205–06.

28 Ibid., 206.

29 Ibid., 212.

30 Ibid., 207.

31 Abu Abdur Rahman Ahmad bin Shu'aib bin 'Ali an-Nasa'i, *Sunan an-Nasa'i*, translated by Nasiruddin al-Khattab, bk. 25, ch. 41, no. 3175 (Darussalam, 2007).

32 Ibid., no. 3177.

33 Al-Tabari, *The History of al-Tabari*, vol. 24, *The Empire in Transition*, translated by David Stephan Powers (State University of New York Press, 1989), 40.

34 Ibid.

35 Ibid.

36 Ibid., 40–41.

37 Ibid., 41.

38 H. A. R. Gibb, *The Arab Conquests in Central Asia* (AMS Press, 1970), 65–66.

39 G. R. Hawting, *The First Dynasty of Islam: The Umayyad Caliphate AD 661-750* (Routledge, 1986), 86.

40 Ibid., 80.

41 Al-Tabari, *The History of al-Tabari*, vol. 25, *The End of Expansion*, translated by Khalid Yahya Blankinship (State University of New York Press, 1989), 127–28.

42 Ibid., 128.

43 Ibid.

44 Ibid., 126.

45 Tabatabai, *Shi'ite Islam*, 202–03.

46 Al-Tabari, *The History of al-Tabari*, vol. 26, *The Waning of the Umayyad Caliphate*, translated by Carole Hillenbrand (State University of New York Press, 1989), 24.

47 Ibid., 24–25.

48 Carroll, *The Building of Christendom*, 274.

49 Gibbon, *The History of the Decline and Fall of the Roman Empire*, vol. 5, ch. 52, part 2, 301.

50 *Hitler's Table Talk 1941–1944*, translated by Norman Cameron and R. H. Stevens (Enigma Books, 2000), 667.

51 Al-Tabari, *The History of al-Tabari*, vol. 27, *The Abbasid Revolution*, translated by John Alden Williams (State University of New York Press, 1985), 174.

52 Najeebabadi, *The History of Islam*, vol. 3, 68.

53 Michael the Syrian, *The Chronicle of Michael the Great, Patriarch of the Syrians*, translated by Robert Bedrosian (Sources of the Armenian Tradition, 2013), 144.

54 Ibid., 145.

55 Theophanes, *The Chronicle of Theophanes*, 142.

56 Najeebabadi, *The History of Islam*, vol. 2, 333.

57 Gibbon, *The History of the Decline and Fall of the Roman Empire*, vol. 5, ch. 52, part 3, 322–23.

58 Ibid., 323.

59 Ibid.

60 Antoine Fattal, *Le statut légal des non-Musulmans en pays d'Islam* (Université Saint-Joseph Institut de lettres orientales, 1958), 188.

61 Michael the Syrian, *The Chronicle of Michael the Great*, 145.

62 Theophanes, *The Chronicle of Theophanes*, 163.

63 Ibid.

64   Ibid.

65   Bat Ye'or, *The Decline of Eastern Christianity Under Islam*, 302.

66   Karen Armstrong, *Islam: A Short History* (Modern Library, 2002), 55.

67   Najeebabadi, *The History of Islam*, vol. 3, 82.

68   Gibbon, *The History of the Decline and Fall of the Roman Empire*, vol. 5, ch. 52, part 4, 325.

69   Ibid., 325–26.

70   Ibid., 326.

71   Ibid., 327.

72   Al-Tabari, *The History of al-Tabari*, vol. 32, *The Reunification of the Abbasid Caliphate*, translated by C. E. Bosworth (State University of New York Press, 1987), 196–97. Bracketed material added by the English translator.

73   Michael the Syrian, *The Chronicle of Michael the Great*, 151.

74   Ibid.

75   Al-Tabari, *The History of al-Tabari*, vol. 32, 224.

76   Michael the Syrian, *The Chronicle of Michael the Great*, 153.

77   Ibid., 154.

78   Ahmed ibn Naqib al-Misri, *Reliance of the Traveller ('Umdat al-Salik): A Classic Manual of Islamic Sacred Law*, translated by Nuh Ha Mim Keller (Amana Publications, 1999), section o4.9.

79   Gibbon, *The History of the Decline and Fall of the Roman Empire*, vol. 5, ch. 56, part 1, 468.

80   Bat Ye'or, *The Dhimmi*, 186.

81   Bernard Lewis, *The Jews of Islam* (Princeton University Press, 1984), 47–48.

82   Ibid., 48–49.

83   Paul Markham, "The Battle of Manzikert: Military Disaster or Political Failure?" De Re Militari: The Society for Medieval Military History, August 1, 2005, http://deremilitari. org/2013/09/the-battle-of-manzikert-military-disaster-or-political-failure/.

84   Tabatabai, *Shi'ite Islam*, 208–09.

85   Ibid., 209-210.

86   "Qarmatiyyah," Overview of World Religions, St. Martin's College, https://web.archive. org/web/20070428055134/http://philtar.ucsm.ac.uk/encyclopedia/islam/shia/qarma. html.

87   J. J. Saunders, *A History of Medieval Islam* (Routledge, 1965), 130–31.

88   Ibid., 130.

89   Cyril Glassé, *The New Encyclopedia of Islam* (Rowman & Littlefield, 1989), 91.

Chapter Four

1   Karen Armstrong, "The curse of the infidel: A century ago Muslim intellectuals admired the west. Why did we lose their goodwill?" *The Guardian*, June 20, 2002.

2   María Rosa Menocal, *The Ornament of the World: How Muslims, Jews, and Christians Created a Culture of Tolerance in Medieval Spain* (Little, Brown, 2002), 29–30.

3   Barack Obama, "Remarks by the President on a New Beginning," Cairo, June 4, 2009.

4   Richard Fletcher, *Moorish Spain* (University of California Press, 1992), 172–73.

5   Fletcher, *Moorish Spain*, 93.

6   Menocal, *The Ornament of the World*, 72–73.

7   Kenneth Baxter Wolf, *Christian Martyrs in Muslim Spain* (Cambridge University Press, 1988), 9, 10.

8   Ibid., 12.

9   Ibid.

10   Menocal, *The Ornament of the World*, 70.

11   Wolf, *Christian Martyrs in Muslim Spain*, 12.

12   Ibid., 34.

13   Darío Fernández-Morera, *The Myth of the Andalusian Paradise* (ISI Books, 2016), 126–27.

14   Ibid., 128–29.

15   Ibid., 130–31.

16   Ibid., 130.

17   Ibid., 131–32.

18   Ibid., 132.

19   Ibid.

20   Carroll, *The Building of Christendom*, 412.

21   Fernández-Morera, *The Myth of the Andalusian Paradise*, 129.

22   Ibid., 130.

23   Reinhart Dozy, *Spanish Islam: A History of the Muslims in Spain*, translated by Francis Griffin Stokes (Goodword Books, 2001), 497.

24   Carroll, *The Building of Christendom*, 428.

25   Dozy, *Spanish Islam*, 498.

26   Ibid., 504.

27   Ibid., 520.

28   Ibid., 523.

29   Paul Johnson, *A History of the Jews* (Perennial Library, 1987), 178.

30   Bernard F. Reilly, *The Kingdom of León-Castilla under King Alfonso VI, 1065-1109*, Library of Iberian Resources Online, chs. 10–12, http://libro.uca.edu/alfonso6/index.htm.

31   Fletcher, *Moorish Spain*, 108.

32   Fernández-Morera, *The Myth of the Andalusian Paradise*, 182–83.

33   Richard Gottheil and Meyer Kayserling, "Granada," *Jewish Encyclopedia* (1906), accessed at http://jewishencyclopedia.com/articles/6855-granada.

34   David Levering Lewis, *God's Crucible: Islam and the Making of Europe, 570-1215* (W. W. Norton, 2008), 364.

35   Carroll, *The Building of Christendom*, 523.

36   Ibid., 523.

37   Al-Misri, *Reliance of the Traveller*, section o11.9, 11.

38 Bat Ye'or, *The Dhimmi*, 187.

39 Fletcher, *Moorish Spain*, 172; Joseph Kenny, *The Spread of Islam Through North to West Africa* (Dominican Publications, 2000).

40 Fernández-Morera, *The Myth of the Andalusian Paradise*, 158.

41 Ibid., 159.

42 Ibid.

43 Hogendorn, "The Hideous Trade: Economic Aspects of the 'Manufacture' and Sale of Eunuchs," 139.

44 Saunders, *A History of Medieval Islam*, 144.

45 Ibid., 147.

46 Ahmad Shayeq Qassem, *Afghanistan's Political Stability: A Dream Unrealised* (Ashgate Publishing, 2009), 19.

47 Saunders, *A History of Medieval Islam*, 144.

48 Shourie, et al., *Hindu Temples*, 211.

49 Ambedkar, *Thoughts on Pakistan*, 51.

50 Shourie et al., *Hindu Temples*, 212.

51 Ibid., 212.

52 Ibid., 233.

53 Ibid., 234–35.

54 Ibid., 203–04.

55 Ibid., 204.

56 Ibid.

57 Ibid., 203.

58 Sita Ram Goel, *The Story of Islamic Imperialism in India* (Voice of India, 1982), 45–46.

59 Ibid., 46.

60 Ibid.

61 Ibid.

62 Ibid., 46–47.

63 Ambedkar, *Thoughts on Pakistan*, 50.

64 Shourie et al., *Hindu Temples*, 210.

65 Ibid.

66 Ibid., 211.

67 M. J. Akbar, *The Shade of Swords: Jihad and the Conflict between Islam and Christianity* (Routledge, 2002), 101.

68 J. J. Saunders, *A History of Medieval Islam*, 144.

69 Shourie et al., *Hindu Temples*, 219.

70 Ibid., 229.

71 Ibid., 211.

72 Saunders, *A History of Medieval Islam*, 144.

73 Goel, *The Story of Islamic Imperialism in India*, 47.

74   Bat Ye'or, *The Dhimmi*, 188.

75   Robert Hoyland, "The Rise of Islam," in *The Oxford History of Byzantium*, edited by Cyril Mango (Oxford University Press, 2002).

76   Aristakes Lastiverts'i, *History*, translated by Robert Bedrosian (Sources of the Armenian Tradition, 1985), 55.

77   Markham, "The Battle of Manzikert."

78   Lastiverts'i, *History*, 57.

79   Markham, "The Battle of Manzikert."

80   Lastiverts'i, *History*, 121.

81   John Julius Norwich, *Byzantium: The Apogee* (Alfred A. Knopf, 1992), 341.

82   Ibid., 342–43.

83   Markham, "The Battle of Manzikert."

84   Norwich, *Byzantium*, 346.

85   Markham, "The Battle of Manzikert."

86   Norwich, *Byzantium*, 354.

87   R. Scott Peoples, *Crusade of Kings* (Wildside Press LLC, 2007,) 13.

88   Moshe Gil, *A History of Palestine 634-1099* (Cambridge University Press, 1992), 412.

89   Halil Inalcik, "Osman Ghazi's Siege of Nicaea and the Battle of Bapheus," in *The Ottoman Emirate, 1300-1389: Halcyon Days in Crete I—A Symposium Held in Rethymnon, 11-13 January 1991*, edited by Elizabeth Zachariadou (Crete University Press, 1993), 77.

90   Gil, *A History of Palestine 634-1099*, 473–76. To his credit, Caliph al-Muqtadir did respond to the 923 persecutions by ordering the church rebuilt.

91   Ibid.

92   Runciman, *A History of the Crusades*, vol. 1, 30–32.

93   Carole Hillenbrand, *The Crusades: Islamic Perspectives* (Routledge, 2000), 101.

94   Gil, *A History of Palestine 634-1099*, 376.

95   Runciman, *A History of the Crusades,* vol. 1, 35–36; Hillenbrand, *The Crusades*, 16–17; Jonathan Riley-Smith, *The Crusades: A Short History* (Yale University Press, 1987), 44.

96   Runciman, vol. 1, 49.

Chapter Five

1   Pope Urban II, "Speech at Council of Clermont, 1095, According to Fulcher of Chartres," quoted in *Gesta Dei per Francos* by Bongars, 1, 382 f., translated in *A Source Book for Medieval History*, edited by Oliver J. Thatcher and Edgar Holmes McNeal (Scribners, 1905), 513–17, http://www.fordham.edu/halsall/source/urban2-fulcher.html.

2   James Harvey Robinson, ed., *Readings in European History*, vol. 1 (Ginn and Co., 1904), 312–16. Reprinted at *Medieval Sourcebook*, http://www.fordham.edu/halsall/source/urban2a.html.

3   Ibid.

4   Thomas Madden, *The New Concise History of the Crusades* (Rowman & Littlefield, 2005), 17–18.

5   Ibid., 18.

6   Ibid., 19.

7   Amin Maalouf, *The Crusades Through Arab Eyes* (Schocken Books, 1984), 44.

8   Ibid., 19.

9   Ibid.

10   Ibid., 39.

11   Ibid.

12   Ibid., 40.

13   Ibid., 39.

14   R. G. D. Laffan, ed. and trans., *Select Documents of European History 800-1492*, vol. 1 (Henry Holt, 1929). See also "The Crusaders Capture Jerusalem, 1099," EyeWitness to History, http://www.eyewitnesstohistory.com/crusades.htm.

15   Archbishop Daimbert, Duke Godfrey, and Count Raymond, "Letter to Pope Paschal II, September, 1099," in *Readings In Church History*, edited by Colman J. Barry (Christian Classics, 1985), 328.

16   Gil, *A History of Palestine 634-1099*, 827.

17   Hillenbrand, *The Crusades*, 64–65.

18   Maalouf, *The Crusades Through Arab Eyes*, 50.

19   "Remarks as Delivered by President William Jefferson Clinton, Georgetown University, November 7, 2001," Georgetown University Office of Protocol and Events, www.georgetown.edu.

20   Maalouf, *The Crusades Through Arab Eyes*, xvi.

21   John Esposito, *Islam: The Straight Path*, 3rd ed. (Oxford University Press, 1998), 58.

22   Hillenbrand, *The Crusades*, 70–71.

23   Robinson, *Readings in European History*.

24   Madden, *The New Concise History of the Crusades*, 19–20.

25   Maalouf, *The Crusades Through Arab Eyes*, 263.

26   Ibid., 136.

27   Hillenbrand, *The Crusades*, 111.

28   Ibid., 112.

29   Maalouf, *The Crusades Through Arab Eyes*, 138.

30   Ibid., 144.

31   Ibid., 145.

32   Ibid.

33   Ibid., 151–52.

34   Bernard Lewis, *The Assassins: A Radical Sect In Islam* (Basic Books, 1967), 2–3.

35   Ibid., 3–4.

36   Ibid., 4–5.

37   Marco Polo, *The Travels of Marco Polo*, translated by Henry Yule, edited and annotated by Henri Cordier (John Murray, 1920), ch. 23.

38   Lewis, *The Assassins*, 12.

39   Polo, *The Travels of Marco Polo*, ch. 24.

40   Ibid.

41   Michael the Syrian, *The Chronicle of Michael the Great*, 190.

42   Maalouf, *The Crusades Through Arab Eyes*, 179.

43   Madden, *The New Concise History of the Crusades*, 74.

44   Ibid., 76.

45   Ibid.

46   Ibid., 78.

47   Runciman, *A History of the Crusades*, vol. 2, *The Kingdom of Jerusalem and the Frankish East, 1100-1187* (Cambridge University Press, 1951), 487.

48   Madden, *The New Concise History of the Crusades*, 80.

49   Ibid., 81–82.

50   Ibid., 70.

51   Pope Innocent III, *Quia Maior*, April 19–29, 1213, https://genius.com/Pope-innocent-iii-quia-maior-annotated.

52   Ibid.

53   Ibid.

54   Madden, *The New Concise History of the Crusades*, 181–82.

55   John Esposito, ed., *The Oxford History of Islam* (Oxford University Press, 1999), 692.

56   Runciman, *A History of the Crusades*, vol. 3 (Cambridge University Press, 1951), 398–402.

57   Kenneth Meyer Setton, *The Papacy and the Levant, 1204-1571: The thirteenth and fourteenth centuries* (American Philosophical Society, 1976), 146.

58   Runciman, *A History of the Crusades*, vol. 3, 398–402.

59   Ibid.

60   Ibid.

61   Ibid.

62   Richard Bonney, *Jihad from Qur'an to bin Laden* (Palgrave Macmillan, 2004), 159–60.

63   Madden, *The New Concise History of the Crusades*, 189.

64   Bat Ye'or, *The Dhimmi*, 196–97.

65   Fletcher, *Moorish Spain*, 120.

66   Andrew Bostom, *The Legacy of Islamic Antisemitism* (Prometheus, 2007), 102.

67   Ibid., 104.

68   Bat Ye'or, *The Dhimmi*, 189.

69   Ibid.

70   Damian J. Smith, "The Papacy, the Spanish Kingdoms and Las Navas de Tolosa," *Anuario de Historia de la Iglesia* 20 (2011): 171.

71   Ibid., 174.

72   Ibid., 175.

73   Ibid., 177.

74   Fletcher, *Moorish Spain*, 124.

75   Lal, *The Legacy of Muslim Rule in India*, 49–50.

76   Goel, *The Story of Islamic Imperialism in India*, 45–48.

77   Ibid., 48.

78   Ibid.

79   Ambedkar, *Thoughts on Pakistan*, 52.

80   Goel, *The Story of Islamic Imperialism in India*, 48.

81   Ibid.

82   Ibid.

83   Ambedkar, *Thoughts on Pakistan*, 50.

84   Goel, *The Story of Islamic Imperialism in India*, 48.

85   Ibid., 49.

86   Ibid.

87   Ibid.

88   Ambedkar, *Thoughts on Pakistan*, 57.

89   Lal, *The Legacy of Muslim Rule in India*, 119.

90   Ibid., 50–51.

91   Ibid., 119–20.

92   Ibid., 119.

Chapter Six

1   Lord Kinross, *The Ottoman Centuries: The Rise and Fall of the Turkish Empire* (Morrow Quill Publishers, 1977), 23.

2   Inalcik, "Osman Ghazi's Siege of Nicaea and the Battle of Bapheus," 77.

3   Caroline Finkel, *Osman's Dream: The History of the Ottoman Empire* (Basic Books, 2007), 5.

4   Michael G. Knapp, "The Concept and Practice of Jihad in Islam," *Parameters* (Spring 2003): 83.

5   Lewis, *The Assassins*, 1–2.

6   Kinross, *The Ottoman Centuries*, 55.

7   Gibbon, *The History of the Decline and Fall of the Roman Empire*, vol. 2, ch. 66, part 1, https://www.ccel.org/g/gibbon/decline/volume2/chap66.htm.

8   Ibid.

9   Kinross, *The Ottoman Centuries*, 38.

10   Ibid.

11   Gibbon, *The History of the Decline and Fall of the Roman Empire*, vol. 2, ch. 64, part 48, https://www.ccel.org/g/gibbon/decline/volume2/chap64.htm.

12   Ibid.

13   Ibid.

14   Kinross, *The Ottoman Centuries*, 55.

15   Ibid.

16   Ibid.

17   Ibid., 42–43.

18   Gibbon, *The History of the Decline and Fall of the Roman Empire*, vol. 2, ch. 64, part 48, https://www.ccel.org/g/gibbon/decline/volume2/chap64.htm.

19   Ibid.

20   Godfrey Goodwin, *The Janissaries* (Saqi Books, 1997), 36–37.

21   Gibbon, *The History of the Decline and Fall of the Roman Empire*, vol. 2, ch. 64, part 53, https://www.ccel.org/g/gibbon/decline/volume2/chap64.htm.

22   Bat Ye'or, *The Decline of Eastern Christianity Under Islam*, 115.

23   Thomas Sowell, *Conquests and Cultures: An International History* (Basic Books, 1998), 192.

24   Kinross, *The Ottoman Centuries*, 46.

25   Gibbon, *The History of the Decline and Fall of the Roman Empire*, vol. 2, ch. 64, part 54, https://www.ccel.org/g/gibbon/decline/volume2/chap64.htm.

26   Ibid.

27   Ibid.

28   Leslie Peirce, *The Imperial Harem: Women and Sovereignty in the Ottoman Empire* (Oxford University Press, 1993), 158; Wilhelm Baum, "Manuel II Palaiologos (1391-1425 A.D.)," De Imperatoribus Romanis, http://www.roman-emperors.org/manuel2.htm.

29   Baum, "Manuel II Palaiologos (1391-1425 A.D.)."

30   Ibid.

31   Gibbon, *The History of the Decline and Fall of the Roman Empire*, vol. 2, ch. 64, part 66, https://www.ccel.org/g/gibbon/decline/volume2/chap64.htm.

32   Kinross, *The Ottoman Centuries*, 65.

33   Finkel, *Osman's Dream*, 23.

34   Baum, "Manuel II Palaiologos (1391-1425 A.D.)."

35   Gibbon, *The History of the Decline and Fall of the Roman Empire*, vol. 2, ch. 64, part 60, https://www.ccel.org/g/gibbon/decline/volume2/chap64.htm.

36   Baum, "Manuel II Palaiologos (1391-1425 A.D.)."

37   Gibbon, *The History of the Decline and Fall of the Roman Empire*, vol. 2, ch. 65, part 29, https://www.ccel.org/g/gibbon/decline/volume2/chap65.htm.

38   Ibid.

39   Ibid.

40   Baum, "Manuel II Palaiologos (1391-1425 A.D.)."

41   Gibbon, *The History of the Decline and Fall of the Roman Empire*, vol. 2, ch. 65, part 46, https://www.ccel.org/g/gibbon/decline/volume2/chap65.htm.

42   John Julius Norwich, *A Short History of Byzantium* (Vintage Books, 1999), 362.

43   Justin Marozzi, *Tamerlane: Sword of Islam, Conqueror of the World* (Da Capo Press, 2004), 358.

44   Ibid., 344.

45   Gibbon, *The History of the Decline and Fall of the Roman Empire*, vol. 2, ch. 66, part 32, https://www.ccel.org/g/gibbon/decline/volume2/chap66.htm.

46   Pope Benedict XVI, "Faith, reason and the university: memories and reflections," address at University of Regensburg, September 12, 2006.

47   Ibid.

48   Khaled Abu Toameh, "Gazans warn pope to accept Islam," *Jerusalem Post*, September 18, 2006.

49   Kinross, *The Ottoman Centuries: The Rise and Fall of the Turkish Empire*, 115.

50   Ibid., 91.

51   Steven Runciman, *The Fall of Constantinople 1453* (Cambridge University Press, 1965), 145.

52   Andrew Wheatcroft, *Infidels: A History of the Conflict Between Christendom and Islam* (Random House, 2005), 195.

53   "Leading Sunni Sheikh Yousef Al-Qaradhawi and Other Sheikhs Herald the Coming Conquest of Rome," MEMRI, December 6, 2002, https://www.memri.org/reports/leading-sunni-sheikh-yousef-al-qaradhawi-and-other-sheikhs-herald-coming-conquest-rome.

54   Runciman, *The Fall of Constantinople 1453*, 149.

55   Kinross, *The Ottoman Centuries*, 115–16.

56   Ibid., 129.

57   Warren Carroll: *The Glory of Christendom: A History of Christendom*, vol. 3 (Christendom Press, 1993), p. 571.

58   Kinross, *The Ottoman Centuries*, 130–31.

59   Ibid., 131.

60   Ibid., 133.

61   Ibid., 139.

62   Bat Ye'or, *The Dhimmi*, 192.

63   Ibid., 193.

64   Ibid.

65   Ibid.

66   Ibid.

67   Ibid.

68   Ibid.

69   Ibid.

70   Ibid., 198–99.

71   Ibid., 201; John Hunwick, *Jews of a Saharan Oasis: The Elimination of the Tamantit Community* (n.d., Markus Wiener Publishers).

72   Goel, *The Story of Islamic Imperialism in India*, 50.

73   Lal, *The Legacy of Muslim Rule in India*, 130.

74   Ibid.

75   Vincent Arthur Smith, *The Oxford History of India: From the Earliest Times to the End of 1911* (Clarendon Press, 1920), 245.

76   Ibid., 241–42.

77   Lal, *The Legacy of Muslim Rule in India*, 131.

78   Goel, *The Story of Islamic Imperialism in India*, 50–51.

79   Ibid., 51.

80   Ibid.

81 Ibid.

82 Smith, *The Oxford History of India*, 248–49.

83 Ibid., 250.

84 Ibid.

85 Ibid.

86 Ibid., 251.

87 Ibid., 250.

88 Ibid.

89 Ibid.

90 Ibid.

91 Ibid., 250–51.

92 Goel, *The Story of Islamic Imperialism in India*, 55.

93 Shourie et al., *Hindu Temples*, 239.

94 Ibid.

95 Goel, *The Story of Islamic Imperialism in India*, 55–56.

96 Shourie et al., *Hindu Temples*, 240.

97 Goel, *The Story of Islamic Imperialism in India*, 55–56; Shourie et al., *Hindu Temples*, 240.

98 Goel, *The Story of Islamic Imperialism in India*, 55–56.

99 Shourie et al., *Hindu Temples*, 240.

100 Ahmad Shayeq Qassem, *Afghanistan's Political Stability: A Dream Unrealised* (Ashgate Publishing, 2009), 20.

101 Marozzi, *Tamerlane*, 394.

102 Goel, *The Story of Islamic Imperialism in India*, 51.

103 Ibid.

104 Ibid.

105 Ibid., 51–52.

106 Ibid., 52.

107 Ibid.

108 Ibid.

109 Ibid.

110 Ibid.

111 Ibid.

112 Ibid.

113 Ibid., 52–53.

114 Ibid., 53.

115 Marozzi, *Tamerlane*, 355.

116 Ibid., 360–61.

117 Ibid.

118 Ibid., 361–62.

119   Ibid., 396.

120   Ibid., 396–97.

121   Ibid., 399.

122   Ibid., 400.

123   Goel, *The Story of Islamic Imperialism in India*, 56.

124   Shourie, et al., *Hindu Temples*, 240.

125   Ibid., 238.

126   Ibid., 238–39.

127   Ibid., 239.

128   Goel, *The Story of Islamic Imperialism in India*, 56.

129   Ibid.

130   Ibid.

131   Smith, *The Oxford History of India*, 280.

132   Ibid., 281.

133   Ibid.

134   Ibid., 253–54.

135   Shourie et al., *Hindu Temples*, 269.

136   Ibid., 240.

137   Ibid., 232–33.

Chapter Seven

1   Finkel, *Osman's Dream*, 104.

2   Ibid., 105.

3   Esposito, *The Oxford History of Islam*, 692.

4   Martin Luther, "On war against the Turk," 1528, http://www.lutherdansk.dk/On%20 war%20against%20Islamic%20reign%20of%20terror/On%20war%20against%20Islam-ic%20reign%20of%20terror1.htm

5   Martin Luther, *Works*, Weimar ed., 28, 365*f*; 30 II, 195; 47, 175, in *Luther on Islam and the Papacy* by Francis Nigel Lee (Queensland Presbyterian Theological College, 2000), 4.

6   Kinross, *The Ottoman Centuries*, 147.

7   Ibid.

8   Ibid., 176, 179.

9   Finkel, *Osman's Dream*, 119.

10   Kinross, *The Ottoman Centuries*, 185.

11   Ibid.

12   Ibid., 187.

13   Ibid.

14   Ibid.

15   Ibid.

16   Ibid.

17 Ibid.

18 Ibid., 188.

19 Finkel, *Osman's Dream*, 124.

20 Kinross, *The Ottoman Centuries*, 192.

21 Finkel, *Osman's Dream*, 129.

22 Ronald Segal, *Islam's Black Slaves: The Other Black Diaspora* (Farrar, Straus and Giroux, 2001), 114.

23 Finkel, *Osman's Dream*, 150.

24 Ibid., 151.

25 Ibid.

26 Ibid., 152.

27 Gábor Ágoston, "Muslim Cultural Enclaves in Hungary Under Ottoman Rule," *Acta Orientalia Academiae Scientiarum Hungaricae* 45, no. 2/3 (1991): 197.

28 Ibid., 156.

29 Ibid., 157.

30 Ibid., 156.

31 Kinross, *The Ottoman Centuries*, 264.

32 Finkel, *Osman's Dream*, 159.

33 Ibid.

34 Wheatcroft, *Infidels*, 27.

35 Ibid.

36 Kinross, *The Ottoman Centuries*, 270.

37 Ibid., 270–71.

38 Ibid., 271.

39 Wheatcroft, *Infidels*, 31.

40 Ibid.

41 Kinross, *The Ottoman Centuries*, 273.

42 Ibid., 275.

43 Ibid., 276.

44 Finkel, *Osman's Dream*, 192.

45 Kinross, *The Ottoman Centuries*, 288–89.

46 Ibid., 319.

47 Ibid., 292.

48 Finkel, *Osman's Dream*, 213.

49 Kinross, *The Ottoman Centuries*, 315.

50 Ibid., 315–16.

51 Finkel, *Osman's Dream*, 279–80.

52 Kinross, *The Ottoman Centuries*, 339.

53 Ibid., 343.

54   Ibid.

55   Ibid., 346.

56   Ibid., 347.

57   Giles Milton, *White Gold: The Extraordinary Story of Thomas Pellow and Islam's One Million White Slaves* (Farrar, Straus and Giroux), 12.

58   Murray Gordon, *Slavery in the Arab World* (New Amsterdam Books, 1989), 33.

59   Milton, *White Gold*, 12.

60   Ibid., 13.

61   Ibid., 22.

62   Ibid., 23.

63   Ibid., 28.

64   Ibid., 30.

65   Al-Misri, *Reliance of the Traveller*, section o9.14.

66   Abu'l Hasan al-Mawardi, *Al-Ahkam as-Sultaniyyah (The Laws of Islamic Governance)* (Ta-Ha Publishers, 1996), 192.

67   Shourie et al., *Hindu Temples*, 268.

68   Ibid., 237.

69   Ibid., 244.

70   Ibid., 269.

71   Ibid., 233.

72   Ibid., 269.

73   Ibid.

74   Ibid., 229.

75   Ibid.

76   Goel, *The Story of Islamic Imperialism in India*, 57.

77   Ibid.

78   Ibid.

79   Ibid., 57–58.

80   Hermann Kulke and Dietmar Rothermund, *A History of India* (Routledge, 2016), 344.

81   Smith, *The Oxford History of India*, 295.

82   Ibid., 310.

83   Ibid., 306.

84   Ibid., 307.

85   Goel, *The Story of Islamic Imperialism in India*, 57–58.

86   Ibid.

87   Kulke and Rothermund, *A History of India*, 361; Smith, *The Oxford History of India*, 350.

88   Smith, *The Oxford History of India*, 357.

89   Ibid., 358.

90   Kulke and Rothermund, *A History of India*, 368.

91   Smith, *The Oxford History of India*, 359–60.

92   Ibid., 360.

93   Shourie et al., *Hindu Temples*, 242.

94   *Memoirs of the Emperor Jahangueir, written by himself; and translated from a Persian manuscript, by Major David Price* (Oriental Translation Committee, 1829), 33.

95   Ibid.

96   Goel, *The Story of Islamic Imperialism in India*, 59; Smith, *The Oxford History of India*, 376.

97   Goel, *The Story of Islamic Imperialism in India*, 59.

98   Ibid.

99   Shourie et al., *Hindu Temples*, 272.

100   Ibid.

101   Ibid., 246.

102   Ibid., 266.

103   *Memoirs of the Emperor Jahangueir*, 14–15.

104   Ibid., 15.

105   Lal, *The Legacy of Muslim Rule in India*, 330.

106   Ibid., 271–72.

107   Abdul Hamid Lahori, *Badshanama of Abdul Hamid Lahori*, translated by Henry Miers Elliot (Hafiz Press, 1875), 39.

108   Ibid., 46.

109   Ibid., 55.

110   Shourie, et al., *Hindu Temples*, 278.

111   Smith, *The Oxford History of India*, 409.

112   Ibid., 411–15.

113   Shourie et al., *Hindu Temples*, 279; Goel, *The Story of Islamic Imperialism in India*, 61.

114   Ibid., 280.

115   Ibid., 61.

116   Ibid., 62.

117   Ibid., 280.

118   Ibid., 281; Goel, *The Story of Islamic Imperialism in India*, 62.

119   Shourie et al., *Hindu Temples*, 281.

120   Ibid.

121   Ibid.

122   Ibid.

123   Ibid., 284.

124   Ibid., 286.

125   Ibid., 285.

126   Goel, *The Story of Islamic Imperialism in India*, 63.

127   Shourie et al., *Hindu Temples*, 285.

128 Ibid.

129 Shourie et al., *Hindu Temples*, 288; Smith, *The Oxford History of India*, 438.

130 Kulke and Rothermund, *A History of India*, 379; Goel, *The Story of Islamic Imperialism in India*, 62.

131 Smith, *The Oxford History of India*, 438–39.

132 Shourie et al., *Hindu Temples*, 289.

133 Ibid., 282.

134 Ibid., 279.

Chapter Eight

1   "Sweden, the Ottoman Empire and the Crimean Tartars, c 1580-1714—The Realpolitik of a Christian Kingdom," *Världsinbördeskriget, February 14, 2011, https://varldsinbor-deskriget.wordpress.com/2011/02/14/sweden-the-ottoman-empire-and-the-crimean-tar-tars-c-1580-%E2%80%93-1714-%E2%80%93-the-realpolitik-of-a-christian-kingdom/.*

2   Kinross, *The Ottoman Centuries*, 372–73.

3   Ibid., 374–76.

4   Umar Busnavi, *History of the War in Bosnia During the Years 1737-1739*, translated by C. Fraser (Oriental Translation Fund, 1830), 2–3.

5   Ibid., 86.

6   Hamid Algar, *Wahhabism: A Critical Essay* (Islamic Publications International, 2002), 13.

7   Ibid., 13–14.

8   Bonney, *Jihad from Qur'an to bin Laden*, 159–60.

9   Algar, *Wahhabism*, 18.

10 Ibid., 18–19.

11 Ibid., 22–23.

12 Charles Allen, *God's Terrorists: The Wahhabi Cult and the Hidden Roots of Modern Jihad* (Da Capo Press, 2006), 61.

13 Kinross, *The Ottoman Centuries*, 395.

14 Ibid., 405.

15 Finkel, *Osman's Dream*, 383.

16 Ibid.

17 Andrew Roberts, *Napoleon: A Life* (Penguin, 2014), 201.

18 Ibid.

19 Ibid., 222.

20 Ibid., 199.

21 Ibid., 202.

22 Ibid., 200.

23 "Halabi, Suleiman al-," Damascus Online, https://web.archive.org/web/20091231235534/http://damascus-online.com/se/bio/halabi_suleiman.htm.

24 Andrew James McGregor, *A Military History of Modern Egypt: From the Ottoman Conquest to the Ramadan War* (Greenwood Publishing Group, 2006), 48.

25 Roberts, *Napoleon*, 199.

26 "Kuwaiti preacher, ISIS call for demolition of Egypt's Sphinx, pyramids," RT, March 9, 2015, https://www.rt.com/news/239093-islamist-calls-destroy-pyramids/.

27 Algar, *Wahhabism*, 21.

28 Ibid., 30.

29 Ibid., 37.

30 Ibid., 38.

31 Wheatcroft, *Infidels*, 233.

32 Thomas Gordon, *History of the Greek Revolution* (T. Cadell, 1833), 147.

33 Ibid., 148.

34 Ibid., 148–49.

35 Kinross, *The Ottoman Centuries*, 444.

36 Ibid.

37 Gordon, *History of the Greek Revolution*, 156.

38 Ibid.

39 Nomikos Michael Vaporis, *Witnesses for Christ: Orthodox Christians, Neomartyrs of the Ottoman Period 1437-1860* (St. Vladimir's Seminary Press, 2000), 340.

40 Ibid.; Gordon, *History of the Greek Revolution*, 187.

41 Gordon, *History of the Greek Revolution*, 187.

42 Kinross, *The Ottoman Centuries*, 477.

43 Ibid.

44 Ibid.

45 Ibid.

46 Bat Ye'or, *The Decline of Eastern Christianity Under Islam*, 399–400.

47 Ibid., 406.

48 Ibid., 417.

49 Finkel, *Osman's Dream*, 470–71.

50 Bonney, *Jihad from Qur'an to bin Laden*, 149.

51 Segal, *Islam's Black Slaves*, 132.

52 Ibid., 133.

53 Ibid., 133–34.

54 Bernard Lewis, *Race and Slavery in the Middle East* (Oxford University Press, 1994), http://www.fordham.edu/halsall/med/lewis1.html.

55 Ibid.

56 Segal, *Islam's Black Slaves*, 56.

57 Bat Ye'or, *The Dhimmi*, 321.

58 Tudor Parfitt, "*Dhimma* Versus Protection in Nineteenth Century Morocco," in *Israel and Ishmael: Studies in Muslim-Jewish Relations*, edited by Tudor Parfitt (Palgrave Macmillan, 2000), 157–59.

59 Vahakn N. Dadrian, *The History of the Armenian Genocide* (Berghahn Books, 1995), 147.

60   Ibid., 117.

61   Ibid.

62   Ibid.

63   Ibid.

64   Ibid.

65   Ibid.

66   Ibid., 144.

67   Ibid.

68   Ibid., 144–45.

69   Ibid., 146.

70   Kinross, *The Ottoman Centuries*, 560.

71   Dadrian, *The History of the Armenian Genocide*, 146.

72   Ibid.

73   Ibid., 169, note 121.

74   Andrew G. Bostom, "A Modern Jihad Genocide," FrontPageMagazine.com, April 28, 2003, http://archive.frontpagemag.com/readArticle.aspx?ARTID=18489.

75   Dadrian, *The History of the Armenian Genocide*, 156.

76   Ibid., 59.

77   Frank Lambert, *The Barbary Wars* (Hill and Wang, 2005), 4.

78   Ibid.

79   Ibid., 92–93.

80   "Treaty of Peace and Friendship between the United States of America and the Bey and Subjects of Tripoli of Barbary," Library of Congress, https://www.loc.gov/law/help/us-treaties/bevans/b-tripoli-ust000011-1070.pdf.

81   Ibid.

82   Ibid.

83   United States Department of State, *The Diplomatic Correspondence of the United States of America*, vol. 1 (Blair & Rives, 1837), 605.

84   Shourie et al., *Hindu Temples*, 287.

85   Ibid.

86   Ibid.

87   Ibid., 287–88.

88   Smith, *The Oxford History of India*, 462.

89   Bonney, *Jihad from Qur'an to bin Laden*, 101.

90   Ibid., 102.

91   Ibid., 103.

92   Ibid., 104.

93   Smith, *The Oxford History of India*, 462.

94   Ibid., 465.

95 Rudolph Peters, *Islam and Colonialism: The Doctrine of Jihad in Modern History* (Mouton Publishers, 1979), 46.

96 Ibid., 47.

97 Ibid.

98 Ibid., 48–49.

99 Ibid., 50–51.

100 Al-Misri, *Reliance of the Traveller*, section o9.2.

101 Peters, *Islam and Colonialism*, 51.

102 Ibid., 51–52.

103 Muslim ibn al-Hajjaj, *Sahih Muslim*, rev. ed., translated by Abdul Hamid Siddiqi (Kitab Bhavan, 2000), no. 4553.

104 Sanjeev Nayyar, "So who was really responsible for Partition?" Rediff News, September 17, 2009, http://news.rediff.com/column/2009/sep/17/so-who-was-really-responsible-for-partition.htm.

105 Ibid.

106 Peters, *Islam and Colonialism*, 54–55.

107 Ibid., 56.

108 Ibid., 54–55.

109 Bonney, *Jihad from Qur'an to bin Laden*, 183–84.

110 Daniel Allen Butler, *The First Jihad: The Battle for Khartoum and the Dawn of Militant Islam* (Casemate, 2006), 42.

111 Ibid., 43.

112 Peters, *Islam and Colonialism*, 66–67.

113 Ibid., 69.

114 Ibid., 70.

115 Ibid., 79.

116 Butler, *The First Jihad*, 53–54.

117 Peters, *Islam and Colonialism*, 67.

118 Butler, *The First Jihad*, 105.

119 Ibid.

120 Ibid., 195–96.

Chapter Nine

1 Al-Misri, *Reliance of the Traveller*, section o9.1.

2 Ibid.

3 Rudolph Peters, *Jihad in Classical and Modern Islam: A Reader* (Markus Wiener Publishers, 1996), 53.

4 Peters, *Islam and Colonialism*, 86.

5 Ibid., 87.

6 Ibid., 90.

7   Ibid.

8   Niall Ferguson, *The War of the World: Twentieth-century Conflict and the Descent of the West* (Penguin, 2006), 180.

9   Manus I. Midlarsky, *The Killing Trap: Genocide in the Twentieth Century* (Cambridge University Press, 2005), 342.

10   "Turks Are Evicting Native Christians: Greeks and Armenians Driven From Homes and Converted by the Sword, Assert Americans," *The New York Times*, July 11, 1915.

11   Bonney, *Jihad from Qur'an to bin Laden*, 150–51.

12   Ibid., 151.

13   "Turkish Massacres: 47,000 Refugees Reach Mesopotamia," *The Times* (London), October 11, 1918.

14   "Turks are Evicting Native Christians," *The New York Times*, July 11, 1915.

15   "Frequently Asked Questions about the Armenian Genocide," Armenian National Institute, http://www.armenian-genocide.org/genocidefaq.html; "700,000 Greeks Victims of Turks," *The New York Times*, July 10, 1921.

16   Philip Mansel, *Constantinople: City of the World's Desire, 1453-1924* (St. Martin's Griffin, 1995), 437.

17   "1930: The City of Constantinople Renamed to 'Istanbul,'" History.info, http://history.info/on-this-day/1930-the-city-of-constantinople-renamed-to-istanbul/.

18   Kevork B. Bardakjian, *Hitler and the Armenian Genocide* (Zoryan Institute, 1985), 17.

19   Kinross, *The Ottoman Centuries*, 410.

20   H. C. Armstrong, *The Gray Wolf* (Penguin Books, 1937), 206.

21   Ibid.

22   Mansel, *Constantinople*, 414.

23   Armstrong, *The Gray Wolf*, 205.

24   Alexei Vassiliev, *The History of Saudi Arabia* (New York University Press, 2000), 212–13.

25   Ibid., 221.

26   Ibid.

27   Ibid., 233.

28   Ibid., 284.

29   Ibid., 295.

30   Will Martin, "From an unexplored desert to a $2 trillion IPO: The 84-year history of Saudi Aramco in pictures," Business Insider, December 4, 2017, https://www.businessinsider.my/the-history-of-saudi-aramco-timeline-2017-11/.

31   Malo Tresca, "How Saudi Arabia exports Wahhabism," LaCroix International, August 22, 2017, https://international.la-croix.com/news/how-saudi-arabia-exports-wahhabism/5095.

32   Carlotta Gall, "How Kosovo Was Turned Into Fertile Ground for ISIS," *The New York Times*, May 21, 2016.

33   Ibid.

34   Ibid.

35   Tresca, "How Saudi Arabia exports Wahhabism."

36 "What is Wahhabism? The reactionary branch of Islam from Saudi Arabia said to be 'the main source of global terrorism,'" *The Telegraph*, May 19, 2017, https://www.telegraph.co.uk/news/2016/03/29/what-is-wahhabism-the-reactionary-branch-of-islam-said-to-be-the/.

37 Brynjar Lia, *The Society of the Muslim Brothers in Egypt* (Ithaca Press, 1998), 28.

38 Ibid.

39 Ibid., 33.

40 Ibid., 68–69, 75–76.

41 Ibid., 80.

42 Ibid., 153–54.

43 Ibid., 155.

44 Jonathan Raban, "Truly, madly, deeply devout," *The Guardian*, March 2, 2002.

45 John Roy Carlson, *Cairo to Damascus* (Alfred A. Knopf, 1951), 89–90.

46 Shaker El-sayed, "Hassan al-Banna: The leader and the Movement," Muslim American Society, http://www.maschicago.org/library/misc_articles/hassan_banna.htm.

47 Carlson, *Cairo to Damascus*, 91.

48 Ibid., 91–92.

49 Robert Irwin, "Is this the man who inspired Bin Laden?" *The Guardian*, November 1, 2001.

50 John Calvert, "'The World is an Undutiful Boy!' Sayyid Qutb's American experience," *Islam and Christian-Muslim Relations* 11, no. 1 (2000): 95, 99, 100.

51 Ibid.

52 Ibid.

53 Ibid.

54 Sayyid Qutb, *Milestones,* The Mother Mosque Foundation, n.d., 7.

55 Ibid., 10–11.

56 Ibid., 58.

57 Ibid., 58–59.

58 Ibid., 59–60.

59 Carlson, *Cairo to Damascus*, 92.

60 Ibid., 90–91.

61 Martin Kramer, "Fundamentalist Islam at Large: The Drive for Power," *Middle East Quarterly* (June 1996).

62 Calvert, "'The World is an Undutiful Boy!" 94.

63 David Pryce-Jones, *The Closed Circle: An Interpretation of the Arabs* (Ivan R. Dee, 2002), 251–52.

64 Lawrence Wright, *The Looming Tower: Al-Qaeda and the Road to 9/11* (Vintage Books, 1996), 36.

65 Ibid.

66 Edy Cohen, "How the Mufti of Jerusalem Created the Permanent Problem of Palestinian Violence," The Tower, November 2015, http://www.thetower.org/article/how-the-mufti-of-jerusalem-created-the-permanent-problem-of-palestinian-violence/.

67   Ibid.

68   Ibid.

69   Jeffrey Herf, "Haj Amin al-Husseini, the Nazis and the Holocaust: The Origins, Nature and Aftereffects of Collaboration," Jerusalem Center for Public Affairs, January 5, 2016, http://jcpa.org/article/haj-amin-al-husseini-the-nazis-and-the-holocaust-the-origins-nature-and-aftereffects-of-collaboration/.

70   Saul S. Friedman, A History of the Middle East (McFarland, 2006), 243; David G. Dalin, "Hitler's Mufti," First Things, August 2005, https://www.firstthings.com/article/2005/08/hitlers-mufti.

71   Jeffrey Herf, Nazi Propaganda for the Arab World (Yale University Press, 2009), 125–26.

72   "The Arab Higher Committee: its origins, personnel and purposes, the documentary record submitted to the United Nations, May, 1947," (The Nation Associates, 1947).

73   Ibid.

74   Friedman, A History of the Middle East, 243.

75   Dalin, "Hitler's Mufti."

76   Gilbert Achcar, The Arabs and the Holocaust: The Arab-Israeli War of Narratives (Henry Holt and Company, 2010), 157.

77   "Hajj Amin al-Husayni: Arab Nationalist and Muslim Leader," United States Holocaust Memorial Museum, https://www.ushmm.org/wlc/en/article.php?ModuleId=10007666.

78   Dalin, "Hitler's Mufti."

79   Ibid.

80   Richard Paul Mitchell, The Society of the Muslim Brothers (Oxford University Press, 1993), 56.

81   Ibid.

82   Joseph Lelyveld, His Final Battle: The Last Months of Franklin Roosevelt (Knopf Doubleday Publishing Group, 2017), 79.

83   Joseph B. Schechtman, The United States and the Jewish State Movement: The Crucial Decade, 1939-1949 (Herzl Press, 1966), 110.

84   Friedman, A History of the Middle East, 249.

85   David Barnett and Efraim Karsh, "Azzam's Genocidal Threat," Middle East Quarterly (Fall 2011): 85–88.

86   Friedman, A History of the Middle East, 249.

87   Ibid.

88   Bruce Hoffman, Anonymous Soldiers: The Struggle for Israel, 1917-1947 (Knopf Doubleday Publishing Group, 2015), 10.

89   Mark Urban, Generals: Ten British Commanders Who Shaped the World (Faber and Faber, 2005), 233.

90   Bruce Hoffman, Anonymous Soldiers, 10–11.

91   Carlson, Cairo to Damascus, 110.

92   Ibid., 163.

93   Ibid., 60.

94   Al-Bukhari, Sahih al-Bukhari, vol. 4, bk. 56, no. 3030.

95   Jamie Glazov, "From Russia With Terror," FrontPageMagazine.com, March 31, 2004, http://archive.frontpagemag.com/readArticle.aspx?ARTID=13975.

96   Ion Mihai Pacepa, "The KGB's Man," *The Wall Street Journal*, September 22, 2003.

97   Ion Mihai Pacepa, "Russian Footprints," *National Review*, August 24, 2006.

98   James Dorsey, "Wij zijn alleen Palestijn om politieke redden," Trouw, March 31, 1977. https://brabosh.com/2016/02/18/pqpct-bbo/

99   Ion Mihai Pacepa, "The KGB's Man."

100   "The Charter of Allah: The Platform of the Islamic Resistance movement (Hamas)," translated and annotated by Raphael Israeli, The International Policy Institute for Counter-Terrorism, April 5, 1998. http://www.ict.org.il/documents/documentdet.cfm?docid=14.

101   Ibid.

102   Ibid.

103   Ibid.

104   Ibid.

105   Ibid.

106   Ibid.

107   Esther Schapira and Georg M. Hafner, *Muhammad Al Dura: the TV Drama: Our Search for the Truth in the Middle East Media War* (La Maison d'Edition, 2016).

108   Sanjeev Nayyar, "So who was really responsible for Partition?" Rediff News, September 17, 2009, http://www.rediff.com/news/column/so-who-was-really-responsible-for-partition/20090917.htm.

109   Jeff Kingston, "The unfinished business of Indian partition," *The Japan Times*, August 12, 2017.

110   Shamil Shams, "India's partition and 70 years of proxy jihad," DW, August 14, 2017, http://www.dw.com/en/indias-partition-and-70-years-of-proxy-jihad/a-40083688.

111   Ibid.

112   Ibid.

113   Praveen Swami, *India, Pakistan and the Secret Jihad: The Covert War in Kashmir, 1947-2004*, (Routledge, 2006), 53–54.

114   Hari Om Mahajan, "What's political now? It's Islamic jihad," The Pioneer, May 26, 2017, http://www.dailypioneer.com/columnists/big-story/whats-political-now-its-islamic-jihad.html.

115   Baqer Moin, *Khomeini: Life of the Ayatollah* (St. Martin's Press, 1999), 75.

116   Ibid., 78.

117   Ibid., 84.

118   Ibid., 88.

119   Ruhollah Khomeini, "Islamic Government," in *Islam and Revolution: Writings and Declarations of Imam Khomeini*, translated by Hamid Algar (Mizan, 1981), 40.

120   Ibid.

121   Ibid., 55.

122   Homa Katouzian, *The Persians: Ancient, Medieval and Modern Iran* (Yale University Press, 2009), 322.

123 Ibid.

124 Mark Bowden, *Guests of the Ayatollah: The Iran Hostage Crisis—The First Battle in America's War with Militant Islam* (Grove/Atlantic, 2006), 70.

125 James Buchan, *Days of God: The Revolution In Iran and Its Consequences* (Simon & Schuster, 2012), 257.

126 Ibid., 265.

127 Moin, *Khomeini*, 228.

128 "Iran Hostage Crisis Fast Facts," CNN, December 25, 2015, updated October 20, 2017, https://www.cnn.com/2013/09/15/world/meast/iran-hostage-crisis-fast-facts/index.html.

129 Elaine Sciolino, *Persian Mirrors: The Elusive Face of Iran* (Free Press, 2000), 68.

130 Shaul Bakhash, *The Reign of the Ayatollahs: Iran and the Islamic Revolution* (Basic Books, 1990), 111, 221–22; Moin, *Khomeini*, 219–20.

131 Moin, *Khomeini*, 219.

132 Amir Taheri, *The Spirit of Allah: Khomeini and the Islamic Revolution* (Hutchinson, 1985), 20, 45.

133 Amir Taheri, *Holy Terror: Inside the World of Islamic Terrorism* (Sphere, 1987), 225–26.

134 Ibid., 226–27.

135 Taheri, *The Spirit of Allah*, 263–64.

136 "Iran Responsible for 1983 Marine Barracks Bombing, Judge Rules," CNN, May 30, 2003, https://archive.li/TX460.

137 Gordon Thomas, "William Buckley: The Spy Who Never Came in from the Cold," Canada Free Press, October 25, 2006, https://canadafreepress.com/2006/thomas102506.htm.

138 Ibid.

139 "Hizballah's Brash U.S. Supporters," IPT News, November 18, 2010, https://www.investigativeproject.org/2331/hizballah-brash-us-supporters; "Hassan Nasrallah: In His Own Words," Committee for Accuracy in Middle East Reporting in America (CAMERA), July 26, 2006, http://www.camera.org/index.asp?x_context=7&x_issue=11&x_article=1158.

140 Phil Hirschkorn, Rohan Gunaratna, Ed Blanche, and Stefan Leader, "Blowback," *Jane's Intelligence Review*, August 1, 2001.

141 Al-Misri, *Reliance of the Traveller*, section k29.5; r40,1–3.

142 Abdullah Azzam, "Who was Abdullah Azzam?" in *Join the Caravan* (Azzam Publications, 2001), 8.

143 Ibid., 9.

144 Tayseer Allouni with Usamah bin Laden, "A Discussion on the New Crusader Wars," translated by Muawiya ibn Abi Sufyan (Markaz Derasat, October 2001). Pious exclamations of peace upon Muhammad removed for ease of reading.

145 Azzam, *Join the Caravan*, 51.

146 Al-Bukhari, *Sahih al-Bukhari*, vol. 4, bk. 56, no. 2790; *cf.* Azzam, *Join the Caravan*, 40.

147 Tawfiq Tabib, "Interview with Sheikh al-Mujahideen Abu Abdel Aziz," *Al-Sirat Al-Mustaqeem* [The straight path], August 1994, http://www.seprin.com/laden/barbaros.html.

148 Azzam, *Join the Caravan*, 39.

149 Ibid., 39.

150 Ibid., 23.

151 "What is Wahhabism? The reactionary branch of Islam from Saudi Arabia said to be 'the main source of global terrorism,'" *The Telegraph*, May 19, 2017.

152 Andrew Wander, "A history of terror: Al-Qaeda 1988-2008," *The Guardian*, July 12, 2008, https://www.theguardian.com/world/2008/jul/13/history.alqaida.

153 Gilles Kepel, *Jihad: The Trail of Political Islam*, translated by Anthony F. Roberts (The Belknap Press, 2002), 250.

154 Tabib, "Interview with Sheikh al-Mujahideen Abu Abdel Aziz."

155 Kerim Fenari, "The Jihad of Imam Shamyl," Q-News, http://www.amina.com/article/jihad_imamshamyl.html.

156 Mark Riebling and R. P. Eddy, "Jihad @ Work," *National Review*, October 24, 2002.

157 Osama bin Laden, "Declaration of War against the Americans Occupying the Land of the Two Holy Places," August 1996, https://is.muni.cz/el/1423/jaro2010/MVZ203/OBL___AQ__Fatwa_1996.pdf.

158 Ibid.

159 Ibid.

160 Ibid.

161 World Islamic Front, "Jihad Against Jews and Crusaders," February 23, 1998, https://fas.org/irp/world/para/docs/980223-fatwa.htm.

162 Ibid.

163 Ibid.

164 Wander, "A history of terror."

165 Bill Clinton, "Remarks by the President to the Opening Session of the 53rd United Nations General Assembly," White House Press Release, September 21, 1998.

Chapter Ten

1 "Bin Laden: Goal is to bankrupt U.S.," CNN, November 1, 2004, http://www.cnn.com/2004/WORLD/meast/11/01/binladen.tape/.

2 Ibid.

3 Ibid.

4 Osama bin Laden, "Letter to the American People," *The Guardian*, November 24, 2002, https://www.theguardian.com/world/2002/nov/24/theobserver.

5 Ibid.

6 Khalid Sheikh Mohammed, Walid bin 'Attash, Ramzi bin As-Shibh, 'Ali 'Abd Al-'Aziz 'Ali, and "Mustafa Ahmed Al-Hawsawi, "The Islamic Response to the Government's Nine Accusations," Jihad Watch, March 11, 2009. https://www.jihadwatch.org/2009/03/911-defendants-we-ask-to-be-near-to-god-we-fight-you-and-destroy-you-and-terrorize-you-the-jihad-in

7 "'Islam is Peace' Says President: Remarks by the President at Islamic Center of Washington, D.C.," The White House, September 17, 2001. https://georgewbush-whitehouse.archives.gov/news/releases/2001/09/20010917-11.html.

8 Ibid.

9 Jim Sciutto, Ryan Browne, and Deirdre Walsh, "Congress releases secret '28 pages' on

alleged Saudi 9/11 ties," CNN, July 15, 2016, https://www.cnn.com/2016/07/15/politics/congress-releases-28-pages-saudis-9-11/index.html; Fred Kaplan, "The Idealist in the Bluebonnets: What Bush's meeting with the Saudi ruler really means," *Slate*, April 26, 2005. http://www.slate.com/articles/news_and_politics/war_stories/2005/04/the_idealist_in_the_bluebonnets.html; Alex Spillius, "Barack Obama criticised for 'bowing' to King Abdullah of Saudi Arabia," *The Telegraph*, April 8, 2009, https://www.telegraph.co.uk/news/worldnews/barackobama/5128171/Barack-Obama-criticised-for-bowing-to-King-Abdullah-of-Saudi-Arabia.html.

10   "Declassified '28 pages' on 9/11—full text," CNN, July 15, 2016, https://www.cnn.com/2016/07/15/politics/28-pages-released-full-text/index.html.

11   Ibid.

12   Ibid.

13   Ibid.

14   Rowan Scarborough, "Saudi government funded extremism in U.S. mosques and charities: report," *The Washington Times*, July 19, 2016, https://www.washingtontimes.com/news/2016/jul/19/911-report-details-saudi-arabia-funding-of-muslim-/.

15   "Declassified '28 pages' on 9/11," CNN.

16   Ibid.

17   Ibid.

18   Helene Cooper and Jim Rutenberg, "A Saudi Prince Tied to Bush Is Sounding Off-Key," *The New York Times*, April 29, 2007, http://www.nytimes.com/2007/04/29/washington/29saudi.html.

19   Scarborough, "Saudi government funded extremism in U.S. mosques and charities: report."

20   "Declassified '28 pages' on 9/11," CNN.

21   Ibid.

22   Ibid.

23   Ibid.

24   Ibid.

25   Ibid.

26   Ibid.

27   Scarborough, "Saudi government funded extremism in U.S. mosques and charities: report."

28   Ibid.

29   David Aufhauser, "An Assessment of Current Efforts to Combat Terrorism Financing," testimony of Hon. David D Aufhauser (Government Printing Office, June 15, 2004), 46. Hearing before the Committee on Governmental Affairs, United States Senate. https://www.gpo.gov/fdsys/pkg/CHRG-108shrg95189/html/CHRG-108shrg95189.htm

30   Haviv Rettig, "Expert: Saudis have radicalized 80% of US mosques," *The Jerusalem Post*, December 5, 2005, http://www.jpost.com/International/Expert-Saudis-have-radicalized-80-percent-of-US-mosques.

31   Justin Huggler, "German vice-chancellor accuses Saudi Arabia of funding Islamic extremism in the West," *The Telegraph*, December 6, 2015, https://www.telegraph.co.uk/news/worldnews/europe/germany/12035838/German-vice-chancellor-accuses-Saudi-Arabia-of-funding-Islamic-extremism-in-the-West.html.

32   "Extremist Recruitment on the Rise in Southern Punjab," WikiLeaks, November 13, 2008, https://wikileaks.org/plusd/cables/08LAHORE302_a.html.

33   Office of the Secretary of State, "Terrorist Finance: Action Request for Senior Level Engagement on Terrorism Finance,'" WikiLeaks, December 30, 2009, https://wikileaks.org/plusd/cables/09STATE131801_a.html.

34   Zaid Jilani, "In Secret Goldman Sachs Speech, Hillary Clinton Admitted No-Fly Zone Would 'Kill a Lot of Syrians,'" The Intercept, October 10, 2016, https://theintercept.com/2016/10/10/in-secret-goldman-sachs-speech-hillary-clinton-admitted-no-fly-zone-would-kill-a-lot-of-syrians/.

35   "U.S. District Court Rules Iran Behind 9/11 Attacks," PR Newswire, December 23, 2011, https://www.prnewswire.com/news-releases/us-district-court-rules-iran-behind-911-attacks-136148008.html.

36   Ibid.

37   Ibid.

38   Ibid.

39   Ibid.

40   Kenneth R. Timmerman, "Iran's Dirty 9/11 Secrets," Frontpage Mag, September 8, 2011, https://www.frontpagemag.com/fpm/104395/irans-dirty-911-secrets-kenneth-r-timmerman.

41   Ibid.

42   "U.S. District Court Rules Iran Behind 9/11 Attacks," PR Newswire.

43   Timmerman, "Iran's Dirty 9/11 Secrets."

44   Ibid.

45   "U.S. District Court Rules Iran Behind 9/11 Attacks," PR Newswire.

46   United States District Court, Southern District of New York, affidavit of Clare M. Lopez and Dr. Bruce D. Tefft, March 26, 2010. https://www.yumpu.com/en/document/view/51049000/affidavit-of-clare-m-lopez-and-dr-bruce-d-tefft-iran-911-case

47   Timmerman, "Iran's Dirty 9/11 Secrets."

48   "U.S. District Court Rules Iran Behind 9/11 Attacks," PR Newswire.

49   "9/11 Lawsuit: Federal Court Awards $7 billion in final judgment against Iran and Hezbollah," Winder & Counsel, n.d., http://www.winderfirm.com/library/9-11-lawsuit-federal-court-awards-7-billion-in-final-judgment.html.

50   Daniel Beekman, "Terrorism Victims Win Right to Seize $500M Midtown Office Tower Linked to Iran after Long Legal Battle," The New York Daily News, April 2, 2014.

51   Josie Ensor, "Trove of Bin Laden documents reveal Iran's secret dealings with al-Qaeda," The Telegraph, November 1, 2017, https://www.telegraph.co.uk/news/2017/11/01/iran-relationship-al-qaeda-revealed-newly-released-trove-bin/.

52   Helen Kennedy, "Israel Foe's Donation Draws Flak," The New York Daily News, January 10, 2002.

53   Ibid.; Kate O'Beirne, "The Chaplain Problem," National Review, October 27, 2003.

54   "Rally at Lafayette Park: Alamoudi," IPT, October 28, 2000, https://www.investigative-project.org/218/rally-at-lafayette-park-alamoudi.

55   Ibid.

56   Ibid.

57   Matt Continetti, "Mueller's Misstep: The FBI director befriends apologists for terror," *National Review*, June 12, 2002.

58   Mary Beth Sheridan and Douglas Farah, "Jailed Muslim Had Made a Name in Washington: Alamoudi Won Respect as a Moderate Advocate," *The Washington Post*, December 1, 2003.

59   "Abdurahman Alamoudi Sentenced to Jail in Terrorism Financing Case," Department of Justice press release, October 15, 2004.

60   "Alamoudi Sentence Cut by Six Years," IPT, July 25, 2011, https://www.investigativeproject.org/3059/alamoudi-sentence-cut-by-six-years.

61   Interview with Dick Cheney, moderated by Tim Russert, *Meet the Press*, September 14, 2003; transcript at http://www.nbcnews.com/id/3080244/ns/meet_the_press/t/transcript-sept/#.WpYG-hPwaV4.

62   Mohamed Akram, "An Explanatory Memorandum on the General Strategic Goal for the Group in North America," May 22, 1991, Government Exhibit 003-0085, U.S. vs. HLF, et al. 7 (21).

63   Ibid.

64   Ibid.

65   United States Department of State, *The Diplomatic Correspondence of the United States of America*, vol. 1, 605.

66   Barack Obama, "Remarks by the President on a New Beginning," The White House, June 4, 2009.

67   "Obama: 'The future must not belong to those who slander the prophet of Islam,'" *The Washington Post*, September 26, 2012.

68   Tomer Ovadia, "Rep. Keith Ellison: Bachmann 'wanted attention,'" Politico, July 20, 2012. https://www.politico.com/story/2012/07/ellison-bachmann-wanted-attention-078784

69   Jennifer Bendery, "Keith Ellison: Michele Bachmann Thinks Muslims 'Are Evil,'" Huffington Post, July 19, 2012, https://www.huffingtonpost.com/2012/07/19/keith-ellison-michele-bachmann_n_1688150.html.

70   "Democrats' dilemma," *The Washington Times*, September 24, 2006.

71   Patrick Poole, "Rep. Keith Ellison Rewrites History on his Muslim Brotherhood, CAIR Ties," PJ Media, July 21, 2012, https://pjmedia.com/blog/rep-keith-ellison-rewrites-history-on-his-muslim-brotherhood-cair-ties/.

72   Ibid.

73   Mitch Anderson, "Ellison: Hajj was transformative," *StarTribune* (Minneapolis/St. Paul), December 18, 2008.

74   Ahmed Shawki, "A man and 6 of the Brotherhood in the White House!" *Rose El-Youssef*, December 22, 2012. http://www.investigativeproject.org/3868/a-man-and-6-of-the-brotherhood-in-the-white-house.

75   Ibid.

76   Robert Spencer, "Dhimmitude and stealth jihad at Fort Hood," Jihad Watch, December 2, 2009 https://www.jihadwatch.org/2009/12/dhimmitude-and-stealth-jihad-at-fort-hood; Brooks Egerton, "Syrian opposition figure trained U.S. soldiers but was suspended over extremist ties after Fort Hood massacre," Dallas Morning News,

September 5, 2013. https://www.dallasnews.com/news/watchdog/2013/09/05/syrian-opposition-figure-trained-u-s-soldiers-but-was-suspended-over-extremist-ties-after-fort-hood-massacre

77   Ben Hubbard, "Islamist Rebels Create Dilemma on Syria Policy," *The New York Times*, April 27, 2013.

78   Adam Kredo, "Muslim Brotherhood Official, Former Clinton Foundation Employee Arrested," Washington Free Beacon, September 18, 2013, http://freebeacon.com/national-security/muslim-brotherhood-official-former-clinton-foundation-employee-arrested/.

79   Ibid.

80   Eileen F. Toplansky, "The Muslim Brotherhood and Weiner," American Thinker, June 19, 2011, https://www.americanthinker.com/articles/2011/06/the_muslim_brotherhood_and_weiner.html.

81   "Huma Abedin & Hillary Clinton—Abedin Family Ties to Al-Qaeda," Free Republic, November 11, 2007, http://www.freerepublic.com/focus/f-news/1924323/posts.

82   Andrew C. McCarthy, "The Huma Unmentionables," *National Review*, July 24, 2013, https://www.nationalreview.com/blog/corner/huma-unmentionables-andrew-c-mccarthy/.

83   "FBI removes hundreds of training documents after probe on treatment of Islam," Fox News, February 21, 2012, http://www.foxnews.com/politics/2012/02/21/fbi-purges-hundreds-training-documents-after-probe-on-treatment-islam.html.

84   "CAIR: Jesse Jackson, ICNA Endorse Letter on Anti-Islam FBI Training," Council on American-Islamic Relations press release, August 6, 2010.

85   Spencer Ackerman, "FBI Teaches Agents: 'Mainstream' Muslims Are 'Violent, Radical,'" Wired, September 14, 2011, https://www.wired.com/2011/09/fbi-muslims-radical/.

86   Associated Press, "FBI drops lecture that was critical of Islam," NDTV, September 16, 2011, https://www.ndtv.com/world-news/fbi-drops-lecture-that-was-critical-of-islam-467796.

87   Salam al-Marayati, "The wrong way to fight terrorism," *The Los Angeles Times*, October 19, 2011.

88   "Letter to DHS John Brennan on FBI's Use of Biased Experts and Training Materials," Muslim Advocates, October 27, 2011. https://www.muslimadvocates.org/letter-to-dhs-john-brennan-on-fbis-use-of-biased-experts-and-training-materials/

89   Ibid.

90   Ibid.

91   Letter from John Brennan to Farhana Khera, November 3, 2011, in "Emerson, IPT Expose Brennan Letter: FBI Training 'Substandard and Offensive' to Muslims" by AWR Hawkins, Breitbart, February 8, 2013, http://www.breitbart.com/big-government/2013/02/08/nov-3-2011-letter-from-john-brennan-capitulating-to-muslim-complaints-against-fbi/.

92   Ibid.

93   Ibid.

94   John Brennan, "A New Approach for Safeguarding Americans," Center for Strategic and International Studies, August 6, 2009, http://csis.org/files/attachments/090806_brennan_transcript.pdf.

95   Steven Emerson and John Rossomando, "Obama CIA Nominee John Brennan Wrong for the Job," IPT, February 5, 2013, https://www.investigativeproject.org/3902/obama-cia-nominee-john-brennan-wrong-for-the-job.

96 "Counterterror Adviser Defends Jihad as 'Legitimate Tenet of Islam,'" Fox News, May 27, 2010, http://www.foxnews.com/politics/2010/05/27/counterterror-adviser-defends-jihad-legitimate-tenet-islam.html.

97 "CAIR Welcomes New Security Strategy's Focus on Confronting Al-Qaeda," Council on American-Islamic Relations press release, May 27, 2010, http://cairunmasked.org/wp-content/uploads/2010/06/quote.pdf.

98 John Brennan, "Securing the Homeland by Renewing America's Strengths, Resilience, and Values," Center for Strategic and International Studies, May 26, 2010, http://www.whitehouse.gov/the-press-office/remarks-assistant-president-homeland-security-and-counterterrorism-john-brennan-csi.

99 "WH counter-terrorism adviser Brennan storms out of TWT offices," The Washington Times, August 23, 2010.

100 Ibid.

101 Ibid.

102 Ibid.

103 Manasi Gopalakrishnan, "'Islamic State' reportedly training terrorists to enter Europe as asylum seekers," DW, November 14, 2016, http://www.dw.com/en/islamic-state-reportedly-training-terrorists-to-enter-europe-as-asylum-seekers/a-36389389.

104 Jacob Bojesson, "German Intel Agency Says Hundreds of Jihadis Arrived Among Refugees," The Daily Caller, July 5, 2017, http://dailycaller.com/2017/07/05/german-intel-agency-says-hundreds-of-jihadis-arrived-among-refugees/.

105 Julian Robinson, "Angela Merkel under more pressure over refugee policy as it is revealed migrants committed 142,500 crimes in Germany during the first six months of 2016," Daily Mail, November 1, 2016, http://www.dailymail.co.uk/news/article-3893436/Angela-Merkel-pressure-refugee-policy-revealed-migrants-committed-142-500-crimes-Germany-six-months-2016.html.

106 Ivar Arpi, "It's not only Germany that covers up mass sex attacks by migrant men… Sweden's record is shameful," The Spectator, December 27, 2016, https://www.spectator.co.uk/2016/01/its-not-only-germany-that-covers-up-mass-sex-attacks-by-migrant-men-swedens-record-is-shameful/.

107 "Opinion: Welcome to Sweden, the rape capital of the world," NA, February 28, 2017, http://www.na.se/opinion/ledare/opinion-welcome-to-sweden-the-rape-capital-of-the-world.

108 Michael Qazvini, "How Muslim Migration Made Malmo, Sweden a Crime Capital," Daily Wire, January 16, 2017, https://www.dailywire.com/news/12466/how-muslim-migration-made-malmo-sweden-crime-michael-qazvini.

109 Nicolai Sennels, "Dangerous refugees: Afghan Muslim migrants 79 times more likely to rape," Jihad Watch, July 1, 2017, https://www.jihadwatch.org/2017/07/dangerous-refugees-afghan-muslim-migrants-79-times-more-likely-to-rape.

110 "Rotherham child abuse scandal: 1,400 children exploited, report finds," BBC News, August 26, 2014, http://www.bbc.com/news/uk-england-south-yorkshire-28939089.

111 Przemek Skwirczynski, "Polish MP: Germans Going to Great Lengths to Cover Crimes of Their Arab Guests," Breitbart, July 30, 2016, http://www.breitbart.com/london/2016/07/30/polish-mp-germans-going-great-lengths-cover-crimes-arab-guests/.

112 Liam Deacon, "Claim: Dutch Police Bribe Newspaper to Bury Data on Criminal Asylum Seekers," Breitbart, May 4, 2017, http://www.breitbart.com/london/2017/05/04/

dutch-police-allegedly-bribe-newspaper-to-bury-data-on-criminal-asylum-seekers/; Donna Rachel Edmunds, "Swedish Police Stop Reporting Suspects' Ethnicity for Fear of Being Branded Racist," Breitbart, January 15, 2016, http://www.breitbart.com/london/2016/01/15/2784799/.

113   Pope Francis, "Apostolic Exhortation Evangelii Gaudium of the Holy Father Francis to the Bishops, Clergy, Consecrated Persons and the Lay Faithful on the Proclamation of the Gospel in Today's World," The Holy See, November 24, 2013, http://w2.vatican.va/content/francesco/en/apost_exhortations/documents/papa-francesco_esortazione-ap_20131124_evangelii-gaudium.html.

114   Philip Pullella, "After Paris attacks, Pope speaks out against insulting religions," Reuters, January 15, 2015, https://uk.reuters.com/article/uk-france-shooting-pope/after-paris-attacks-pope-speaks-out-against-insulting-religions-idUKKBN0KO16Q20150115.

115   Pope Francis, "Message of His Holiness Pope Francis on the Occasion of the World Meetings of Popular Movements in Modesto (California) [16-18 February 2017]," The Holy See, February 10, 2017, https://w2.vatican.va/content/francesco/en/messages/pont-messages/2017/documents/papa-francesco_20170210_movimenti-popolari-modesto.html.

116   Ibid.

117   Elise Harris, "Vatican, al-Azhar focus on papal trip speeches in latest meeting," Catholic News Agency, July 7, 2017, https://www.catholicnewsagency.com/news/vatican-al-azhar-focus-on-papal-trip-speeches-in-latest-meeting-88693.

118   Thomas D. Williams, "Pope Francis Welcomes Leader of Muslim World League to Vatican," Breitbart, September 21, 2017, http://www.breitbart.com/national-security/2017/09/21/pope-francis-welcomes-leader-of-muslim-world-league-to-vatican/.

119   Ibid.

120   "Message of His Holiness Pope Francis For the Celebration of the 51st World Day of Peace," The Holy See, January 1, 2018, http://w2.vatican.va/content/francesco/en/messages/peace/documents/papa-francesco_20171113_messaggio-51giornatamondiale-pace2018.html.

121   Gopalakrishnan, "'Islamic State' reportedly training terrorists to enter Europe as asylum seekers."

122   Hannah Roberts, "ISIS threatens to send 500,000 migrants to Europe as a 'psychological weapon' in chilling echo of Gaddafi's prophecy that the Mediterranean 'will become a sea of chaos,'" Daily Mail, February 18, 2015, http://www.dailymail.co.uk/news/article-2958517/The-Mediterranean-sea-chaos-Gaddafi-s-chilling-prophecy-interview-ISIS-threatens-send-500-000-migrants-Europe-psychological-weapon-bombed.html.

123   Jack Blanchard, "Officials warn 20,000 ISIS jihadis 'have infiltrated Syrian refugee camps,'" Mirror, September 14, 2015, https://www.mirror.co.uk/news/uk-news/officials-warn-20000-isis-jihadis-6443516.

124   Ian Drury, "Four out of five migrants are *not* from Syria: EU figures expose the 'lie' that the majority of refugees are fleeing war zone," Daily Mail, September 18, 2015, http://www.dailymail.co.uk/news/article-3240010/Number-refugees-arriving-Europe-soars-85-year-just-one-five-war-torn-Syria.html.

125   Aaron Brown, "'Just wait…' Islamic State reveals it has smuggled thousands of extremists into Europe," Express, November 18, 2015, https://www.express.co.uk/news/world/555434/Islamic-State-ISIS-Smuggler-THOUSANDS-Extremists-into-Europe-Refugees.

126 Ibid.

127 John Irish, "French security chief warns Islamic State plans wave of attacks in France," Reuters, May 19, 2016, https://www.reuters.com/article/us-france-security/french-security-chief-warns-islamic-state-plans-wave-of-attacks-in-france-idUSKCN0YA1HO.

128 DPA, "Pope denounces Christians who don't want refugees as 'hypocrites,'" EBL News, October 13, 2016, https://eblnews.com//news/world/pope-denounces-christians-who-dont-want-refugees-hypocrites-40253?.

129 Ibid.

130 Bridget Johnson, "ISIS Group Releases Image of 'Beheaded' Pope Francis," PJ Media, November 17, 2017, https://pjmedia.com/homeland-security/isis-group-releases-image-beheaded-pope-francis/.

131 Jon Dean, "'Why we hate you': ISIS reveal 6 reasons why they despise Westerners in jihadi magazine," Mirror, August 1, 2016. https://www.mirror.co.uk/news/world-news/why-isis-hate-you-reasons-8533563

132 Islamic State, "This is the Promise of Allah," June 29, 2014, http://myreader.toile-libre.org/uploads/My_53b039f00cb03.pdf.

133 Ibid.

134 Ibid.

135 Ibid.

136 Ibid.

137 Ibid.

138 Ibid.

139 "Isis video 'shows al-Baghdadi alive' after death rumours," BBC News, July 5, 2014, http://www.bbc.com/news/av/world-middle-east-28178272/isis-video-shows-al-baghdadi-alive-after-death-rumours.

140 Abu Bakr al-Husayni al-Qurashi al-Baghdadi, "A Message to the Mujahidin and the Muslim Ummah in the Month of Ramadan," Al-Hayat Media Center, n.d., https://scholarship.tricolib.brynmawr.edu/bitstream/handle/10066/14241/ABB20140701.pdf.

141 Ibid.

142 Ibid.

143 "Crowd Gathers to Show Support of ISIS Takeover of Mosul," MEMRI, June 12, 2014, https://www.memri.org/tv/crowd-gathers-show-support-isis-takeover-mosul.

144 Brittany M. Hughes, "State Dept. on Beheading of U.S. Journalist: 'This Is Not About the United States,'" CNS News, August 21, 2014, https://www.cnsnews.com/news/article/brittany-m-hughes/state-dept-beheading-us-journalist-not-about-united-states.

145 Reena Flores, "CIA director on ISIS: They aren't Muslims—they're 'psychopathic thugs,'" CBS News, March 13, 2015, https://www.cbsnews.com/news/cia-director-isis-not-muslims-psychopathic-thugs/.

146 "French govt to use Arabic 'Daesh' for Islamic State group," France 24, September 18, 2014, updated December 5, 2015, http://www.france24.com/en/20140917-france-switches-arabic-daesh-acronym-islamic-state.

147 Abu Muhammad al-Adnani ash-Shami, "Indeed Your Lord Is Ever Watchful," September 21, 2014, https://ia801400.us.archive.org/34/items/mir225/English_Translation.pdf.

148 Al-Misri, Reliance of the Traveller, section o9.13.

149 "Video: Kuwaiti Activist: 'I Hope that Kuwait Will Enact a Law for…Sex Slaves,'" Jihad Watch, June 22, 2011. https://www.jihadwatch.org/2011/06/i-hope-that-kuwait-will-en-act-the-law-forsex-slaves

150 "Islamic State (ISIS) Publishes Penal Code, Says It Will Be Vigilantly Enforced," MEM-RI, December 17, 2014, https://www.memri.org/jttm/islamic-state-isis-publishes-penal-code-says-it-will-be-vigilantly-enforced.

151 Al-Bukhari, *Sahih al-Bukhari*, vol. 8, bk. 86, no. 6829.

152 Abu Dawud, *Sunan Abu Dawud, English Translation with Explanatory Notes*, translated by Ahmad Hasan (Kitab Bhavan, 1990), Section 38, number 4447.

153 Bethan McKernan, "Hillary Clinton emails leak: Wikileaks documents claim Democratic nominee 'thinks Saudi Arabia and Qatar fund Isis,'" Independent, October 11, 2016, http://www.independent.co.uk/news/world/politics/hillary-clinton-emails-leak-wikileaks-saudi-arabia-qatar-isis-podesta-latest-a7355466.html.

154 *Time* Magazine, July 1, 2013.

155 Arnel Hecimovic, "Rohingya Muslims flee ethnic violence in Myanmar - in pictures," *The Guardian*, September 17, 2017.

156 Wa Lone, "Myanmar military denies atrocities against Rohingya, replaces general," Reuters, November 13, 2017.

157 "Myanmar: 71 dead in militant attacks on police, border posts," Associated Press, August 25, 2017

158 Aye Chan, "The Development of a Muslim Enclave in Arakan (Rakhine) State of Burma (Myanmar)," SOAS Bulletin of Burma Research, Vol. 3, No. 2, Autumn 2005, p. 399.

159 Aye Chan, "The Development of a Muslim Enclave in Arakan (Rakhine) State of Burma (Myanmar)," SOAS Bulletin of Burma Research, Vol. 3, No. 2, Autumn 2005, p. 406.

160 Kyaw Zan Tha, "Background of Rohingya Problem," Scribd, December 28, 2008.

161 Angsuman Chakraborty, "Complete Background of Rohingya crisis," Medium, September 15, 2017.

162 Angsuman Chakraborty, "Complete Background of Rohingya crisis," Medium, September 15, 2017.

163 George Sprantzes, "Constantine Palaologus XI speaks before his officers and allies before the final siege of Constantinople by the Ottoman Sultan Mehmed Bey," World Historia, June 24, 2009, http://www.worldhistoria.com/speech-by-constantine-xi_topic124058.html.

164 Al-Bukhari, *Sahih al-Bukhari*, vol. 4, bk. 56, no. 2977.

ACKNOWLEDGMENTS

This book represents the crown and summit of everything I have to say that anyone who doesn't know me personally may care to listen to. I've written a guide to the Qur'an and a biography of Muhammad, and with this book, the case is complete—that is, the case that there are elements within Islam that pose a challenge to free societies, and that free people need to pay attention to this fact before it is, quite literally, too late. It is necessary for me to repeat yet again that this does not mean that every individual Muslim, or any given Muslim, embodies that challenge and is posing it individually, but as this book makes clear, the Islamic jihad imperative remains regardless of whether or not any Muslim individual decides to take it up.

I am grateful to David S. Bernstein of Bombardier Books for giving me the chance to write this book, and for his careful and insightful editorial touch, as well as that of Elena Vega and J. M. Martin. Thanks also to Hugh Fitzgerald, the most erudite and engaging commentator on the contemporary scene, for his extraordinarily helpful suggestions and guidance; Pamela Geller for alerting me to some original and important documents on the Mufti of Jerusalem; and Ibn Warraq for his keen historian's eye. I'm grateful also to the eagle-eyed Loren Rosson for his proofreading help.

Hugh and Christine Douglass-Williams have valiantly held the fort at our news and commentary site on contemporary jihad activity, Jihad Watch (www.jihadwatch.org), which is held together in the face of regular and massive cyber jihad assaults by the mysterious and indefatigable technical expert known to the world only as Marc. What would I do without them, or without David Horowitz and Mike Finch of the David Horowitz Freedom Center, whose ongoing support makes it all possible?

There are so many others. As always, I cannot name them all, for fear of giving today's jihadis marching orders. But I would be remiss if I did not once again thank the man without whom none of this would ever have happened, Mr. Jeffrey Rubin.

If any of my work over the years has had any value, I owe it to these folks, and to the others who shine no less brightly for remaining unnamed.

BIBLIOGRAPHY

Hadith and Life of Muhammad

Muhammed Ibn Ismaiel Al-Bukhari, *Sahih al-Bukhari: The Translation of the Meanings*, translated by Muhammad M. Khan (Darussalam, 1997).

Abu-Dawud Sulaiman bin Al-Aash'ath Al-Azdi as-Sijistani, *Sunan abu-Dawud*, translated by Ahmad Hasan, bk. 38, no. 4390 (Kitab Bhavan, 1990).

Ibn Ishaq, *The Life of Muhammad: A Translation of Ibn Ishaq's Sirat Rasul Allah*, translated by Alfred Guillaume (Oxford University Press, 1955).

Muslim ibn al-Hajjaj, *Sahih Muslim*, rev. ed., translated by Abdul Hamid Siddiqi (Kitab Bhavan, 2000).

Abu Abdur Rahman Ahmad bin Shu'aib bin 'Ali an-Nasa'i, *Sunan an-Nasa'i*, translated by Nasiruddin al-Khattab, (Darussalam, 2007).

Maxime Rodinson, *Muhammad*, translated by Anne Carter (Pantheon Books, 1971).

Ibn Sa'd, *Kitab Al-Tabaqat Al-Kabir*, translated by S. Moinul Haq and H. K. Ghazanfar, two vols. (Kitab Bhavan, n.d.).

Abu Ja'far Muhammad bin Jarir al-Tabari, *The History of al-Tabari*, vol. 7, *The Foundation of the Community*, translated by M. V. McDonald (State University of New York Press, 1987).

Abu Ja'far Muhammad bin Jarir al-Tabari, *The History of al-Tabari*, vol. 8, *The Victory of Islam*, translated by Michael Fishbein (State University of New York Press, 1997).

Abu Ja'far Muhammad bin Jarir al-Tabari, *The History of al-Tabari*, vol. 10, *The Conquest of Arabia*, translated by Fred M. Donner (State University of New York Press, 1993).

Origins of Islam

Fred Donner, *Muhammad and the Believers at the Origins of Islam* (The Belknap Press of Harvard University Press, 2010).

Ignaz Goldziher, *Muslim Studies*, translated by C. R. Barber and S. M. Stern (George Allen & Unwin Ltd., 1971).

Robert G. Hoyland, *Seeing Islam As Others Saw It: A Survey and Evaluation of Christian, Jewish and Zoroastrian Writings On Early Islam* (Darwin Press, 1997).

Yehuda D. Nevo and Judith Koren, *Crossroads to Islam* (Prometheus Books, 2003).

Robert Spencer, *Did Muhammad Exist? An Inquiry Into Islam's Obscure Origins* (ISI Books,

2010).

Robert Spencer, *The Truth About Muhammad: Founder of the World's Most Intolerant Religion* (Regnery, 2006).

The Rightly-Guided Caliphs

Agha Ibrahim Akram, *Islamic Historical General Khalid Bin Waleed* (Lulu Press, 2016).

Abu Ja'far Muhammad bin Jarir al-Tabari, *The History of al-Tabari*, vol. 11, *The Challenge to the Empires*, translated by Khalid Yahya Blankinship (State University of New York Press, 1993).

Abu Ja'far Muhammad bin Jarir al-Tabari, *The History of al-Tabari*, vol. 12, *The Battle of al-Qadisiyyah and the Conquest of Syria and Palestine*, translated by Yohanan Friedman (State University of New York Press, 1992).

Abu Ja'far Muhammad bin Jarir al-Tabari, *The History of al-Tabari*, vol. 13, *The Conquest of Iraq, Southwestern Persia, and Egypt*, translated by Gautier H. A. Juynboll (State University of New York Press, 1989).

The Sunni/Shi'a split

Abu Ja'far Muhammad bin Jarir al-Tabari, *The History of al-Tabari*, vol. 15, *The Crisis of the Early Caliphate*, translated by R. Stephen Humphreys (State University of New York Press, 1990).

Abu Ja'far Muhammad bin Jarir al-Tabari, *The History of al-Tabari*, vol. 16, *The Community Divided*, translated by Adrian Brockett (State University of New York Press, 1997).

Abu Ja'far Muhammad bin Jarir al-Tabari, *The History of al-Tabari*, vol. 17, *The First Civil War*, translated by G. R. Hawting (State University of New York Press, 1996).

Allamah Sayyid Muhammad Husayn Tabatabai, *Shi'ite Islam*, 2nd ed., translated by Seyyed Hossein Nasr (State University of New York Press, 1977).

The Umayyad Caliphate

G. R. Hawting, *The First Dynasty of Islam: The Umayyad Caliphate AD 661-750* (Routledge, 1986).

Abu Ja'far Muhammad bin Jarir al-Tabari, *The History of al-Tabari*, vol. 18, *Between Civil Wars: The Caliphate of Mu'awiyah*, translated by Michael G. Morony (State University of New York Press, 1987).

Abu Ja'far Muhammad bin Jarir al-Tabari, *The History of al-Tabari*, vol. 19, *The Caliphate of Yazid b. Mu'awiyah*, translated by I. K. A. Howard (State University of New York Press, 1990).

Abu Ja'far Muhammad bin Jarir al-Tabari, *The History of al-Tabari*, vol. 24, *The Empire in Transition*, translated by David Stephan Powers (State University of New York Press, 1989).

Abu Ja'far Muhammad bin Jarir al-Tabari, *The History of al-Tabari*, vol. 25, *The End of Expansion*, translated by Khalid Yahya Blankinship (State University of New York Press, 1989).

Abu Ja'far Muhammad bin Jarir al-Tabari, *The History of al-Tabari*, vol. 26, *The Waning of the Umayyad Caliphate*, translated by Carole Hillenbrand (State University of New York Press, 1989).

Dhimmitude

Bat Ye'or, *The Decline of Eastern Christianity Under Islam: From Jihad to Dhimmitude* (Fairleigh Dickinson University Press, 1996).

Bat Ye'or, *The Dhimmi: Jews and Christians Under Islam*, translated by David Maisel, Paul Fenton, and David Littman (Fairleigh Dickinson University Press, 1985).

Andrew Bostom, *The Legacy of Islamic Antisemitism* (Prometheus, 2007).

Antoine Fattal, *Le statut légal des non-Musulmans en pays d'Islam* (Université Saint-Joseph Institut de lettres orientales, 1958).

John Hunwick, *Jews of a Saharan Oasis: The Elimination of the Tamantit Community* (Markus Wiener Publishers, n.d.).

Israel and Ishmael: Studies in Muslim-Jewish Relations, edited by Tudor Parfitt (Palgrave Macmillan, 2000).

Paul Johnson, *A History of the Jews* (Perennial Library, 1987).

Bernard Lewis, *The Jews of Islam* (Princeton University Press, 1984).

The Byzantine Empire

L. W. Barnard, *The Graeco-Roman and Oriental Background of the Iconoclastic Controversy* (E. J. Brill, 1974).

Warren Carroll: *The Glory of Christendom: A History of Christendom*, vol. 3 (Christendom Press, 1993).

Edward Gibbon, *The History of the Decline and Fall of the Roman Empire* (1782).

Aristakes Lastiverts'i, *History*, translated by Robert Bedrosian (Sources of the Armenian Tradition, 1985).

Michael the Syrian, *The Chronicle of Michael the Great, Patriarch of the Syrians*, translated by Robert Bedrosian (Sources of the Armenian Tradition, 2013).

John Julius Norwich, *Byzantium: The Apogee* (Alfred A. Knopf, 1992).

John Julius Norwich, *A Short History of Byzantium* (Vintage Books, 1999).

Theophanes the Confessor, *The Chronicle of Theophanes: Anni Mundi 6095-6305 (A.D. 602-813)*, translated by Harry Turtledove (University of Pennsylvania Press, 1982).

The Jihad in Spain

Warren H. Carroll, *The Building of Christendom* (Christendom College Press, 1987).

Reinhart Dozy, *Spanish Islam: A History of the Muslims in Spain*, translated by Francis Griffin Stokes (Goodword Books, 2001).

Darío Fernández-Morera, *The Myth of the Andalusian Paradise* (ISI Books, 2016).

Richard Fletcher, *Moorish Spain* (University of California Press, 1992).

Ibn Abd al-Hakam, *Dhikr Fath Al-Andalus* (*History of the Conquest of Spain*), translated by John Harris Jones (Williams & Norgate, 1858).

Bernard F. Reilly, *The Kingdom of León-Castilla under King Alfonso VI, 1065-1109*, Library of Iberian Resources Online, n.d..

Kenneth Baxter Wolf, *Christian Martyrs in Muslim Spain* (Cambridge University Press, 1988).

The Abbasid Caliphate

J. J. Saunders, *A History of Medieval Islam* (Routledge, 1965).

Abu Ja'far Muhammad bin Jarir al-Tabari, *The History of al-Tabari*, vol. 27, *The Abbasid Revolution*, translated by John Alden Williams (State University of New York Press, 1985).

Abu Ja'far Muhammad bin Jarir al-Tabari, *The History of al-Tabari*, vol. 32, *The Reunification of the Abbasid Caliphate*, translated by C. E. Bosworth (State University of New York Press, 1987).

The Crusades

Moshe Gil, *A History of Palestine 634-1099* (Cambridge University Press, 1992).

Carole Hillenbrand, *The Crusades: Islamic Perspectives* (Routledge, 2000).

Amin Maalouf, *The Crusades Through Arab Eyes* (Schocken Books, 1984).

Thomas Madden, *The New Concise History of the Crusades* (Rowman & Littlefield, 2005).

R. Scott Peoples, *Crusade of Kings* (Wildside Press LLC, 2007).

Jonathan Riley-Smith, *The Crusades: A Short History* (Yale University Press, 1987).

James Harvey Robinson, ed., *Readings in European History*, vol. 1 (Ginn and Co., 1904).

Steven Runciman, *A History of the Crusades*, 3 vols. (Cambridge University Press, 1951).

Steven Runciman, *The Fall of Constantinople 1453* (Cambridge University Press, 1965).

Kenneth Meyer Setton, *The Papacy and the Levant, 1204-1571: The thirteenth and fourteenth centuries* (American Philosophical Society, 1976).

Slavery

Murray Gordon, *Slavery in the Arab World* (New Amsterdam Books, 1989).

Jan Hogendorn, "The Hideous Trade: Economic Aspects of the 'Manufacture' and Sale of Eunuchs," *Paideuma* 45 (1999).

Joseph Kenny, *The Spread of Islam Through North to West Africa* (Dominican Publications, 2000).

Bernard Lewis, *Race and Slavery in the Middle East* (Oxford University Press, 1994).

Giles Milton, *White Gold: The Extraordinary Story of Thomas Pellow and Islam's One Million White Slaves* (Farrar, Straus and Giroux, 2004).

Ronald Segal, *Islam's Black Slaves: The Other Black Diaspora* (Farrar, Straus and Giroux, 2001).

The Jihad in India and Central Asia

B. R. Ambedkar, *Thoughts on Pakistan* (Thacker and Company Ltd., 1941).

H. A. R. Gibb, *The Arab Conquests in Central Asia* (AMS Press, 1970).

Sita Ram Goel, *The Story of Islamic Imperialism in India* (Voice of India, 1982).

Hermann Kulke and Dietmar Rothermund, *A History of India* (Routledge, 2016).

Memoirs of the Emperor Jahangueir, written by himself, and translated from a Persian manuscript, by Major David Price (Oriental Translation Committee, 1829).

Abdul Hamid Lahori, *Badshanama of Abdul Hamid Lahori*, translated by Henry Miers Elliot (Hafiz Press, 1875).

K. S. Lal, *The Legacy of Muslim Rule in India* (Aditya Prakashan, 1992).

Derryl N. MacLean, *Religion and Society in Arab Sind* (Brill, 1989).

Ahmad Shayeq Qassem, *Afghanistan's Political Stability: A Dream Unrealised* (Ashgate Publishing, 2009).

Justin Marozzi, *Tamerlane: Sword of Islam, Conqueror of the World* (Da Capo Press, 2004).

Rudolph Peters, *Islam and Colonialism: The Doctrine of Jihad in Modern History* (Mouton Publishers, 1979).

Arun Shourie, Harsh Narain, Jay Dubashi, Ram Swarup, and Sita Ram Goel, *Hindu Temples: What Happened to Them*, 2 vols. (Voice of India, 1990).

Vincent Arthur Smith, *The Oxford History of India: From the Earliest Times to the End of 1911* (Clarendon Press, 1920).

Praveen Swami, *India, Pakistan and the Secret Jihad: The Covert War in Kashmir, 1947-2004*, (Routledge, 2006).

The Assassins

Bernard Lewis, *The Assassins: A Radical Sect In Islam* (Basic Books, 1967).

Marco Polo, *The Travels of Marco Polo*, translated by Henry Yule, edited and annotated by Henri Cordier (John Murray, 1920).

The Ottoman Empire

H. C. Armstrong, *The Gray Wolf* (Penguin Books, 1937).

Gábor Ágoston, "Muslim Cultural Enclaves in Hungary Under Ottoman Rule," *Acta Orientalia Academiae Scientiarum Hungaricae* 45, no. 2/3 (1991).

Richard Bonney, *Jihad from Qur'an to bin Laden* (Palgrave Macmillan, 2004)

Umar Busnavi, *History of the War in Bosnia During the Years 1737-1739*, translated by C. Fraser (Oriental Translation Fund, 1830).

Vahakn N. Dadrian, *The History of the Armenian Genocide* (Berghahn Books, 1995).

Caroline Finkel, *Osman's Dream: The History of the Ottoman Empire* (Basic Books, 2007).

Godfrey Goodwin, *The Janissaries* (Saqi Books, 1997).

Thomas Gordon, *History of the Greek Revolution* (T. Cadell, 1833).

Lord Kinross, *The Ottoman Centuries: The Rise and Fall of the Turkish Empire* (Morrow Quill Publishers, 1977).

Philip Mansel, *Constantinople: City of the World's Desire, 1453-1924* (St. Martin's Griffin, 1995).

Andrew James McGregor, *A Military History of Modern Egypt: From the Ottoman Conquest to the Ramadan War* (Greenwood Publishing Group, 2006).

Leslie Peirce, *The Imperial Harem: Women and Sovereignty in the Ottoman Empire* (Oxford University Press, 1993).

Nomikos Michael Vaporis, *Witnesses for Christ: Orthodox Christians, Neomartyrs of the Ottoman Period 1437-1860* (St. Vladimir's Seminary Press, 2000).

Andrew Wheatcroft, *Infidels: A History of the Conflict Between Christendom and Islam* (Random House, 2005), 195.

Wahhabism and Saudi Arabia

Hamid Algar, *Wahhabism: A Critical Essay* (Islamic Publications International, 2002).

Charles Allen, *God's Terrorists: The Wahhabi Cult and the Hidden Roots of Modern Jihad* (Da Capo Press, 2006).

Alexei Vassiliev, *The History of Saudi Arabia* (New York University Press, 2000).

The Barbary Wars

Frank Lambert, *The Barbary Wars* (Hill and Wang, 2005).

United States Department of State, *The Diplomatic Correspondence of the United States of America*, vol. 1 (Blair & Rives, 1837).

The Mahdi revolt

Daniel Allen Butler, *The First Jihad: The Battle for Khartoum and the Dawn of Militant Islam* (Casemate, 2006).

Rudolph Peters, *Jihad in Classical and Modern Islam: A Reader* (Markus Wiener Publishers, 1996).

The Muslim Brotherhood

John Roy Carlson, *Cairo to Damascus* (Alfred A. Knopf, 1951).

Brynjar Lia, *The Society of the Muslim Brothers in Egypt* (Ithaca Press, 1998).

Richard Paul Mitchell, *The Society of the Muslim Brothers* (Oxford University Press, 1993).

Sayyid Qutb, *Milestones,* The Mother Mosque Foundation, n.d.

The Nazis and the Jihad

Gilbert Achcar, *The Arabs and the Holocaust: The Arab-Israeli War of Narratives* (Henry Holt and Company, 2010).

The Arab Higher Committee: its origins, personnel and purposes, the documentary record submitted to the United Nations, May, 1947, The Nation Associates, 1947.

Kevork B. Bardakjian, *Hitler and the Armenian Genocide* (Zoryan Institute, 1985).

Jeffrey Herf, *Nazi Propaganda for the Arab World* (Yale University Press, 2009).

Niall Ferguson, *The War of the World: Twentieth-century Conflict and the Descent of the West* (Penguin, 2006).

Manus I. Midlarsky, *The Killing Trap: Genocide in the Twentieth Century* (Cambridge University Press, 2005).

The Jihad in Israel

"The Charter of Allah: The Platform of the Islamic Resistance movement (Hamas)," translated and annotated by Raphael Israeli, The International Policy Institute for Counter-Terrorism, April 5, 1998.

Saul S. Friedman, *A History of the Middle East* (McFarland, 2006).

Bruce Hoffman, *Anonymous Soldiers: The Struggle for Israel, 1917-1947* (Knopf Doubleday Publishing Group, 2015).

Esther Schapira and Georg M. Hafner, *Muhammad Al Dura: the TV Drama: Our Search for the Truth in the Middle East Media War* (La Maison d'Edition, 2016).

Joseph B. Schechtman, *The United States and the Jewish State Movement: The Crucial Decade, 1939-1949* (Herzl Press, 1966).

Iran's Islamic Revolution

Shaul Bakhash, *The Reign of the Ayatollahs: Iran and the Islamic Revolution* (Basic Books, 1990).

Mark Bowden, *Guests of the Ayatollah: The Iran Hostage Crisis—The First Battle in America's War with Militant Islam* (Grove/Atlantic, 2006).

James Buchan, *Days of God: The Revolution in Iran and Its Consequences* (Simon & Schuster, 2012).

Ruhollah Khomeini, *Islam and Revolution: Writings and Declarations of Imam Khomeini*, translated by Hamid Algar (Mizan, 1981).

Homa Katouzian, *The Persians: Ancient, Medieval and Modern Iran* (Yale University Press, 2009).

Baqer Moin, *Khomeini: Life of the Ayatollah* (St. Martin's Press, 1999), 75.

Elaine Sciolino, *Persian Mirrors: The Elusive Face of Iran* (Free Press, 2000).

Robert Spencer, *The Complete Infidel's Guide to Iran* (Regnery, 2016).

Amir Taheri, *Holy Terror: Inside the World of Islamic Terrorism* (Sphere, 1987).

Amir Taheri, *The Spirit of Allah: Khomeini and the Islamic Revolution* (Hutchinson, 1985).

Al-Qaeda

Abdullah Azzam, *Join the Caravan* (Azzam Publications, 2001).

Gilles Kepel, *Jihad: The Trail of Political Islam*, translated by Anthony F. Roberts (The Belknap Press, 2002).

Lawrence Wright, *The Looming Tower: Al-Qaeda and the Road to 9/11* (Vintage Books, 1996).

ISIS

Robert Spencer, *The Complete Infidel's Guide to ISIS* (Regnery, 2015).

INDEX

ABOUT THE AUTHOR

Robert Spencer is director of Jihad Watch, a program of the David Horowitz Freedom Center, where he is a Shillman Fellow. He is the author of eighteen books, including *The New York Times* bestsellers *The Politically Incorrect Guide to Islam (and the Crusades)* and *The Truth About Muhammad.* Spencer has led seminars on Islam and jihad for the FBI, the United States Central Command, United States Army Command and General Staff College, the U.S. Army's Asymmetric Warfare Group, the Joint Terrorism Task Force (JTTF), the Justice Department's Anti-Terrorism Advisory Council, and the U.S. intelligence community. He has discussed jihad, Islam, and terrorism at a workshop sponsored by the U.S. State Department and the German Foreign Ministry. He is a consultant with the Center for Security Policy.